"Roger Copeland's book about the sixty-year career of Merce Cunningham is also a brilliant sixty-year history of theater, dance, art, music and intellectual movements in America. *Merce Cunningham: The Modernizing of Modern Dance* represents almost three decades of work, displayed in a rare depth and scope of ideas. A stylish writer and hard-core analytic thinker, Copeland crosses disciplines with ease. Finally, in an age of turgid theoretical writing, students will see that theory can be delivered in clear prose. An eclectic historian, Copeland relates the past to the present and shows how the multiple arts merge in Cunningham's choreography. I admire his nimble connections. This is the heart of the matter in Cunningham's work, and it is what distinguishes this book."
    —*Sally Sommer, Professor of American Dance Studies at Florida State University*

"Roger Copeland's book examines the trajectory of Merce The Choreographer and places him just where I think he belongs—as a global artist of the twentieth century moving in all directions into the twenty-first."
    —*Valda Setterfield, Member of MCDC 1964–1974*

"The best book I've read on Cunningham, and by far the most probing—I love it. It places Cunningham squarely in context, delving beyond his well-known use of chance, music, and technology. The connections to Wagner and Brecht are intriguing, as is the relationship of Cunningham to arts other than dance. The book is the first I know to examine Cunningham as part of the circle of musicians around John Cage, so I hope that it reaches a wider audience than the dance community per se; scholars and enthusiasts of Cage, Feldman, Brown, Wolff, Oliveros, and others should take a good look at it. Furthermore, the book shows Cunningham's constant interest in exploring movement and how we see it."
    —*Allen Fogelsanger Director of Music for Dance, Cornell University*

"Roger Copeland's opus on Merce Cunningham and his Dance Company examines the nature of a maverick career which reinvented an art form. We know what happened to Modern Dance and Ballet in America: they were shaken to their dimensional roots in space and time. Copeland gives us a mature thesis of how it happened and compiles philosophies, art and dance history to propose why it happened—why we all dance the way we currently do."

—*Steve Paxton*

"Copeland's *Merce Cunningham: The Modernizing of Modern Dance* is a must read for anyone who has an avid interest in contemporary culture. The breath of his vision encompasses many divergent yet complimentary artistic worlds as he reveals the inherent complexities of arguably the worlds most influential choreographer."

—*Joseph V. Melillo, Executive Producer, BAM*

Merce Cunningham
The Modernizing of Modern Dance

Roger Copeland

ROUTLEDGE
NEW YORK AND LONDON

Published in 2004 by
Routledge
29 West 35th Street
New York, NY 10001
www.routledge-ny.com

Published in Great Britain by
Routledge
11 New Fetter Lane
London EC4P 4EE
www.routledge.co.uk

Copyright © 2004 by Routledge

Routledge is an imprint of the Taylor & Francis Group.

Printed in the United States of America on acid-free paper.

10   9   8   7   6   5   4   3   2   1

Cataloging-in-Publication Data is available from the Library of Congress.

ISBN 0-415-96574-8 (hb)   0-415-96575-6 (pb)

For my parents, Marjorie Ann Copeland
and Hyman Lawrence Copeland

"What I am saying does not mean that there will henceforth be no form in art. It only means that there will be new form, and that this form will be of such a type that it admits chaos and does not try to say that the chaos is really something else.... To find a form that accommodates the mess, that is the task of the artist now."

—Samuel Beckett, 1961

A. A Violent Order is Disorder; And
B. A Great Disorder Is An Order.
These Two Things Are One. [Pages of Illustrations]
—Wallace Stevens, "Connoisseur Of Chaos," 1942

"The logic of one event coming as responsive to another seems inadequate now. We look at and listen to several at once. For dancing, it was all those words about meaning that got in the way. Right now, they are broken up.
they
do not
quite
fit,
we have
to shuffle
and deal
them out
again."

—Merce Cunningham, *Changes*, 1968

"If Cunningham's work doesn't add up in a linear way, that doesn't mean it's abstract. It means that life doesn't add up in a linear way.... It may not look like Red Riding Hood and the wolf, but that's still who it is."
—Mark Morris, as quoted by Joan Acocella in *Mark Morris*, 1993

"Does dance depend? Or is it independent? Questions that seem political. They arose in an aesthetic situation. What's to be said? People and sounds interpenetrate."
—John Cage, "Where Do We Go From Here?," 1963

Contents

Acknowledgments

This book has been a long time comin'. It started life as an essay in *The New Republic* nearly a quarter-century ago. Over the years, early drafts of various chapters have appeared in *Partisan Review, Dance Theatre Journal, The Drama Review, Performing Arts Journal* and other publications. But why has it taken so long to complete? "Complete" is a very odd word to invoke with regard to Merce Cunningham, who—84 years old as of this writing—shows no signs of slowing his choreographic output. Alas, one of the problems with writing about an artist as prolific as Cunningham is that he enables you to procrastinate in good conscience.

There was that moment in the early 1980's—I remember it well—when I took a deep breath and declared, "Now or never.... Time to bring this project to some sort of completion." But a second voice in the back of my head whispered "Not so fast." What about all those new works for film and video that Cunningham was then creating in collaboration with artists like Charles Atlas and (a little later) Elliot Caplan? Wouldn't it be wise to wait and see where all that fresh work is heading? Ten years later, in the early 1990's, I felt a similar determination to finish . . . until it dawned on me that Cunningham was just then embarking on a seminal series of explorations involving the computer and other forms of digital technology. What looked like light at the end of the publication tunnel turned out to be the flicker of the computer screen on which Cunningham was now composing his dances.

And on it went, until just a few years ago when I came to the sobering realization that 2003 would mark the 50th anniversary of the founding of the Merce Cunningham Dance Company. Arbitrary though they may be, deadlines—like anniversaries—serve necessary purposes. Without them, the waiting game could continue indefinitely. To wit: as this manuscript goes to press, Cunningham is preparing to collaborate with two of the most adventurous art rock bands on the planet: Radiohead and Sigur Rós. After decades of working primarily with the electronic avant-garde, this may well inaugurate a new era of partnership between Cunningham and the outer fringes of popular music. As usual, I feel a strong temptation to pull the emergency brake; but for better or for worse, we're past the point of no return.

When a project takes this long to complete, it accumulates a long list of debts, both personal and professional. I'm especially grateful to the many friends and colleagues who read and commented on portions of the manuscript: Sally Banes, Steve Paxton, Valda Setterfield, Lynn Garafola, Mindy Aloff, Roger Shattuck, Stanley Kauffmann, Allen Fogelsanger, and Laura Jacobs. Lisa Naugle and the late Iris Garland helped me to understand some of the ways in which Cunningham utilizes computer software as a choreographic tool. The National Endowment for the Humanities and The Rockefeller Foundation were both generous enough to grant me fellowships that permitted time for research and writing that would otherwise have been devoted to teaching. For archival assistance, I want to thank David Vaughan of The Cunningham Dance Foundation, Laura Kuhn at the John Cage Trust, and Madeline Nichols and her marvelous staff at the Dance Collection of the New York Public Library at Lincoln Center for the Performing Arts.

Naomi Stern indirectly subsidized my near monthly trips into New York City by both putting me up in her apartment and putting up with me. I'm deeply indebted to Raphael Martin and (especially) Ruth Mercer for undertaking the laborious task of organizing and fact-checking the bibliographic notes. My thanks to Richard Carlin, Shannon McLachlan, and Danielle Savin at Routledge for shepherding the manuscript through the production process. (They all know how to crack the whip without leaving any permanent scars.) And even though he bears no responsibility whatsoever for the approach to his work that informs this book, I'd be shamefully remiss in not thanking Merce Cunningham for having choreographed the remarkable dances that made me want to write about him in the first place. The final expression of gratitude goes to my wife Michele Gross and my son Colin who continued to love me even when my stubborn attachment to this project made me utterly unloveable.

Introduction

Less than a year into the new millennium—October 7, 2000, to be more precise—*The Guardian* of London ran a 4,000-word profile of the choreographer Merce Cunningham. Several paragraphs into the essay, readers were matter of factly informed that "Merce Cunningham is, without doubt, the world's greatest living choreographer." The most remarkable thing about this declaration was how utterly unremarkable it proved to be. Rather than provoking a flurry of outraged letter writing from the partisans of other major living choreographers, the phrase "without doubt" seemed simply to underscore the obvious. Imagine if the newspaper had stated, with self-evident certitude, that Frank Gehry is "without doubt" the world's greatest living architect, Gerhart Richter is "without doubt" the world's greatest living painter, or Arvo Pärt is "without doubt" the world's greatest living composer. In any of those alternative scenarios, the ensuing controversy would have been both swift and clamorous. But given that George Balanchine and Martha Graham are no longer with us, Merce Cunningham is the last of the great, groundbreaking 20th century choreographers. It's not that Pina Bausch doesn't have her fierce partisans, especially in Europe. And, in this country, one could reasonably nominate Paul Taylor, Twyla Tharp, or, perhaps, even Mark Morris. All are great choreographers, but none has exerted the sort of influence that makes Cunningham such a logical—some would say inevitable—choice for this honor.

It's my guess that many of the other contenders to the crown would quickly defer to Cunningham. Consider the case of Mark Morris, arguably the most celebrated American choreographer to have emerged in the past two decades. In 1995, the dance critic Tobi Tobias asked Morris the following questions:

> Tobias: Is there any choreographer producing work now whose concerts you always try to go to, and always expect to have a very interesting time?
> Mark Morris: Merce Cunningham.
> Tobias: Anyone else?
> Morris: No. (58)

He neither hesitates nor equivocates. Indeed, Morris's admiration for Merce Cunningham's work is virtually unqualified—which is all the more impressive given the fact that he and Cunningham seem to share so little in common. Morris is arguably the most "musical" choreographer since Balanchine. His dances are almost always inspired by music and often derive their spatial—not just their rhythmic—structure from the musical score that accompanies them. By contrast, Cunningham is famous (alas, in some quarters, infamous) for having "liberated" dance from its traditional dependence upon music. Yet Morris continues to find Cunningham the most consistently "interesting" choreographer around. This testifies to the unique place Merce Cunningham occupies in the landscape of contemporary dance. No serious choreographer of the past few decades can avoid defining his or her own achievements in relation to Cunningham's—even if that relationship ultimately proves adversarial.

No one has revised "the fundamentals" more fundamentally than Merce Cunningham; for example: the relationship between movement, music, and rhythm; the way choreographic time can transfigure an audience's perception of space; the evolution of a codifiable technique that forges fresh connections between the dancer's head, back, pelvis, legs, and feet (resulting in an unprecedented rapprochement between ballet and modern dance); compositional practices based on the use of "chance operations," (producing new strategies for linking together disparate phrases of movement); a radical reenvisioning of which locations on a proscenium stage are most likely to command an audience's attention—this list could go on and on. No other choreographer has challenged as many "givens," paved as many new pathways, opened as many doors.

More radically than any other figure in the second half of the 20th century, Merce Cunningham has redefined what we think of as "modern dance." Indeed, he almost single-handedly *modernized* modern dance by rejecting the basic impulse that animated so much of the long tradition stretching from Isadora Duncan through Martha Graham, the desire to seek inspiration from so-called primitive sources. One of the great pioneers of pre-Cunningham modern dance, Doris Humphrey, described this primitivist yearning as follows:

> He [the modern dancer] is, in a sense, a throwback. He is aware of this but believes
> that his art is rooted so deeply in Man's fundamental instincts that he can read
> back into His unconscious remembrance before the atrophy of civilization set
> in. (1998, 59)

In other words, pre-Cunningham modern dance strove to take us *back*
to the future. Of course, "primitivism" is itself a time-honored mode of
modernism, one of modernity's most strenuous and heroic attempts at
self-criticism. Yet in most of the other arts, so-called primitive inspira-
tions (African masks for Picasso; Slavic folk melodies for Stravinsky) find
themselves absorbed into a distinctively contemporary context; and the resulting attitude toward history and progress is no less "forward-looking"
than, say, Marinetti's conception of futurism. Perhaps it's a difference of
degree rather than kind, but in the world of modern dance (prior to
Cunningham), primitivism plays a rather different role. Indeed, the very
concept of innovation, of "originality" for these pre-Cunningham, modern
dance pioneers implied a return to *origins,* a quest for the most "natural"—
perhaps even primordial—way of moving. Hence Doris Humphrey's desire
to return to the source (i.e., the sort of movement that might have existed
"before the atrophy of civilization set in").

By contrast, Cunningham choreographs dances that both acknowledge
and celebrate the speed, fragmentation, simultaneity of stimuli, and peculiar perceptual demands unique to the contemporary city. Granted,
Cunningham, in close association with his partner and musical collaborator, John Cage, has drawn inspiration from a variety of ancient Asian
sources such as the *I Ching* and key practices of Zen Buddhism. But, the
actual use Cunningham and Cage made of these influences was not only
distinctively "Western" but also distinctively urban—light-years away from
the steady-state world of Noh drama or Japanese tea ceremonies (to cite
but two of the cultural practices that owe their provenance in part to the
teachings of Zen masters). The actual sensory experience communicated
by most of Cunningham's and Cage's work has little to do with emotional
tranquility or relaxed contemplation. This is nowhere more evident than in
Merce Cunningham's complicated relationship to the conventions of classical ballet.

Before Cunningham, modern dance was so obsessed with the search
for "healthier" and earthier ways of moving that its practitioners often
dismissed the ballet vocabulary outright, demonizing it with adjectives such
as "artificial," "mechanical," and "puppetlike." On the evolutionary ladder,
ballet dancers were thought to reside in the general vicinity of performing

seals: "Execute 32 flawless fouettés and we'll throw you a slice of mackerel." Indeed, when Cunningham first began to choreograph professionally in the 1940s, ballet was located on the "other side" of a virtual Mason-Dixon line that modern dancers were sternly instructed not to cross. (Ironically, it had already become commonplace for ballet choreographers to borrow from the varied vocabularies of modern dance. Fokine, Nijinsky, Massine, Balanchine, and Robbins—in their very different ways—were all modernizers of ballet.) But Cunningham was the first *modern dance* choreographer to arrange for a truce of sorts between these once-warring antagonists. The result was an unprecedented fusion between balletic convention (upright carriage, lightning-fast footwork) *and* the curvaceous, sometimes convulsive, flexibility of torso and back we associate more often with modern dance.

Who would have guessed that the *modernization* of modern dance would depend in part on its rapprochement with classical ballet? Only Merce Cunningham—the very same choreographer who would subsequently pioneer many of the innovations that set the stage for what's come to be known as postmodern dance. The idea that any movement, no matter how pedestrian, can be regarded as a "dance movement"—providing that it's properly "framed"—is one of many postmodern notions that can be traced back to Merce Cunningham. It's no coincidence that a number of the original members of the Judson Dance Theater (the principal spawning ground for postmodern dance) had either studied with Cunningham or had actually danced in his company. Granted, Cunningham's movement vocabulary remains, for the most part, highly virtuosic rather than pedestrian or vernacular. But, as Carolyn Brown, one of the great founding members of the Cunningham Company, once put it, "Merce opened more doors for succeeding generations than he himself was willing to walk through" (1992, 122).

Thus far, I've focused on the way Cunningham enlarged the sheer range of movement available to the modern dancer. But Cunningham's innovations are by no means confined to the realm of movement invention. No one since Diaghilev had convinced so many advanced composers and visual artists to create sound scores, décor, and costumes for a dance company. When the curtain rose on the New York premiere of Cunningham's "Way Station" in 2001, what first caught the eye was some of the most stunning décor designed for any dance performance anywhere over the past quarter century. More tellingly, Charles Long's brilliantly colored, three-legged, biomorphic abstractions could easily have held their own alongside any new work of sculpture acquired by a gallery or museum in recent years.

Equally important, though, is the fact that Cunningham radically redefined what it means for choreographers, composers, and visual artists to "collaborate" with one another. In Cunningham's dances, choreography, music, and décor are all conceived in mutual isolation, often encountering one another for the very first time on opening night. Cunningham pioneered a new model of media-mixing that might be called "collaboration at a distance." Even in performance, the movement, the sound, and the décor in a Cunningham dance remain fiercely independent of one another.

Furthermore, the complex strategies Cunningham utilizes to compose his dances are equally innovative. Under the influence of his chief musical collaborator, John Cage, Cunningham has introduced the dance world to utterly iconoclastic ideas about the role that "chance operations" can play in the choreographic process. Similarly, his "decentralizing" of stage space—whereby a dancer positioned, say, downstage center assumes no automatic pride of place over dancers positioned upstage left or right—has challenged inherited ideas about spatial organization that have literally "held the stage" since the introduction of the proscenium arch and single-point perspective scenic design in the early 17th century.

In recent years, Cunningham has received a great deal of attention—much of it in the mainstream media—for having facilitated a marriage between dance and digital technology. Since the early 1990s, he's been the only dance-maker of international renown to routinely utilize computer technology (a software program called LifeForms) as an essential component of his choreographic process. This is immensely significant in its own right; but it also tells us a great deal about the unceasingly innovative nature of Merce Cunningham's long career. (Cunningham was already in his 70s when he initiated these experiments with the computer.) Traditionally, when a great artist lives into his 7th or 8th decade, the birthday becomes a retrospective occasion, an opportunity to look back—with immense satisfaction, but also a touch of nostalgia—on a substantially completed body of work whose high-water marks are all securely situated in the past. But when the perpetually prodigious Merce Cunningham turned 80 on April 16, 1999, there was very little time for backward glances or historical reassessments. The ever-busy Mr. Cunningham was hard at work on his latest dance: a high-tech, multimedia, digital collaboration called "Biped."

Cunningham's uninterrupted productivity is impressive enough all by itself. (His choreographic career can be traced back to the late 1930s.) But what made "Biped" truly astonishing was the fact that it pioneered an unprecedented fusion of concert dance and state-of-the-art computer and video technology known as "motion capture" (which—in effect—propelled his dancers into cyberspace). So much for the widespread assumption that the digital revolution is being driven entirely by whiz kids who look too young to shave. Of course, Cunningham's involvement with advanced technology is nothing new. Over the course of the last 50 years, he has presided over collaborations that incorporate electronic tape splicing and *musique concrète*, video synthesizers, FM telemetry, radar and ultrasonic transmissions, sound scores produced by the dancers in performance as they dart past strategically placed photoelectric cells—not to mention the more recent digital developments such as LifeForms and "motion capture."

But the *deeper*, more significant, connection between Cunningham's work and that of other artists who utilize advanced technologies is a shared commitment to the rigorously impersonal *methods* of scientific inquiry. This is true even of those Cunningham dances that don't incorporate some easily recognizable form of "technology." For example, when Cunningham and Cage speak of "chance methods," their emphasis lies as much or more on the rigor of the methods as on the randomness of the chance. By contrast, the long tradition of modern dance that preceded Cunningham was motivated more by a retreat from 20th-century scientific methodology than by an embrace of it. And this provides yet another example of what I mean when I say that Cunningham "modernized" modern dance.

A thorough examination of Merce Cunningham's work at the dawn of the 21st century will also, inevitably, entail an examination of the changing place of the human body in a world whose daily business is increasingly conducted in cyberspace rather than physically palpable space. Kenneth King, one of Cunningham's most important legatees, has long been fascinated by the relationship(s) between the dancer's body and "thinking machines." In an essay written in the 1990s, King called Cunningham "the most advanced choreographer on the planet;" and he subsequently went on to declare that "Merce's dance is already a kind of futuristic Artificial Intelligence... " (1992, 187). Even if we dismiss this claim as the exaggerated enthusiasm of a mind a bit too mired in science fiction, it's no coincidence that the choreographer who inspired this flight of fancy is Merce Cunningham.

But, these flirtations with cyberspace notwithstanding, Cunningham is also one of the great pioneers of contemporary *classicism* in dance. Indeed, it's become commonplace to refer to Cunningham's choreography as "classical," largely because the basic look and feel of his dances is so much more "balletic" than Martha Graham's. But the true nature of this classicism has been fundamentally misunderstood. Cunningham's classicism has at least as much to do with his use of chance as with his re-balleticizing of modern dance. This puzzles many people for whom it seems not only ironic—but downright oxymoronic—that the same choreographer could be simultaneously attracted to a movement vocabulary markedly more balletic than Graham's *and* to compositional strategies based on chance-methodologies. But for Cunningham, chance and the ballet vocabulary are two means toward the same end: they help to liberate the choreographer from the limitations of his own instincts. The ballet lexicon offers up a preexisting body of movement considerably more impersonal than the vocabularies of earlier modern dance choreographers. Similarly, chance methods are a strategy for making aesthetic decisions in a manner that transcends purely personal inclinations. Cunningham's use of chance is based on a very rigorous methodology, the utter antithesis of spontaneity or improvisation. Cunningham's way of working can therefore be labeled as "classical," assuming that a classical artist is one who both recognizes and celebrates the limits of self-expression—one who conceives of creativity not as pure, unrestricted, personal invention, but as a *collaboration* between his own subjectivity and some impersonal tradition, set of laws, or preexisting system of technique. When Cunningham incorporates both chance methodologies and aspects of the ballet lexicon into his work, the result is a uniquely *contemporary* brand of classicism.

Cunningham's Legacy

It's my belief that Merce Cunningham will eventually be regarded—if he isn't already—as one of the three most important choreographers of the 20th century (along with George Balanchine and Martha Graham). His influence is visible almost anywhere one cares to look in the world of contemporary dance and performance: When Stephen Petronio creates movement phrases based on "cut-up" photo-montages or when Karole Armitage treats classical movement in a thoroughly "drastic" way, they are following paths first paved by Cunningham. Similarly, when Trisha Brown says that collaborating with visual artists such as Robert Rauschenberg creates "the most interesting interference," or when she conceives of a new work (called "Newark") as a turf war between the dancers and Donald Judd's scenery, she, too, is exhibiting the influence of Cunningham, who often positions elements of decor directly between the dancers and the audience. A similar claim can be made for Cunningham's impact on Twyla Tharp's 1966 "Re-Moves," a portion of which was obscured by an eight-foot-high plywood box. The final section of the dance took place inside the box, leaving the audience with nothing to perceive but the sound of internal scurrying.

Cunningham's influence is by no means confined to the "dance world." When Robert Wilson organizes stage space in a thoroughly "decentralized" way, or when he devises an "image track" and a "sound track" that are totally autonomous of one another, he also demonstrates his indebtedness to Cunningham (a debt that Wilson is quick to acknowledge). Peter Brock's seminal theater piece *US*, produced by the Royal Shakespeare Company in the mid-1960's, contains a sequence directly inspired by the work of Cage and Cunningham.

Needless to say, Cunningham's influence now extends far beyond the borders of the United States. Frederick Ashton's "Monotones" in 1965 (set to Satie's "Trois Gymnopedies") is arguably the purist and most abstract ballet ever created by that great British choreographer. Would Ashton have proceeded in this direction had he not seen two of Cunningham's loveliest dances set to music by Satie ("Nocturnes" and "Septet") in London the previous season? I doubt it. Or—for a more recent example of Cunningham's influence on a major European choreographer—one need only consider Angelin Preljocaj, whose choreographic vocabulary often appears to be based on a fusion (or more accurately, a standoff) between Cunningham and Pina Bausch. Preljocaj's "Romeo and Juliet" (1990) is an almost literal confrontation between Bausch and Cunningham technique. The ruling Capulets move in a spare, abrupt, hard-edged style that is unmistakably Cunninghamesque; the Montagues, by contrast, are more likely to perform the sort of lush, impulsive, smotheringly erotic embraces that energize so much of the dancing of Bausch and her disciples.

The difficulty of attempting to summarize the range of Cunningham's achievements—or the pervasiveness of his influence—in these sorts of laundry lists is that, the longer the lists become, the more arbitrary they begin to feel. Is there a way of zeroing in on the very "heart" of his accomplishment?

Beyond the Ethos of Abstract Expressionism

We can take a tentative step in that direction by arguing that Merce Cunningham is the only choreographer whose work is central to one of the great sea-changes or "paradigm shifts" in the arts of the last 50 years, an artistic revolution associated most often with two of Cunningham's best-known collaborators, Robert Rauschenberg and Jasper Johns, his earliest "artistic directors" (i.e., the visual artists responsible for overseeing the design of decor and costumes for his dances). Johns and Rauschenberg are commonly credited with having led the move away from the hot, anguished, deeply personal energies of abstract expressionism toward a much cooler and impersonal mode of art-making. Cunningham pioneered an almost identical transition beyond the sort of id-obsessed, psychologically driven modern dance that reached its apotheosis in the work of Martha Graham. Ironically, dance critics have traditionally analogized Cunningham to the very painter with whom he has the *least* in common: Jackson Pollock. But Cunningham's deeper allegiances are, logically enough, with the painters with whom he actually collaborated, who defined themselves in opposition to Pollock and abstract expressionism. Thus the underlying argument of this book is that Cunningham is to Graham as Johns and Rauschenberg are to a painter like Pollock.

Perhaps the following anecdote will help to illuminate this parallel. During the late 1970s, when the Sony Walkman craze was still in full, fashionable swing, it was not uncommon for members of the Cunningham/Cage audience to bring battery-powered headsets along with them to the company's performances—in effect, providing their own auditory accompaniment as

Cunningham's dancers went through their cool, brainy, elegant paces. At the time, this struck me as a perfectly logical extension of the Cunningham/Cage aesthetic in which movement, sound, and décor are all conceived and executed independently of one another, adamantly refusing to meld into a fixed, organic whole. The separate elements all exist simultaneously before us, inhabiting what Cunningham calls an "open field." The order and manner in which we "connect the dots" is left open. I thought to myself: If Cunningham refuses to tell us how to look at and listen to his work, what's wrong with seizing the initiative and maximizing one's auditory options?

A few years later, I asked John Cage what he thought of this practice. Cage's generosity was legendary and his tolerance for eccentricity seemingly boundless. So I fully expected him to nod his approval and murmur "Why not?"—perhaps even issue a full-fledged endorsement. But, much to my surprise, he raised a series of objections, the most trenchant of which was: "How do we know what these audience members are listening to? What if the sound they supply hasn't been composed by chance operations?" And, if so, how can it possibly be considered an appropriate accompaniment for a dance by Merce Cunningham, where chance methods routinely determine a number of variables such as spatial arrangement of the dancers and the order in which disparate choreographic phrases follow one another? His comments struck me with the force of an epiphany because they made me realize that, contrary to received wisdom, the relationship of sound, movement, and décor in a Cunningham dance is *not* entirely arbitrary. Granted, the sound and the movement don't provide a metrical support structure for one another. Similarly, the décor and costumes do not set out to embody a central concept that governs the entire enterprise. But there *is* a shared sensibility at work.

Chance may determine many aspects of the Cunningham experience, but Cunningham does not choose his collaborators by chance. They all belong, we might say, to the Cunningham circle. In addition to Cage, the "founding members" included the composers Earle Brown, Morton Feldman, David Tudor, and Christian Wolff (who collectively constituted a "New York School" of composition in the mid-1950s). Likewise, Robert Rauschenberg and Jasper Johns, whom Cunningham and Cage recruited to oversee the design of décor and costumes for the company, shared a similar sensibility. Johns and Rauschenberg made extensive use of silkscreen, blueprint paper, plexiglass, and modes of mechanical reproduction, resulting in images that are less obviously "self-expressive" than those of the abstract expressionists. In place of the personal, gestural, virtually calligraphic brushstrokes of abstract expressionism, they began to incorporate the sort of objective, "ready-made" icons that would begin to dominate pop and minimal art (e.g., Johns's flags and targets—images that are appropriated from the external world in the manner of Marcel Duchamp's ready-mades—rather than generated "instinctively" or dredged up from the depths of the unconscious).

Abstract expressionism also was characterized by the intense *physicality* of its brushstrokes, the involvement of a significant portion of the artist's *body,* not just his hand, wrist, or fingers. What Rauschenberg and Johns progressively eliminated from their work was nothing less than the "bodily" dimension of abstract expressionism (which is not to say that their art— especially Rauschenberg's—didn't engage the body of the *viewer* in distinctive ways). Something quite similar occurs in the work of the composers with whom Cunningham first collaborated. Almost all of them relied on electronic modes of sound generation and/or modification (utilizing sine-wave generators, oscillators, reverberators, modulators, and so on). The *body* of the musician plays a much less central role in the creation of such sounds than it does when working with acoustic instruments.

Is there a name for this "shared sensibility" that dethroned the overheated, highly *physicalized* energies of abstract expressionism? No one, to the best of my knowledge, has managed to pin a convincing label on this group of artists, at least not the sort of label that both defines common ground and makes an indelible impression on the memory. But there *have* been attempts, however tentative, to place Cunningham's work in this broader context. In 1968, Calvin Tomkins published an expanded edition of his book *The Bride and the Bachelors,* adding a chapter on Cunningham to his earlier study of Duchamp, Tinguely, Cage, and Rauschenberg. Tomkins's book was invaluable as an introduction to the work of five discreet individuals. But when it came to describing the sensibility they share, he all but abandoned the effort early on. Consider this paragraph from his introduction:

> Marcel Duchamp, John Cage, Jean Tinguely, Robert Rauschenberg, and Merce Cunningham do not constitute a movement or a school, nor do they even share a common point of view. Cage, the composer, and Cunningham, the modern dancer and choreographer, have worked in close collaboration for many years, and yet the intellectual rigor with which Cage charts his aesthetic course is quite foreign to Cunningham's more instinctive way of working. (1968, 1)

Really? Cunningham, it seems to me, is no more "instinctive" in his approach to movement than Cage is in his approach to music. But in order to understand why that's so, we need to uncover the "family resemblances" that unite this unique group of artists. Tomkins continues:

> Although Duchamp's infinitely subtle play of ideas has obvious reverberations in the ideas of all the others, none of them has been directly influenced by Duchamp (their discovery of him served rather to reinforce ideas arrived at independently), and none of them shows much of his ironical detachment.

Again, I would argue, Tomkins has missed the forest for the trees. Irony—and a virtually unlimited admiration for Duchamp—are but two of many qualities shared by Cunningham, Cage, and the visual artists they collaborated with most often.

To my mind, the most useful—certainly, the most provocative—account of Cunningham, Cage, and their cohorts in the art world comes from a writer much less sympathetic to them than Tomkins. Duchamp once referred to "the beauty of indifference"; and the art critic Moira Roth, seizing on his term, published a book in 1998 (based on an earlier essay from 1977) that lumps Duchamp, Cage, Cunningham, Johns, and Rauschenberg together as practitioners of what she calls "The Aesthetic of Indifference." Her account was intended as a severe rebuke to these artists. Indeed, she milks the word "indifference" for every imaginable antisocial connotation it can generate. Even so, Roth does a better job than Tomkins of defining the sensibility that Cunningham, Cage, Johns, and Rauschenberg (her gang of four) share with Duchamp. Although she fails to acknowledge its more positive qualities, Roth accurately describes the chief attributes of this sensibility:

> Coolness and intelligence were the hallmarks of the Aesthetic of Indifference and, as a concomitant, there was among the new group a widespread disdain for traditional artistic manual skills and the artist's personal "touch." (1977, 50)

This leads to an important question, one that bears directly on Cunningham's relationship to the rest of this group: How can a choreographer, an artist whose very *medium* is the human body, feel at home in such "untactile" company? It's doubly difficult to imagine a *modern dance* choreographer deemphasizing "personal touch" (and the broader category of "the tactile," a clear prerequisite for the sort of kinetic empathy most modern dancers wanted their audiences to experience). That question constitutes both the starting point for this study and the key to what makes Merce Cunningham's work so distinctive. "Cool intelligence" was not a quality that anyone would have associated with modern dance prior to Cunningham.

The Place of the Body

In many ways, this book is less a conventional biography of a particular artist than a cultural history of that moment when American art moved beyond the ethos of abstract expressionism. This "ethos" involves much more than a specific moment (or movement) in the history of painting. It implies a deep-set attitude toward art-making in the late 1940s and 1950s that places a very high premium on the full participation of the artist's *body*. Broadly construed, it includes not only that variety of "action painting" made famous by Jackson Pollock but also the highly physicalized, method-based acting styles of Marlon Brando, James Dean, and Montgomery Clift; the primal scream at the root of Allen Ginsberg's "Howl"; the Artaud-influenced work of The Living Theatre; Norman Mailer's Beat-generation manifesto "The White Negro"; and much of the art of the postwar years that drew its principle inspiration from Freudian or Jungian views of the unconscious. The single best example of this belief in the supreme wisdom of the *body* is probably the work of Martha Graham. "Bodies never lie," Graham famously declared. She believed that modern dance can reestablish contact with those ancient, natural, and mythic energies that (presumably) lie dormant beneath the surface of contemporary culture.

Merce Cunningham was one of Martha Graham's principal dancers between 1939 and 1945. But, by 1953, when Cunningham formed his first dance company, he had eliminated virtually every vestige of Graham's influence from his own dancing and choreography. Significantly, 1953 was also the year in which Rauschenberg created his "Erased DeKooning Drawing," thereby declaring *his* independence from the ethos of abstract expressionism. Thus, Cunningham's rejection of the Graham aesthetic is paralleled almost exactly by Johns's and Rauschenberg's repudiation of abstract expressionism. For Cunningham, the principal emphasis for both artist and audience is on "seeing clearly" rather than "feeling deeply." The action painter's dependence on anguished inspiration gives way to a much more aloof and brainy mode of aesthetic "problem solving." Neither Graham nor Pollock would, I suspect, have regarded the adjective "brainy" as much of a compliment. (And, before Cunningham, the word "brainy" rarely appeared in writing about modern dance.)

But a choreographer who began his professional career as a principal dancer for Martha Graham is the very last person one would have expected to spearhead such an un-Dionysian movement. Modern dance—especially Graham's variety of modern dance—is widely regarded as a "hot" rather than a "cool" medium, as the most tactile and perhaps the most primal of the arts. What then becomes of modern dance when choreographers such as Cunningham begin to cultivate the cool, detached, impersonal sensibility that characterized the New York art world following the repudiation of abstract expressionism? What becomes of dance when choreographers no longer fully trust "the wisdom of the body" and begin, at least implicitly, to challenge the modern dance world's most cherished belief: that *tactile*, physical knowledge is the most profound and ultimately, the most reliable, way of knowing the world? Yet another name for this deeply held belief (that animates so much of pre-Cunningham modern dance) is *primitivism*: the idea that dancing is the most "primitive" of the arts and that it can help restore a sense of tactile health and wholeness otherwise alien to the modern world. Again, we return to Doris Humphrey's belief that modern dance can reconnect us with that era of prehistory "before the atrophy of civilization set in." Cunningham's moderizing of modern dance entails the repudiating of primitivism.

Primitivism, in this context, connotes a dense constellation of beliefs about the nature and function of dancing, the idea that dance: is the oldest and most primal of the arts; originates in and harks back to a period before the self and the world were divided; is both preverbal and nonverbal in nature (and therefore immune to the abstractions and putative deceptions of language); is the most participatory of the performing arts (because it always preserves at least a vestigial sense of ritual involvement); and that, ultimately, the mission of dance—even in the most purely aesthetic and theatrical of contexts—is always, at least implicitly, *therapeutic*. Dance, in other words, can offer us alternatives to the spiritually impoverished condition of contemporary life. These are bold claims (to put it mildly); but, as we'll soon see, the rhetoric of pre-Cunningham modern dance is nothing if not redemptive.

City Life

It's with regard to this sort of "primitivism" that the contrast between Cunningham and Graham falls into sharpest relief. Cunningham is probably the first modern dance choreographer to part ways with primitivism by embracing—rather than lamenting—the basic conditions of city life. Andy Warhol, whose silver-mylar pillows for Cunningham's "Rainforest" (1968) lend a distinctly urban flavor to what might otherwise pass as an evocation of the "natural" world, once described himself as someone who enjoyed "all the great modern things that the Abstract Expressionists tried so hard not to notice at all" (1989, 605)—which is to say: *urban* things, man-made things. And Cunningham could describe his relationship to Graham and the primitivists in much the same way.

Cunningham is widely regarded as a choreographic formalist who believes that movement is no longer obligated to represent anything other than itself. At the same time, it's difficult to think of another choreographer whose work provides a more vivid sense of contemporary urban life. Granted, he never gives us "stories" about the city featuring briefcase-wielding characters who dash about in the fast track or walk on the wild side. What he offers us instead is the dense spatial and rhythmic texture of urban life embodied in simultaneous occurrences, the dissociation of what we hear from what we see, sudden reversals of direction, and unpredictable entrances and exits. The resulting images capture the unmistakable look and feel of busy people going about their business. In the world of Cunningham's dances, the driving impulse is to hurry up, then stop: Race to the street corner, but then stop at the traffic light; run for the elevator; but then wait—impatiently—while it descends to the ground floor. There is no need to commission backdrops painted with likenesses of traffic lights or stop signs. What we witness is the deep structure of urban life, not the photographic surface. On more than one occasion, John Cage utilized the image of traffic to represent the characteristic "patterns" of contemporary experience. And it's no coincidence that Cunningham and Cage lived for most of their adult lives in New York City, the international capitol of the accelerated clock.

Thus, Cunningham's "formalism"—his rejection of the narrative structure in Martha Graham's choreography of the 1940s—is *not* a shift from a representational art (Graham's) to a nonrepresentational art (Cunningham's); it's a shift from an older mode of mimesis to one that more accurately mirrors the complexity, simultaneity, and non-Aristotelian causality that characterize contemporary, urban life. This is more than a matter of rejecting causal linkages. Every undergraduate who has ever taken a course in "The Theater of the Absurd" is well aware of the extent to which artists in the second half of the 20th century routinely replaced "causality" with mere sequence. But the "nonlinear," collagelike structures that result from Cunningham's and Cage's use of chance operations have more in common with the sort of complex systems that function in weather forecasting or predictions about the global economy. This is the sort of causality that links events that *appear* to be widely separated by intervals of both space and time (e.g., what effect does the devaluation of Asian currencies have on fluctuation in the marginal rates of U.S. Treasury Bonds?) This is a world in which causality still exists, but manifests itself in complex, chaotic, and nonlinear ways. And this sort of complexity is one of the chief characteristics of what we've come to call globalization, a world of indirect interconnectedness, where very small differences of "input" in one part of a dynamic system can cause massive differences of "output" in another part of the same system— or, as chaos theorist Edward Lorenz asked in a now-famous 1979 paper, "Does the Flap of a Butterfly's Wings in Brazil Set Off a Tornado in Texas?"

Systems of this sort provide an accurate analogy for the extraordinarily complicated interactions(s) that occur between movement, sound, and décor in a work by Cunningham. Despite frequent appearances to the contrary, the relationship among these elements is not utterly random. "Chance *operations*" is the marvelously oxymoronic phrase that Cunningham and Cage employ to describe the "rules" (or "operations") that govern these interactions. As with many complex systems, the resulting behavior is *both* deterministic and unpredictable. "To find a form that accommodates the mess, that is the task of the artist now," Samuel Beckett once declared. Finding that form is one of the tasks that Cunningham and Cage assigned themselves. By contrast, the long tradition of modern dance that extends from Duncan through Graham almost always rejected the "mess" of urban life by reaching "back" toward something primitive. Hence, Graham's works with titles such as "Primitive Mysteries" or her remarkable string of dances in the 1940s inspired by Greek mythology. (Both Duncan and Graham, in their very different ways, laid claim to the inspiration of ancient Greece.) But Graham in particular proceeds on the belief—and I mean belief with a capital "B"—that modern dance can perform a quasi-ritualistic function: that it can reawaken primal memories that have been buried beneath the various repressions we call urban "civilization."

A slightly different, if less utopian, version of this primitivist ethos was almost as central to abstract expressionism. Primitivism fuels one of the great myths of modern art: the idea that the "primitive" (e.g., motifs derived from African, Native American, or Oceanic art) and/or the unconscious (the supposed repository of all that's most primitive within the self) offer the artist a source of inviolable purity, enabling him or her to escape the corruptions of contemporary urban culture. Martha Graham and Jackson Pollock therefore function in this book as prime examples of the modernist-as-primitivist. By contrast, Cunningham, Cage, Johns, and Rauschenberg seem much less confident about the ability of these two "safe houses" (the unconscious and the primitive) to remain insulated from the incursions of urban life. Cunningham has always been skeptical about the role that unconscious impulses play (or were thought to play) in the creative process. Here we begin to encounter the profound influence of John Cage on his work; it was in tandem with Cage that Cunningham began to employ utterly impersonal, chance-generated procedures to dictate the sort of aesthetic decisions that a Graham or a Pollock would have consigned to the realm of unconscious inspiration.

The Politics of Perception

But *why* did Cunningham and company move beyond the ethos of abstract expressionism? What I will argue—surprising as this may sound at first—has a great deal to do with *politics*. I say "surprising," because it's become fashionable to categorize Cunningham's work as a "purely formal" (and thus *apolitical*) exploration of movement-as-an-end-in itself. Especially today, when our notion of what constitutes political art is dominated by the race/class/gender mantra of identity politics, there's a very strong tendency to think of artists like Cunningham and Cage as being willfully insulated from social realities. Yvonne Rainer, one of the principle pioneers of postmodern dance (and someone who is quick to acknowledge the many debts she owes to Cunningham), has nonetheless argued that:

> Cage's and Cunningham's insistence on the autoreferentiality of sound and movement resulted in performances that denied or at least ignored the political and ideological significance of the body. (Foster 1986, 259)

Moira Roth goes considerably further; arguing that the "aesthetic of indifference" she attributes to Cunningham and company is actually a product of McCarthyism and the chilling effect it exerted on artists who might have otherwise been inclined to deal with politically engaged subjects:

> [These] artists loosely came together, intellectually and psychologically, in terms of a shared aesthetic during and just after the McCarthy period.... It is time to see their art and artistic stands in the Cold War context.... These artists made and talked about an art characterized by tones of neutrality, passivity, irony, and often negation. "Amusement" and "indifference" became positive values.... In its deliberately apolitical and generally neutral stance, the Aesthetic of Indifference represented a new breed of artist, an alternative to the politically concerned Abstract Expressionists. (1977, 49)

One of my principle goals in writing this book is to reclaim the concept of "the political" from those current denizens of "the cultural left" who cavalierly dismiss the so-called detachment of artists like Cunningham and Cage as socially irresponsible.

My first encounter with the work of Cunningham and Cage took place during that most "political" of months, May of 1968 (see Chapter 1). Suffice it to say that the experience did not strike me as apolitical. Indeed, in the context of the 1960s, what Roth called "indifference" (Cunningham's impersonal cool, his sense of "distance," his ironic detachment) struck me as an avoidance of didacticism—not just political didacticism but many other sorts of sensory and intellectual manipulation as well. The work of Cunningham, Cage, Rauschenberg, and Johns functioned for me as a welcome antidote to an increasingly manipulative urban environment of relentless sensory overload, of steady bombardment by messages of all kinds, subliminal as well as overt. In some contexts, a politics of *dis*engagement can perform a more radical function than a politics that is more conventionally "engaged." Many of Cunningham's innovations—the independence of movement, sound, and décor in his dances, the decentralizing of stage space, the physical obstacles that sometimes impede or obscure one's view of the dancers—serve the ultimate goal of increasing the spectator's perceptual freedom, of providing us with opportunities to choose when and where to focus our visual and auditory attention. Cunningham and Cage practice (quite consciously) a politics of perception.

In Antonioni's great film *Red Desert*, there's a marvelous moment that illuminates this connection between perception and politics. Richard Harris says to Monica Vitti, "You wonder what to look at. I wonder how to live. Same thing." Cunningham and company realize that at the deepest level—the only one that matters in any lasting way—morality and politics are rooted in the nature of our perceptual habits. Choosing, really *choosing*, where to direct one's attention is a vital component of the free moral life.

I make no grand, overarching claims about the ability of Cunningham's dances to improve the world. Neither Cunningham, nor any other serious artist I can think of in the second half of the 20th century, functioned as an "unacknowledged legislator" of the age. Indeed, when it comes to the relationship between art and social action, I'm inclined to agree with W. H. Auden, who wrote in his "Elegy to William Butler Yeats": "Poetry makes nothing happen. It survives in the valley of its saying." What poetry, or any other art, can do—and what Cunningham's art does quite magnificently— is to help freshen and clarify perception. Cunningham's works challenge existing relations between seeing and hearing; and by stretching the interval between stimulus and response, they help to inoculate us against the many forms of (virtually) Pavlovian conditioning that play an increasingly dominant role in our daily lives.

Cunningham's major innovations were pioneered in the early 1950s. These were the years in which the American advertising industry was learning how to systematically utilize theories of depth psychology in order to stimulate consumerist desires that have little relation to instinctive need. (Vance Packard's classic study of these phenomena, *The Hidden Persuaders*, was published in 1957.) In the intervening decades, the sheer pervasiveness of information-technologies—omnipresent television screens, Walkmans, laptop computers, CD-ROMs—have conspired to insure that there's no escape from the "virtual realities" of popular culture. (Try using a search engine on the Internet today without having your peripheral vision invaded by blinking, attention-grabbing advertisements.) Significantly, Packard's 1957 introduction was titled "the depth approach." He understood the ease with and the extent to which the most seductive of these sounds and images can colonize our imaginations and perhaps even the *depths* of our unconscious. Thus, behavior that *feels* self-motivated and perfectly "natural" often turns out to be culturally conditioned. (That's usually what we mean when we speak of "second nature.")

But simply being aware of the way these image-industries operate does little to immunize us against their methods. Seen in this light, Cunningham's decision in the early 1950s to circumvent personal taste and "unconscious" instinct begins to assume a distinctly *political* character. (Cunningham routinely employs chance procedures to dictate the sort of aesthetic decisions that most artists consign to the realm of personal "style.") This use of chance methodology as a compositional tool enables

Cunningham to avoid placing himself at the mercy of creative "impulses" that might *feel* natural, that might *appear* to originate in the unconscious, but that may in fact be a product of cultural conditioning (i.e., "second nature" posing as nature). Similarly, the "indeterminate" elements in the sound scores John Cage composed for Cunningham's dances utilize noise, randomness, and entropy to subvert even the most unconscious varieties of intention. In harboring these doubts about the presumed "purity" of unconscious instinct, Cunningham, Cage, Johns, and Rauschenberg reject one of the key aspirations of high modernism. Indeed, in moving beyond the energies and assumptions that fueled the ethos of abstract expressionism, they helped to pioneer the transition from modernism to postmodernism (a connection that's examined in Chapter 11.)

Cunningham's Collaborations

One of the basic premises of this book is that Merce Cunningham's significance cannot be fully appreciated without considering his relationship to the composers and visual artists with whom he works. Most dance critics have consistently ignored (or even dismissed) the importance of his collaborations with Cage, Feldman, Wolff, Johns, Rauschenberg, Stella, Warhol, and others. Alas, even Cunningham's most ardent admirers within the dance world continue to complain about the collaborative element of his work. As recently as the 1990s, a critic who considers herself a great fan of his wrote:

> ... Cunningham's dances look best with the simplest settings and costumes, and it is arguably in the area of decor that the Cunningham repertory has been most often hoist by the Cage-Cunningham petard. (1992, 192)

The sound scores that accompany Cunningham's dances are even more of a problem for most dance critics, who—as we'll see in Chapter 1—tend to regard them as little more than a distraction, annoyance, or worse. In 1970, Clive Barnes said this about Cunningham's "Canfield" at The Brooklyn Academy of Music:

> The score, attributed to Pauline Oliveros, consists in large part of acoustical experiments, all of them arcane, but boring, carried out by a peripatetic Mr. Cage at the instructions of his fellow musical warlocks, David Tudor and Gordon Mumma. All of them seemed to be having a good time—which was agreeable—but their activities were distracting to anyone who had come to see Mr. Cunningham dance rather than Mr. Cage make a fool of himself.

The most basic questions about the sorts of music Cunningham utilizes are rarely raised—let alone answered. For example, most critics understand why Cunningham would be reluctant to choreograph to a score by Aaron

Copland or Samuel Barber; but few could explain why Cunningham would consider it equally inappropriate to dance to an electronic score by say, Milton Babbitt (or any other composer who set out to reconcile the world of electronic sound with the ordering principles of strict serial structures). It seems to me essential to explain why Cunningham usually works with *particular* varieties of live, "indeterminate," electronic sound. So this book is, among other things, an attempt to restore his dances to their proper context: to acknowledge and celebrate the importance of the *collaborative* element in his work.

The Limits of Descriptive Criticism

This book is not the long-awaited biography of Merce Cunningham. This book has nothing whatsoever to say about Cunningham's private life. Inquiring minds who want to know whether or not he sleeps in the nude (and with whom), how his living quarters are decorated, or even—less frivolously— how personal experiences have been refracted into or reflected in his art, had best look elsewhere. This study proceeds on the assumption that Merce Cunningham's work—to a very considerable extent—*is* his life. (Although, in Chapter 12, I *will* talk about the extent to which the current proponents of identity politics tend to challenge this assumption.) I make no attempt to conceal the fact that Merce Cunningham and John Cage did not merely work together for many years; they *lived together* (quite openly) for most of that long artistic partnership. But recent attempts to draw a connection between their sexual preferences and their artistic practices strike me as woefully misguided.

The pages that follow constitute one possible response to the hunger I sense for a different kind of writing about Cunningham, one that's less descriptive and more interpretive (above all, more richly contextualized, both intellectually and culturally) than much of the criticism his work has elicited. Kenneth King, one of the most provocative experimental choreographers of the 1960s and one of Cunningham's most important legatees, once wrote,

> We've had descriptive journalistic criticism instead of a dance literature. Merce, though, is worthy of a Paul Valery, Maurice Merleau-Ponty, or a Jacques Derrida. (1992, 189)

Then again, one *could* argue that descriptive, journalistic criticism is the most appropriate way of writing about a choreographer who speaks openly of his desire to create a variety of dance "unprompted by references other than to its own life." It would seem to acknowledge and honor the fact that Cunningham is, among other things, a great formalist who broke with the mythic and narrative dimensions of modern dance so central to the work of Graham. Surely at its best, descriptive criticism performs an invaluable service by providing the reader with a closely observed, physically palpable sense of the Cunningham body in motion.

Furthermore, one mustn't underestimate the sheer difficulty of this task. In so far as Cunningham avoids not only narrative storytelling but also conventional notions of musicality, his work is especially difficult to write about. In a panel discussion at the Brooklyn Academy of Music in 1997, Joan Acocella argued that Cunningham's choreography is

> not just non-narrative, but actively resistant to narrative. . . . The pattern-making mechanism in the mind gets sand thrown in it. . . . There seems to be something about Cunningham that repels criticism, discourages it, embarrasses it.

So, it's no small achievement simply to *describe* a Cunningham performance in ways that are both precise and evocative. But even the best descriptive criticism can do Cunningham an inadvertent disservice. The problem is that critics have been so eager to credit Cunningham with having liberated dance from the burden of projecting various sorts of meaning—narrative, symbolism, personal expression, and so on—that they fail to properly consider the *meaning* of this liberation. In this regard, it's instructive to contrast the extraordinarily sophisticated body of criticism and scholarship that John Cage's work has generated with the comparatively meager critical oeuvre Cunningham has elicited.

Descriptive criticism thus constitutes only the first, most tentative step toward accounting for Cunningham's ultimate significance. If it ignores the underlying sensibility that informs his repudiation of the Graham aesthetic, an essentially descriptive criticism can misconstrue Cunningham's significance just as surely as the more literal minded, politically motivated criticism that dismisses him as a "mere" formalist or as a practitioner of the (presumably escapist) "aesthetic of indifference." In fact, it sometimes seems easier to defend Cunningham against his enemies than to save him from his friends. In 1968, Arlene Croce, a great admirer of Cunningham's, wrote: "I thought, watching Merce's dances, that I was being subjected to a theory about dancing. I was too worried about the theory to look at the dancing (1968, 24). Given Cunningham's distaste for didacticism and manipulation, I don't think of him as the kind of artist who ever "subjects" his audiences to anything. Nonetheless, I think I know what Croce means. Cunningham's dances are often exercises in problem solving, exemplary instances of the mind and the body—the audiences' as well as the performers'—connecting and cross-fertilizing in new and unexpected ways. If ever a choreographer has offered us a portrait of the "thinking body" and of the mind-in-motion, that choreographer is Cunningham. Croce senses this, but unfortunately, she resolves the dilemma in a way that impoverishes the experience:

> I don't remember just when it was that I stopped making a terrific mental
> effort to understand Merce and just began enjoying him. Today it seems just as
> preposterous to make a mental effort over Merce as it does over Fred Astaire.

But for me, it was never a matter of "making a mental effort" over
Cunningham, an activity that sounds ancillary to (and dissociated from)
the sensory experience of watching his dances. I don't regard the thinking
that informs this book as an act of mental "effort" at all—but, rather, as
an attempt to trace a chain of associations that flow quite effortlessly from
the experience of watching his dancers perform. Carolyn Brown, surely one
of the greatest Cunningham dancers of all time, once had this to say about
dance criticism:

> I don't believe the written word can recreate the experience of seeing *any*
> dancing. Should it try, is the question. It seems to me that dance writing has to
> do something else. (1992, 122)

For better or for worse, this book tries to do something else, which is
not to imply that it won't attempt to convey what it's like to experience
Cunningham's work in the theater. But I make no effort to recreate entire dances through moment-by-moment description—if only because such
"close readings" tend to lose the generalist reader in a thicket of undifferen-
tiated detail. I believe that the best way of providing the nonspecialist reader
with a composite portrait of Cunningham's choreography is through the
steady accumulation of precisely described moments from many different
works—rather than relying on extended descriptions of a few particular
dances.

The dirty little secret of dance scholarship is that the least helpful (and
probably least read) passages in many otherwise good books are those that
attempt to reconstruct whole dances on paper. One of the most basic differences between dance criticism and film or theater criticism is that unless the
reader has already *seen* the work being discussed, he or she will not derive an
especially vivid sense of it from even the most detailed verbal description.
(There are, of course, some glorious exceptions to this rule—Edwin Denby
on "Agon," Arlene Croce on "The Four Temperaments"—but I don't pretend
to possess their all-too-rare powers of evocation.) Still, I've done my best
to capture and convey the special aura that infused Cunningham's work in
the late 1960s: the relationship between the dancers' bodies and the elegant
objects designed by Johns, Warhol, and Stella; the sensuous intelligence; the
cool, detached euphoria. I also make a great many connections between the
sensibility that informed his dances and many other cultural landmarks of
the 1960s: the films of Godard and Antonioni, the plays of Pinter, the novels

of Pynchon, and the essays of Susan Sontag. Cunningham stands at the very center of a great sea-change in taste; and to isolate him from these broader cultural currents is to deny the art of dance its hard-earned place at the table.

The most succinct description of the sort of scholarship I've attempted in this book comes from a great classicist, Kevin Dover, who argues that:

> The physical unearthing of new material is not in all circumstances more exciting than that kind of discovery which is ultimately the product of reflection; and a spark is often kindled by the mere juxtaposition of facts long familiar in isolation. (Nagler, 1981, 1)

Although many of the facts reported in this book have never before appeared in print, I readily concede that *Merce Cunningham: The Modernizing of Modern Dance* is not an exercise in scholarly sleuthing or archival unearthing. Much of this book is an act of reflection on "facts long familiar in isolation." To cite only the most obvious example: We know that many years ago Cunningham made the revolutionary decision to create dances in which movement, sound, and décor coexist in the same space and time while remaining autonomous of one another. But this fact assumes a considerably greater significance when we contrast it with primitivist theories of wholeness: the idea that modern dance is assumed to be the most holistic of the arts, the one best equipped to "heal" any number of dualities that bedevil the modern world. Another piece of received wisdom—the idea that Cunningham is a practitioner of the "collage" aesthetic—takes on a richer, more resonant meaning when juxtaposed against its antithesis, the Wagnerian impulse toward a "Gesamtkunstwerk" (or synthesis of the arts) that underlies so much of modernist primitivism. The Wagnerian aesthetic embodies the primitivist hunger for wholeness. By contrast, collage is the art of an age that has come to distrust the claims of wholeness. And the category of dances that Merce Cunningham refers to as "Events" is probably the best example anyone has yet produced of the collage aesthetic translated into the realm of performance.

These examples demonstrate the delicate relationship between "subjective" ideas and "objective" facts in this book. Obviously, *Merce Cunningham: The Modernizing of Modern Dance* is principally a book of ideas. And, even though the ideas are carefully grounded in fact(s), I readily concede that anyone looking for *all* of the relevant facts about *all* of Cunningham's major works will be sorely disappointed. (Readers in search of a Jack Webb–style "Just the facts, Ma'am" approach to Cunningham should consult David Vaughan's invaluable catalogue raisonné, *Merce Cunningham: Fifty Years.*) Similarly—and even though my focus is the "work," rather than the "life"—I make no attempt to document Cunningham's oeuvre in a dance-by-dance, chronological fashion. This book is organized thematically, not chronologically. Nevertheless, when it comes to Cunningham's chief innovations (e.g., the autonomy of movement and sound, the use of chance as a compositional strategy, etc.), I've attempted to trace the evolution of these practices more thoroughly, sequentially, and clearly than comparable accounts in previous studies.

This is especially true with regard to those periods of time (e.g., 1952–53) when an astonishing number of advances were pioneered simultaneously. For example, "Suite by Chance" in 1953 was not only the first dance of Cunningham's in which all essential space/time variables were arrived at by chance modes of composition. It also was his first dance set to a wholly electronic score—as well as the first dance in which movement and sound were entirely autonomous of one another. (The list goes on: "Suite" also marked Cunningham's first use of the stopwatch as a controlling device.) Similarly, in 1952, Cunningham became the first choreographer to utilize *musique-concrète* (specifically, a score by Pierre Henry and Pierre Schaeffer) as an accompaniment for dance. One can argue that Henry and Schaeffer were attempting the acoustical equivalent of the collage tradition in the visual arts. And, a year later, when Cunningham restaged this dance for his newly formed company, he retitled it (significantly) "Collage."

These years were just as seminal for his chief collaborators. In 1952, Cage, Cunningham, and Rauschenberg staged an untitled work (often referred to as "Theater Piece") at Black Mountain College, a work now widely regarded as the most important forerunner of those "art world" performances that just a few years later would be labeled "happenings." Cage encountered Rauschenberg's "white" and "black" paintings that same year; and their "musical equivalent," "4′33″"—Cage's legendary "silent" piece—premiered a few months later. In 1952–53 Cage—in collaboration with Earle Brown, Christian Wolff, and Morton Feldman—created "Williams Mix," an elaborately spliced audiotape recording that anticipated many of William Burrough's "cut up" and "fold in" techniques (as well as Burroughs's own subsequent experiments with audiotape). No less significant is the fact that 1953 was the year that Rauschenberg demonstrated the extent to which he (along with Jasper Johns) would oppose, perhaps even "erase," much of the heritage of abstract expressionism.

Merce Cunningham: The Modernizing of Modern Dance is a book that many readers will find unabashedly argumentative: It *argues* with much of the received wisdom that has stubbornly attached itself to Cunningham's work over the years. I take issue with many of the prevailing notions about Cunningham's relationship to the natural world, the way in which his choreography is said to have been influenced by the philosophy of Zen Buddhists such as D. T. Suzuki, and the impact that television is thought to have had on his work. This book challenges equally familiar notions about the connections between Cunningham's compositional procedures and those of abstract expressionism, the ways in which his choreography relates to conceptions of contemporary classicism, and the deeper significance of his attraction to the vocabulary of classical ballet. Certainly, when it comes to current academic fashion(s), this book is vigorously polemical. It champions a number of the ideas most vilified by the race/class/gender gurus: formalism, objectivity, disinterestedness, the value of the visual (as opposed to the tactile)—terms often associated (naively, in my view) with patriarchy, "the prevailing culture," the West, phallocentrism, and so on, ad infinitum, ad nauseam. Indeed, the primitivism that Cunningham, Johns, and Rauschenberg collectively repudiated has enjoyed a revival of sorts in recent years in the work of many feminist choreographers and performance artists.

But before we soar into the heady realms of primitivist theory, I'd like to begin on terra firma with the most vivid account I can muster of what it was like to first discover Cunningham's work in the late 1960s. What Moira Roth refers to derisively as "the aesthetic of indifference" is a pretty good description of my own emerging sensibility. And that helps to explain some of the peculiarities of my "taste" in modern dance: the reason I was slow to develop an appreciation for Martha Graham but felt an instant affinity with Merce Cunningham.

1
From Graham to Cunningham
An Unsentimental Education

The Persistence of Dandyism

> "A person appears comic to us if in comparison with ourselves he makes too great an expenditure on his bodily functions and too little on his mental ones."
> —Sigmund Freud, "Jokes and the Comic" (1965, 255)

> "The distinguishing characteristic of the dandy's beauty consists above all in an air of coldness which comes from an unshakable determination not to be moved."
> —Charles Baudelaire, "The Dandy" (1965, 29)

One would have thought the 1960s an ideal (perhaps *the* ideal) time for a first encounter with the primitive mysteries of Martha Graham. The cultural signposts all seemed to point in her direction: a renewal of interest in myth and ritual; the meteoric rise of "Dionysian" intellectuals such as Norman O. Brown; the pervasive body-consciousness; a sexualizing of the culture at large. Why then, on first encountering Graham's choreography, during the summer of 1967 (the notorious Summer of Love, no less), did I find her work rather . . . unlovable? Why did I behave so inappropriately, biting my tongue in a vain attempt to stifle a bad case of the giggles? No doubt, the narrow (some might say, ideological) confines of my sensibility were at fault. I was a precocious 17-year-old, eager to appear More-Sophisticated-Than-Thou. It was essential to my fragile, still-evolving sensibility that my enthusiasms all be certifiably modern. But Graham's work seemed most distinctive for its atavism, its willed primitivism. Hers were dances that harked back to the primordial ooze. Thus, it wasn't altogether apparent to me why modern dance was called *modern* dance.

What is apparent in retrospect is that I was already one of those fanatical high modernists, those purists who believed in the autonomy and separateness of every art form. I wanted dance to do something unique to dance. I didn't want choreographers "using" the body to tell stories, especially not stories that had already been given shape and urgency by great playwrights and novelists. So, obviously, there was going to be a "problem" with Graham. The very *names* of her characters, so literary, so burdened with overly generalized Meaning, tended to put me off: "He Who Summons"; "She of the Ground"; "The One Who Speaks"; "The One Who Dances" ... all of which made me feel like "The One Whose Head Ached From Allegory."

But the real obstacle in my path wasn't so much this ideological commitment to purity of medium but, rather, my temperamental commitment to coolness, distance, and irony—an "unshakable determination not to be moved." We think of the 1960s as a very "hot" decade, but that's only half-true. Those who came of intellectual age in the 1960s wanted to have it both ways (perhaps every which way): immediacy *and* distance, sensuality *and* irony. As a result, any adequate account of the 1960s and its cultural context will have to consider the cult of cool, in both the literal and the figurative sense of the term: hip; with-it; the-last-word-in-sophistication; but also cool as a matter of temperament, if not literally, temperature, as in: "Don't feel anything and if you do, don't show it." Graham, it seemed to me at the time, was not cool; worse, she was unfashionably "hot." (For Marshall McLuhan, one of the decade's chief taste-makers, "cool" was the ultimate compliment. Hence, television was defined as a "cool" medium; print culture was demonized as "hot.") From this cool (and distinctly aloof) point of view, Graham's work struck me as both oversized and overwrought, a casebook example of Freud's criterion for comedy, where the body is a little too much in evidence (or at least more in evidence than the mind). Stark Young's notorious wisecrack about Graham ("She looks as though she were about to give birth to a cube") succinctly summarized my sentiments.

Perhaps because Graham's work seemed so heavy (literally and figuratively), so humorless and devoid of irony, I seized on any moment that might provide some comic relief, no matter how unintended. Actually ... the *less* intended, the better: Tiresias in "Night Journey" bouncing on his seer's staff like a pogo stick; or Oedipus, in the same work, throwing his weight around so stiffly that he functioned as little more than a priapic prick. I think, too, of those little agitated knee runs Graham was so fond of. When The Penitent in "El Penitente" or Medea in "Cave of the Heart" pitter-patted to the left or the right on their knees, my response was to either laugh or wince or both.

The situations the characters found themselves in called for emotions of the most elemental sort; but that bourrée-on-the-knees seemed a bit prissy for the occasion. I also had a terrible time figuring out exactly what was supposed to be happening in many of these dances on a strictly narrative level. And a mind unsure of who's doing what to whom can distract one's attention from the serious business of looking. This was nowhere more of a problem than in "Deaths and Entrances," which I found both inscrutable and interminable. "Too many entrances and not enough deaths," I quipped to myself.

I'm not particularly proud of this behavior. In fact, I now consider it a grave lapse (or under nourishment) of taste. "Dark Meadow"—which I didn't discover until years later—now strikes me as one of the masterworks of the 20th century. But I hope that this retracing of my own aesthetic learning curve will reveal something of interest about a sensibility that was by no means unique to me, a mode of thinking and feeling that became quite fashionable in the mid-to-late 1960s. (It was of course the very sensibility that Moira Roth disparages as the "Aesthetic of Indifference." Had I known her essay at the time, I might well have proclaimed, "Vive la Indifference.") This sensibility can best be portrayed as a latter-day variety of dandyism, the phenomenon that Baudelaire described in his classic essay of 1863. One hundred years later, dandyism, with its "air of coldness," "its unshakable determination not to be *moved*," became a major—if undeclared—theme in the life of the 1960s counterculture. Certainly it was central to the massive transition that had already occurred in the visual arts: a move away from the hot, romantic, angst-ridden ethos of abstract expressionism toward the cooler, more impersonal detachment of pop and minimal art. Indeed, it's no coincidence that when Moira Roth contrasted the physical appearance of the abstract expressionists with that of the practitioners of the aesthetic of indifference, the image of the dandy figured into her comparison:

> In its deliberately apolitical and generally neutral stance, the Aesthetic of Indifference represented a new breed of artist, an alternative to the politically concerned Abstract Expressionists. George Segal, a young artist at this time, has described his memory of the typical abstract expressionist's heavy set appearance with drooping moustache and corduroy jacket...Duchamp and Cage, who struck him as models for a new 'slender, cerebral, philosophical, iconoclastic type', physically and intellectually very different from the Abstract Expressionist one. For Segal and others, the new artist had a dandy-like elegance of body build and a manner which delighted in cool and elegant plays of the mind: playfulness indeed was a key characteristic in most of this new breed of artist. (1977, 49)

References—invariably unflattering—to dandyism occur a number of times in the course of her essay. But what interests me at the moment is the effect that this latter-day dandyism had on the dance-going tastes of people like myself. The dandy's determination "not to be moved" is, above all, a fear of being emotionally overpowered, a fear of seduction. Perhaps laughter is the inevitable (if lamentable) response of the dandy to work that is unafraid of trafficking in large, overheated emotions. Laughter induces (or is induced by) a distancing of emotion—what Henri Bergson once described as a "momentary anesthesia of the heart," a condition woefully at odds with the "primitive" sense of awe and wonder that Graham was so determined to conjure up. And that's why Graham, at least at the time, didn't strike me as "cool." At least not in the manner of my other, recently acquired, certifiably "modern" enthusiasms (circa 1967, as I was about to enter college): The Peter Hall/RSC production of Pinter's *The Homecoming;* Andy Warhol's silk-screen portraits of Marilyn Monroe and Jackie Kennedy; the music of the Velvet Underground (often thought of as Andy Warhol's rock group); and films such as Resnais's *Last Year at Marienbad,* Antonioni's *Red Desert* and *Blow Up,* Michael Snow's "underground" classic *Wavelength,* and virtually everything by that most Brechtian of film directors, Jean-Luc Godard. Favorite novels included Robbe-Grillet's *The Erasers,* William Burroughs's *The Ticket That Exploded,* and Thomas Pynchon's study of technoparanoia, *The Crying of Lot 49.*

Earlier I used the word "Brechtian" in relation to the films of Godard. "Brechtian" was perhaps my favorite adjective of those years (although my ideas about Brecht were derived more from his manifestoes than from his plays). The critic, or, more properly, essayist whom I read with the greatest enthusiasm was Susan Sontag, whose essays "Against Interpretation," "The Aesthetics of Silence," and "One Culture and the New Sensibility" had, no doubt, a great deal to do with shaping the sensibility I've just sketched. By current standards of taste, this is a highly rarefied catalogue of enthusiasms. (In fact, their collective emotional temperature is so ice-cold that some may wonder about my use of the word "Enthusiasm.") The shared sensibility is hard-edged, ruthlessly nonsentimental, objectivist, and unapologetically brainy. Dance, you may have noticed, is conspicuously absent from the list. But what sort of dance would have been at home in this celestial pantheon?

Deep down, in my secret heart of hearts, I loved ballet: the space-devouring leaps, the ultra-high extensions, the superhuman majesty of it all. And, at its best (which is to say, in the work of Balanchine), the speed and the clarity—qualities that both quickened the pulse and sharpened the eye. Frank O'Hara, in a tribute to Maria Tallchief, wrote " . . . her breathing limbs tear ugliness out of our lives." I felt much the same way about Suzanne Farrell. But the late 1960s was not the time to admit to a fascination with something as traditional-sounding as "ballet." I was still intimidated by the externals: its history (the fact that it had a history!), its existence as "an institution," its presumed connection to, and dependence on, the citadels of wealth and power. How, one wondered, could anything performed in a great Edifice Complex like Lincoln Center possibly be relevant (oh, that awful 1960s word!), up-to-the-second, and so on. Of course, I would eventually realize that not being wholly indebted to the present is a virtue rather than a vice. But this, remember, was still the late 1960s. . . . Where, oh where, could one find the icy, dandified virtuosity of ballet outside the world of institutionalized art and beyond the precincts of tradition? The answer turned out to be the work of Merce Cunningham.

Human Bodies and Inanimate Objects: Savoring the Surface

The timing of my first encounter couldn't have been more propitious: May 1968, the month of months in the year of years, in the decade of decades (at least it felt that way at the time!). But even from the jaded—and perhaps a wee bit envious—vantage point of the early 21st century, 1968 remains the annus mirabilis of the decade that's become synonymous with radicalism of every kind, aesthetic as well as political. I don't mean to imply that the impact Cunningham's work made on me in May 1968 was entirely attributable to its fortuitous historical context, but the heady, intoxicating, convulsive character of the moment surely played a part. The site of my initiation— my sacre du printemps—was The Brooklyn Academy of Music (BAM). Cunningham's season at BAM opened on May 15, one day after the official beginning of the "worker-student" alliance on the barricades of Paris.

The political connotations of the moment were full of resonance for me; but I want first to focus on aesthetic impressions that were less dependent on the political passions of the moment. In the course of the next seven days in May, I had the great good fortune to see an astonishing number of the works that I still regard as some of Cunningham's greatest accomplishments: "Scramble," "Rainforest," "How to Pass, Kick, Fall and Run," "Winterbranch," "Walkaround Time," "Untitled Solo," "Place," and "Variations V." Over the course of the next several years, I became acquainted with other works that made a comparably indelible impression: "Tread," "Crises," "Canfield," and "Signals."

What first struck me about the company—and what distinguished Cunningham's dancers most clearly in my mind from Graham's—was their dandified detachment, not an "air of coldness" per se, but their collective sense of hyperalertness: the high carriage, the flexible head, the level gaze, the ultra-articulated feet, the aura of sangfroid. One of Cunningham's movement signatures was the highly propulsive off-center jeté, in which the dancers seemed to hurl their bodies in several directions simultaneously (but remaining—this is key—supremely balanced all the while). Frequently off-center, but rarely off-balance: that's one generalization we can safely make about Cunningham's choreography. Typically, the head cocks backward, the ribcage wrenches to one side, the left arm sculpts the third dimension while the right arm (defying Newton, embracing Einstein) explores the fourth. With Cunningham, body sculpture is not just a matter of which direction the dancer is traveling but also which way the performer faces while moving there. (Many choreographers think in terms of four directions: upstage, downstage, left, and right. Cunningham routinely utilizes *at least* eight: for example, the legs move on a diagonal upstage left while the head turns downstage left, and so on.)

The company members in 1968 were a remarkably diverse and idiosyncratic lot. Carolyn Brown was the paragon of classical purity, an ice queen who could give Suzanne Farrell a run for her money. Gus Solomons Jr., the only African American member of the company, was a long-limbed, lyrical contortionist. British-born Valda Setterfield displayed an odd mix of regal elegance and blunt prosiness. Watching her was a little like imagining a member of the Royal Family doing her own shopping at the local grocery store; even when dancing with great speed, she never seemed to be in a hurry. Clearly, the emotional temperature of Cunningham style has something in common with British reserve. Sandra Neels, more exuberantly "All American," was a pert brunette with long, lean legs who excelled at lyrical adagios. Barbara Lloyd, the pip-squeak of the bunch, moved with the greatest abandon, the most convincing appearance of "spontaneity." She was the only company member who seemed to luxuriate, unselfconsciously, in the sheer act—the sheer *joy*—of moving. And Cunningham was . . . well . . . a cunning ham, a great comic actor as well as a lithe, blithe, impish mover. Unlike the other male dancers who had been featured performers with Martha Graham, Cunningham was always more Ariel than Caliban, light and brainy rather than monumental or "earthy." The aura of tough-minded intelligence that radiated from the Cunningham company was more than a matter of onstage "attitude." Reportedly, the sort of conversation one overheard in the studio was a heady brew that freely mixed dance-related matters with philosophical aesthetics and terminology drawn from the visual arts. Gus Solomons Jr. held a degree in architecture from MIT. Carolyn Brown had been a philosophy major at Columbia. This was a brainy bunch. By contrast, the sort of conversation one overheard in other dance studios of the period sounded more like that of the Brady Bunch.

But the most distinctive thing about the Cunningham company's collective intelligence was the sensuous way it manifested itself in movement. Cunningham wasn't the only member of the group who exhibited a kind of cunning. Many of his dancers exuded a sly dexterity that called to mind the great tricksters in literature. There was something . . . ambidextrous about them. The isolation of one part of the body from another made them masters of rubbing the head while patting the stomach. (Typically, one leg would be elevated in demi-pointe while the other was raised in attitude.) The resulting sense of fragmentation began to intensify when one realized that the dancers merely shared the same space and time with the music, but that none of their movements were triggered or guided by it. (I was reminded of that scene in *Blow Up* in which David Hemmings teaches a very stoned Vanessa Redgrave how to move *against* the grain of the music she's listening to: how not to go with the flow.)

In Cunningham's "Untitled Solo" (originally choreographed in 1953 but revived for the 1968 season), his head, arms, and legs appeared so oblivious to one another that they could have been grafted together from three different bodies, moving at three different speeds. Indeed, "the Cunningham body" often looked as if it had been *assembled* by a practitioner of cubist collage. It emphasized the flexing and unflexing of the joints. And its great clarity of articulation derived in part from the way its allegro passages called attention to the *jointedness* of the body. Cunningham's dancers could move from whiplash fouette to penchee arabesque without apparent transition. (The resulting effect was not unlike those jarring jump cuts in Godard's *Breathless*: an exercise in rapid continuity without flow.) Of course, there also were quiet, comparatively tender, adagio sequences in many Cunningham pieces—as well as suspended balances that evoked an eerie tranquillity. Yet the stillness remained pregnant, active—not so much suspended animation as animated suspension. And there were often extended silences that sensitized one's ears to the soft brushing of feet against floor. The dominant quality was one of darting to and fro, what balletomanes would call "elance." (The most characteristic moments involved rapid shifts not only of direction, but of weight as well.)

With their unpredictable entrances and exits that seemed to tug at the outermost corners of one's attention, Cunningham's dancers seemed to be "here and there and yonder" all at once. And their faces were unlike those of any other dancers I'd seen. They avoided the pert, strained, plastered-on smiles of the ballet dancer as well as the dramatized angst that sometimes made modern dancers look hopelessly melodramatic. What one saw was the thought-process-made-visible: a complete concentration on the task at hand. Above all, they didn't seem silent in the way that Martha Graham's dancers did. They looked smart and wise (a little mischievous, no doubt), maybe even "smart ass," as if they had chosen to be silent, as if it was *cool* to be silent. In other words, they weren't silent because they were too emotionally overwrought to speak (or even worse, because they feared they might have nothing to say). No other dance company—certainly none that I knew of at the time—exuded a comparably mute cool, the sort of "advanced" (and highly "dandified") sensibility that, up until then, I associated almost exclusively with the world of painting and sculpture. This "art world" connection was an essential component of what made the company unique, and it took a variety of forms. For example, even on the most conventional of proscenium stages, it often seemed as if the dancers were performing in an art gallery or museum. Perhaps because the lighting never tried to "partner" the dancers or to focus one's attention in particular ways, the space felt clean and open. In other words, as in the gallery or museum, one's eyes enjoyed the liberating freedom to roam, to cruise, to savor those elegant surfaces.

Of course, the museum analogy is no mere metaphor, because the dancers, especially in those days, often shared the space with uncommonly curious objects designed by the same artists whose work was found in the leading galleries: Johns, Rauschenberg, Warhol, Stella, Morris, Nauman, and so on. Décor played an active (never merely decorative) role in many of these dances. Indeed, in a number of the works I first encountered between 1968 and 1970, the décor would interfere in some active way with one's perception of the dancing, throwing visual obstacles in the path of vision—in effect, demanding that we "look harder." For "Walkaround Time" (1968), Jasper Johns designed movable vinyl rectangles emblazoned with iconography from Duchamp's "Large Glass." These translucent "windows" often mediated the audience's relationship to the performers. In "Scramble" (1967), one's view of the dancing was sometimes obscured by Frank Stella's mobile aluminum frames, over which were stretched pieces of brightly colored cloth. Quintessentially, in "Tread" (1970), with decor by Bruce Nauman, the downstage edge of the proscenium was lined with 10 massive electric fans, half of which whirled at high speeds throughout the course of the performance. (Whenever one would view a dancer through the blades of the spinning fans, his or her body would briefly appear to be vivisected, an apt visual metaphor for the dissociation of body parts so central to Cunningham's choreographic style.)

I thought of this aspect of Cunningham's work as his "Antonioni connection," the practice that linked his handling of objects in space with the visual strategies so evident in some of my favorite Antonioni films from the 1960s. *Red Desert* (1964) for example, is filled with visual obstacles—railings, beams, furniture—that often come directly between the camera and the actors. Parenthetically, one might compare Antonioni's composition of the frame with Cunningham's overall organization of stage space. Antonioni often eschews the resources of montage (and even the more conventional editing techniques of "shot/reverse shot") in order to maximize the viewer's perceptual freedom. Significant information will sometimes appear only in the corner of a widescreen composition—and Antonioni refused to didactically manipulate the viewer's focus so as to insure that he or she notices it. Another consequence of this strategy is the poignant isolation of human beings against vast, flat backgrounds that are stark, white, and clinical.

Isolation—of one human being from another, even of one *body part* from another—is a key characteristic of Cunningham's work as well. And, despite the 1960s richly deserved reputation for communal activity, Antonioni-style *ennui* was showing up in some pretty unlikely places—even in the more advanced pop music of the period (most prominently, in the work of Lou Reed and the Velvet Underground, a group with extremely close ties to Andy Warhol and his galaxy of self-proclaimed "superstars"). Lou Reed, in his characteristic black leather jacket and mirror shades, was the very model of the thoroughly modern dandy. And the Velvet Underground was one of the few pop groups of the era that shared with John Cage an interest in industrial-strength noise. Thus, it felt like divine coincidence that the Velvet Underground played at a benefit party for the Cunningham company following the opening night performance at BAM in May 1968. I wasn't there, alas; but my dandy-wannabe sensibility envisioned this event as the last word in ultra-chic, ultra-cool.

Cunningham's "Place" (1966) exuded the same look and feel of urban detritus and anomie that pervaded the world of Warhol and the Velvet Underground. And Cunningham's sense of "isolation"—especially the final image of him thrashing violently across the floor, encased in a plastic garbage bag—suggested an almost infinite *distance* between himself, the other dancers, and the audience. And where precisely was "Place" *placed*? The title functioned ironically. Perhaps the best description of both the "action" and the "place" in "Place" appears in Mallarmé's poem "Coup de dés": "Nothing shall have taken place but place . . . except perhaps at an altitude so remote that any locality fuses with the beyond . . . a constellation, chilled with oblivion." Images of Mallarmé's ice-cold "beyond" were very much a part of the late 1960 Zeitgeist. Kubrick's *2001: A Space Odyssey*—which emphasized not the "excitement" of space travel but the loneliness and isolation of it—premiered in 1968. David Bowie, admittedly influenced by both Kubrick and the Velvet Underground (as well as by his close friendship with Warhol), subsequently produced his *Space Oddity* album, filled (and chilled) with references to distant space travel (e.g., "Ground Control to Major Tom"). Images of free-floating, isolated astronauts appeared in the film sequences of Cunningham's "Variations V" (1965); and, following the moon landing in 1969, Cunningham said that the quality of light and sound in the live television transmission of Neil Armstrong's first steps on the lunar surface were exactly what he'd been aiming for in "Canfield" that same year.

For me, the strangest, most intriguing (and for a while at least, most inexplicable) element of Cunningham's performances was the utter *isolation* of the design elements, their essential obliviousness to one another: their unshakable determination not to be moved, swayed, or in any way affected by each other. This was probably most apparent in the lighting designs for works such as "Canfield" and "Winterbranch" (1964). In both pieces, the play of light throughout the stage space was essentially indeterminate. Put bluntly: Light didn't serve the customary end of illuminating the dancers. If lighting instruments happened to fade up as the dancers darted past them— well and good. But the dimmer board had its own agenda, independent of the audience's (perfectly understandable) desire to see the dancing.

For "Canfield," Robert Morris designed a vertical column adorned with blazingly bright white lights focused on the back wall of the stage. Moving on a trolley that glided from side to side, the lighting began by establishing a predictable back-and-forth rhythm. But then—as if breaking down internally or simply becoming "indeterminate"—the trolley would unexpectedly reverse direction (just like a Cunningham dancer!) By displaying a "will of its own"—and no special propensity for focusing on "the human element," let alone the *dance* element—it erased many seemingly important distinctions between the animate and the inanimate. The lighting displayed all the brutal impersonality of a bank surveillance camera, recording blankly, without "human interest," oblivious to anything—no matter how conventionally significant—that might lay just beyond the perimeters of the viewfinder. A totally disinterested gaze that any aspiring dandy might envy! Yet another variation on the fixed, unblinking stare of the camera in Andy Warhol's films from the early 1960s. (The most sophisticated variation on this strategy occurred in Michael Snow's "Wavelength" [1967] where the camera takes a full 45 minutes to zoom glacially, but inexorably, toward one inanimate spot on the wall of a room, utterly indifferent to what sounds suspiciously like a murder occurring just outside the frame.)

This attitude of "indifference" was equally evident in Pauline Oliveros's sound score for "Canfield"—which assigned the musicians the task of scientifically testing the acoustical properties of the performance space. As the lights dimmed out at BAM, one could hear Cage, David Tudor, and Gordon Mumma communicating with one another over walkie-talkies. With a cool and scrupulous objectivity, they discussed the acoustical properties of the opera house. The Holy Grail for these techno-musicians was a search for what they called the "resonant frequency" of the performance space. Theoretically—if they could then match the desired frequency with that of their instruments—a deep, audible pulse would result. (This seemed to me about as likely as Abbie Hoffman's chances of levitating the Pentagon; but what mattered most was the audacity of the ambition.) Indifferent to the "dance performance" occurring in their midst, the techno-musicians proceeded with an overt series of experiments, a disinterested "sizing up" of the auditorium, an icily objective examination of its acoustical dimensions.

There was something a little scary about the single-mindedness with which these sound-crazed fanatics went about their mission. You sensed that even if someone were to yell "Fire" in this crowded theater, they'd continue to go about their business in a business-like way.

I distinctly recall Gordon Mumma blowing short blasts on a bugle while scrupulously turning a full 360 degrees. The sound ping-ponged off a variety of surfaces (including the bodies of the dancers). That some of these "surfaces" were human appeared to be of no special concern to him. Cunningham seemed to be contemplating that most frightening of all possibilities: a posthuman world. Like Warhol and Michael Snow, he evoked, without any apocalyptic melodrama or self-pity, an "inhuman" landscape that refuses to lend human beings or human consciousness any special pride of place. (The art critic Leo Steinberg once suggested that Jasper Johns's early work is "about human absence." Johns then "absented" himself even further by protesting that Steinberg's comment misleadingly implied "he had been there" in the first place! Those early works, Johns insisted, were "objects alone." [Francis 1984, 50]) Of course, it's one thing to praise a visual artist for creating "pure" objects, and quite another to praise a *choreographer* for deemphasizing the differences between his highly trained dancers and the inanimate objects with which they shared the stage. But, for me, this was the practice that lent Cunningham's dances their special flavor, their mentholated cool. Cunningham was a Pygmalion in reverse, choreographing dances in which performers seemed to acquire the emotional reticence and palpable physicality of objects. (One thinks, quintessentially, of Cunningham dancing with a chair strapped to his back in "Antic Meet" [1958].) It was only a matter of time, it seemed, before Cunningham choreographed a dance called "Objects" (a work with that title premiered in 1970).

How very different this approach to the inanimate was from the world in which Martha Graham set her dances: a "magical" place of primitive animism—where objects, active and transformational, were no less alive than people (e.g., the stretch of rope that serves variously as suicide noose and umbilical cord in "Night Journey"; that shimmering, wiry cage that Medea dons in "Cave of the Heart"; the bar of metal that functions alternately as crucifix and banner in "El Penitente"; the section of cloth in "Clytemnestra" that does triple duty as queenly robe, Agamemnon's "welcome mat" and funereal drape). In Graham's work, the décor, no less than the characters, felt organic and alive. Both seemed to possess an inner dynamism. Noguchi once described the sculptural settings he designed for Graham as "an extension of her body." But in Cunningham's pieces, dancers aspired to the quiet, *inanimate* elegance of objects. (Today, no doubt, we'd accuse Cunningham of having "objectified" his dancers, thereby subjecting them to the predatory "male gaze." What a pity. How myopic!) For many artists in the 1960s, "the object" had achieved virtual cult status; indeed, objects were *the* privileged icons of high modernism. "In the early '60s the formula was art = object," declared Mel Bochner (quoted by Johnson [1976, 10]). Rainer Crone put the matter more aphoristically when he argued that in Warhol's silkscreen portraits of the widowed Jacqueline Kennedy "the emotions of mourning become object" (Johnson 1976, 11). This helps to explain why Cunningham's work, unlike Graham's, could (and inevitably *would*) insinuate itself effortlessly into the company of those cool passions I alluded to earlier—the work of Robbe-Grillet, Pinter, Antonioni, Michael Snow, Susan Sontag, and so on—all of which, in one way or another, seemed to endorse or promote a "cult of the object" and the implicit sensuousness of its surface.

For example, in Robbe-Grillet's and Alain Resnais's film *Last Year at Marienbad*, it was often difficult to tell whether one was looking at a living actor, frozen in objectlike immobility or at a genuinely inanimate object, a mannequin. But again, in this context, to treat people like objects was not to "objectify" them in the current, highly pejorative, politically incorrect sense but, rather, to liberate them from the limitations of strictly psychological modes of explanation. And, at the same time, to "objectify" people was also to reinvest them with what Robbe-Grillet liked to call "être-la," a sense of sheer *thereness*, of palpable physicality. In his seminal essay, "For a New Novel" (1965), Robbe-Grillet made the definitive argument against allegorical modes of representation, complaining about the process by which physical realities are transformed (or "deformed") into "mere" symbols and metaphors, thereby forsaking their concreteness:

> At every moment, a continuous fringe of culture (psychology, ethics, metaphysics, etc) is added to things, giving them a less alien aspect, one that is more comprehensible, more reassuring. Sometimes the camouflage is complete: a gesture vanishes from our mind, supplanted by the emotions which supposedly produced it, and we remember a landscape as austere or calm without being able to evoke a single outline, a single determining element. (1967, 274–75)

The physicality of the landscape is in danger of being subsumed by the adjectives we use to describe it. In Robbe-Grillet's novels and films, by contrast, objects are divested of meaning (which he referred to derisively as "the fog of meaning"). "Around us, defying the noisy pack of our animistic or protective adjectives, things are there," he noted with elegant matter-of-factness.

Cunningham's determination to cut through the "fog of meaning" was especially evident in his approach to male/female partnering. Traditionally, in both ballet and modern dance, one of the functions of the pas de deux or the duet was to signify romantic and/or erotic entanglement. But in Cunningham's work, partnering is often executed in such an impersonal way that it's divested of such connotations. (Even when bodies are pressed tightly together, the dancer's attention seems focused on something other than his or her partner's flesh.) The audience's attention thus shifts to what the movement "is," not what the movement "means."

Another way in which Cunningham encourages us to focus on what the movement "*is*" (rather than on what it "means" or what it appears to be "leading up to") is by refusing to differentiate in any hierarchical way between steps that are traditionally preparatory (e.g., a plié that precedes a jeté) and the steps that normally serve as climax or exclamatory punctuation for a phrase. In the fractured causality of Merce Cunningham's universe, one moment doesn't "lead" to the next. Each moment—each instant of the present—is given the full weight of his attention. As Cunningham once wrote, "If one thinks of dance as an errand to accomplish, as a message to be sent, then one misses the *spring* along the way" (1957, 22). Cunningham's emphasis on the here and now sounds very much like the goal for art that Gertrude Stein articulated in her 1935 "Lectures in America": "The Business of Art is to Live in the actual Present, That is, the complete actual present, and to express that complete actual present" (1975, 59).

Certainly, there are parallels to be drawn between Stein's dislocations of syntax and Cunningham's chance-generated ordering of phrases. (Cage, for example, often spoke of his desire to "demilitarize syntax," to radically rearrange linear habits of association.) But it's also essential to point out that Cunningham's sense of "presence" is never uncomplicated and rarely unmediated. The visual obstacles in works such as "Tread" and "Walka-round Time" and the many ways in which Cunningham acknowledges the impact of the electronic and the digital revolution on our lives all conspire to create an active tension between "presence" and mediation. But, like Robbe-Grillet, Cunningham emphasizes the physical palpability of the body-as-object (even if our ultimate relationship to that body is mediated in a variety of ways.) By contrast, the moment the body on stage begins to function as a representation of (say) Medea, Jocasta, or Clytemnestra, its locus of reality moves *elsewhere*, into an imaginary, less physically palpable realm, somewhere other than here (and now). As Cage wrote in a program note for the 1968 BAM season, "By not relying on psychology, this 'modern' dance is freed from the concerns of most such dancing. What comes through, though different for each observer, is *clear*—since one can only approach it directly, not through an idea of something else than itself and [the dancers] do not cover themselves with disguising costumes."

Cunningham's dancers exemplified the beauty (but never the superficiality) of surface: clean, sensuous, self-sufficient, rarely invoking inner depths or hidden mysteries. As a result, Cunningham's dancers seemed utterly unlike most actors in the theater, whose protean, chameleon-like transformations suggested that they were always hiding something—or that their "essence" lay elsewhere. ("I have that within which passes show," says Hamlet.) But, in Cunningham's choreography, the reigning sensibility was closer to Frank Stella's description of his own work from that period: "My painting is based on the fact that only what can be seen there *is* there. It really is an object" (cited in Galser [1968, 158]). Perhaps Cunningham was echoing Stella when he said of his choreography: "What is seen is what it is" (Vaughan 1997, 67).

There was though, one theater experience in the late 1960s that affected me in much the same way Cunningham's work did: Peter Hall's glacially elegant production of Pinter's *The Homecoming* (1965) performed by the Royal Shakespeare Company (RSC). (The painter Larry Rivers paid *The Homecoming* the ultimate art-world compliment when he stated that "Mr. Pinter has created an object" [Landau 1973, n.p.].) Hall's production was itself the consequence of a sea-change in British theater that bears a close (if not exact) resemblance to the shift in sensibility from Pollock and Graham to Johns, Rauschenberg, and Cunningham. *The Homecoming* was first produced by the Royal Shakespeare Company, whose new "house style" of the 1960s was based on a rejection of emotional bombast in favor of cool, clean intelligence (a "cleansing" intelligence designed to purge the theater of every vestige of 19th-century histrionics and pageantry). Shakespeare was now being performed with the same lean, minimalist precision that characterized Hall's approach to Pinter. John Barton's new "rational style" of verse speaking was matched by a revolution in scene design as evident in Peter Brook's legendary productions of *King Lear* (1962) and *A Midsummer Night's Dream* (1970) as in John Bury's setting for *The Homecoming*. (Brook's *Dream*, for example, did away with moonlit forests and gossamer-clad fairies in favor of gleaming white plastic and chrome.) Kenneth Tynan summed up this revolution as follows: The RSC, he wrote "has developed . . . a classical style of its own. How is it to be recognized? By solid Brechtian settings that emphasize wood and metal instead of paint and canvas" (Steinberg 1985, 85). Paint and canvas implied painted illusionism (i.e., imaginary environments). The RSC's settings by contrast, were minimalistic art objects that refused to disguise their own raw materials. To paraphrase Frank Stella: "Only what could be seen was there."

This production of Pinter's play, just as surely as Cunningham's dances, helped me to understand what Susan Sontag must have meant when she wrote in "Against Interpretation" (1964), an essay that became for many of us a virtually sacred text in the late 1960s, "Transparence is the highest, most liberating value in art . . . . Transparence means experiencing the luminousness of the thing in itself, of things being what they are" (1966, 13). As in Pinter's *The Homecoming*, this savoring of surface is as much a sensual, as a cerebral, pleasure. And in Sontag's oft-quoted, aphoristic conclusion to the essay, she maintained, "In place of a hermeneutics we need an erotics of art" (14). Cunningham's work offered an erotics fit for a dandy, a sensuality more visual than tactile, designed for the observer whose eyes derived pleasure from their sheer mobility, scanning and cruising at will. His dances exuded other forms of cool eroticism as well. "Rainforest" (1968), with its luxuriously sexy, gently wafting, helium-filled, silver-mylar pillows (designed by that king of cool, Andy Warhol) seemed to me an urban "Schéhérazade," the last word in chic sensuality. I think, too, of Cage sipping champagne as he read quirky anecdotes in 1965's "How to Pass, Kick, Fall, and Run." (The sharp thud of the cork popping from his champagne bottle struck me as one of the most elegant and aristocratic sounds I'd ever heard.) How very different this dandified sensuality was from the fashionable narcissism of the emerging dance boom. Cunningham's dancers never wallowed so visibly in their own physicality that they seemed to be nuzzling or licking themselves on stage.

Cunningham's eroticism also had little or nothing to do with "the natural." By contrast, the body, especially the naked body, functioned in much of the art of the late 1960s as the very symbol of "naturalness." This, after all, was the decade in which the dress rehearsal was less common than the *undress* rehearsal. However, you don't have to be a semiotician to realize that a body minus clothing is still a product of its cultural conditioning. (Even naked, we continue to move in ways that are dictated by the clothes we've just discarded.) But, unlike most of the great pioneers of modern dance, Cunningham never embarked on a quest for the most "natural" way of moving; his style often seemed willfully inorganic. Given the chance-dictated nature of movement sequences in his work, it's not surprising that the ordering of phrases rarely seemed guided by a "natural" sense of flow (or even by anatomical logic).

Not Going With the Flow

Accordingly, the Cunningham company also avoided any trace of hippie-dippie, touchie-feelie, ersatz ritual: no mystical rites of initiation, no facile invocations of oneness with the audience—a far cry from those exotic (but sanitized) theatricalizations of "primitive" ritual that were so much a part of the dance boom at its peak. (Remember those hideous Gerald Arpino ballets with titles like "The Sacred Grove on Mt. Tamalpais"?) In 1968, The Living Theater toured the United States with its most utopian work, *Paradise Now*, featuring "the rite of universal intercourse," in which the audience was invited to join the performers in an extended group-grope. By contrast, Cunningham—with his insistence on preserving the autonomy of every element—countered that tendency of the "counterculture" that was all about fusion, audience-interaction, and going with the flow. (Those fans in "Tread" that blew air in your face, seemed to be saying "Keep your distance. . . . Do not under any circumstances mistake what you see on stage for a participatory rite.")

Furthermore, one rarely if ever saw images of togetherness or "communality" on stage. Body-to-body contact in Cunningham's choreography is usually impersonal and asexual. Dancers are often handled by one another like inanimate objects. (This is especially true in works such as "Tread" and "How to Pass, Kick, Fall, and Run.") The effect frequently resembles a speeded up, deadpan parody of "touchie-feelie" encounter group exercises. In "Crises" (1960), the dancers wore elastic bands around various parts of their bodies. By inserting a hand or an arm through the stretch band surrounding another dancer's wrist or waist, the performers could momentarily bind themselves together—but the key word is "momentarily." Social bonds in Cunningham's dances are, literally and figuratively, *elastic* and predicated on principles of individual liberty. (His choreography seemed to heed the advice of Kahlil Gibran: "Let there be spaces in your togetherness.")

But the culture at large in the late 1960s seemed intent on fusion, not separation. The dominant sentiment of the period was probably best summed up by the opening lines of The Beatles' "I Am The Walrus": "I am he as you are he as you are me and we are all together"—culture as a psychedelicatessen where all the ingredients flowed together in a sort of paisley update of Art Nouveau. The most common artistic and technological embodiment of this craving for oneness was mixed-media of the sort one found at "psychedelic discotheques," the multiscreen projection systems that wowed the crowds at Expo '67, or that were featured in a good deal of intermedia art. Nam June Paik, a key proponent of such mixes, discerned a sexual metaphor beneath much of this multimedia mania: "Male human body has nine holes. Female body has ten. When all holes are filled, you have satisfaction. Purpose of inter-media art is to plug all holes as fast and efficiently as you can."

Without a doubt, the best-known, mixed-media dance work that sought to plug all the holes was Robert Joffrey's "Astarte" (1967). Certainly when it came to publicizing the many connections between dance and the counterculture, it left no hole unplugged. On March 15, 1968—exactly two months before the beginning of Cunningham's season at BAM—a psychedelicized photo of Trinette Singleton as "Astarte" graced the cover of *Time* magazine. Clearly, "Astarte" had succeeded in fingering the Zeitgeist. Here was a work dedicated to the blurring of boundaries: film/live action; audience/performers; inside of the theater/outside on the street. While Singleton gyrated in her paisley leotard, Max Zomoso—dressed in jacket and tie and cunningly planted in the front row of the house (a symbolic surrogate for the audience)—gradually rose from his seat, enraptured by this ancient Moon Goddess. Slowly, as if hypnotized, he stripped down to his underwear and surrendered to her primitive power. All the while, gigantic filmed images of Singleton were projected onto an undulating scrim curtain. "Astarte" ended with Zomoso drifting somnambulistically out the back door of the theater, while film footage purported to show him exiting, into an alley, totally tranced-out. This was it: the bridging of the gaps, the plugging of the holes between art and life, live action and filmed overlay, the space of the performance and the "real" world of the street.

By contrast, Cunningham's "Variations V" (1965), with film projection by Stan Van Der Beek and video by Nam June Paik, seemed utterly unlike the garden variety (the "got-to get-ourselves-*back*-to-the-Garden" variety), multimedia—or multi*mediocrity*—of the period. This was not Fillmore East or the Electric Circus. The images didn't meld seamlessly into one another. There was no attempt to clobber the audience into blissed-out submission. If "Astarte" epitomized the "mixed media" of the period, "Variations V" was an example of *un-mixed*-media. Those whose idea of a good time was to drop acid and then crash the last 10, solarized minutes of *2001*—sitting as close to the screen as possible—would not find comfort here. If there was any sort of connectedness to be found in this work, it was not the tactile, sensory massage variety. In "Variations V," the dancers moved through a series of electromagnetic fields, triggering bleeps and blurts of electronic sound as they darted in and around antenna-like poles. When Cunningham's dancers "reached out to touch someone," it was more likely to remind you of Ma Bell rather than the sort of touch-therapy then being practiced at places such as The Esalen Institute. This was the electronic interconnectedness of long distance. In "Walkaround Time" (1968), when Carolyn Brown performed slow developpés on demi-pointe, she "swept" her working leg like an electronic antenna picking up otherwise invisible signals. And a year later, when Cunningham choreographed a work called "Signals," the title felt entirely appropriate—maybe even inevitable. In "Signals," the dancers often stood in one place with feet firmly planted, while their torsos tilted and twisted like radar scanners. Furthermore, one dancer wielded a stick in a way that both delineated and enforced the physical distance between the performers.

Although we weren't quite ready to describe it as such at the time, this was dancing for the electronic age. Even the most cursory glance at the orchestra pit made it immediately apparent that we had entered a brave new world. The electronic paraphernalia included wave function generators, pitch sensors, signal modifiers, frequency shifters, VU meters, oscilloscopes. . . . But what made this strange universe seem less forbidding to the layperson was the aura of happy chaos that permeated the pit: What we actually saw resembled a bunch of overgrown kids playing with their expensive toys. Between Cage and his cohorts, it looked as if the Hardy Boys had commandeered their way into mission control at the Kennedy Space Center: lots of dials and switches, criss-crossing wires, a maze of electronic circuitry.

In April 1969, prior to the company's next season at BAM, a controversy arose that illustrates Cunningham's ambiguous relationship to the very idea of "music" for dance. Two different unions, Local 802 of The American Federation of Musicians and Local 4 of The International Alliance of Stage Employees (the electricians), fought one another for jurisdiction over the activities in the orchestra pit. The electricians claimed that the strange sound-producing equipment it contained was too dependent on electronics to qualify as musical instrumentation. Suffice it say that the sounds emanating from this high-tech pit were rarely acoustical. They were usually generated electronically in ways that eliminated the role that the *body* of the musician had traditionally played in the creation of sound on more traditional instruments: *sound from which the body has been excluded.* (Even Pierre Schaeffer, whom we think of as the founder of *musique-concrète,* was opposed to the use of electronic oscillators as sound sources. He feared that the resulting sounds would feel "inhuman.")

So what happens when an all-too-human dancer's body moves through that kind of auditory environment? What sort of movement is stylistically consistent with such sounds? Inorganic movement... choreography that never pretends or presumes to have discovered the most "natural" way of moving. And, despite the clarity and concreteness of the physical images, both sound and décor often worked to impose a layer of mediation between the dancers and the audience. Cunningham seemed to acknowledge that the privileged place of physical presence in our lives had been challenged— perhaps irreversibly—by electronics. His dancers often appeared to inhabit the landscape of the sci-fi, technobody that Thomas Pynchon had described in novels like *The Crying of Lot 49.* Cunningham wasn't the only choreographer to acknowledge this new electronic universe, but he responded to the Zeitgeist with deadpan acceptance rather than moralistic condemnation. (Again, it's evidence of the sensibility that Moira Roth would dismiss as "indifference.") By contrast, the dance theater pieces of Alwin Nikolais (which also employed electronic sound scores) often took the form of neat and simpleminded allegories about the dangers of mechanical reproduction, the invasions of the body snatchers, and so on—conventional, soft-headed, humanist "messages." And ironically, even though the bodies of Nikolais's dancers were often completely disguised beneath body tubes, stretch jersey, and slide projections, the end result was much more familiar and recognizably "human" than Cunningham's world where the most fundamental differences between human beings and inanimate objects were virtually ignored.

But the most revealing contrast was, once again, with the work of Martha Graham. While Graham and so much of the modern dance world exuded a sentimental primitivism, a longing for lost Edens (or at least a yearning for a long-lost sense of "the organic," the natural), Cunningham seemed fully reconciled to the city. What might have struck Graham as urban blight became for Cunningham a potential delight, a source of complexity. There were no rhapsodies to the world of lost unity or wholeness; but rather a celebration of fragmentation and simultaneity—an acceptance, in other words, of the world we actually inhabit.

Clarity Amid Clamor

Of course, in May 1968 many aspects of that world seemed difficult to accept, let alone celebrate. Halfway through that convulsive year, we were already feeling psychically numbed. In April, Martin Luther King Jr. was assassinated; in June, Bobby Kennedy. July saw the demonstrations and the police riot that disrupted the Democratic Convention in Chicago. In August, Soviet tanks rolled into Prague, effectively ending the Velvet Revolution. One psychic depth charge after another, each searing its way into wounds that never quite managed to heal. Dandified detachment was difficult to achieve and even harder to maintain. Warhol's silver pillows, so buoyantly detached, became a case in point: On June 3, just a few days after the conclusion of the Cunningham season at BAM (and two days before the assassination of Robert Kennedy), Andy Warhol was shot eight times by a would-be assassin. Warhol, who liked to hover "above it all," perhaps in emulation of his "Silver Clouds," was literally brought down to earth. Thus in May 1968, the perceptual skills that one developed and honed at a Cunningham performance began to feel strangely like a mode of survival training. How to maintain one's sense of clarity, of perceptual freedom in the midst of sensory assault? That was one of the key questions Cunningham's work raised for me.

The sound scores could be excruciatingly loud and aggressive. La Monte Young's metal-against-glass assault on the ears in "Winterbranch" made even the shrillest chunk-of-chalk-on-the-blackboard seem soothing by comparison. Yet the accompanying stage pictures maintained great clarity amid the clamor. One's neck and shoulders would tense tightly from the sound—like a cat under threat from a dog. But the lucidity of line and shape helped to restore one's equilibrium. Cunningham's dancers were ports in a storm: islands of icy, elegant detachment.

Similarly, Cunningham's work taught one how to practice a kind of selective inattention, necessitated by the competing and often irreconcilable claims being made on one's sensorium. Often, it was impossible to "take it all in." To make everything fit, to make it cohere: that way lay madness. Only a conspiracy theorist out of Pynchon's *The Crying of Lot 49* would even attempt it. Pynchon wrote about "the true paranoid, for whom all is organized in spheres joyful or threatening about the central pulse of himself." And in *Gravity's Rainbow* (1973), Pynchon would write about the other side of the perceptual coin, the state of "anti-paranoia, where nothing is connected to anything, a condition not many of us can bear for long." The alternative to both was solipsism: a crowding out, a turning inward, a refusal to confront complexity and simultaneity. The dandy, by contrast, is someone who pulls back without turning inward. To Moira Roth, the dandy's "unshakable determination not to be moved" (or in her words, his "indifference") is apolitical—or worse. But the jarring events of 1968 convinced me that the dandy's detachment *could* become an essential ingredient of radical politics.

Cunningham's performances provided a special space, a "manipulation-free zone" in which you could begin to reclaim control over your own sensorium. Consider the relationship between movement and sound in a Cunningham dance. In order for the movement to remain independent of the sound, it was necessary for Cunningham's dancers to perform a remarkable feat of selective concentration. It's one thing (and no easy thing) to execute ruthlessly complicated rhythmic counts in silence, without musical accompaniment. But it's infinitely more difficult to do what Cunningham asks of his dancers: to focus in such a way that your concentration isn't broken by seemingly random, easily distracting eruptions of sound. Here the dandy's "unshakable determination not to be *moved*" takes on a literal, not just a figurative, meaning.

If some of Cunningham's works were exercises in sensory overload, others were studies in silence. The sound scores for a number of dances were set at the very lowest threshold of auditory perception. Cage, for example, claimed he could never hear any of Gordon Mumma's contribution to "Landrover" (1972). Sensory overload and silence; bone-crushing energy and perceptual clarity: the two complimentary poles of Cunningham performance in the late 1960s and early 1970s. Herbert Marcuse, an eminence grise of the New Left in the 1960's, argued that "There is no free society without silence" (1980, n.p.). Cunningham seemed to embody this Marcuseian sentiment. His distaste for manipulation seemed to parallel one of the more important differences between The New Left and its older, stodgier predecessor from the 1930s. The New Left claimed to be suspicious of the very concept of leadership, the idea that a progressive political movement might depend on the all-too-manipulative exhortations of charismatic leaders. Thus, in theory (if not in practice), the very distinction between "leaders" and "followers" disappeared for The New Left. In his aptly titled *Revolution for the Hell of It*, Abbie Hoffman wrote: "We are printing 20,000 buttons that say 'Yippie Leader'. . . . The only way to support a revolution is to make your own" (1968, 187–88).

But whenever I wanted to make "political" claims for Merce Cunningham's art (or whenever I needed to defend his work against charges of mere "formalism" or "indifference"), I invariably turned for support to Bertolt Brecht, the artist who (to my mind) had achieved the most convincing synthesis of aesthetic *and* political radicalism. Brecht, in his play *Galileo* (1938), provided a devastating critique of leadership: "Unhappy is the country that breeds no hero," states one character. To which Galileo replies: "Unhappy is the country that *needs* a hero." It was also Brecht who formulated the theory of the *Verfremdungseffekt*, the estrangement or alienation effect, which places a positive premium on emotional detachment. Of course, people continue to complain that Brecht failed to practice what he preached and that his theories—as exciting as they might sound in the abstract—had little bearing on the eventual success or failure of his plays. Anyone searching for concrete examples of how Brecht's theories might function in actual performance practice need look no further than the nearest collaboration of Cunningham and Cage. Not that the two of them shared anything remotely resembling Brecht's Marxist politics—far from it. Cage once titled an installment of his *Diaries*, "how to improve the world (you will only make matters worse)." But that didn't prevent their work from functioning in a variety of Brechtian ways. As Emile de Antonio said of Andy Warhol: "Andy's not radical, but his work is radical." I would make the same claim for Cunningham. (And, Cage's brand of libertarian anarchism may not be Marxist, but it's certainly politically radical.)

Brecht envisioned his ideal spectator as a sort of dandy: someone who would smoke throughout the entire performance, remaining relaxed, disengaged, unflappable. The smoke would help create a zone of distance between the spectator and the spectacle. Brecht wanted his audiences "not only awake, but alert." At the conclusion of his play *The Resistible Rise of Arturo Ui* (1941), Brecht's spokesperson declares, "If only we could learn to look, rather than gape." "Looking" connoted an active, agile, and voluntary use of one's eyes; "gaping" implied stupefaction, passivity, perhaps even hypnosis. Cunningham's organization of stage space promotes looking rather than gaping. By rejecting Renaissance models of perspectival space, he avoids creating what Giorgio Vasari called "magnets to the eye," the sort of vanishing point that lures visual attention involuntarily upstage. While watching a Cunningham piece, one tends to scan left and right rather than zooming in on a single point set in deep space.

Cunningham's collaborations also seemed to me to provide the best available example of what Brecht was after when he criticized Wagner's ideas about theatrical synthesis. Brecht advocated a "separation of the elements," an anti-Gesamtkunstwerk, in which each collaborative element maintained its autonomy. Thus, for me, Brecht and Cunningham began to resonate off of one another in mutually enriching ways: Cunningham provided concrete examples of what Brecht (in many instances) had only theorized; and Brecht's theories helped me to understand the ways in which Cunningham's collaborations were actually functioning in performance. Increasingly, it seemed to me that the heart of Cunningham's achievement lay in these collaborations. It was only by considering Cunningham's movement *in relation* to the music of Cage or the decor of Johns and Rauschenberg that one fully understood just how radical this whole enterprise really was.

Saving Cunningham From Himself

Shortly after the BAM concert, I began to read everything about Cunningham I could get my hands on. Clearly, by 1968, most reputable dance critics had developed at least a grudging admiration for his choreography. But there remained one aspect of Cunningham's work that even his most enthusiastic supporters couldn't bring themselves to accept. Selma Jeanne Cohen's *Dance Magazine* review of the May 1968 season contains an all-too-typical example of this prejudice: "About the only complaint anyone could register against 'How to Pass . . . ' was the difficulty of listening to John Cage's wry stories and concentrating on the dancers at the same time." For most dance critics, sound and decor in a Cunningham work are thought to interfere with—to distract our attention from—all that really matters: the movement. Given the artistic stature of Cunningham's collaborators, this is excruciatingly ironic. Not since the Diaghilev era had so renowned a group of composers and visual artists agreed to design sound scores, costumes, and décor for a dance company. (On this point, at least, everyone seems to agree.) Given this fact, one would expect a small scholarly industry to have arisen for the purpose of defining and examining the sensibility that Cunningham shares with Rauschenberg, Johns, Cage, and the other members of his illustrious circle.

But the plain, sad truth of the matter is that the dance community has always been a bit impatient with, embarrassed by, and ultimately condescending toward the sound scores and décor that Cunningham commissions from advanced composers and visual artists. Even the most superficial survey of what's been written about Cunningham over the years reveals that Selma Jeanne Cohen's comments constitute the rule rather than the exception. In a

1954 *Dance Magazine* review of the seminal "Suite by Chance," Doris Hering wrote:

> This nihilistic excursion used something called "For Magnetic Tape" by Christian Wolff. To a series of silences and squeals that set the teeth on edge, Mr. Cunningham and his group meandered about unrelated to each other and unrelated to the audience. It was an ordeal. (1954, 70)

A decade later, little had changed. In a Sunday *New York Times* essay from August 1963, then dance critic Allen Hughes quoted a letter from an audience member who felt put-upon by John Cage's scores for Cunningham's "Aeon" (1961) and "Antic Meet" (1958):

> My friend and I so enjoyed the wonderful performance (titled) the "Modern Dance" on Aug. 6 (a program shared by the companies of Paul Taylor and Donald McKayle) that we not only bought tickets for the following two performances, but also persuaded our young daughters to spend their baby-sitting money on tickets too. I must ask you to be good enough to refund at least their two tickets, because . . . we were not forewarned of the type of 'music' we would be subjected to . . .

After quoting another such letter, Hughes chastised Cunningham as follows:

> Because modern dance, with its admittedly confusing diversity offers more than enough surprises (some unpleasant) of its own, it seems too bad that it must also be saddled with those of another art, even when a relationship exists between the two. . . . Something must be wrong somewhere when decisions about watching dancing depend on the ability to tolerate the music that goes with it.

The dance critic Walter Terry, in a 1965 review of "Winterbranch," complained that not only are the sound and the light distracting, but also that they constitute an unconscionably aggressive and painful assault on the sensorium of the spectator. (Terry's essay was titled "Show a Little Mercy, Merce"):

> ticket purchasing dance followers should not be physically tortured by amplified sounds that literally pain the eardrums or by blinding lights suddenly turned upon them, without warning, from the stage. In "Winterbranch," both these methods of torture are employed.

Then the concluding paragraph, the cri de coeur:

> What Mr. Cunningham does in his own studio or backyard for an invited group is his own business; what he does in the theater is theatrical business. There is such a thing as a paying customer, and that customer is sometimes right, especially if he doesn't find it an unalloyed delight to be abused. (1978, 479, 481)

In 1970, Clive Barnes had this to say about Cunningham's "Canfield" at The Brooklyn Academy of Music:

> The score, attributed to Pauline Oliveros, consists in large part of acousti-
> cal experiments, all of them arcane, but boring, carried out by a peripatetic
> Mr. Cage at the instructions of his fellow musical warlocks, David Tudor and
> Gordon Mumma. All of them seemed to be having a good time—which was
> agreeable—but their activities were distracting to anyone who had come to see
> Mr. Cunningham dance rather than Mr. Cage make a fool of himself.

Arlene Croce registered a similar complaint against Cunningham's "Exchange" in 1978:

> I wish I had been able to watch it more closely, but my concentration broke
> about halfway through under the battering of David Tudor's score.... How can
> you watch a dance with V2 Rockets whistling overhead? (1982, 130)

She concluded by criticizing the nondance elements of Cunningham's work for being so "interfering and dictatorial." Several weeks later, Croce echoed Selma Jeanne Cohen's 1968 complaint about "How to Pass...":

> When Merce Cunningham and John Cage combined forces in "How to Pass,
> Kick, Fall, and Run." ... they kept the words and the dancing on separate planes,
> and the result was that Cage distracted us every time he opened his mouth. (130)

And in a 1987 *New Yorker* piece, Croce objects once again to "the more intrusive sound scores devised for Merce Cunningham by John Cage and his school of intruders." (Too bad Cage never played the Mudd Club or CBGBs. What a great name for a new music ensemble!).

But there was one concert, above all others, that best illustrates the dance world's attitude toward Cunningham's collaborations: opening night at BAM in April 1969. The instruments in the pit included electronic versions of French horns and violins; and, as we've already seen, a dispute erupted between the musician's union and the electrician's union over which of them would assume responsibility for the unconventional activities taking place in the pit. With the disagreement still unresolved by curtain time, the company decided—much to the delight of most of the dance community—to per-form in silence. Over the years, many dance writers have admitted to me that this performance was—for obvious reasons—their favorite Cunningham concert of all time. The next day, Joseph Gale wrote in *The Newark Evening News:* "The unions did Cunningham a favor, and if they never settle their dispute, it would be too soon." Marcia Siegel stuck a similar note in her review of the same concert:

> I don't know if the auditory documents of John Cage and his colleagues are
> becoming more violent, or if urban life has had a sensitizing effect on our

hearing, but I find I have less tolerance for Cunningham's noise today than I had five years ago. Opening night at Brooklyn was performed in silence because of a dispute between the musicians' and the stagehands' unions as to who had jurisdiction over the indefinable activities in the pit. Several of Cunningham's most ardent admirers who were there remarked how lovely that concert was. (1992, 71)

Like other unruly children, Cunningham and company are presumed to be on their best behavior when seen and not heard. But in actual practice, sound is only one irritant among many. Décor proves no less distracting to those who resent the way Cunningham asks us to shift and divide our attention between dancers and inanimate objects. In 1969, Croce wrote that:

> *Walkaround Time* doesn't, as they say, "work." I took it as one of Cunningham's lesser projects in demystifying Art. It has something to do with a Jasper Johns assemblage (which is assembled only in the last minute by the dancers, after they've used it as environmental decor) based on the Marcel Duchamp construction called "The Large Glass." (1977, 339)

Referring to the décor (or lack of it) in Cunningham's program at BAM in 1972, Marcia Siegel wrote:

> Two of his three new works ("Landrover" and "TV Rerun") . . . involved a minimum of pop-art gadgetry, and they looked so bare and complete that I really got involved in them. Bizarre decors and sonic environments lend theatricality and sometimes fun to Cunningham's dances, but his unadorned works are as starkly satisfying to me as a tree against a February hillside . . . .

After this audible sigh of relief, Siegel goes on to complain about the third work on the program:

> "Borst Park," the last of the new works, seems of lesser importance, containing less dancing and more tricks than I care for. (1977, 274, 276)

Nancy Dalva, in 1992, summed up the dance world's attitude toward Cunningham's collaborative ventures:

> . . . Cunningham's dances look best with the simplest settings and costumes, and it is arguably in the area of décor that the Cunningham repertory has been most often hoist by the Cage-Cunningham petard. (1992, 180)

A few pages later in the same essay she says of Cunningham's "Field and Figures" (1989):

> It is a dance with a very clear scheme—once you filter out the terrific distraction of the vastly irritating Duchamp based read-aloud score (Ivan Tcherepnin's *The Creative Act*) and recover from the shock of Kristin Jones' and Andrew Ginzel's futuristic set . . . (1992, 184–85)

The Doris Hering essay was written in the 1950s, Nancy Dalva's in the 1990s. Thus—at least with regard to Cunningham's collaborative activity—one is tempted to conclude: La plus que les choses changent la plus qu'ils restent la même chose.

No doubt, many of these dance writers would like to believe that by denouncing those obstreperous visual and sonic environments, they're simply saving Cunningham from himself, from his own cheerful brand of nihilism. Ideally, these writers would like to see Cunningham released from auditory bondage to the composers with whom he collaborates; they want him "un-Caged" (so to speak). But here one is reminded of Cage's great revelation: that even when sealed inside a "soundless" chamber, he continued to hear two things: his heartbeat and the coursing of blood through his circulatory system. Still, Cunningham's critics insist on pretending that movement *can* occur in absolute silence. All of these writers proceed on the assumption that sound and décor exist for one reason and one reason only: to support and better illuminate the movement. Apparently, it never occurs to them that Cunningham's approach to collaboration might be *about* the nature of interference, static, signal-to-noise ratios, audio/visual discontinuity—and about the habits of attention one needs to cultivate in an urban environment of unceasing sensory overload.

Alaistair Macaulay inadvertently gave the game away when he complained about the sound score for Cunningham's "Eleven" (1988): "Fending off the wretched music, as I tried to do at a second performance, I isolated several new aspects of movement information" (1992, 177). One needn't employ the arcane terminology of "information theory" to recognize the distinction in Macaulay's mind between "information" and mere noise. But such objections play right into Cage and Cunningham's hands. One of the their key concerns is the way in which "noise" is defined in the second half of the 20th century. Noise is *unwanted* information; and the difference between noise and information is not always so easily established. (We'll explore this issue in much greater detail in Chapters 7 and 13.) As Cage wrote of a mixed-media work by Rauschenberg:

> Now that Rauschenberg has made a painting with radios in it, does that mean that even without radios, I must go on listening even while I'm looking, everything at once in order not to be run over? (1961, 101)

Thus, to complain about distraction and intrusion in a Cunningham/Cage concert, is—as Brecht so succinctly put it—reproaching the linden tree for not being an oak. In order to fully appreciate Cunningham's modernization of modern dance, we need to conduct a detailed examination of the sensibility he shares with visual artists such as Rauschenberg. Cunningham's relationship to his great predecessor Martha Graham is paralleled almost exactly by Rauschenberg's (and Johns's) relationship to the great tradition that preceded them in the visual arts: abstract expressionism. This is another way of saying that we need to take the collaborative aspect of Cunningham's work *seriously*, rather than superciliously dismissing it as irrelevant, distracting, or just plain self-indulgent. The next three chapters aim to flesh out this portion of my argument: that Cunningham is to Martha Graham as Rauschenberg and Johns are to Jackson Pollock.

2

Portrait of the Artist as a Jung Man

"When Martha had been creating 'Letter to the World' at Bennington in 1940, she had also been thinking about the dance that three years later was to become 'Deaths and Entrances.' One evening in the sitting room at Bennington which she and Erick (Hawkins) shared with Jean Erdman and her husband, Joe Campell, Martha spoke of these mysterious sisters, the Brontes, and their kinship to the wild spirits of the moor, the *sidh* of Celtic folklore, the fairy folk."

" 'Martha,' said Joe Campbell, 'when you talk about fairy folk you are really entering the world of the unconscious, and these creatures that come out of the fairy hills are manifestations of the psyche. You are now tapping the unconscious memories of the race.' Martha's eyes opened wide like the eyes of a young student just getting a new idea. 'Tell me,' she said, and Campbell, who taught mythology and the Greek classics, explained. And Martha, in his words, "went to town." Graham had entered a new era of development."
—Agnes de Mille, *Martha* (1991, 249–250)

Painting as Dancing

In 1950, the photographer and filmmaker Hans Namuth persuaded a reluctant Jackson Pollock to execute one of his famous "action paintings" on a canvas of glass while the camera recorded Pollock's bodily gyrations from below the transparent pane. Pollock's body dips as his paint brush drips; and the resulting rhythmic improvisation—we might call it "dip and drip"—seems to parallel the rhythms of the jazz recordings that Pollock often listened to as he painted (e.g., the music of Fats Waller, T -Bone Walker, Jelly Roll

Morton.) Although neither Pollock nor Namuth realized it at the time, their collaboration had produced one of the world's most eccentric *dance* films. It demonstrated (in a way the paintings alone rarely do) that abstract expressionism was animated in part by a *desire to transform painting into dancing*.

In the introduction to his biography of Pollock, *Energy Made Visible*, B. H. Friedman wrote, "This was the man who had 'danced' 'Autumn Rhythm' and 'Lavender Mist' and 'Blue Poles' and maybe a dozen more of the most graceful paintings ever made in America or anywhere else" (1972, xx). Allan Kaprow, in an essay titled, "The Legacy of Jackson Pollock," written in 1958, referred to " ... (his) so called 'dance' of dripping, slashing, squeezing, daubing ... " (1998, 46). But Pollock wasn't the only abstract expressionist who thought of his art in "dancerly" terms: Arshile Gorky hired a Hungarian violinist to inspire his students while they painted. One of Franz Kline's works from 1950 is titled "Nijinsky (Petrushka)." Still, it's only after watching Namuth's film of Pollock-in-motion that one can fully appreciate Harold Rosenberg's claim that at the dawn of the abstract expressionist movement:

> the canvas began to appear to one American painter after another as an arena in which to act—rather than as a space in which to reproduce, re-design, or "express" an object, actual or imagined. What was to go on the canvas was not a picture but an event. (1952, 39)

Rosenberg calls our attention to the highly physicalized way these paintings were executed. And Namuth's film is a vivid reminder of the fact that Pollock painted in a hunkered down (rather than upright) position. Which is to say: his canvases lay on the ground. Alas, art history has subsequently concealed—or at least deemphasized—the "earthly" origins of these paintings by hanging them conventionally on the walls of museums. I'm not proposing an alternative mode of exhibition, but the relationship of these art works to the ground, much like the "dance" that brought them into being, is an essential (if often neglected) component of their identity.

Abstract expressionism—or at least the bodily and gestural phase of it that Rosenberg called action painting—can be regarded as the culmination of modern art's love affair with "the primitive." I'll wait until Chapter 6 to discuss the full range of associations between primitivism, the body, and dance. For now, suffice it to say that ecstatic dancing is often regarded (rightly or wrongly) as a central element of "primitive" ritual. As we'll see in due course, Western preconceptions about "the primitive" routinely assign a privileged place to the body and its presumably organic relationship to the earth.

Pollock's conception of painting-as-dancing evolved directly out of those works he executed in the 1940s, works that derived their primary inspiration from images of primitive ritual and mythology. (He was deeply influenced by three exhibitions at The Museum of Modern Art in the late 1930s and early 1940s: the "African Negro Art Exhibition" of 1935, "Prehistoric Rock Pictures" in 1937, and "Indian Art of the United States" in 1941.) But now, rather than alluding to the iconography of primitive art, Pollock attempted to "dance" himself into an altered state of consciousness (that "liminal" blurring of boundaries between conscious and unconscious experience we associate with many "primitive" rituals). "When I am *in* my painting," Pollock once declared, "I'm not aware of what I'm doing" (Shiff 1987, 95). Jackson Pollock wanted to express himself (his inner, most "authentic" self) in the most unmediated manner possible. His conception of painting-as-dancing could well have been inspired by Havelock Ellis, who wrote that "dancing... is no mere translation or abstraction from life, it is life itself" (1983, 494). Harold Rosenberg emphasizes the fact that Pollock didn't "translate" onto the canvas an image that had already taken shape in his conscious mind or in preliminary sketches:

> The painter no longer approached his easel with an image in mind; he went up to it with material in his hand to do something to that other piece of material in front of him. The image would be the result of this encounter. (1952, 39)

The "trance-dance" dimension of Pollock's action painting also provides a provisional solution to the problem that Harold Bloom calls "the anxiety of influence" (i.e., the intimidating weight of tradition, the steadily increasing fear that "there's nothing new under the sun.") In *The Genealogy of Morals,* Nietzsche uses the image of the dancer to embody his concept of "active forgetfulness" (a Dionysian reclaiming of innocence). Jacob Wasserman makes much the same point in *The World's Illusion* when he suggests that: "To dance means to be new, to be fresh at every moment, as though one had just issued from the hand of God" (1920, 77). The abstract expressionists tried to convince themselves that every painting was a fresh beginning: "I start each painting as if I had never painted before," boasted Barnett Newman (Schiff 1987, 95). This sense of having escaped the shadow of history, of falling back on nothing but one's own interior resources, was central to abstract expressionism.

Interior Voyages: Pollock and Graham

Of course, it was central to modern dance as well. Indeed, one might argue that the action painter's metaphysical credo was much the same as Martha Graham's: "Bodies never lie." Needless to say, no one watching Namuth's film has ever mistaken Jackson Pollock for a Graham dancer. But Graham's variety of modern dance, as it evolved in the 1940s and 1950s, had much in common with abstract expressionism: Both were Jungian, gravity-ridden, and emotionally overwrought. Compare the titles of the major works that Pollock and Graham created in the 1940s. Pollock painted "She Wolf" (1943), "Pasiphae"(1943), "Guardians of the Secret," (1943), "Totem, Lesson I" (1944), and "Night Sounds" (1944). Graham choreographed works bearing equally incantatory names: "Cave of the Heart" (1946), "Errand into the Maze" (1947), and "Night Journey" (1947). (Pollock's "Guardians of the Secret" from 1943 alludes abstractly to priests and priestesses who "stand guard" over a mysterious biomorphic web of paint in the center of the canvas. In Graham's great duet of 1947, "Errand into the Maze," the female protagonist journeys "into the maze of the heart's darkness.")

If one translates the primal, sexually charged forms in Pollock's "Pasiphae" (1943) into three-dimensional space, the result is a set of biomorphic forms remarkably similar to Isamu Noguchi's decor for Graham's "Night Journey" (1947). In that great collaboration between Graham and Noguchi, we see what looks like fossilized versions of massive genitals: a phallus and vagina carved from what could be dinosaur bones. It's easy to see why Noguchi was often referred to as "an abstract expressionist sculptor." Similarly, both Graham and Pollock tended to view the floor of stage or studio as a metaphorical substitute for "the earth." "Your spine," Graham told her students, "is the line connecting heaven and earth" (1974, 139). According to Tony Smith, Pollock conceived of his canvases in much the same way:

> His feeling for the land had something to do with his painting canvases on the floor. I don't recall if I ever thought of this before seeing Hans Namuth's film. When he was shown painting on glass, seen from below and through the glass, it seemed that the glass was the earth, that he was distributing flowers over it, that it was spring. (Friedman 1972, 163)

Brian O'Doherty elaborates on the role played by "nature" in Pollock's work:

> The few paintings Pollock did on glass are especially revealing when set up outdoors against the landscape, to which the eye can penetrate between the paint. The work is referred to its natural context, and human nature is joined to both, composing the organic trinity to which Pollock presumably laid claim in his unusually extravagant reply to [Hans] Hofmann: "I am Nature" (1973, 106).

The art historian Richard Shiff has written of Pollock's drip paintings, "As if tracing his own moving shadow, he fixed his presence on the ground" (1977, 112). A careful examination of works like "Vortex," "Watery Paths," and "Full Fathom Five" attests to the horizontal position of the canvas as Pollock dripped and splattered it with paint. The surface is dotted with thick puddles of paint that show no evidence of "vertical runoff." (It was a standard joke in the New York art world of the mid-1950s to suggest that the abstract expressionists left much of their best work on the floors of their studios.) Both the image and the texture of *mud* are central to many of Pollock's best paintings. Even Clement Greenberg, the ultimate formalist, was willing to concede that the earthen tones and textures in Pollock's work were evocations of the *ground* rather than exercises in "pure," nonreferential color. Speaking of paintings such as "Guardians of the Secret," Greenberg wrote, "The mud abounds in Pollock's larger works" (Danto 1997, 72). Analogously, in Graham's masterwork of 1947, "Dark Meadow," a central character is named "She of the Ground." Her flatfooted, downward motion beckons and guides the character named "The One Who Seeks." And what the protagonist (originally portrayed by Graham herself) *seeks* is nothing less than The Thing Itself: The Instinctive, The Natural, The Archetypal, The Authentic, The Mythic—all of those ancient "truths" that have presumably been repressed by an urbanized, industrialized, and all too secularized "civilization."

Both Pollock and Graham believed that they knew where the treasure is buried: deep down under. Ernestine Stodelle describes the choreography of "Dark Meadow": "Movement burst forth as though the choreographer had suddenly touched subterranean springs of compulsive-impulsive gesture" (Shelton 1983, 123). The contractions in "Dark Meadow" are like excavations of the earth, an uncovering and dredging up of all those "primal energies" that are normally repressed ("kept down") by polite society. For Graham—and presumably for Pollock as well—the unconscious was literally a *sub*conscious, a dark, subterranean realm located below consciousness and eternally associated with earth. This idea that meaning is located in the nether regions ("buried," "below," "underneath," etc.) is also relevant to one *apparent* difference between Pollock and Graham: the fact that Pollock's best works—the drip and splatter paintings created between 1947 and 1951—appear to be entirely abstract, whereas Graham's great myth-inspired, dance-dramas are invariably more figurative. I say "apparent" difference, because many critics are convinced that even Pollock's most abstract works possess a hidden, figurative dimension.

Pepe Karmel, in the course of examining what Namuth's still photos of Pollock-at-work reveal about the artist's penchant for "painting over"—and thereby concealing—images, writes:

> This process of creating figures, obscuring them, and then overpainting them with new figures is evident not just in Pollock's drip paintings but throughout his oeuvre. Comparison between the finished version of the 1943 canvas "Guardians

of the Secret" and the earlier state visible in a photograph of Pollock's 8th St. apartment for instance, reveals that the upper registers of the painting were originally occupied by a completely different set of heads. These seem to have been painted out and replaced with new versions. (1998, 127)

Thomas Hess goes a step farther, arguing that subject matter—indeed, "literary" subject matter—remains central to Pollock's most "abstract" works from the late 1940s. Representational imagery is still very much a part of Pollock's process, Hess maintains, "but it disappeared beneath the interlacing drips and streamers. The 'literary' image was the secret at the heart of a labyrinth" (Karmel 1998, 103). "The secret at the heart of a labyrinth"—a phrase equally evocative of Graham's "Night Journey," "Cave of the Hearth," or "Errand into the Maze." Here we see both Graham and Pollock acting out one of the great founding myths of modernism: the idea that through some strenuous inner voyage or convulsive transformation of consciousness, the artist can reestablish contact with these disguised and/or *buried* truths. "This is an ecstatic voyage," writes Graham in her *Notebooks,* "Please do not embark with me unless you know the destination, an arrivement [*sic*] at a port of call (the self) where the cargo is demanded" (1973, 177). Graham's conception of art-as-voyage places her in a long and distinguished modernist tradition. Rimbaud's famous letter of 1871 contains a classic description of this arduous, self-sacrificing journey toward authentic Vision: "The poet makes himself into a visionary by means of a long, immense, and calculated disordering (*dereglement*) of all his senses" (Hayman 1977, 32). Of course, this "disordering" presumes that it's still possible to escape the confines of the prevailing culture, the very culture that has presumably repressed the truths of the body and insulated us from authentic extremes of feeling.

The prescribed escape route for the visionary modernist led in two principal directions: the unconscious and/or the primitive—both of which were presumed to be pristine, unspoiled, uncolonized. Of course, the two aren't mutually exclusive. For Freud and Jung, the unconscious, the primitive (and the infantile) were closely connected. But, in actual modernist practice, the unconscious and the primitive offer alternative paths toward authenticity. The first leads to the innermost recesses of self; the second to the outermost reaches of exotic "otherness." Rilke, in the seventh of his "Duino Elegies," advocates the first route. His search for purity leads him to the following conclusion: "Nowhere beloved can world exist but within." Gaughin moves in the opposite direction, sailing for Tahiti. In an 1891 interview, he declared:

It is necessary for me to immerse myself in virgin nature, see no one but savages, live their life, with no one other thought in mind but to render, the way a child would, the concepts formed in my brain, and to do this with nothing but the primitive means of art, the only means that are good and true.

The idea—or more properly the *ideal*—of "Nature" is the destination where the inward journey and the outward voyage meet. As Cezanne once wrote: "Nature is on the inside."

Pollock and Graham derive inspiration from both extremes: the depth psychology of Jung as well as the iconography of tribal cultures. Significantly, both Graham and Pollock consulted Jungian analysts in the 1940s. Pollock sometimes communicated with his analyst, Dr. Joseph L. Henderson, by drawing for him. A major phase of Pollock scholarship—devoted to symbolic representations of the artist's innermost, private demons—began in 1970 when a treasure-trove of drawings that Pollock had bequeathed to Henderson was made public. (One of the untitled "psychoanalytic drawings" from 1940 shows a figure reclining on a modernistic couch.)

In Graham's *Notebooks,* we find this quotation from Jung: "If the ego arrogates to itself power over the unconscious, the unconscious responds with a subtle attack." Graham follows that quote with these words of her own: "provoking the unconscious as tho' it were a wrathful and offended deity." This is Graham's psychoanalytic gloss on those climactic moments in so many of her works when the heroine's repressed fears are exorcised ("Errand into the Maze") or her primal memories are recollected ("Night Journey"). These epiphanies create the flashes of blinding revelation that transform the heroine into a Visionary. In the *Notebooks,* Graham writes

> The summons
> The Entrance—(The Dark Door)
> The one spoken to—enters—
> ... Voices—no words...
> She who is entranced by Vision
> Blinded by light... (1973, 26)

These are also the moments that provide the great climaxes in Graham. (Mark Ryder, who first danced the role of "The Creature of Fear" in "Errand... ", has said of that work: "One must be raped by one's subconscious... ".) As in Pollock's "Guardians of the Secret," the buried Jungian key-to-life's-puzzle is so well protected that only the most intrepid explorer can hope to encounter it face to face and then bear the full weight of its revelation. Writing about the element of visionary "quest" in abstract expressionism, Harold Rosenberg has suggested that "The American vanguard painter took to the white expanse of the canvas as Melville's Ishmael took to the sea." *Moby Dick* was one of Pollock's favorite books; and it's clear that he identified with Ahab's epic quest for the whale. Perhaps it's no coincidence that the titles of two of the paintings he completed in the years just before his death in 1956 were "Search" and "The Deep."

Despite their mutual fascination with spiritual strenuousness, visionary experience, and the exotic "other," Graham and Pollock both exemplify a specifically American primitivism: the idea of starting from scratch—the radical freshness that comes from conceiving of oneself as an American "Adam" (or "Eve"). Pollock's wild-west swagger and ever-present cowboy boots helped define his self-image as frontiersman and noble savage. In retrospect, we might say that Pollock aspired to be one part Rimbaud and one part Rambo. And it's no coincidence—prosaic though it may at first sound—that Pollock studied under Thomas Hart Benton and that his earliest works were "American Scene" paintings. According to Brian O'Doherty:

> [Pollock's] "honest" exploitation of the national physiognomy (both of land-scape and character) "exposed" Europe as overcivilized and spiritually exhausted. The idea of the new beginning, the devaluation of foreign culture, and the aggressive posture of Abstract Expressionism's myth in the fifties, came . . . as much from American Scene painting as from the Futurism that subliminally runs through twentieth-century American art (1973, 106).

The analog in Graham's work is of course her fascination with the American frontier (in dances such as "Appalachian Spring" [1944], or, even earlier, her great solo, "Frontier" from 1935.) And perhaps paradoxically, Graham made a point of emphasizing the "purity" of her American identity: She was fond of claiming that her mother's ancestors could be traced back six generations to the Mayflower.

Graham and Pollock both derived inspiration from more specific primitivist sources as well, especially the American Indian culture of the Southwest. Pollock was deeply influenced by Native American sand painting. Animal figures and totems abound in his work from the late 1930s and early 1940s. He also drew inspiration from the vast canvases of the great Mexican muralists, Clemente Orozco and David Siqueiros. (Pollock even studied with Siqueiros in 1936; and it was Siqueiros who first encouraged him to experiment with the techniques of pouring and spattering.) Similarly, the hieratic gestures of Graham's "Primitive Mysteries" (1931) and "El Penitente" (1940) are deeply indebted to the mystical blend of Native American ritual and Mexican Catholicism that she associated with the Southwest. Graham had always wanted to choreograph a dance based on the story of "Pocahontas"; and in her notes for this (never realized) work, she wrote:

> The women of the court eye her—she watches the men and gradually the court men are replaced in her eyes by very elegant Indian warriors in ritual dances.

> The women of the court eye her and seem to strip her of her court clothes and
> she becomes the beautiful savage again (1973, 37).

In addition, many elements of Graham's standard vocabulary (the knee walks, the flexed feet) are non-Western (in fact, South East Asian) in origin. Her working notes for "Night Journey" and "Cave of the Heart" for example, are rife with references to "Bali turns" and "Javanese foot movement." African influences came filtered through Picasso and his generation of modern primitivists. Pollock read—and claimed to be a great fan of—John Graham's 1937 essay, "Primitive Art and Picasso." John Graham's article is pervaded by the sort of sentimental primitivism we'll examine more fully in Chapter 6 (e.g., "Primitive races and primitive genius have readier access to their unconscious minds than so-called civilized peoples" [Rubin 1984, 337]). And even though African American movement motifs aren't readily discernible in her choreography, Martha Graham spoke of a dynamic balance between the Native American and the Afro-American strains of primitivism in the American arts:

> We have two primitive sources, dangerous and hard to handle in the arts, but
> of intense psychic significance—the Indian and the Negro. That these influence
> us is certain—the Negro with his rhythms of disintegration, the Indian by his
> intense integration, his sense of ritualistic tribal drama (1930, 87)

Abstract Expressionism and Modern Dance: The Shared Cultural Context

Of course, by the late 1940s and early 1950s, Graham and Pollock, though exemplary, were hardly alone. The inward journey, the quest for "more life"—for authentic, transformative, physical experience (if not "primitivism" per se)—was an integral part of the cultural landscape they inhabited. Norman Mailer's essay *The White Negro* drew an explicit connection between primitivism and the American bohemia of the Beat generation. Mailer's thesis is that the white hipster escapes the confines of America's increasingly suburban and conformist culture by emulating the more bodily life of the black man. (His conception of the African American has much in common with Graham's):

> The hipster had absorbed the existentialist synapses of the Negro, and for practi-
> cal purposes could be considered a white Negro.... For Hip is the sophistication
> of the wise primitive in a giant jungle, and so its appeal is still beyond the civilized
> man. (1968, 6)

A passion for black jazz was virtually de rigeur for the "white negro"; and Pollock was no exception. In the words of Lee Krasner, "He thought it was the only other really creative thing happening in this country." The music he listened to while executing his great "liquid line" paintings in the late 1940s included Jelly Roll Morton's "Beale Street Blues," Louis Armstrong's "Lazy River," Fats Waller's "Carolina Shout," and T-Bone Walker's "I Got a Break, Baby." For the Beats, jazz constituted the most direct, unmediated conduit between bodily motion and sound. Allen Ginsberg perpetuates the myth of black primitivism when he treats the sort of improvisation so central to jazz as if it was purely "natural," untutored, and spontaneous:

> Jazz gives us a way of expressing the spontaneous motions of the heart. It's like a fountain of inspiration that's available to everybody. All you got to do is tune on your radio or put on your record or pick up an ax yourself and blow. (Ward 2001, 51)

Mailer alluded to "the existentialist synapses of the Negro," which reminds us that this period was also the heyday of existentialism. (Sartre's influential work of that title was translated into English in 1947.) Existentialism's emphasis on "risk"—its view of humankind as having been "thrown" into being—is a virtual recipe for "action" painting. Applied to art making, the ethos of existentialism encouraged the creator to hurl himself into situations with unpredictable results. This "existential ethic" provides an important bridge between the surrealist movement and the postwar emergence of action painters such as Pollock. As a result of World War II, Breton, Ernst, Masson, Matta, and a number of other surrealists all immigrated to New York. Pollock in particular was influenced by the sheer *speed* with which Matta wielded the brush; and he may have been inspired to paint his own "Pasiphae" after seeing a Masson with that title in New York in 1944.

But it was actually the waning fortunes of surrealism and the subsequent emergence of existentialism that helped create the proper climate for the acceptance of action painting. *Time* magazine in 1945 summed up Sartre's philosophy in the following aphorism: "One is free to act, but one must act to be free." Stella Brooks, a Greenwich Village bohemian chanteuse, began to sing "The Existentialism Blues." And in a wonderful account of this period, *Surrealism in Exile and the Beginning of the New York School,* Martica Sawin cites an exchange that reportedly took place during the late 1940s in the offices of *View,* a magazine closely associated with the surrealist movement:

> "I think," said Charles one afternoon, "that Surrealism is on its way out."
> "And what is on its way in?" I asked.
> "Existentialism, Honey. Existentialism." (1995, 375)

But before it passed from the scene, surrealism helped pave the way for the popularization of psychoanalysis. Broadway and Hollywood discovered their own versions of the unconscious a few years before Martha Graham saw the inner light in her works from 1946 to 1947. Moss Hart and Kurt Weill's *Lady in the Dark,* with its famous "Circus Dream," offered Broadway theatergoers a bargain-basement version of psychoanalysis in 1941. Agnes de Mille's "Laurey Makes Up Her Mind" ("the Dream Ballet") in *Oklahoma!* (1943) featured some of the most starkly surrealistic decor in the history of Broadway (especially that famous staircase leading-into-the-abyss). Hollywood quickly transformed the mechanics of psychoanalysis into a formulaic detective mystery. In Hitchcock's *Spellbound* (1945), Ingrid Bergman portrays a sexually repressed psychiatrist who refers to herself as a "dream detective." When Bergman's character experiences her sexual awakening (the moment she first kisses Gregory Peck), a vast corridor of doors open one-after-the-other. *Spellbound* concerns the disappearance (which may or may not involve murder) of a psychiatrist-author whose best-known book is titled *Labyrinth of the Guilt Complex.* (Graham, in the *Notebooks,* refers to her character from "Errand into the Maze" as the "Lady of the Labyrinth"; and Adolph Gottlieb painted his "Labyrinth" series in the early 1950s. *Labyrinth* was also the title of a leading postwar French intellectual journal that published the work of *both* Breton and Sartre.) Key fragments of the jigsaw-puzzle-answer to *Spellbound*'s detective mystery are revealed in a labyrinthine dream sequence designed by Salvador Dali. And the kindly psychiatric father figure (an avuncular version of the elderly Freud) is played by Mikhail Chekhov, who trained with Stanislavsky at the Moscow Art Theater and later taught his own version of psychologically-based acting in New York City.

Indeed, we find a similar ethos in the most celebrated American acting style of the period. The Actor's Studio version of "the method"—by far the best-known bastardization of Stanislavsky technique—emphasized the importance of drawing on one's own authentic "emotion memories" and of elucidating the interior "subtext" that lay *below* the surface of the character's speech. By the early 1950s, Marlon Brando, James Dean, and Montgomery Clift were creating screen characters full of inner anguish and inarticulate sensitivity. The contortions of Dean's body in *East of Eden* (1954) are as kinetically and emotionally expressive as the most violent Graham contraction. (And they're infinitely more revealing than any of the words he mumbles in that film.) The dominant forms of training for both method actors and modern dancers were fundamentally concerned with the elimination of "blockages"—sexual reticence, emotional evasion, intellectual equivocation—anything that might inhibit the exploration of one's "true inner self." Graham in fact taught movement at the Neighborhood Playhouse, a leading school for actors that helped promote the Method. Marian Seldes, arguably the greatest actress to have trained at the Playhouse, once declared "I learned everything I know from Graham." That may well be true; but the official instructor of acting at the Neighborhood Playhouse was Sanford Meisner, the most anti-intellectual of the Stanislavsky-inspired method-gurus. ("I am against the head," he declared famously. And his physical exercises were designed, he once boasted, "to eliminate all intellectuality from the actor's instrument.")

The connection between modern dance and Stanislavsky-derived approaches to actor training was made official in the mid-1960s, when Valentina Litvinoff, a former student of Graham's, began to publish the essays that were later collected in *The Use of Stanislavsky Within Modern Dance*. The heart of her argument is summarized in the following passage:

> Martha [Graham] is a living embodiment of Stanislavsky. Her every movement on the stage, beginning earlier than the "Lamentation" and extending beyond the "Clytemnestra" is an illustration of the use of The Method, whether it is so labeled or not. Big gestures and small are all motivated. (1972, 11)

But, in actual practice, it was Graham technique that facilitated the goals of method-acting, not the other way around. Anne Jackson, another great actress who studied movement with Graham, told about the use she made of the contraction in an interview conducted for the documentary film *Martha Graham: The Dancer Revealed:*

> My first film was called *So Young, So Bad* and I played a disturbed young woman.... I had to look through a window, see this friend of mine hold a baby; and I [had to] turn into camera and break into tears. Well, I thought, "I don't know how to do that." So what I did was a Martha Graham contraction... that gut thing... and I sank down and just sobbed.

In 1947, Graham and Meisner collaborated on a production of *The Eumenides* with students at The Playhouse. That same year, Anna Sokolow, a member of Graham's original company and a choreographer of considerable distinction, began to teach movement for Elia Kazan at The Actor's Studio. Sokolow's masterwork "Rooms" (1955), a harrowing study of urban alienation, grew out of improvisations—verbal as well as physical—with the acting students at the Studio.

Graham and Sokolow both derived their movement aesthetic from the basic rhythms of breathing. This illustrates another significant connection between method actors and Graham-trained modern dancers: a mutual determination to locate the right "breath-rhythm." (Method actors will often say that the key to a character lies in the way he or she breathes.) Charles Olson's 1950 manifesto "Projective Verse" argued that poetry should be animated (or "motivated") by the actual rhythm of the writer's breathing as he or she composes the poem. As with the Graham contraction, Olson's poetry is born of the "natural," bodily rhythms of breath. Likewise, Ginsberg's "Howl" (1956) is a long, unedited "barbaric yawp" that seems to erupt from the body with the inexorability of lava flowing from a volcano. This was the verbal equivalent of Pollock's drips and splatters. Just as Pollock's action painting draws on more of the body than simply the artist's hand, Ginsberg's "Howl" celebrates body and vilifies mind ("Moloch whose name is the Mind! . . . Moloch in whom I am a consciousness without a body!"). In other words—and consistent with the "ethos" of both abstract expressionism and modern dance—only those experiences which are grounded in the *body* offer the promise of authenticity.

Stan Brakhage, who brought the spirit of abstract expressionism to "underground" filmmaking, created an almost exact, cinematic equivalent for Pollock's drip paintings and Graham's "fever chart of the heart." In *Anticipation of the Night* (1958), Brakhage's handheld camera becomes a direct extension of the nervous system as his body darts and weaves its way across the landscapes he's photographing. The darkness of "night" is of course a key obsession for both Graham and Pollock ("Night Journey," 1947; "Night Sounds," 1944). Brakhage even formulated a theory he called "closed-eye vision," which emphasized the interior landscape of "true vision" rather than the outer-directed experience of mere eyesight.

If Brakhage is the Jackson Pollock of underground film (allowing his entire body to dictate the trajectory of his camera), then Maya Deren is the Martha Graham of the medium. In her earliest films, a female protagonist—often portrayed by Deren herself—wanders through mysterious terrain in search of self-realization. Balinese and Haitian possession rituals were her most potent source of inspiration. The titles of Deren's films in the 1940s and 1950s (*Ritual in Transfigured Time, The Very Eye of Night*) are virtually interchangeable with the titles of Graham's dances. And it's probably no coincidence that Deren's *A Study in Choreography for Camera* (1945) may well be the most perfect dance film ever made.

In 1948, even George Balanchine made a contribution to modernist primitivism. His "Orpheus," designed by Noguchi, looks—at least from today's vantage point—much more like a "Noguchi" ballet than a Balanchine ballet. Lincoln Kirstein refers to the work's "ritual choreography," but it's Noguchi's décor and properties—his exquisitely curved lyre, his luminous Stone Age rock carvings—that lend a primeval feel to the work. Granted, Balanchine ended the ballet with a characteristically Apollonian apotheosis (Apollo himself bestows immortality on Orpheus' lyre). But along the way, Orpheus is ritualistically dismembered by the Dionysian Bacchantes.

Finally, no account of modernist primitivism in the 1940s and 1950s would be complete without at least passing reference to the work of Tennessee Williams. *Suddenly Last Summer* (1958), explores the labyrinth in which depth psychology meets naked primitivism in the form of ritual sacrifice. Here, a psychiatrist plumbs the depths of his patient's psyche in search of a repressed memory (which turns out to be an act of cannibalistic dismemberment in a remote part of Mexico). The conclusion is William's gloss on Euripides's *The Bacchae;* and the climactic recollection is punctuated by a full-fledged primal scream (or what Antonin Artaud—whose *Theater and its Double* was first translated into English that same year—referred to as "speech before words").

Anna Sokolow had worked as Kazan's assistant on the Broadway production of William's *Camino Real* (1953). And reportedly, when Williams attended the premiere of Sokolow's "Rooms" in 1955, he said of one lonely, deluded female character who dances with a wholly imaginary lover: "That's Blanche . . . ," a comment that leads us directly to William's greatest success, *A Streetcar Named Desire.* It was in *Streetcar,* of course, that Brando uttered (or muttered) his immortal cry, "Stella!" Above all, it's the image of Brando as Stanley Kowalski in Kazan's film version of *Streetcar* (1952) that stands alongside Namuth's still photos of Pollock as one of the great archetypal emblems of alternative American culture in the 1950s. Williams has Blanche describe Stanley in overtly primitivist terms:

> He acts like an animal, has an animal's habits! Eats like one, moves like one, talks like one! There's even something—subhuman—something not quite to the stage of humanity yet! Yes, something ape-like about him, like one of those pictures I've seen in—anthropological studies! Thousands and thousands of years have passed him right by, and there he is—Stanley Kowalski—survivor of the Stone Age!

In her biography of Jackson Pollock, Ellen Landau, seizing on the fact that Williams apparently met the young Pollock in 1944, suggests that Stanley Kowalski may actually have been modeled on him. This seems to me highly improbable. (Although it's tempting to reimagine the scene in which Stanley snarls at Blanche: "Don't call me a Polack." Perhaps some revisionist director—fresh from a reading of Landau's book—will have Blanche alter her pronunciation of "Polack" ever so slightly.) Still, the mythic fusion of Brando and Pollock informs virtually every frame of Ed Harris's cinematic biography of Jackson Pollock (2000). In his *New York Times* review of *Pollock*—which Harris conceived and directed in addition to playing the title role—Stephen Holden observes,

> . . . in *Pollock,* the tense domestic clashes between the artist and his wife, the painter Lee Krasner (Marcia Gay Hayden), are subtly staged to recall the electrifying chemistry of Marlon Brando and Kim Hunter in the film version of *Streetcar.* (Holden 2000, B23)

There's no denying the range of primitivist sources—from tribal ritual to Brando's myth-making characterization of Stanley Kowalski—that may well have influenced the way Hans Namuth immortalized Pollock in those famous still photos of the artist-at-work. According to Pepe Karmel (1998, 90):

> If Pollock appears as a kind of shaman, enacting enigmatic rituals in a sacred space, this is probably at least in part because Namuth had photographed actual shamans on his 1947 trip to Guatemala. If Pollock seems at other moments like a real life version of Stanley Kowalski, it is not merely because he wears a proletarian T-shirt and jeans. Namuth, with his background in the theater, would probably have seen Marlon Brando's searing performance in the original production of Tennessee William's *A Streetcar Named Desire*, and would have recognized in Pollock another avatar of American sincerity, straining to express the inexpressible with strands of paint instead of mumbled words.

More than any of the paintings themselves, it was Namuth's widely disseminated images of Pollock-in-motion that helped create the ethos—indeed, the Mythos—of abstract expressionism. Even Julien Beck and Judith Malina, cofounders of The Living Theatre, were quick to acknowledge their primary debt to the spirit of action painting. Significantly, when Beck discussed the genesis of The Living Theatre in the documentary film *Signals Through the Flames,* he insisted that "Our own work came out of the abstract expressionist movement in New York in the 1940s." This was a full 10 years before Beck and Malina discovered the seminal ravings of Antonin Artaud; and this reminds us that the *ethos* of abstract expressionism applies to more (much more) than a specific movement in the history of painting. It refers in fact to all of the art created in the late 1940s and 1950s that places a special premium on the full participation of the artist's *body.*

3
Beyond The Ethos of Abstract Expressionism

"How can we know the dancer from the dance?" asked Yeats in "Among School Children." Pre-Cunningham modern dance proceeds on the assumption that we can't. Graham once boasted that her dances fit her as her skin fit her. José Limón, another great pioneer of pre-Cunningham modern dance, insisted that "All choreography is autobiographical, whether one knows it or not, whether one intends it or not" (Vachon 2002). This same notion applies equally well to *all* of the art created in the spirit of abstract expressionism. The ethos of action painting is predicated on the assumption that the same sacred, indissoluble bond exists between all "authentic" works of art and the inner lives of their creators. As Harold Rosenberg put it, "A painting that is an act is inseparable from the biography of the artist" (Jones 1998, 74). Again, we return to Martha Graham's credo, as recounted by Agnes de Mille:

> [Martha] once told me that Dr. Graham [her father] had said, "Bodies never lie." This statement had profound meaning for Martha.... Now we have the lie detector, which is based on just this principle: The body cannot lie. (1991, 22)

But two events, both of which took place in 1953, signaled an imminent departure from this belief—indeed, a decisive break with the legacies of both abstract expressionism and modern dance: Rauschenberg created his "Erased DeKooning Drawing," and Merce Cunningham formed his first dance company.

1953

Let's begin by focusing on the "paradigm shift" that Rauschenberg (and subsequently, Johns) pioneered in the visual arts. In 1953, Rauschenberg asked Willem DeKooning for a drawing he could *erase;* and DeKooning, perhaps surprisingly, provided one. (The erasure didn't come easily. According to Rauschenberg, the insistent rubbing wore down 40 erasers over the course of a month!) No doubt this gesture was too playful to qualify as a passionate declaration of war on abstract expressionism. (And DeKooning, as we've seen, was a willing participant.) But it's certainly no coincidence that the art Rauschenberg chose to erase belonged to a legendary abstract expressionist. At the very least, his erasure was an ironic dismissal of all that soul-churning, existential angst Rauschenberg associated with painters like DeKooning and Pollock. "The kind of talk you heard then in the art world was so hard to take," Rauschenberg has said of the abstract expressionists. "It was all about suffering and self-expression and The State of Things" (1965, 210).

In 1957 (less than a year after Pollock's death) Rauschenberg created "Factum I and II"—his notorious "double paintings" (technically collages of oil, fabric, and paper images of postcards and calendars). The two collages appear to be identical, even though the first incorporates elements of spontaneity and accident; the second is a meticulously recreated duplicate. Rauschenberg thereby demonstrates that the final product is not necessarily dependent on the process. The same result can be achieved without the anguished gestures, the one-time-only, "my-guts-are-on-this-canvas," outpourings of emotion that signified "authenticity" for the abstract expressionists. And note that the moment this sort of angst-ridden, high seriousness disappears from the creative process, critics like Moira Roth accuse artists like Rauschenberg and Johns of "indifference."

In 1959, Rauschenberg created his most direct and stinging parody of Pollock, "Winter Pool," which parodies the action painter's famous statements about always being "in" his own paintings. Rauschenberg's work includes a ladder that invites the viewer to, in effect, "climb in." During this same period (1959–1960), Johns too produced some exceptionally funny parodies of the abstract expressionist ethos. His "Thermometer" (1959) plays with the idea of literally "taking the temperature" of abstract expressionist brushstrokes (i.e., Johns places a functioning thermometer in the middle of a field of "hot," gestural smearings of oil paint on canvas). Of course, we conventionally refer to colors as "warm" or "cool." But in the objectivist universe of Jasper Johns, the thermometer will register only the temperature of the room, not the subjective, psychologized "heat" of the color. And in "Painting with Two Balls," (1960) Johns—beginning with the title—satirizes the overheated sexual drive that seems to animate so much of abstract expressionism. (Here, he situates two tiny wooden balls between separate panels of wildly gestural red, green, blue, and yellow brushstrokes.) Note, too, that the ambiguity of the title refers both to process (the "act" of painting) and to the product (i.e., the painting as object). Rauschenberg had already toyed with similar ambiguities in "Factum I and II."

It's not terribly surprising that Rauschenberg received very little encouragement from the art world in the early 1950s, immersed as it was in the ethos of abstract expressionism. (Johns's mature work doesn't really begin until the mid-1950s). What *is* perhaps surprising is the fact that one of Rauschenberg's earliest admirers was a former Graham dancer he met in New York in 1951 and subsequently worked with at Black Mountain College in North Carolina. The dancer was, of course, Merce Cunningham. But the dances Cunningham now performed displayed little evidence of Graham's influence.

Beginning in 1951 with his "16 Dances for Soloist and Company of Three," Cunningham had decided to determine the arrangement of sequences by tossing coins, thereby utilizing an "impersonal" (and much more objective) mode of aesthetic decision making, rather than structuring the dance according to the subjective dictates of his own instincts or taste— which is another way of saying that, unlike Graham, he made little or no attempt to draw inspiration from the pristine, "primitivist" sanctuary of the unconscious. Of course, this repudiation of primitivism did not occur over night. No one who danced with Graham from 1939 to 1945 could have entirely escaped the influence of primitivist themes and movement motifs. Cunningham's "16 Dances..." is an important transitional work in this regard, because its structure was derived at least as much from psychological archetypes as from chance operations. Each of its separate sections was intended to embody a specific emotional archetype (sorrow, fear, wonder, eroticism, tranquillity, etc.) These archetypes in turn were derived from the nine "permanent" emotions embodied in classical Indian art. For the "wondrous" solo, Cunningham wore a costume indirectly inspired by the ceremonial masks of Native Americans from the Pacific Northwest. (A photograph by Gerda Peterich of Cunningham posed as the "Odious Warrior" looks as fiercely combative as those Ted Shawn all-male exercises in macho muscle flexing.)

I've argued that the work of Cunningham, Cage, Johns, and Rauschenberg is inextricably tied to the life of New York City. But it's also important to note that none of them grew up in Manhattan (or for that matter, even in the Northeast). Cunningham's early years were spent in Centralia, Washington, where he developed a lifelong fascination with the distinctive, fog-enveloped typography of the Pacific Northwest. Cunningham's original title for "The Seasons" (1947) was "Northwestern Rite"; and he had initially hoped to convince another artist from Washington State, Morris Graves—a native of the scenically spectacular Puget Sound area—to design the decor and costumes. Eventually, however, Cunningham found himself collaborating on "The Seasons" with none other than Isamu Noguchi, whose décor and costumes for Graham made an essential contribution to the primitivism we associate with her dances. And speaking of Graham—or at least of dances whose titles remind one of her repertory from the 1940s—Cunningham even choreographed a work called "Orestes" at Black Mountain College in 1948.

Aside from their titles, we know very little about the works Cunningham choreographed prior to "16 Dances..." in 1951. But their names alone would seem to suggest that they shared many of Graham's preoccupations: e.g. "Totem Ancestor" (1942), "Spontaneous Earth" (1944), "Mysterious Adventure" (1945), "The Encounter" (1946). In 1944, Barbara Morgan shot a now famous photograph of Cunningham performing a solo he choreographed that year called "Root of an Unfocus." It's a haunting image, in part because it captures both Cunningham in the foreground of the frame and his mirrored image in the background. But what's disquieting about the photograph isn't entirely attributable to Morgan's stunning double-exposure technique, which serves to double Cunningham's impact. The power of the photograph has at least as much to do with Cunningham's facial expression, which looks tense and adrenalized, suggesting that his coiled body in the foreground is ready to confront some sort of mysterious but clearly imminent threat. Of course, still photos—especially ones as carefully posed as Morgan's appears to be—often misrepresent works that unfold in time. But, judging from the visual evidence, it seems difficult not to conclude that Cunningham's choreography in the mid-1940s still placed a considerable emphasis on psychological motivation and emotional expressivity.

This evidence suggests that Cunningham's rejection of Graham's primitivism took the form of a gradual evolution, not a sudden repudiation. It's also important to point out that Cunningham feels no compunction whatsoever about returning on occasion to these earlier obsessions. For example, in 1977, when the long-awaited opportunity to collaborate with Morris Graves finally arrived, the result was the magically atmospheric "Inlets" (which evoked, in an almost literal way, the mist-enshrouded landscapes of Washington State). Not since "Noctures" had a Cunningham dance made such "moody" use of a scrim curtain; and Graves designed a mysterious disk (rather like a glowing theatrical "moonbox") that floated dreamily across the stage. Cunningham's choreography even utilized flattened-out, "archaic" primitivist poses—reminiscent of Nijinsky in "Faun."

Rauschenberg followed a similar evolutionary path away from the concerns of the abstract expressionist era. Two titles from 1950, "Mother of God" and "Crucifixion and Reflection," are both worthy of a mythically motivated, abstract expressionist. And his "Untitled (Elemental Sculpture)" from 1953 appears remarkably like Noguchi at his most primitivist. As its title suggests, this is still very much a work of "elemental" sculpture. A twisted, serpentine piece of metal spirals up and away from a stone that would not look out of place on the set of Graham's "Dark Meadow." Even Rauschenberg's 1953 "erasure" of DeKooning remains a physical, gestural act (i.e., action painting becomes action *erasure*). That same year, Rauschenberg and Cage collaborated on their "Automobile Tire Print" in which Cage drove his Model A Ford (whose tires had been covered in ink) over a 22-foot-long strip of paper. The resulting "scroll" exhibits what C. S. Peirce would call an "indexical" relationship with the automobile tire: a directly physical, even "existential" bond that mirrors the action painter's calligraphic brushstrokes and drip patterns. But here, of course, the "painter" has been both urbanized and mechanized.

Taking A Chance on Chance

Regardless of how long it may have taken Cunningham to break decisively with his Graham inheritance, there's no denying that "16 Dances . . ." (1951) marked a sharp, seminal divide in his early development—perhaps even a point of no return. At the very least, its use of chance-generated juxtapositions denied the dance any sense of "organic" continuity. Cunningham himself has commented on the unprecedented difficulty of performing it:

> It was the first time where you encountered a coordination, going from one thing to another that I had not encountered before, physically—so how do you do it if you're going to accept this idea at all (the idea of chance-generated composition), how do you manage to do it? You have to just fight with it and struggle, and try to find the most direct way to go from one of these things to the other. (Vaughan 1997, 59)

In composing "Sixteen Dances . . . ," Cunningham's use of chance was largely confined to determining the order of the separate sections. But for one of the dances (a quartet), decisions concerning sequence, duration, and the direction of movements for each dancer were also arrived at by tossing coins. This was a significant turning point. In virtually all of Cunningham's subsequent works, numerous variables (e.g., the locations of the dancers, the speed with which phrases are performed, the order in which steps are combined, the number of dancers who appear in each sequence) were arrived at *not* by intuition, instinct, or even the faculty of "taste," but by a wide variety of chance methods, including: rolling dice, picking cards, tossing coins, consulting the *I Ching*, numbering imperfections—specks, watermarks—on pieces of paper (each page is "keyed" to areas of the performance space; and when held up to the light, the location of the imperfections on the pieces of paper serve to position the dancer on stage). Of all these various methods, one—the use of the *I Ching*—has proved incomparably more important than any other. If Cunningham has a "favorite number," it's likely to be 64, the total of symbolic hexagrams in the *I Ching*, the ancient Chinese book of divination, one of the five classic texts of Confucianism. The hexagrams are formed by combining eight basic trigrams in different pairs (one above the other).

This helps explain the sheer number of Cunningham dances that are composed from a field of 64 possible movements. (A partial listing of such works, confined solely to the past quarter century, includes "Ocean" [1994], "Inventions" [1989], "Five Stone Wind" [1988], "Fabrications" [1987], "Phrases" [1984], "Pictures" [1984], "Inlets II" [1983], "Fielding Sixes" [1980], "Roadrunners" [1979], and "Torse" [1976].) The literal translation of the words "I Ching" is "Classic of Changes." And it's no coincidence that *Changes* is the title that Cunningham gave his 1968 book about compositional practices (subtitled "Notes on Choreography"). Many people have concluded that Cunningham's extensive use of the *I Ching* demonstrates that his dances are no less indebted to non-Western philosophies than were those of Martha Graham. (In a subsequent chapter, I'll explain why I adamantly disagree with this argument. Cunningham, it seems to me, "appropriates" the *I Ching* for his own, very different purposes that have little or nothing to do with traditional Confucian ideas about divination.)

Detailed accounts of the way Cunningham actually utilizes these chance-generating procedures (the process behind the product) can make for laborious, even tortured, reading. But it's essential to understand just how mathematically—or at least, procedurally—rigorous these practices are. Here, for example, is Cunningham's own description of the compositional methods he employed in creating "Summerspace" (1958):

> From each number in space (upstage right was no.1, upstage left no. 2, center right no. 3, center left no. 4, downstage right no. 5, downstage left no. 6) to each other number went a line, each presuming the reverse so there were 21 in all. Each one had a sequence of movement relating to it, ranging from simple to complex.
>
> To this gamut of movement in given space-directions was applied a chance procedure. It was done in this order:
>
> 1. Direction, e.g. from where to where. This gave the movement its basic form.
> 2. Whether the movement was done fast, medium, or slow.

3. Whether the movement happened in the air, across the surface, or on the ground.
4. Length of time in seconds, assuming 5″ as a minimum.
5. Shape of space, i.e. in what way the space was covered (straight lines, diagonal lines, circular, and so on).
6. Number of dancers involved in this particular action.
7. Did they perform this action together or separately.
8. Did they end the action on or off stage. (Vaughan 1997, 109)

One more example, drawn from Cunningham's recollection of the playful (but no less exacting) way he utilized chance to govern compositional decisions in the making of "Canfield" (1969). In his book of interviews with Jacqueline Lesschaeve, Cunningham says of this dance:

> The title is from the game of solitaire. While playing it one summer day on vacation in Cadaques, I decided the procedure could be used for choreography. The various components of a deck of cards were allotted to aspects of dance. To each of the fifty-two cards I related a word that implied movement, for example, the Queen of Spades indicated leap; the Ten of Diamonds lurch; the Seven of Hearts bounce, continuing for all fifty-two. Then I used the idea of thirteen cards in a suit to indicate the number of dances comprised in the whole work. To red and black were allotted fast and slow. When two or three face cards came up in succession, they referred to the possibility of duets and trios. . . . A card game seems to me to be a formal procedure, the rules and continuity of playing being rigorously set. (1985, 115–16)

Needless to say, these passages from Cunningham's *Changes* and Lesschaeve's *The Dancer and The Dance* will never be mistaken for quotations from the writings of Martha Graham. In her *Notebooks*, Graham cites the following line from Schiller's *Wallenstein:* "There is no chance; And what seems hazard in our eyes/Arises from the deepest source" (1973, 168). Unless one really believes that "chance *is* the fool's name for fate," it's difficult not to conclude that Cunningham's use of chance procedures as a compositional tool marked a major departure from the Gospel According to Graham.

Similarly—and despite the fact that Pollock's dripped and poured paintings were created spontaneously—Pollock himself always insisted that they were ordered by a mystical sense of inevitability: "I deny the accident . . ." he once famously declared (Updike 1998, 12). Significantly, it was in 1953 that Cunningham premiered "Suite by Chance," the first dance in which *all* of the variables of space and time were determined by chance procedures. 1953 was, of course, also the year that Rauschenberg created his "Erased DeKooning."

It's thus entirely appropriate that the Cunningham Company (or, as it was then called, "Merce Cunningham and Company") was officially founded that year. For all practical purposes, Cunningham had "erased" most vestiges of the Graham legacy as well. The dances he now choreographed were much more upright and balletic than Graham's; the emphasis was on "line and placement." (Perhaps not precisely the same line and placement one found in ballet—but line and placement nonetheless). The choreography emphasized brisk tendus, razor-sharp dégagés, and high passés. Certainly, the dancers' long, probing legs were as active and articulate as any ballerina's. (A year earlier, in 1952, Louis Horst, speaking of the inverted cabrioles, entrechats, and rond de jambes in Cunningham's "Variation," wrote that they "seemed to have no place on a modern dance program.")

Getting Down: Early Modern Dance and the Rejection of Ballet

The early pioneers of modern dance—from Duncan through Graham— rejected what they believed to be the "artificial" (and orthopedically un- healthy) vocabulary of ballet in favor of movements more in keeping with the "natural" inclinations of the body. Duncan criticizes ballet for defy- ing the "natural" law of gravity and for linking steps and phrases together inorganically. In "The Dance of the Future" she writes:

> The school of the ballet of today, vainly striving against the natural laws of gravitation or the natural will of the individual, and working in discord in its form and movement with the form and movement of nature, produces a sterile movement which gives no birth to future movements, but dies as it is made. The expression of the modern school of ballet, wherein each action is an end, and no movement, pose, or rhythm is successive or can be made to evolve succeeding action, is an expression of degeneration, or living death. All the movements of our modern ballet school are sterile movements because they are unnatural; their purpose is to create the delusion that the law of gravitation does not exist for them. (1977, 55)

For Duncan, natural movement—organically conceived and executed— could only originate in the solar plexus, which she identified as "the central spring of all movement." By contrast, the elongated back of the ballet dancer was thoroughly demonized:

> The ballet school taught the pupils that this spring was found in the center of the back at the base of the spine. From this axis, says the ballet master, arms, legs and trunk must move freely, giving the result of an articulated puppet. This method produces an artificial mechanical movement not worthy of the soul. (1927, 67)

Although she lays claim to the inspiration of ancient Greece, Duncan's movement discoveries were motivated as much by her detestation of bal- let as by her attraction to "primitive" images of bacchantes, nymphs, and satyrs. The natural movement that Duncan purports to have (re)discovered was—perhaps unsurprisingly—the very antithesis of ballet. Still, in practice, much of Duncan's dancing remained sprightly and vertical: hops and skips performed with an infectious, childlike abandon. It wasn't until the heyday of Martha Graham that modern dance truly came to terms with gravity and declared its determination to "get down." Thus, by the late 1940s, almost everyone in the world of modern dance was carrying the weight of the universe on his or her shoulders and affirming the elemental (i.e., natural) force of *gravity*—everyone that is, except Merce Cunningham. Cunningham was busy cultivating his lightness, uprightness, and speed.

This is not to imply that the Cunningham vocabulary is *essentially* balletic. In the early 1950s it stood in marked contrast to *both* ballet and the prevailing conceptions of modern dance. Cunningham, for example, spoke during that decade of his "eight basic movements, with variations: bending, rising, extending, turning, sliding, skimming and brushing, jumping, and falling" (Ludlow 1959, 10)—hardly a description of the standard ballet lexicon. (By 1976, when he was choreographing "Torse"—a work that focuses on the unballetic flexibility of the torso—Cunningham discussed another five basic positions for the back: upright, arch, tilt, twist, and curve.) Gus Solomons Jr., who danced with the company between 1965 and 1968, has pinpointed the way in which Cunningham "uses the spine as another *limb*, with equal articulation in all the joints of that spine, and reduces the center from the whole torso to just the pelvis so that the spine becomes free as a limb" (Brown, et al. 1992, 118).

"Summerspace," from 1958, remains one of the best examples of what Cunningham did "with" ballet, and what, at the same time, he did "to" ballet. It begins with a female dancer running—not bourrée-ing but running—in a circle. Yet "Summerspace" feels balletic in its uncompromising uprightness and in its emphasis on legs and feet. But partnered lifts are few and far between because this is a dance that continually reinforces each performer's sense of separateness. Light jumps are often executed with arms pressed firmly against the dancers' sides rather than opened into the surrounding space in a more balletically conventional port de bras. When "Summerspace" was restaged in 1966 for The New York City Ballet, Balanchine's dancers had considerable trouble executing its unpredictable transitions from andante to allegro.

Like "Summerspace," Cunningham's dances created in the 1950s were often fast, light, coolly ironic in tone, and increasingly devoid of narrative or symbolic elements: no mythic heroes or heroines, no inner voyages, no "exotic," primitivist movement motifs, no climactic moments of visionary revelation. Nothing, in other words, comparable to the suicide of Jocasta in "Night Journey" or the murder of the title character in "Clytemnestra." In an essay published in 1952, Cunningham suggests that his dances are more likely to evoke the collagelike juxtaposition of seemingly unrelated articles in a newspaper than any sort of crisis or *climax:*

> Now I can't see that crisis any longer means a climax, unless we are willing to grant that every breath of wind has a climax (which I am), but then that obliterates climax, being a surfeit of such. And since our lives, both by nature and by the newspapers, are so full of crisis that one is no longer aware of it, then it is clear that life goes on regardless, and further that each thing can be and is separate from each and every other, viz: the continuity of the newspaper headlines. Climax is for those who are swept by New Year's Eve. (Rose 1968, 278)

This aversion to climax also amounts to a desexualizing of modern dance. Graham, by contrast, never concealed her belief that the contraction is intimately related to the orgasm. Indeed, Graham once claimed that her works are set in "the house of pelvic truth." Pearl Lang, discussing Graham's floor work once observed that "The breath in the body goes way down from the genitals up through the waist, through the throat, and through the top of the head, and then down again" (de Mille 1991, 251). More succinctly, Mark Ryder once described Graham technique as "crotch-sprung." (And recall Jasper John's sly reference to abstract expressionism as "painting with two balls.") Compared to Graham (or for that matter, Pollock) Cunningham's work is both literally and figuratively, *anticlimactic.*

Indeed, Cunningham's dances rarely "build" to any sort of climax: sexual, narrative, or otherwise. In Cunningham's choreographic universe, steps that are conventionally regarded as "preparatory" are no more or less significant than the steps that precede or follow them. Of the vocabulary in "Minutiae" (1954) Cunningham has noted, "They were mostly movements anyone does when getting set to do a larger movement. They were (and are) the movements before the effort" (1968, n.p.). Applying (successfully) for a Guggenheim Fellowship that same year, Cunningham wrote to the foundation about his interest in "chance as a method of finding continuity, that is, continuity thought of as being the continuum of one thing after another, rather than being related by psychological or thematic or other cause-and-effect devices" (*Dance Observer,* 1954, 107). Early on, this absence of linear, causal "continuity" gave rise to considerable consternation among dance critics. P. W. Manchester for example, complained that "Summerspace" "straggle(s) all over the stage with no beginning, no middle and no end" (1960, 11). (This of course, is a little like complaining that *Waiting for Godot* is a play in which "nothing happens.")

But even more perplexing was Cunningham's insistence on "freeing" choreography from its former dependence on music. In Cunningham's work, movement and sound went their separate ways, almost always independent of one another. "Suite by Chance,"(1953) with music composed by Christian Wolff, was the first Cunningham dance whose score was entirely electronic (oscillator sounds on magnetic tape). Cunningham was originally expecting a piano score from Wolff, who subsequently threw him a curve. Thus Cunningham found himself having to accommodate to a very different type of sound, one that could no longer be rhythmically "counted." As he would later admit:

> This changed the way I worked with time. Originally we had expected to be able to connect in some way with the piano sounds or with counts, but we no longer could do that. Consequently I had to connect through minutes and seconds. I used a stop watch for the first time. (1984, 90)

Martha Graham by contrast viewed musical accompaniment as an objectification of the inner landscape she sought to externalize. Music embodied the propulsive energy that drives her protagonists "beyond" the assumptions of the prevailing culture, beyond the outer world of mere appearances. In her *Notebooks*, Graham quotes Schopenhauer's *Metaphysics of Music*: "Music expresses the inner being, the essence of phenomena, the will itself, the thing per se, which lies behind all appearance" (1973, 176).

In Cunningham's earlier solos (e.g., "Root of An Unfocus," from 1944, with music by Cage) the score is divided into time units. The movement and the music enjoyed a "point" of correspondence at both the beginning and the end of each unit, but were otherwise autonomous of each other. By 1953, sound and image in Cunningham's work had become—with only occasional exceptions—completely independent of one another.

Creatures From Another Planet

During that seminal year of 1953, Cunningham performed his groundbreaking "16 Dances . . . " in New York City on a program that included May O'Donnell's "Dance Sonata," Nina Fonaroff's "Lazarus," Pauline Koner and José Limón in "Deep Rhythm," and Pearl Lang in Graham's "Canticle for Innocent Comedians." (Needless to say, most of these dancers and choreographers had long-standing associations with Graham.) Doris Hering, reviewing the concert for *Dance Magazine*, wrote:

> Although Merce Cunningham was also raised in the Graham cradle, he has completely severed himself from her sphere of influence. And on these programs, where so many of the choreographers were Graham bred, he seemed like a creature from another planet. (1953, 15)

This other planet was situated Beyond the Valley of Abstract Expressionism. The atmosphere was much cooler and less steamy. The air there was drier, and also clearer. Visibility in fact, was almost unlimited. It was a world that emphasized *seeing clearly* rather than *feeling deeply;* and it was of course the land of painters such as Rauschenberg and Johns as well as choreographers such as Cunningham.

In other words, the visual artists, too, seemed like creatures from another planet when compared to Pollock and the abstract expressionists. The resulting sea change in sensibility was later vividly evoked by the art critic Peter Schjeldahl. Writing in 1984, he described the visceral impact one experiences at the Museum of Modern Art (MOMA) when moving directly from the paintings of Pollock and Rothko to those of Johns:

> One of several pedagogical coups in the recent rehanging of The Museum of Modern Art's permanent collection comes right after the singing grandeurs of Pollock and Rothko. Entering the next space, one is confronted—with a sensation like that of being hit in the face with a bucket of ice—by one of Johns' 'Flags' of the late 1950s. The conjunction is incredibly rich and, in terms of a sea change in American culture at the time, dead accurate. What we notice right off about Johns' elegant icon, in context, is what it *leaves out:* self. Subjectivity is reduced to a wandering, empty signature: sensitive, waxen brushstrokes which, like the bleats of lambs without a shepherd, call feebly after the missing figure of the artist. At MOMA, this painting acts as a kind of Ur-form, and common denominator, of the American Pop and Minimal works that shortly follow it. (13)

It should be evident by now that Cunningham shared many preoccupations with the visual artists who challenged the intensely subjective practices at the heart of abstract expressionism. And thus it makes perfect sense that, beginning in 1954, Robert Rauschenberg designed the majority of Cunningham's settings and costumes for the next 10 years. Rauchenberg's décor for "Minutiae" (1954), the first of the dances he designed for Cunningham and Company, vividly illustrates the intimate connection between his works for the gallery and his works for the theater. "Minutiae"'s decor consists of a series of freestanding panels that inhabit a middle-ground between abstract expressionism and pop art. The panels are painted with a basic coat of reddish-orange, and Rauschenberg's vigorous brushstrokes are still very much in evidence. But barely visible beneath the thick encrustations of paint are pasted-on comic strips. Similarly, the downstage panel suggests the lingering influence of a painter like Rothko: amorphous patches of deep, dark colors—azure and purple—seem to hover above the softer, reddish undercoating. The dancer's unitards were dyed in overlapping variations on this same set of colors. But the middle of the downstage panel contains a detail that an abstract expressionist like Rothko would have considered sacrilegious: a small, circular, rotating mirror which catches reflections of both dancers and spectators (not unlike the way some of Rauschenberg's "white paintings" reflected the shadows of movement throughout the performance space during Cage's untitled "Theater Piece" two years earlier at Black Mountain College). The panel below the mirror also contains kitschy, commercial images of apples that look as if they might have been appropriated from the ad pages of *The Saturday Evening Post*. (This mixing of "high" and "low," abstract and representational, would have been taboo for the abstract expressionists.) And the panel above the mirror contains a sheet of transparent gauze that allows us to see a filtered image of the upper bodies of the dancers as they pass behind it. Rauschenberg's freestanding sculpture for "Minutiae" is one of many settings designed for Cunningham that serve in part to mediate the spectator's relationship to the dancers.

When "Minutiae" was first performed, in December 1954, the Charles Egan Gallery in New York was exhibiting Rauschenberg's "Red Paintings." That same year, Rauschenberg began to work on his earliest "combines" (almost all of which *combined* spattered paint, newsprint, photographs, and small, attached objects). The "combines" evolved directly from the heavily "collaged" surfaces of the Red Paintings. Thus, Rauschenberg's decor for "Minutiae" functioned as a bridge between the Red Paintings and the Combines.

During the London performances of Cunningham's "Story" 10 years later, Rauschenberg constructed a combine "live" on the stage of the Phoenix Theatre as the dance progressed. (The design concept for "Story" specified that Rauschenberg construct a new object for each performance, usually from materials found in the theater that same day.) The resulting assemblage (also titled "Story") features a number of "found" images and objects unique to London and to the backstage area of the theater (e.g. fragments of faded ads for Harp Lager and Outspan Oranges as well as an actual wheel from a child's scooter attached to the top edge of the right-hand panel).

Three years earlier, in 1961, the American Embassy in Paris had hosted an evening titled "Homage to David Tudor." As part of the performance, Rauschenberg, in full view of the audience, worked on his "First Time Painting." The canvas itself was turned away from the spectators. But despite the fact that the audience never directly saw the surface of the painting, they were able to hear the amplified sounds of Rauschenberg's brushstrokes and hammer blows (because the canvas had several live contact mikes attached to it). The "finished" work was subsequently exhibited for the first time the following day as part of Rauschenberg's one-man show at the Galerie Daniel Cordier.

Between 1961 and 1964, there is an absolute continuity—a dynamic give and take—between Rauschenberg's work for the galleries and his work for the stage. The "Time Paintings" (the first of which was executed during the homage to Tudor) are combines, all of which contain working clocks. They boldly announce that Rauschenberg's work possesses a temporal (and thus performative) dimension even when exhibited in a "static" museum context. Rauschenberg readily acknowledges the extent to which his involvement with Cunningham and Cage helped to generate one of the key innovations in his visual art. "My relationship to dance..." he once admitted, "is directly responsible for my new interest in the spectator's active role" (Spector 1997, 233). And when he won first prize at the Venice Biennale in 1964 (while on tour with the Cunningham company), he declared that "the Merce Cunningham Dance company is my biggest canvas" (Fenton 1997, 12).

Aside from Rauschenberg, the visual artist most instrumental in forging a cooler, more impersonal alternative to the ethos of abstract expressionism is, of course, Jasper Johns. And in 1967, Johns began to oversee decor and costume for the Cunningham company (a responsibility that he continued to exercise until 1980). But the commonalties between his work and Cunningham's had already been evident for many years. In 1963 for example, Cunningham choreographed a new piece called "Field Dances." That same year, Johns began work on his seminal "Field Painting."

"Field Dances" is one of those anomalous Cunningham works in which the dancers are free to make a specified number of movement decisions (e.g., when to enter and exit, where the phrases assigned to them will be performed.) But Cunningham is insistent that these choices be exercised within the confines of a strict time frame. Johns's painting is inspired by similar concerns: Two canvases are juxtaposed side by side. The left panel appears to have been painted in a quick and improvised way; the canvas to the right looks cooler and more deliberate. (In this regard, it recalls Rauschenberg's "Factum I and II.") Cage's contribution to "Field Dances" is similarly "divided." The sounds in his score are sometimes recorded, sometimes produced by live radios. But regardless of the source of the sound, Cage specifies that it should originate in a second space: *outside* the theater in which the dancing takes place. Cage also wanted his score for "Field Dances" to be dominated by "found" sounds ("real" sounds); and Cunningham, perhaps under the influence of the Judson Dance Theater experiments then in progress, incorporated a great deal of nontechnical, even pedestrian, movement. Similarly, Johns in "Field Painting" was also experimenting with the introduction of real objects (a paintbrush, a printmaking squeegee) into an otherwise "painterly" field. Appropriately, "Field Painting" also contains an homage to the originator of the concept of the ready-made: Marcel Duchamp. (An outline of Duchamp's "Female Fig Leaf" is visible in the upper right corner of the painting.)

This sort of dynamic interplay between the work of Cunningham, Cage, Rauschenberg, and Johns illustrates my central assertion: that Cunningham's repudiation of Graham and modern dance directly paralleled Rauschenberg's and Johns's repudiation of Pollock and abstract expressionism. As we've seen, the very titles of Graham's greatest works from the 1940s ("Cave of the Heart," "Night Journey") often suggest a voyage into darkness or the inner self—a movement away from the neon-bright, clamorously noisy world of day-to-day urban experience. Indeed, Graham's self-professed goal was to "make visible the *interior* landscape." (Frances Wickes, the Jungian analyst whom Graham befriended, wrote a series of books whose titles include *The Inner World of Childhood, The Inner World of Man,* and *The Inner World of Choice.*) By contrast, Rauschenberg, Johns—and, for that matter, Cage—often employ "found" materials that come from the world of "outer" rather than "inner" experience (what Jasper Johns once called "preformed, conventional, depersonalized, factual, exterior elements" [Rosenberg 1964, 176]): Johns's flags, targets, and Ballantine Ale cans; the found objects in the "combines" of Rauschenberg; the non-musical, "found" sounds in the compositions of Cage; and so on.

Cage's use of "found" sound begins at least as early as his score for Cunningham's "Credo in Us" from 1942. Here, door buzzers were deemed no more or less "musical" than piano keys. The raw materials utilized by all of these artists were appropriated from the external world in the manner of Duchamp's ready-mades, rather than generated "instinctively" or dredged up from the depths of the artist's unconscious. As Andy Warhol, another Cunningham collaborator, later said of his own neo-Duchampian images based on Campbell's Soup cans and Brillo Boxes, "Pop comes from the outside" (Cateforis 1999, 11). Warhol credits Johns and Rauschenberg with having conflated the very distinction between "inside" and "outside." In his own words, "Johns and Bob Rauschenberg and others had begun to bring art back from abstract introspective stuff. Then Pop Art took the inside and put it outside, took the outside and put it inside" (Cateforis 1999, 13).

If the distinction between inside and outside no longer obtains, then the modern artist's "voyage to the interior," as exemplified by Graham and Pollock, begins to lose its automatic claim to authenticity and moral superiority. Indeed, by the late 1970s, the atmosphere had changed sufficiently for Christopher Lasch to write:

> The record of the inner life becomes an unintentional parody of the inner life. A literary genre that appears to affirm inwardness actually tells us that inner life is precisely what can no longer be taken seriously. This explains why (Woody) Allen, (Donald) Barthelme, and other satirists so often parody, as a deliberate literary strategy, the confessional style of an earlier time, when the artist bared his inner struggles in the belief that they represented a microcosm of the larger

world. Today the artist's "confessions" are notable only for their utter banality. Woody Allen writes a parody of Van Gogh's letters to his brother, in which the artist becomes a dentist preoccupied with "oral prophylaxis," "root-canal work," and "the proper way to brush." The voyage to the interior discloses nothing but a blank. (1978, 20–21)

Call it the triumph of irony or a new "aesthetic of indifference": Either way, the ethos of abstract expressionism has lost both its innocence and its gravitas, its heroic claims to high seriousness.

4

The Limitations of Instinct

Confusing the Issue: The Cunningham/Pollock Analogy

The proposition that Cunningham is to Graham as Rauschenberg and Johns are to abstract expressionism seems almost too obvious to belabor; but it's a parallel that most dance writers consistently fail to acknowledge. There's a simple, if ultimately exasperating, reason for this: Dance critics have a bad habit of analogizing Cunningham to the painter with whom he has the *least* in common: Jackson Pollock. Of course, Cunningham and Pollock do share some superficial similarities. Neither of them organizes the painting's visual field around a perspectival "vanishing point." But comparing Pollock and Cunningham in this way is a little like suggesting a deep affinity between Mondrian and Roy Lichtenstein simply because they both employ similar figure/ground relationships and both renounce the illusionism of three-dimensional perspective.

Nonetheless, the comparison between Cunningham and Pollock has become de rigueur. Jill Johnston, in 1967 argued that: "It has often been remarked that Pollock's paintings suggest an infinite extension beyond the picture plane. Cunningham's dances suggest the same extension" (1976, 156). Robert Coe, in 1985, paraphrased Harold Rosenberg's famous description of Pollock-in-action and applied it to Cunningham:

> The "triumph of American painting" was in the making, with the gestural energy of abstract expressionism transforming the artist's canvas into an arena of spontaneous physicality. A painting was to be conceived as a field of action producing not a picture but an *event* informed by the artist's existential confrontation with the materials of craft. (1985, 165)

In 1988 Anna Kisselgoff said of Cunningham's "Eleven," "This is one of Mr. Cunningham's decentralized dances, whose spatial arrangements have often been compared to the abstract expressionism of Jackson Pollock" (1988, C3). Similarly, Arlene Croce wrote, "If there has been any abstract expressionism in dance, it has been by no one but Cunningham" (1982, 122). Even Calvin Tomkins, whose book *The Bride and the Bachelors* discusses Cunningham in an expanded context that includes Rauschenberg, has invoked this standard comparison from time to time: "The over-all paintings of Jackson Pollock and others of his generation had helped Cunningham to arrive at his own method of making dances in which there is no single center of interest" (1992, 46).

The most extensive exploration of the Cunningham/Pollock analogy appears in Deborah Jowitt's book *Time and the Dancing Image.* According to Jowitt:

> The way you look at a painting of Pollock's is similar to the way you watch a Cunningham dance. They're both roomy, the eye wanders at will, caught now by this, now by that.... Their processes too have some kinship. Pollock walked around his paintings. Cunningham makes his dances as if they were to be viewed from all sides. That Pollock never actually touched the canvas with his brush slightly distances, almost undermines, the almighty power of the artist's hand, as chance mildly subverts Cunningham's choreographic taste. (1988, 291–92)

I suspect that most art critics would be startled by Jowitt's suggestion that when viewing a Pollock, the eye wanders at will, caught now by this, now by that (as it surely does during a Cunningham performance). But if ever a painter set out to defeat temporality, to make the entire painting visually manifest in a *single instant,* that painter was Pollock. However, Jowitt's argument that Pollock's process of dripping paint undermines the almighty power of the artist's hand couldn't be further from the truth. The most identifiable characteristic of Pollock's paintings is the virtually calligraphic nature of his drip marks and spatterings. They're as idiosyncratic as his handwriting, as ineluctable as a fingerprint. (Like some legal test of identity, they could belong to no one else.) That's because the process of "action painting" engaged so much of Pollock's *body* and its unique way of moving—rather than somehow holding his "imprint" in check and allowing paint to be applied to canvas in a more impersonal and mediated way. (In Pollock's "No. 1, 1948" we find actual traces of the artist's palm print.) William Seitz, in his *Abstract Expressionist Painting in America,* offers the definitive refutation of Jowitt's argument. Acknowledging that Pollock seldom comes into contact with the actual surface of the canvas, Seitz nevertheless maintains that:

> Individual passages... at no point evidence the direct touch of the painter. Rather, it is his entire bodily activity that from a distance influences, but by no

means determines, his configuration. Accident, gravity, and the fluid response
of the paint combine with human gesture to form a structure that is the result
of their interaction. (Kramer 1999, 16)

Perhaps the full extent of the differences between Cunningham and
Pollock will be easier to perceive if we speculate about *why* Cunningham and
company refuse to harness the sort of impulsive energy that fueled abstract
expressionism.

Infiltrating the Unconscious

Why is it that Cunningham, Cage, Rauschenberg, and Johns made no attempt to "tap" the unconscious and/or the primitive as a deep "wellspring"
of creativity? Why did they place so much emphasis on objectivity (as opposed to subjectivity), on detachment and impersonality, on coolness, play-
fulness, and irony? Or—to return to Moira Roth and her accusation of
"indifference"—"Why this denial of commitment and feeling in art"? And
why did Cunningham and Company care so little for those privileged moments of inspiration, those "spontaneous" *bursts* of creativity, those unself-
conscious spurts of uninterrupted flow?

Both abstract expressionism and modern dance were motivated by
Freud's belief that below the culturally conditioned ego lies the "natural" id
(or in Jung's version of this concept, "the collective unconscious"). In order
to reestablish contact with this unacculturated and "primitive" region of the
self, the artist must loosen the stranglehold of rational consciousness and
cultural conditioning (typically through drugs, sex, alcohol, travel, physical
exertion, or some mode of surrealist-style automatism such as "automatic
writing" or "automatic drawing"). As Pollock put it, "When I am *in* my painting, I'm not aware of what I'm doing" (Friedman 1972, 121). But as Giorgio
de Chirico was among the first to point out, even the unconscious runs the
risk of becoming fully "acculturated" amidst the subliminally manipulative,
sensory overload(ed) environments of 20th-century consumer society. In
an environment designed to stimulate desires that have little relation to instinctive "need," we have no way of confirming that what *feels* natural isn't
actually the result of cultural conditioning. In effect, culture masquerading
as "nature" (or "second nature".) We might paraphrase this notion a bit
more colloquially so as to read: "When I do what I want to do, I feel free."
But then comes the nagging doubt, the paranoid spin—which leads one to
ask "What *makes* me want to do what I want to do?" Especially in an age of
conspicuous consumption, the danger exists that we'll confuse purchasing
power (e.g., 27 different varieties of breakfast cereal, 500 cable channels)
with "freedom," while all the while our most fundamental perceptual habits
have been conditioned by forces we neither control nor even recognize. Or so

the argument goes. (Marcuse's *One Dimensional Man* and Jacques Ellul's *The Technological Society* provide what are probably the most persuasive explorations of this potentially paranoid idea.) "Protect Me From What I Want" reads one of Jenny Holzer's best known aphorisms from the mid-1980s.

Even Lionel Trilling—much less "radical" (politically) than Marcuse, Ellul, or Holzer—said this (in 1955) about the emphasis Freud places on biology and "nature" as an ineluctable component of human personality:

> [This idea] proposes to us that culture is not all-powerful. It suggests that there is a residue of human quality beyond the reach of cultural control, and that this residue of human quality, elemental as it may be, serves to bring culture itself under criticism and keeps it from being absolute.... Nowadays... societies are likely to be all too efficient, whether by coerciveness or seductiveness. In a society like ours, which, despite some appearances to the contrary, tends to be seductive rather than coercive, the individual's old defenses against the domination of the culture become weaker and weaker. (1968, 113–14)

The continuing incursion of "culture" on "nature" created the intellectual climate in which semiology flourished during the 1960s and 1970s. The semiologist proceeds on the assumption that "naturalness" is a bourgeois myth, and that advertising and mass media have conditioned us to accept culturally created needs as natural desires. In his preface to the 1970 edition of *Mythologies* (originally published in 1957), Roland Barthes identifies his project as unmasking "the mystification which transforms petit-bourgeois culture into a universal nature" (9). Today, the realization that "culture" often tries to pass itself off as "nature" seems almost numbingly obvious. But with a bit of elaboration, this idea can lead us toward a radically revised view of both the unconscious and the "primitive." Fredric Jameson's conception of "the political unconscious" reminds us that even the innermost sanctuaries are no longer immune to cultural conditioning. He describes the process by which:

> a prodigious expansion of late capitalism ... penetrates one of the two surviving pre-capitalist enclaves of Nature within the system—namely the Unconscious. (The other one is pre-capitalist agriculture and village culture of the Third World.) (1983, 3)

Indeed, the developing world is no longer immune to the global reach of America's most potent export: its popular culture. Robert Farris Thompson recalls a trip he made to the former nation of Zaire (now the Democratic Republic of Congo) where he came across a villager performing what he took to be the "authentic" African root of the Electric Boogie. Eager to uncover the source, he asked the young man how and where he'd learned the dance. The answer: he'd seen Michael Jackson perform it on MTV! Closer to home, the expansion of "late capitalism" is even more "prodigious." In Wim

Wenders's film *Kings of the Road*, two German vagabonds stumble on a graffito that reads "The Yanks have colonized our subconscious" (an aphorism that recalls Leo Lowenthal's dazzling notion that "mass culture is psychoanalysis in reverse" [cited in Hoberman 1982, 10]). John Cage once described Pop Art as "not a Surrealism of the individual, but a Surrealism of the society" (Kostelanetz 1988, 174)—which is another way of suggesting that images of Campbell's Soup cans and Brillo boxes have by now burrowed their way deep into the collective unconscious. Hence the problem with Graham and Pollock's determination to plumb the pure, uncorrupted "depths" of the *sub*conscious. Vance Packard published his pioneering examination of advertising almost half a century ago. Since that time, the pervasive technological replication of seductive "life style imagery" has upped the consumerist ante in subtle, but powerful ways. According to Greil Marcus in *Lipstick Traces* (1989), the image-industry has:

> turned upon individual men and women, seized their subjective emotions and experiences, changed those once evanescent phenomena into objective, replicatable commodities, placed them on the market, set their prices, and sold them back to those who had, once, brought emotions and experiences out of themselves. (101)

Thus, the buried treasures of depth psychology *and* the pristine purity of "the primitive" are both equally compromised. Contemporary anthropology often seems to specialize in debunking the very idea of "the primitive." Sir Edmund Leach gets right to the heart of the matter when he insists that "the distinction between savage and civilized upon which the whole edifice of traditional anthropology was constructed deserves to be consigned to the trash can" (1971, 45). And in his aptly titled *The Invention of Primitive Society,* Adam Kuper goes ever farther, suggesting that:

> the history of the theory of primitive society is the history of an illusion. It is our phlogiston, our aether; or less grandly, our equivalent to the notion of hysteria.... The theory of primitive society is about something which does not and never has existed. (1988, 8)

That's highly debatable. But it's harder to disagree with an anthropologist like James Clifford when he discusses the way in which tourism and immigration patterns have worked to conflate traditional dichotomies between familiar/exotic, far/near, inside/outside, and authentic/prefabricated:

> In cities on six continents, foreign populations have come to stay—mixing in but often in partial, specific fashions. The "exotic" is uncannily close. Conversely, there seem no distant places left on the planet where the presence of "modern" production, media, and power cannot be felt. An older topography and experience of travel is exploded. One no longer leaves home confident of

finding something new, another time or space. Difference is encountered in the adjoining neighborhood; the familiar turns up at the ends of the earth. (1988, 13–14)

So much for the modernist myth of escaping the prevailing culture by sailing to Tahiti or Bali. The aura of exotic "otherness" is wholly dependent on physical distance and geographical isolation. But today—in the age of cyberspace and the World Wide Web—McLuhan's vision of the global village has finally been realized.

The pervasiveness and interconnectedness of the international computer network has by now completely demystified the quest for some pristine, uncorrupted sanctuary of the natural or the primitive. Indeed, the cyberpunks would like us to believe that "technoculture" is so pervasive that nature itself is no longer anything more than a mode of nostalgia, a semantic convenience. In the words of Allucquere Rosanne Stone:

> the boundaries between technology and nature are themselves in the midst of a deep restructuring. . . . "Nature" instead of representing some pristine category or originary state of being, has taken on an entirely different function in late twentieth-century economies of meaning. Not only has the character of nature as yet another co-construct of culture become more patent, but it has become nothing more (or less) than an ordering factor—a construct by means of which we attempt to *keep technology visible* as something separate from our "natural" selves and our everyday life. In other words, the category "nature," rather than referring to any object or category in the world, is a *strategy* for maintaining boundaries. (1991, 101–2)

One of the earliest—and still most potent—artistic embodiments of this idea (i.e., the vanishing distinction between nature and culture) appears in the work of Nam June Paik, the video artist and composer who has collaborated on a number of occasions with Cunningham and Cage. His video installation, "TV Garden" (1974–78), disperses a vast bank of color television screens amidst a garden of green plants. The imagery of commercial television thereby fuses with the foliage. In "Video Fish" (1975), aquarium-tanks swimming with live fish are placed in front of video monitors broadcasting prerecorded images of aquatic life. And, in "Fish Flies on Sky" (1975), television images on the ceiling beam down toward the viewers in an otherwise darkened gallery. The starry night and the televised night are now hopelessly intermingled. It thus seems entirely appropriate that Paik, who grew up in South Korea, says that the earliest dream image he can recall is of Shirley Temple in a 1930s Hollywood film. The moment we can no longer view the natural, the unconscious, the "non-Western," or "the primitive" as an escape route from the prevailing culture, as a source of inviolable purity, the ethos of both abstract expressionism and modern dance is fatally compromised. (Indeed, as we'll see in Chapter 11, this is also the moment at which "modernism"—broadly construed—gives way to "postmodernism.")

The result is what might be called an aesthetics of suspicion, an attitude that leaves the artist distrustful of inspiration that *feels* natural, instinctual, or mythic—no matter how certain it seems that contact has been established with one's "muse," no matter how pleasurable the sensation of an inwardly (or outwardly) generated "flow" of energy that appears to be dictating the creative process. That, no doubt, is part of what the painter Ad Reinhardt was getting at when he declared (contra Pollock): "One must never let the influence of evil demons gain control of the brush" (1973, 168). Indeed, the entire foundation of modernist primitivism in the 1940s and 1950s—not just abstract expressionism, but the broader cultural landscape we've already examined—is called into question. Peter Brook, for example, expresses the following doubts about "method acting":

> The method actor's freedom in choosing anything whatsoever from the gestures of everyday life is equally restricted. For in basing his gestures on his observation or on his own spontaneity the actor is not drawing on any deep creativity. He is reaching inside himself for an alphabet that is also fossilized, for the language of signs from life that he knows is the language not of invention but of his conditioning. His observations of behavior are often observations of projections of himself. What he thinks to be spontaneous is filtered and monitored many times over. Were Pavlov's dog improvising, he would still salivate when the bell rang, but he would feel sure it was all his own doing: "I'm dribbling," he would say, proud of his daring. (1972, 89)

Brando's version of Actor's Studio style, which in the 1950s was regarded as "unactorish," appears no more "natural" to us today than any other overt "period" style. His ear-tuggings, nose wipings, and T-shirt stretchings are, in fact, no less mannered—no less culturally coded—than the highly conventionalized stage business of Restoration Comedy with its snuff boxes, walking sticks, and powdered wigs.

Roland Barthes takes a comparably skeptical view of the surrealist practice of "automatic writing"; and in so doing, he articulates what has now become the standard "poststructuralist" attitude toward artists—like the surrealists—who tried to directly or "automatically" tap the primitive unconscious:

> I don't like the notion of "automatic" writing at all. Without becoming involved in a now classic and purely art-historical debate ("Did they really perform automatic writing?"), I'll just say that automatism—supposing that we retain this vague notion for the time being—is not rooted at all in the "spontaneous," the "savage," the "pure," the "profound," the "subversive," but originates on the contrary from the "strictly coded." ... If we were to imagine that The Good Fairy

> Automatism were to touch the speaking or writing subject with her wand, the
> toads and vipers that would spring from his mouth would just be stereotypes.
> (1985, 244)

And Richard Howard, in his introduction to Barthes's *S/Z*, dismisses the
very idea of "instinctive" pleasure. What he says here of literature is even
more applicable to dance:

> It is precisely our "instinctive enjoyment" which is acculturated, determined, in
> bondage. Only when we know—and it is a knowledge gained by taking pains, by
> renouncing what Freud calls instinctual gratification—what we are doing when
> we read, are we free to enjoy what we read. As long as our enjoyment is—or is
> said to be—instinctive, it is not enjoyment, it is terrorism. (1974, ix)

Finally, to bring matters closer to home—perhaps even full circle—John
Cage described the surrealist (and abstract expressionist!) goal of automatism in a similarly derisive way: "Automatic art, in fact, has never interested
me, because it is a way of falling back, resting on one's memories and feelings subconsciously, is it not? And I have done my utmost to free people
from that" (Kostelanetz 1988, 173). (Cage particularly detested the most
famous—and ruthlessly self-promoting—of the surrealists, Salvador Dali.)
Later in the same interview (conducted in 1966), Irving Sandler asked Cage
to comment directly on Pollock and abstract expressionism. Cage expressed
his general distaste for Pollock; and then Sandler pressed him a bit harder:
"But what about the pitch of intensity, the excitement?" Cage's response:

> They're precisely the things about abstract expressionism that *didn't* interest me.
> I wanted them to change my way of seeing, not my way of feeling. I'm perfectly
> happy about my feelings.... I don't want to spend my life being pushed around
> by a bunch of artists. (Kostelanetz 1988, 177)

Certainly, many of the dancers who eventually gravitated toward
Cunningham rather than Graham were in complete agreement with Cage:
They wanted their "feelings" left out of the equation. Sandra Neels, who
danced with Cunningham between 1963 and 1973, has complained that
even in classroom situations, Graham's floor work flooded her with emotions she was unprepared to deal with. (Graham, I suspect, would have
considered this a great compliment.) David Gordon, one of the principal pioneers of the Judson Dance Theater (and the husband of former
Cunningham dancer, Valda Setterfield), once said that Graham technique
"demands the sort of attention your family does." The key word here is
"demands." Both Neels and Gordon envisioned dance as something separate
from their private lives; they refused to treat it to as a mode of confession or
therapy.

We might compare Graham's rhythm of "contraction and release" with the abstract expressionist tension that Hans Hoffman called "push and pull." Both techniques seek to elicit an involuntary response from the viewer; and that, I think, is what Cage is objecting to when he speaks of "not wanting to be *pushed* around." Suspicious of the involuntary, the "instinctual," (and the conditioned), artists such as Cunningham, Cage, Rauschenberg, and Johns set out to critically examine that which "feels natural," rather than simply surrendering to it.

The Influence of Duchamp and the Aesthetic of Indifference

Here it's essential to acknowledge the artist who exerted perhaps the greatest influence on Cunningham and company: Marcel Duchamp. (Moira Roth singles out Duchamp, who once praised "the beauty of indifference" as the great grand-dada of "the aesthetic of indifference.") Referring to his work "The Large Glass" Duchamp once noted: "There was nothing spontaneous about it, which of course is a great objection on the part of aestheticians. They want the unconscious to speak by itself. I don't." (Gold 1998).

Allusions to—and quotations from—Duchamp abound in the work of Cunningham, Cage, Johns, and Rauschenberg. Johns's setting for Cunningham's "Walkaround Time" (1968) was an outright homage to Duchamp: an assemblage of clear plastic rectangles imprinted with iconography from Duchamp's "Large Glass." In addition, the section of "Walkaround Time" in which Cunningham crouches down, stripping off one set of tights and pulling on another, was conceived as a visual allusion to Duchamp's "Nude Descending a Staircase." So, too, was Carolyn Brown's solo, with its sharp alternation of allegro movement and stillness. Her phrases were intended to allude to the way Duchamp conflated the distinctions between futurism and cubism: that is, his nude is both "still" in the manner of a cubist painting and "descending" in the manner of a futurist work. Cunningham has also referred to those portions of the choreography adapted directly from his technique class (e.g., the "warm-ups" in the opening section) as "ready-mades." Even earlier, the already mentioned "Homage to David Tudor" (1961) included an allusion to Duchamp's "Bride Stripped Bare . . . ": Jean Tinguely constructed an automated "stripper," an anthropomorphic machine that lurched across the stage, discarding chunks of its metal "costume" along the way—rather like an animated version of the Mechanical Bride.

The spirit of Duchamp hovers over many other Cunningham works as well. Ivan Tcherepnin's score for "Field and Figures" in 1989 incorporated recordings of Duchamp and Cage reading excerpts from Duchamp's widely reprinted 1957 lecture "The Creative Act." Similarly, Cage's score for "Inventions" in 1989 was inspired by a reference he encountered in Duchamp's "Green Box... "

Beyond "Animal Expression"

There are many such specific references to Duchamp throughout the work of Cunningham and company, but what matters more is the Duchampian sensibility these artists share. Duchamp anticipated by many years the spirit of Rauschenberg's and Johns's repudiation of abstract expressionism when he derisively dismissed as "olfactory" those artists who wallow in the aroma of wet paint and wield their brushes in a dazed, semi-intoxicated stupor. To Duchamp, this sort of impulsive, spontaneous behavior was "animal-like." He was especially contemptuous of painters whose brushstrokes are so frenetic and so bodily that they appear to have been produced by "la patte" (the animal's "paw" rather than the human's hand). Duchamp insisted that "the direction in which art should turn is to an intelectual expression, rather than to an animal expression" (d'Harnoncourt 1973, 17). Duchamp's readymades undermine any attempt to establish analogies between the creative process and the natural world. For Duchamp, the operative metaphor for creativity is no longer pregnancy and childbirth but, rather, the "rendezvous" or the blind date. Duchamp merely "encounters" the objects that become his "ready-mades"; he doesn't "create" them. As Richard Wollheim notes, Duchamp poses the question: "What is the meaning of the word 'work' in the phrase 'work of art'? (1995, 395).

In 1911, Duchamp attended a theatrical performance in Paris that had a profound effect on his subsequent development. It was an adaptation of *Impressions of Africa,* a highly eccentric novel by Raymond Roussel in which a group of Europeans, shipwrecked on the coast of an African country, devise a series of "machines" whose express function is to create works of art (e.g., the painting machine consists of a photo-sensitive plate connected to a series of paint brushes that—somehow—render "painterly" versions of the photographic images which form mechanically on the light-sensitive emulsion). The idea that works of art could be created with a minimum of "human" intervention is one of the central passions of Duchamp's career; and it's this haunting sense of human detachment (what Roth dismisses as "indifference") that characterizes the work of Cunningham and company as well.

Duchamp's influence on the Cunningham circle was both direct and readily acknowledged. For example, a reexamination of "that which feels natural" (or at least "habitual") is especially evident in Jasper Johns's early paintings, completed shortly after he first visited the Arensberg Collection of Duchamp's works at the Philadelphia Museum of Art in 1954. Gestural brushstrokes were still in evidence; but the paintings were already far removed from the concerns of abstract expressionism. Johns centered these early works around ready-made images, what he called "things the mind already knows": a map of the United States; the American flag; the alphabet; numbers; and archery targets. Taken collectively, it's almost impossible not to associate these images with early memories of school, learning by rote, and various varieties of conditioning—perhaps even of indoctrination.

It's utterly appropriate that one of Johns's "target" paintings appears on the famous poster he designed for the Cunningham company in 1968. Johns asks us to distribute our visual attention evenly throughout each circular band of the image, despite the fact that we've been conditioned to "zero-in" on the target's bull's-eye. Allowing our focus to be directed toward the center feels perfectly "natural." But Johns and Cunningham, true heirs to Duchamp, ask us to use our eyes in counterintuitive ways. Stage center loses its privileged (i.e., "naturally commanding") status in Cunningham's organization of stage space—just as surely as the bull's-eye does in Johns's target paintings. (Jasper Johns, by the way, also participated in the 1961 "Homage to David Tudor," contributing a bull's eye—assembled from flowers—which served as a target for a sharpshooter who wound up firing instead at a plaster sculpture created by Niki de Saint Phalle.)

Cunningham also makes a point of resisting his own "instinctive" preferences (which is to say: the preferences that *feel* natural). "The trouble is," says Cunningham, echoing Duchamp, "we all tend to fall back on our old habits. Dancing is very tiring: and when you're tired you just do the easy thing, the thing you know" (Tomkins 1968, 276). In other words, you do the thing that seems to come *naturally*.

5
Contemporary Classicism:
Rediscovering Ballet

"That the ballet *has* something seems reasonable to assume. That
what it has is what the modern dance needs is here expressed as an
opinion."
—John Cage, "Grace and Clarity," 1944 (1961, 90)

Duchamp and Ballet Ready-mades

Common sense would seem to suggest that Merce Cunningham's interest
in classical ballet has little or nothing to do with the influence of Marcel
Duchamp. (It's difficult to imagine stranger bedfellows than Duchamp and
classical ballet.) But the modified arabesques and attitudes (indeed all the
readily recognizable elements of the ballet lexicon that figure so prominently
in Cunningham's work) function in much the same way that "ready-made"
objects do in the art of Duchamp: They're movement forms that preexisted
the choreographer, that weren't invented by him. They come from the realm
of "outer" rather than "inner" experience.

Surely, one of the things the classic modern dance choreographers found
most objectionable about ballet was that its vocabulary came—in a sense—
"ready-made," and was therefore presumed incapable of expressing their
singular personal identities. But Cunningham is attracted to ballet at least
in part because he *isn't* attempting to tell a story unique to his own musculature or his innate way of moving. Unlike the great modern-dance pioneers,
his movement vocabulary is not an organic extension of his "nature." As

we've seen, he doesn't undertake either of the time-honored voyages of high modernism: He doesn't hark back to the source, to "primitive" origins; and he doesn't try to tap his own instinctive or unconscious movement preferences. Cunningham once remarked to Carolyn Brown that he doesn't even think of his solos—usually the most "personal" form of dance-making—as an exercise in "choreography."

The very "impersonality" of ballet is one great source of its aesthetic appeal not only to Cunningham, but—perhaps more surprisingly—to Cage as well. Indeed, if any single document can be said to have provided the theoretical foundation for Cunningham's innovations, it is surely John Cage's short essay, "Grace and Clarity," originally published in *Dance Observer* in 1944, the year of Cunningham's first solo concert in New York. Early in the essay, Cage writes,

> Personality is such a flimsy thing on which to build an art. . . . And the ballet is obviously not built on such an ephemeron, for, if it were, it would not at present thrive as it does. . . . That the ballet *has* something seems reasonable to assume. That what it has is what the modern dance needs is here expressed as an opinion. (1961, 90)

The problem with modern dance, Cage goes on to say, is that it "was not impersonal, but was intimately connected with and ultimately dependent on the personalities and even the actual physical bodies of the individuals who imparted it" (1961, 89). Cage even goes so far as to suggest that a typical production of "Swan Lake" (yes, "Swan Lake"!) offers valuable lessons in rhythmic clarity—as well as lessons about impersonality—that the average modern dance choreographer still needs to learn:

> It may seem at first thought that rhythmic structure is not of primary importance. However, a dance, a poem, a piece of music (any of the time arts) occupies a length of time, and the manner in which this length of time is divided first into large parts and then into phrases (or built up from phrases to form eventual larger parts) is the work's very life structure. The ballet is in possession of a tradition of clarity of its rhythmic structure. Essential devices for bringing this about have been handed down generation after generation. . . . The modern dance, on the other hand, is rarely clear. . . .
>
> That one should today, have to see "Swan Lake". . . in order to experience the pleasure of observing clarity and grace in the dance, is, on its face, lamentable. Modern society needs, as usual, and now desperately needs, a strong modern dance. The opinion expressed here is that clarity of rhythmic structure with grace are essential to the time arts, that together they constitute an aesthetic (that is, they lie under and beneath, over and above, physical and personal particularities), and that they rarely occur in the modern dance; that the latter has no aesthetic (its strength having been and being the personal property of

its originators and best exponents), that, in order for it to become strong and useful in society, mature in itself, the modern dance must clarify its rhythmic structure. (1961, 90–1)

Thus, Cage's "Grace and Clarity" functions not only as a manifesto opposing the cult of personality in modern dance, but also as a defense of—indeed a plea for—a rapprochement of sorts between ballet and modern: a new fusion of the two that Cunningham (along with Paul Taylor) would soon pioneer. Note how similar Cage's thesis about the differences between modern dance and ballet is to the argument that Lincoln Kirstein had been advancing since the 1930s. Kirstein, who once proposed that modern dance suffers from "the curse of Isadora," summed up what he believed to be the essential differences between modern and ballet:

> ... accidental idiosyncrasy against tradition, personalism vs. collectivity, discontinuity as opposed to an unbroken line. Modern dance opted for self-expressive originality, defined by a few notable heterodoxies. . . . Self-expression triumphed without providing either a cohesive teaching method or a repertory past individual utterance. (1983, 239)

This comparison leads Kirstein to conclude that "(modern dance) is a self-limited form since it depends on the several selves of the individual performer" (1975, 89). Kirstein and Cage are unlikely allies, to say the least. But this (no doubt, unexpected) area of agreement between two potential adversaries helps explain why ballet played such an essential role in Cunningham's campaign to modernize modern dance. The terms in which Kirstein describes ballet (i.e., "collectivity" as opposed to "personalism"; "an unbroken line" as opposed to "discontinuity") are designed to celebrate the genre's steady, but ever-so-gradual, evolution over a period of 400 years. As a practical matter, ballet has no choice but to absorb and colonize new kinetic territory. Otherwise, it degenerates into Alexandrian stasis. Granted, long periods of academic sterility often seem to be the norm for ballet rather than the exception. (This is the deep subtext to "Sleeping Beauty": the reawakening of classical ballet in late-19th-century Russia after its long mid-century slumber, following the decline of Romanticism in Western Europe.) But precisely because ballet *is* more impersonal than modern dance, precisely because it is *not* inextricably tied to a unique individual's manner of moving, it has often proved more supple than modern dance, more protean and adaptable to new circumstances—better equipped, in other words, to assimilate eclectic movement influences from its surrounding environment.

At the same time, the more impersonal nature of the ballet vocabulary, its grounding in geometric universals, gives it greater immunity than modern dance to changes in taste and fashion. As a result—and we'll encounter some specific examples later in this chapter—the best modern ballets tend, as a rule, to look much less dated 20 or 30 years after their premieres than do their counterparts in pre-Cunningham modern dance. (In the late 1990s, the Limón company added Anthony Tudor's "Dark Elegies" to its repertory. Tudor's great modern ballet from 1937 still looked freshly minted, whereas many of the Limón signature dances had long since assumed the status of "period pieces.")

The suggestion that ballet might have a firmer purchase on "modernity" than does modern dance not only flies in the face of received opinion; it seems contrary to common sense. But if we ask ourselves, "Whose dances most vividly embody the look and the feel of the just-concluded-century?," the names that spring most readily to mind are Balanchine, Cunningham, and perhaps William Forsythe. These are the choreographers whose work is most often characterized by propulsive speed, a voracious appetite for space, sharp angularity of design, sudden reversals of direction, fragmentation and/or isolation of body parts, unpredictable entrances and exits, and so on. Two of these dance-makers are readily categorized as ballet choreographers (albeit creators of modern ballet). The third is the most iconoclastic of modern dance choreographers. But what all three share is surely the use they make—however varied—of the *ballet* vocabulary.

A key component of ballet's forward progression, its ongoing historical evolution, is the way it continually redefines and "ups" its virtuosic ante. And because it tends to define virtuosity in terms of technical accomplishment, ballet takes greater pride than modern in the sheer speed with which dancers can be made to move and the great distances they can correspondingly travel. This linking of ultra-fast footwork with an insatiable hunger for space lend ballet a special purchase on modernity. Pre-Cunningham modern dance by contrast, tends to take a dim view of speed, or at least those varieties of speed we associate with the contemporary city. Most modern dance choreographers attribute the accelerated pace of modern life to one variety or another of urban malady (i.e., the ethos of greed, consumerism, and acquisitiveness that presumably dominates money-driven societies). In another variation on the theme of urban malaise, rapid movement is associated with F. W. Taylor's assembly-line, time-and-motion efficiency studies (otherwise known as "scientific management"). The body becomes an instrument of technocratic precision; and the rhythms of industrial mass production are thought to be ruthlessly imposed on it. This helps explain why the partisans of Graham, Humphrey, and Limón technique were so appalled when they first encountered Cunningham using a stopwatch to time his dancers in the 1950s.

Many works of modern dance reflect this distate for the sheer speed of modern life. A. V. Coton described the conclusion of "The Big City" (1932) by the German modern dance choreographer, Kurt Jooss as follows:

> The lights dim more and more, the maddening stupid rhythm goes on and on, marked by the even stamp and shuffle of the dancing automatons who are happily ignorant and uncaring of the drama that is passing amongst them. (1946, 44)

In Charles Weidman's "Bargain Counter" (1936) the shoppers virtually devour one another in the course of their predatory bargain-hunting. In Weidman's "Stock Exchange" (also 1936), a ruthless tycoon—one part greed, one part fear—brings the rest of the world down with him when his assets begin to head south. Rudolph von Laban succinctly expresses his distaste for urban life when he writes of his dance theater piece, "Die Nacht" from 1927:

> The play opened with a crowd of mechanically grinning society men and women, followed by all I had experienced and felt when I first met life in the big city.... Greed, covetousness, adoration of three idols: dollars, depravity and deceit. The whole wild orgy found no solution and ended in madness. The music was a caricature of jazz. (Laban 1975, 43–4)

Humphrey and Weidman's "Theatre Piece" from 1936, one third of their "New Dance" trilogy, conceives of urban life in terms of two central metaphors: "The Race" (in which the only real motivation is "to win"); and "The Theatre," in which vain, emotionally needy actors constantly compete for the adoration of their audiences. The section titled "Behind Walls" (Humphrey's depiction of the business world) opens with an Alwin Nikolais–like effect. Framed by the sort of box in which magicians saw their assistants in half, a human head moves in one direction while the pair of legs to which it presumably belongs moves in another. Mind and body are split off from each other; and the urban world is represented as a space in which the most radical sorts of dislocations are visited on the human being. (Cunningham by contrast, will approach the topic of urban dislocation in an entirely different spirit, accepting it as a not-particularly-alarming-fact of modern life.) The social structures to which the pre-Cunningham modern dance choreographers lent their seal of approval tended to be those of tightly knit, "organic" communities: either tribal (as in Graham's "Primitive Mysteries") or agrarian-peasant (as in José Limón's "There Is A Time"). Doris Humphrey was strongly attracted to the ecosystems of the natural world ("Water Study," "Life of the Bee") and toward communities that forgo modern conveniences and/or find themselves on the brink of extinction (e.g., "The Shakers").

It's not that speed plays no part in these dances. But it's the sort of speed that takes the shape of an inward spiral generated by religious ecstasy or primal emotion. One thinks of the frenzied spinning of the Eldress in "The Shakers" or The Queen in "Life of the Bee." Or, for that matter, the violent contractions of Medea in Graham's "Cave of the Heart" just before she immeshes herself in Noguchi's vibrating wire-sculpture. When it comes to the hustle and bustle of the contemporary city, pre-Cunningham modern dance choreographers tend either to ignore it or deplore it.

Ballet the Modernizer

But if modern dance rejects modernity, contemporary ballet is much more likely to *reflect* modernity. It was Bronislava Nijinska—not Graham, Jooss, or Humphrey—who envisioned a new breed of dancers capable of embodying "the living movement of the automobile or the airplane, those perfected machines representing the latest achievements of industry" (Baer 1978, 87). It was Balanchine—not Laban or Limón—who argued that theatrical dancing "must be reconstructed for service in our twentieth century, speeded up" (Kirstein 1978, 244).

André Levinson, in a wonderful essay called "The Spirit of the Classic Dance," poses a relevant question: "You may ask whether I'm suggesting that the dancer is a machine? But most certainly!—a machine for manufacturing beauty" (Cohen 1974, 117). Levinson's answer only makes sense when we realize that he's talking about the ballet dancer—certainly not the pre-Cunningham modern dancer. It's no coincidence that we routinely speak of the "Ballet Mécanique" but rarely, if ever, about forms of "modern dance mécanique." (Oscar Schlemmer's best-known Bauhaus dance is titled "Triadisches *Ballet*.")

Ultimately, it was ballet, not modern dance, that proved eager to assimilate uniquely 20th-century movements as various as cubism, dada, futurism, and jazz. "Relâche" (1924), the best-known attempt to infuse dance with the antic spirit of dada (and the only dance performance to feature a cameo appearance by Marcel Duchamp), was staged by Rolf de Maré's Ballets Suedois, not by a self-proclaimed modern dance company. Massine's "Parade" (1917) for The Ballets Russes featured a cubist skyscraper-of-a-costume designed by Picasso for the character called "The New York Manager" as well as affectionately playful references to Charlie Chaplin and "The Perils of Pauline." Satie's musical score incorporates the sort of "concrete sounds" that were characteristic of futurist composition (i.e., the fast clicking of a typewriter and the droning of an airplane engine).

But it was the unmistakably syncopated rhythms of ragtime in Satie's score for "Parade" that marked the great musical divide between modern ballet and modern dance. Recall what Laban said about the music he chose for "The Night"; he referred to it as a "caricature of jazz." To most modern dance choreographers, nothing symbolized urban decadence more palpably than jazz. From Duncan, to St. Denis and Ted Shawn, and on through Martha Graham, there is a widespread loathing of jazz. Ironically, part of the appeal of jazz dance and music—especially in Paris in the 1920s—was unabashedly primitivist (the cult of "negritude," Josephine Baker and the "Danse Sauvage" in the Revue Negre, etc.) But to the modern-dance choreographers, jazz represented a distinctly *urban* primitivism and was therefore off limits. By contrast, for George Balanchine, the greatest of all modernizers of ballet, jazz rhythms helped create a variety of movement unique to the 20th century. Even in a ballet as "chaste" as "Concerto Barocco" (1941), there's a moment when the corps seems to be performing a Charleston on pointe. And in "Agon," (1957), which Balanchine and Kirstein once referred to as "a machine that thinks . . . a measured construction in space . . . ," there are hints of boogie-woogie. As in Mondrian's great tribute to Manhattan, "Broadway Boogie Woogie," abstract forms are animated by jazz-inflected rhythms.

The company that Balanchine founded was never called the Balanchine Ballet but, rather, the New York *City* Ballet. And Manhattan was always more than just the home of his company; it was a principal source of both inspiration and subject matter. Indeed, in Balanchine's great practice-clothes ballets such as "Agon," there is no need to signify "New York" by commissioning cubist images of urban high rises. His tall, leggy, hyperextended ballerinas call to mind the deep iconography of the skyscraper and the construction crane.

Modern Dance, Modern Ballet, Modernism

By the time of "Agon"'s premiere in 1957, a curious exchange of identity was underway with regard to the terms "modern dance," "modern ballet," and "modernism." Put bluntly, a cool, abstract, stripped-down ballet such as "Agon" had much more in common with newly prevailing conceptions of modernism (capital "m") than did the hot, deeply self-expressive, narrative dance-dramas of Martha Graham. In the visual arts—which for most of the 20th century had functioned as the principle modernist taste-maker and avant-garde trendsetter—it was Clement Greenberg's definition of modernism that increasingly held sway. Greenberg argued that the true modernist must "purify" his or her art by stripping away anything and everything extraneous to the underlying nature of the medium. Thus, in what sounds at first like pure paradox, ballet became more modernist than modern dance as Balanchine whittled it down to its classical core. This purist and minimalist conception of modernism was the backdrop against which Cunningham pioneered *his* distinctive form of contemporary classicism. The mid-to-late 1950s were the years in which Cunningham produced some of his most beautiful studies of classic ballet steps and structures: "Suite by Chance" in 1952; "Septet" in 1953 (which alludes directly to the imagery of Apollo posing with his three muses in Balanchine's "Apollo"); "Noctures" in 1957; and "Summerspace" in 1958 (which Lincoln Kirstein would subsequently invite Cunningham to restage for the New York City Ballet in 1966).

Needless to say, at those institutionalized bastions of modern dance such as the American Dance Festival, it was pre-Cunningham modern that still ruled the roost. But, viewed from almost any other cultural vantage point, Graham, Humphrey, and Limón were about to suffer that ultimate American indignity: the perception of beginning to appear "old-fashioned." Nothing dramatized this sea-change of taste quite so effectively as an event that occurred at the very end of the decade, in 1959. The occasion was the premiere of the New York City Ballet's "Episodes," which was billed as a "collaboration" between two presumed antagonists, Martha Graham, the high priestess of modern dance, and George Balanchine, the ostensible keeper of the neoclassical flame. The evening was actually more of a confrontation than a collaboration. Graham and Balanchine each choreographed separate works (although both halves of the program were performed to music by Webern).

Graham contributed a narrative dance-drama depicting the tempestuous relations between Mary Queen of Scots, Queen Elizabeth, and Bothwell. Her dance depended heavily on representational décor and costume. Stage center was a stylized executioner's axe resting on a platform employed variously as a throne and a scaffold. Graham as Mary was costumed in an elegant farthingale. At one point, Mary and Elizabeth played a sinister game of lawn tennis, intended to metaphorically embody their rivalry. Balanchine's portion of "Episodes," which is still in City Ballet's repertory, was performed on a bare stage by dancers stripped down to black-and-white (or in the case of the women, black-and-pink) practice clothes. His nervous, angular choreography told no story. His dancers represented nothing other than themselves—unless it was some normally "invisible" reality—say, the elliptical trajectory of subatomic particles. The irony was obvious: Balanchine, the neoclassicist, had created a work infinitely more abstract, self-contained, and less representational than Graham's highly theatrical narrative. The difference reveals how problematic the term "modern dance" had become by 1959. Within the high-modernist universe of Clement Greenberg and the visual arts, Balanchine was clearly more of a card-carrying modernist than Graham. Even John Martin, one of Graham's earliest partisans in the press, was quick to realize that something fundamental had changed. In his

New York Times review, he described Balanchine's contribution to "Episodes" in stark, Greenbergian terms: "dancers have become essentially an organization of bones and muscles." But he went further. Graham's and Balanchine's sections were separated by a 5-minute pause, which Martin subsequently interpreted as a great philosophical divide: "If only we could locate those five minutes on the universal calendar, we would have the philosophical turning point of human history" (Reynolds 1977, 197).

There's no denying that choreographers such as Balanchine and Cunningham—who exemplified Greenbergian purism—were "cool" in a way that Graham, Humphrey, and Limón were not. In 1970 Shirley Wynne, a historian of baroque dance, published an essay (titled "Complaisance, An Eighteenth-Century Cool") which forges connections between ballet, contemporary cool, and the sort of dandyism I discussed in Chapter 1. Ballet has its origin in baroque modes of comportment; and Wynne drew an analogy between the baroque ideal of "complaisance" and the 1960s cult of cool:

> . . . the two attitudes, so widely separated historically and culturally, share at least one fundamental attribute: the look of nonchalance or easy carelessness which is essentially a disguise, a controlled cooling of emotional responses. If you had "complaisance" your identity could not be confused with the gross, ill-bred, awkward members of society. If you do not have "cool," you are at best pitiable and lose merits among those who live by this elusive code. (1970, 22–3)

That modern dance was being reevaluated during the 1960s in light of this dandified cult of cool becomes evident in an observation by Art Bauman (who had previously danced for Charles Weidman.) Bauman was asked to provide a testimonial to Anna Sokolow, a former Graham dancer who went on to become a major choreographer in her own right (and whose masterpiece, "Rooms" [1955], is the only major work of modern dance I know of set to a jazz score). Note Bauman's allusion to the changing values then being attributed to adjectives such as "hot" and "cool" in the 1960s:

> I always liked dance with a lot of guts. In the mid-sixties, Anna was at the cutting edge of expressionism. By then Graham was old hat. It was Anna who captured my imagination. . . . Only "cool" choreographers missed it. They found it too emotional and therefore old-fashioned. They missed the point that it came screaming out of the zeitgeist of the sixties. (Warren 1991, 280)

But in the *longer* view of history, coolness and impersonality have proven more durable, less time-bound. Which dances look and feel more dated now? Sokolow's "Opus 65" with its rebellious youths making confrontational faces at the audience and raising their fists in clenched, antiestablishment protest? Or Balanchine's portion of "Episodes"? More to the point, compare and contrast Sokolow's work with almost anything choreographed by Cunningham between the late 1950s and early 1960s. In 1987, Gus Solomons Jr., who danced with Cunningham between 1965 and 1968, observed:

> Looking at films of [Cunningham's] early work, I was impressed with how little the movement has aged, and I wondered why. I haven't thought it through fully, but it is probably because it is so pure in its mechanics that it transcends any date, any time—any fashion—and I think that the purity is consistent. (Brown et al. 1992, 115)

Dancing for the Second Half of the 20th Century

Certainly, Cunningham has more in common with Balanchine than he does with Sokolow or Graham. But ultimately, Cunningham and Balanchine also inhabit very different universes. Just for starters, in Balanchine's choreography, the merging of movement and music often borders on synesthesia. Balanchine would not have understood—or at least not have tolerated—Cunningham's and Cage's declaration of independence between movement and sound. Balanchine gave us choreographic experiences emblematic of the first half of the 20th century (speed, coolness, angularity, unexpected rhythms, hard edges). All of these elements are present in Cunningham's work as well. But Cunningham goes much further in his exploration of the urban landscape. He was the first choreographer to embrace the conditions that characterize the *second* half of the century: the ever increasing dissociation of sound and image; information overload; perceptual complexities bordering on chaos; the impact of electronics; the digital revolution, and so on.

It's especially instructive to compare Cunningham's routine reliance on electronic sound scores with Balanchine's occasional forays into the world of electronic music. In 1961, Balanchine choreographed the shortlived (now virtually forgotten) "Electronics," danced to an electronic tape score composed on a Studio Trautonium by Remi Gassman and Oskar Sala. Set in an otherworldly, "futuristic" maze of cellophane, Balanchine's ballet typified the hackneyed, knee-jerk association that most contemporary choreographers have made between electronic music and science fiction. Cunningham by contrast, accepts electronic sound as a basic fact of contemporary life, an unavoidable component of the way we live now—no eerie, flashing green lights or visitations by extraterrestrial creatures.

Ballet and Chance

It may seem ironic that Cunningham could be simultaneously attracted to a movement vocabulary markedly more balletic than Martha Graham's *and* to compositional strategies based on chance. Steve Paxton who danced for Cunningham between 1961 and 1964, has suggested that the balletic dimension of Cunningham's vocabulary served as a necessary, if culturally conservative, counterbalance to the radicalism of his compositional practices in the 1950s. "If he had been working with movement as radical in those days as his compositional means were," Paxton proposed, "it would have been completely undecipherable" (Brown et al. 1992, 117). That may be, but for Cunningham, chance and the ballet vocabulary are essentially two means toward the same end: they liberate the choreographer from the limitations of his own instincts. A choreographer who relies solely on the resources of his or her own "personal" way of moving is unlikely to produce a body of work as varied as Cunningham's. (His oeuvre may not be Shakesperian in range, but one could easily claim that the moonlit "Nocturnes" is his *Midsummer Night's Dream* whereas the apocalyptic "Winterbranch" is his *King Lear.*)

Despite the number of aesthetic decisions that are determined by chance operations, Cunningham's choreography is never so "objective" as to feel anonymous. His quirky, idiosyncratic way of moving is never entirely disguised, and it's as apparent in his group pieces as in his solos. In his Buster Keaton-ish way, Cunningham is also one of America's greatest comic actors. Even after age and arthritis had begun to take a toll on his dancing, he remained a thoroughly mesmerizing Leprechaun-of-a-performer. At the age of 80, he held his own on stage alongside Mikhail Baryshnikov in "Occasion Piece" (1999). Over the years, Cunningham's distinctive eccentricities have been especially evident in the facial animation he practices in works such as "Septet," "Scramble," and "Loops"—dances in which he behaves rather like a clown at a child's birthday party: Typically, he cups his hands over his face, pries them apart like window shutters, and reveals his open mouth stretched as if in a silent scream. And yet, in the final analysis, these personal idiosyncrasies and quirky individualized "choices" are filtered through the austere discipline of chance-generated systems.

Robert Rauschenberg has talked about this sort of relationship between the artist's distinctively "personal" style and the more impersonal dictates of chance. What he says about his own way of working applies equally well to Cunningham:

> I'd really like to think that the artist could be just another kind of material in the picture, working in collaboration with all the other materials. But of course I know this isn't possible, really. I know that the artist can't help exercising his control to a degree and that he makes all the decisions finally. But if I can just throw enough obstacles in the way of my own personal taste, then maybe it won't be *all*-controlling, and maybe the picture will turn out to be more interesting as a result. (Tomkins 1968, 232)

Chance Methods versus Improvisation

Ironically, in *Next Week, Swan Lake*, Selma Jeanne Cohen tells us that "Cunningham relied on certain chance procedures to put his movement in touch with nature" (1982, 34). This is a common misperception, one that fails to distinguish between Cunningham's use of chance and mere improvisation. Cunningham is not attempting to break through the resistance of his rational mind in order to tap unconscious, "natural" or primitive impulses that lie waiting to be unleashed. Quite the contrary: he utilizes utterly impersonal, chance-generating mechanisms (coins, dice, the *I Ching*, etc.) so as to avoid what might otherwise "come naturally."

Carolee Schneemann, arguably the most Dionysian/Artaudian/Reichian choreographer to emerge in America in the 1960s (and certainly one of the choreographers most eager "to put her movement in touch with nature"), was highly critical of the way in which Cunningham's and Cage's chance methods emphasized the "*methods*" (i.e., the structures) underlying their compositional strategies rather than sheer (and to her mind, liberating) spontaneity—the potential for unpredictable eruptions of natural and "unknown forces":

> I don't work with "chance methods" because 'method' does not assume evidence of the senses.... I keep it open, "formless." "Chance method" is a contrary process for my needs and a semantic contradiction... what might happen, possibility, unpredictable agent, unknown forces... so corralled, netted, become a closing in. (Banes 1983, 94)

Actually, Schneemann has an important point to make. There *is* something paradoxical about the concept of "chance *methods*." "Chance" implies a surrender or transcendence of will and volition; "method" implies an opposing force: the application of will and volition. The art of Cunningham and Cage achieves a delicate balance between these two polar extremes. Note, too, the difference between the "methods" of Cunningham and Cage and the exercises of Martha Graham (or, for that matter, the Actor's Studio), in which the goal was to "unblock" the performer's inhibitions. In Cunningham's work, such impulses, as we've seen, rarely "flow." This is one reason why so many dancers complain that Cunningham's choreography is excruciatingly difficult to perform: It doesn't *come naturally* to the human body. Many of Cunningham's favorite anecdotes address this aspect of his work (e.g., "The other day, a dancer who was in the company and is now married and has a baby, came to visit. She said her labor was harder than learning another dance but not as hard as 'Torse'" [Joyce 1999, n.p.]). Indeed, as we've seen, in Cunningham's choreography, a body can be required to move from whiplash fouetté into penchée arabesque without apparent transition.

In the final analysis, what Cunningham and Cage derive from chance-generated systems are the *systems* that underlie apparently random behavior. There are a number of important parallels to be drawn between Cunningham's and Cage's compositional strategies and the contemporary science of chaos, which examines "pattern-bounded" unpredictability. In Cage's and Cunningham's work, we encounter examples of what the mathematician James Yorke has described as "wild disorder embedded in stable structure." For example, one of the most important functions of the unison passages in Cunningham's choreography is help establish this balance between "wild disorder" and "stable structure." What could appear more "stable," more "structured," than unexpected "eruptions" of dancing in unison? Steve Paxton makes this point explicitly:

> As for the unison: I fell for this company in the first year I saw it because of "Rune" [1959], which had some amazing unison work in it, and it was done to music that didn't go with the steps. It was extraordinary in its power. At that point I was trying to understand the philosophy of Merce's work. It seemed to be based in Zen and it seemed to be dealing with chance—that's what was always put forth. And yet here was dancing in unison! Then I thought, "Wait a minute, indeterminacy has to manifest itself somehow. You can't see indeterminacy, except maybe in your mind. You can envision something which is ultimately chaotic, but in terms of actual manifestation in a human way, it has to be organized somehow. This is another manifestation of the possibilities."
>
> There's a new theory about chaos. They say in fluidics that if you have a very clear pattern that becomes chaotic, a more recognizable pattern will emerge again underneath that chaos if you watch it long enough. There are organizing principles which we don't understand yet. The idea of chaos as it is regularly understood doesn't include the full range of its potential. It just sounds like a lot of blather happening—that's the way we use the word 'chaos.' But rigorously applied, it is actually a far more structured phenomenon. (Brown et al. 1992, 108)

Joan Retallack uses similar terms to describe the structuring principles in Cage's later music:

> As with the systems being described in the non-linear sciences, it is not that there is *less* structure, but that the structure is one of greater complexity in a richly dynamic relationship with larger areas of indeterminacy. (1994, 267)

This helps to explain the highly calculated, meticulously ordered nature of Cage's methodology. It often appeared as if Cage was incapable of making a move without first consulting the *I Ching;* and it's important to recall that for the Chinese, the *I Ching* is a *scientific* text, not a New Agey, astrological self-help book.

So clearly, Cunningham's chance-methods are worlds away from what we conventionally think of as improvisation. At the same time, it's also true that every once in a while Cunningham choreographs a dance in which *some* decisions are made by the dancers in the "heat" of performance, according to the rules of "spontaneous determination." In "Field Dances" (1963), each performer was assigned a catalogue of movements that he or she could execute in any order; "Story" (1963) also contained "indeterminate" elements, as did "TV Rerun" in 1972. But Carolyn Brown recalls how quickly Cunningham intervened the moment he felt "spontaneity" was getting out of hand. This was especially true during performances of "Story":

> I remember one situation in which we each had our own phrase to do—it was the "object" phrase—and one of our members stayed out there too long, and he [Cunningham] didn't like it at all. He picked her up bodily and walked her off the stage. Because there were certain things that were extremely important to him—especially timing. Timing as part of the total structure of the piece. (1992, 106)

Thus, even in these rather uncharacteristic circumstances, "personal choice" is still exercised from within the confines of strict structure. As Remy Charlip, a member of the original Cunningham company, once observed, "I don't remember doing anything spontaneous in Merce's dances." (Brown, Charlip, et al. 1992, 51)

Cunningham's Classicism

Largely because of his interest in ballet, it's become a commonplace these days to call Cunningham a "classicist." And there are many examples of what appear to be straightforward, uncomplicated choreographic classicism in the Cunningham oeuvre (movement that even a balletomane would unhesitatingly define as "classical"). One thinks, first and foremost, of the exquisitely pure pas de deux (aptly titled "Suspended Moment") in "Suite for Five" (1956), or "Noctures"—from that same year—which can be thought of as Cunningham's Ballet Blanc. Even those dances in which Cunningham seems to be poking fun at classical ballet—the "Sports and Diversions #1" section of "Antic Meet" for example—rely on cleanly executed, ultra-academic vocabulary (e.g., pas de bourrées and chassés).

But the true nature of Cunningham's classicism has been greatly misunderstood. A classicist can be defined as someone who recognizes the limits of self-expression, the sort of artist who conceives of creativity not as pure, unlimited personal invention, but as a *collaboration* between his own subjectivity and some impersonal tradition, set of laws, or preexisting system of technique. Thus, Cunningham's classicism has *at least* as much to do with his use of chance as with his balleticizing of modern dance. But his is a peculiarly *contemporary* form of classicism, one suited to an era that might be dubbed "the age of suspicion"—a period of time in which it's become increasingly difficult to distinguish between natural "inspiration" and cultural-conditioning. Surrendering to one's Muse (or whatever form classical "inspiration" is thought to take) is no safer—no more immunized against cultural-conditioning—than Martha Graham's "inward journey" (a voyage toward a destination whose pristine purity can no longer be guaranteed). How then does one reconcile this classical impulse—the desire to collaborate with something larger (and more objective) than one's own personality—with the fear of surrendering one's detachment, one's *vigilance*? This is one of the problems that Cunningham's work addresses. And chance—at least provisionally—provides a solution.

Chance is the only impersonal directive that is guaranteed to be free of vested interests (providing that the system for generating it is free of intentionality). As William Burroughs once wrote "Always be fair; but when you can't be fair, be arbitrary." A little latter, we'll explore the similarities between Cage's and Cunningham's use of chance and Burroughs's highly elaborated notion that "noise" and "randomness" can disrupt the "systems" that might otherwise subject us to behavioral conditioning. The result for Cunningham and Cage is the peculiarly contemporary form of classicism embodied in the paradox we know as chance *methods* or chance *operations*. Cunningham's comments about chance make it clear that his goal is to "collaborate" (in a time-honored "classical" fashion) with materials that lie beyond the self:

> When I choreograph a piece by tossing pennies—by chance, that is—I am finding my resources in that play which is not the product of *my* will, but which is an energy and a law which I obey. Some people think it is inhuman and mechanistic to toss pennies in creating a dance instead of chewing the nails or beating the head against a wall or thumbing through old notebooks for ideas. But the feeling I have when I compose in this way is that I am in touch with (something) far greater than my own personal inventiveness could ever be, much more universally human than the particular habits of my own practice. (1968, n.p.)

In other words, rather than attempting to tap the energies of a Jungian "collective unconscious," Cunningham utilizes chance-operations. It may or may not be coincidental that many of the dances in which Cunningham first utilized chance in novel ways are also among his most conventionally *classical* works. For example, "Suite by Chance" from 1953, his first work in which "every single element" was arrived at by chance methods, was also, according to Cunningham, "very classic. . . . The first movement was andante; the second movement was very slow; the third a little faster; the last movement was very fast" (Lesschaeve 1985, 90). "Rune" from 1959, the first of Cunningham's dances in which the order of the individual sections shifted from performance to performance, was also one of those dances that struck even dyed-in-the-wool balletomanes as "classic" in its look and feel. Clearly, there's a connection between the impersonal nature of the "ready-made" ballet vocabulary and the transcendence of personal intention implicit in chance operations. W. H. Auden once defended the impersonal, unspontaneous virtues of verse (as opposed to prose), by insisting "Blessed are all metrical rules that forbid automatic response; Force us to choose second thoughts, free from the fetters of self." Both chance and the ballet vocabulary "forbid *automatic* response." Together, they help free Merce Cunningham from the fetters of self.

Not Going With The Flow: Beyond Freedom and Inspiration

Cunningham's resistance to "automatic response"—his ongoing critique of "that-which-feels-natural"—entails an undeniable sacrifice: It means abandoning that exhilarating feeling of flow, the sensation of having one's hand or body guided by muse, instinct, or unconscious impulse. But it also means no longer being dependent on the vicissitudes of *inspiration.* The dance world lacks a phrase to connote the choreographic equivalent of "writer's block"; but Cunningham's compositional practices effectively immunize him against that sort of creative paralysis. His productivity has been staggering and virtually uninterrupted—over 200 new dances in 50-some years.

In this regard, Cunningham has much in common with the poet Paul Valery, who once quipped that "inspiration consists of pulling your chair up to the desk." In fact, Valery regarded inspiration as a *primitive* notion, "the concept of savages." And I would guess that Cunningham (and Cage) might well agree with Valery's dismissive view of "inspiration":

> Supposing that inspiration is what people think it is—which is absurd, and which implies that a whole poem can be dictated to its author by some deity—this would result precisely in the fact that an inspired person could write just as well in a language other than his own and which he did not know. The inspired person could similarly be unfamiliar with his period, the conditions of taste in his period, the works of his predecessors and his rivals—unless you make inspiration into a power so refined, so articulate, so sagacious, so well informed and so calculating that you might as well call it intelligence and knowledge ... It is an unbearable image for poets which represents them receiving from imaginary creatures the best part of their works. Agents of transmission—that's a concept of savages. As for me, I want none of it. I make use only of that chance which is at the basis of all minds, and add to it stubborn labor, which is opposed to that chance (Grubbs 1968, 91).

(The tension between "chance" and "stubborn labor" is embodied in Cage and Cunningham's concept of "chance operations.") In an essay entitled "The Mythic Act," Harold Rosenberg, in the course of discussing Pollock, invokes the vocabulary that Valery finds most objectionable: the artist as medium through which "divine inspiration" passes:

> In photographs of the artist at work, he wears an expression of extreme concentration, on occasion almost amounting to anguish, and his body is positioned in nervous alertness as if he were expecting signals from above or behind (Jones 1998, 74).

To Pollock, the greatest trauma was to "lose contact" with his source of inspiration while in the process of executing a drip painting. ("It is only when I lose contact with the painting that the result is a mess," he observed.) By contrast, John Cage seems to echo Paul Valery when he declares:

> I don't hear things in my head, nor do I have inspiration. Nor is it right, as some people have said, that because I use chances operations my music is written not by me, but by God. I doubt whether God, say he existed, would take the trouble to write my music (1981, 90).

Cunningham's and Cage's attitude toward inspiration connects them much more strongly to a ballet choreographer such as Balanchine than to a modern dance choreographer such as Graham. "Inspiration," Balanchine once declared, "is for the very young" (1984, 2). Balanchine also insisted on demystifying the process of dance-making: "God creates. I assemble" (1984, 32), he once famously quipped. And in the same spirit: "Choreography is too fancy a word for what I do. Dance supplier is better" (1984, 3). Or, at his most aphoristic: "My muse must come to me on union time" (1984, 7).

This altered attitude toward inspiration also results in a radically revised view of "freedom"—both creative and political. The pioneers of modern dance almost always considered themselves apostles of freedom. To them, "freedom" was a mode of feeling, defined principally in terms of subjective physical sensation. To be "free" meant to liberate oneself from the stuffy conventions of puritanical culture (as symbolized by the corset and all that it embodied). Ballet, of course, was correspondingly vilified as "corseted" movement. The feeling of freedom that resulted from this liberation was above all a feeling of *flow*, of kinetic impulses traveling unimpeded from the torso to other parts of the body. This is what Isadora Duncan meant by "successive" movement (which, in the words of Duncan scholar Ann Daly "implied two things: first that movement should spread seamlessly throughout adjacent body parts; second, that each action should evolve seamlessly into the next" [1995, 35]). Needs to say, this is not the sort of sensation Cunningham offers either his dancers or his audiences. And that's why Graham dancers, among others, often regard Cunningham's technique as cramped, stilted, and terribly unrewarding to perform (indeed, almost as unrewarding to watch). Even Paul Taylor (in his autobiography,

Private Domain) has some disparaging things to say about the way Cunning-ham's and Cage's compositional procedures impede organic continuity:

> Merce had been trying out John's philosophy about chance. I went home and made several dance studies for myself using chance methods . . . [these] tended to look and feel very stick-like when executed—that is, without "natural" flow, muscular density, or sensation. It felt stingy, like something I'd not particularly like to do or see. And instead of being "abstract," as I expected, most of the movements looked like a wooden marionette having difficulty in expressing emotion. So much for making up abstract dances by chance, I reasoned. (1987, 47)

But on Cunningham's dancers, the result of such compositional strategies is anything but "sticklike" (even if it's decidedly inorganic). What we see are *thinking* bodies in the business of frequently "changing their minds"— perhaps even "contradicting themselves"—the very opposite, in other words, of "free" flow. John Cage tells a story about Cunningham that neatly sums up his "fear of flow" and his persistent tendency to "change his mind":

> Every morning Merce Cunningham does his yoga. He is self-taught by means of books he collected on the subject. Aware of the intimate connection of body and mind, and not having a yogi's assistance, he proceeds with caution. Once, while breathing deeply in the lotus position, he noticed that an unfamiliar force seemed to be rising up his spine. He changed his mind and very shortly was standing on his feet. (Kostelanetz 1970, 182–83)

Self-Contradiction

Again, we encounter a definition of "freedom" radically different from that which informed the tradition of pre-Cunningham modern dance. Bertolt Brecht once argued that "Freedom comes with the principle of contradic-tion" (1964, 218). A similar attitude pervades the work of Cunningham and his cohorts. Their motivations may not be as overtly political as Brecht's; but, as we'll see in a subsequent chapter, they have much more in com-mon with Brecht than one might at first suspect. Duchamp for example, wrote "I force myself to contradict myself to avoid conforming to my own taste" (d'Hanoncourt 1973, 16). Rauschenberg also admits to working in this counterintuitive way: "I am trying to check my habits of seeing, to counter them for the sake of greater freshness. I am trying to be unfamiliar with what I'm doing" (Cage 1961, 106). Johns has made similar comments about his own work: "I've attempted to develop my thinking in such a way that the work I've done is not me" (Raynor 1973, 20–21).

Cunningham's use of chance procedures, like Duchamp's before him, promotes this sort of self-contradiction. But one could go further and argue that Cunningham's very style of movement—with its remarkably rapid, turn-on-a-dime reversals of direction, its continual *arresting of organic impulse*—probably comes as close as anyone ever will to embodying this principle of self-contradiction in movement. There's something downright Dostoevskian about Cunningham's seemingly perverse refusal to "go with the flow." It's as if he had translated into movement the false starts and self-interruptions of Dostoevsky's narrator in *Notes From Underground.* Perhaps paradoxically, one result of this refusal to follow the flow is a greater sense of personal freedom (an idea that Dostoevsky's narrator would immediately recognize and endorse).

Cunningham's dancers rarely toss themselves so completely "off-balance" that they can't instantly recover their center and move voluntarily in the opposite direction. Certainly his dancers almost never appear to be buffeted about by invisible or supernatural forces. As Deborah Jowitt astutely observes:

> He has always differed from the modern dancers who were his teachers too, in that you never feel the presence of a force in the center of his body pulling the limbs awry, knocking him off balance. The struggle with gravity, the debilitating whirlwinds—external or internal—that were so much a part of the modernist aesthetic did not apparently preoccupy him. (1988, 281)

"Changeling" (1957), one of three solos that Cunningham set to scores by Christian Wolff, was wrenching, even violent, in its rapid reversals of direction. But the momentum always appeared to originate with Cunningham himself, not from some imaginary, external force. (The very title of the work, "Changeling," seems to embody Cunningham's love of reversal, contradiction, and willed unnaturalness.)

Stillness

Conversely, Cunningham's distaste for "flow" is equally apparent in his attitude toward stillness—which he conceives of in a dialectical (or contradictory) relationship to movement. In this sense, Cunningham is working out his own version of Cage's conception of the reciprocal relationship between sound and silence. "The nature of dancing is stillness in movement and movement in stillness," Cunningham once wrote. "No stillness exists without movement, and no movement is fully expressed without stillness." But—and this is where the influence of Cage becomes most evident— "stillness acts of itself, not hampered before or after. It is not a pause or a premonition" (1957, 22).

Cunningham's use of stillness is especially evident in "Shards" (1987), which is constructed from essentially static poses. Often, only one dancer is in motion, and his or her phrase (invariably short) will be picked up by another dancer located in a different section of the stage. (Watching it is a little like taking the optometrist's test in which blinking dots are detected in the periphery of one's field of vision.) Arguably, the work that most fully embodies Cunningham's love of contradiction is the aptly titled "Polarity" (1990). As with many earlier works, Cunningham's movement vocabulary contrasted stasis and motion. But here he applied this distinction in a highly analytical way to disparate body parts, distinguishing between those that are capable of expansive motion (the legs) and those that must move within a much more limited field of action (the head). As with "Shards," only one dancer at a time appeared to be "in motion," while larger groups remained frozen in statuesque poses.

One senses in Cunningham's style more than a trace of that "air of coldness, that determination not to be *moved*" that Baudelaire associates with the dandy. And Cunningham's own dancing—even at its most frantic—always exudes a slight aura of aloofness, a delicate disdain for unimpeded flow that resists the look of "natural," Dionysian abandon. Cunningham gently parodies Graham's Dionysian ambitions in the hilarious "Bacchus and Cohorts" section of "Antic Meet" from 1958. Here Cunningham finds himself trapped in the "maze" of a sweater with many—too many—arms. And the female chorus (diligently flexing their feet and cupping their hands), forearms raised over their eyes, exudes a sense of frantic foreboding unmistakably reminiscent of the women in "Night Journey." ("Antic Meet"—or at least the section of it that spoofs Martha Graham—might be viewed as the choreographic equivalent of Rauschenberg's parody of Pollock in "Winter Pool.")

Aside from the parodic reference to Graham's "Night Journey" in "Antic Meet," the only other Cunningham work I know of that quotes from or directly alludes to an earlier dance is "Septet." Here, significantly, the reference is to Balanchine's "Apollo," specifically one of the moments when the young Apollo links arms with his three muses. But the Apollonian reference is solemn and dignified; there's not even a hint of parody. That's because Cunningham is declaring his artistic allegiances. The highly articulated nature of his movement is much more Apollonian than Dionysian. In a meditation on Nietzsche's famous distinction between these two symbolic poles of human activity, Thomas McEvilley writes: "In the Apollonian light, each thing is seen clear and separate, as itself; in the Dionysian dark all things merge into a flowing and molten invisibility" (1983, 65).

Redefining Freedom

Of course, this Apollonian tendency to see each thing as clear and separate—and the closely related tendency to sense the contradictoriness of things—can easily be exacerbated to the extreme that Dostoevsky called hyperconsciousness. Earlier in this chapter, I compared Cunningham's penchant for

"self-contradiction" to the willfully perverse behavior of Dostoevsky's narrator in *Notes From Underground*. Dostoevsky's character is the prototype
(indeed the archetype) of "hyperconsciousness" in literature. "An intelligent
man . . . " the narrator declares early in the novella:

> must and morally ought to be pre-eminently a characterless creature; a man of
> character, an active man is pre-eminently a limited creature. . . . I repeat, I repeat
> it emphatically: all straightforward persons and men of action are active just
> because they are stupid and limited.

For "underground man," freedom is achieved only by actively resisting
that which is deemed to be "good *for* him," or which feels seductively "good
to him." Lionel Trilling's seminal essay, "The Fate of Pleasure," is in large part
an examination of what motivates the seemingly self-defeating behavior of
Dostoevsky's "characterless" character. Note how applicable Trilling's words
are to the motivations of Cunningham and company:

> For to want what is commonly thought to be appropriate to men, to want
> whatever it is, high or low, that is believed to yield pleasure, to be active about
> securing it, to use common sense and prudence to the end of gaining it, this is
> to admit and consent to the *conditioned* nature of man. (1968, 73)

Thus, for Cunningham, Cage, Rauschenberg, and Johns, true freedom has
more to do with seeing, hearing, and (ultimately) thinking clearly, than with
the sensation of moving "naturally," "organically," or "freely." Freedom for
these artists is not to be found in "nature" or instinct; it can only be achieved
by refusing to surrender to instincts that may turn out to be considerably
less "natural" (and thus ultimately less liberating) than they *feel*. That's one
of the reasons why Cage asks of the arts only that they change his "way of
seeing" not his "way of feeling." Cunningham has discussed his relationship
to Graham in similar terms:

> My experience with Graham was to see how Martha could do things and how
> marvelous she was to watch, but she could not explain it. She could give you
> some sort of emotional explanation, and I would notice that the dancers had
> some feeling about it very often, but couldn't do it. Then I went to the School of
> American Ballet and there was a particularly wonderful teacher named Obukhov,
> an old Russian. He did very complicated exercises, terribly complex, and they
> were slightly old fashioned in style because that was what he was, but that didn't
> matter because everything was so *clear*. . . . In fact, with Graham, as well as in
> ballet classes, what I wanted to see was how the movement operates, not how
> you think it feels to you. (1985, 67–68)

Clarity

One reason that Cunningham, unlike Graham, regularly interrupts the flow of the movement is to emphasize the clarity of its shape. This clarity of shape is one of Cunningham's guiding principles. Even when he executes a step as seemingly functional as a plié, it's not (entirely) for the purpose of grounding himself; it's also because he likes the *shape* of the plié. Cage places a comparable premium on clarity: "Oriental dancing, for instance, is clear in its phraseology. It has its own devices for obtaining it. Hot jazz is never unclear rhythmically . . . The modern dance, on the other hand, is rarely clear" (1961, 91).

We've already examined the extent to which both Cage's and Cunningham's fascination with ballet is, in large part, attributable to its concern with clarity. The ballet vocabulary has evolved with one principle end in view: theatrical *legibility*. Adrian Stokes, writing about the significance of "en dehors" in classical ballet, argues that "Turning out is the essence of ballet. . . . Turning out means that the dancer, whatever the convolutions of the dance, continually shows as much of himself as possible to the spectator." Note how similar Lincoln Kirstein sounds when he discusses the function of the pirouette:

> The effect of the well-executed pirouette is to present the dancer's body in its full plasticity, front and back superimposed on one another, almost as in a double-exposure. An audience necessarily remains stationary in its seat. If the seats could be imagined to revolve rapidly to enable spectators to see back and front in a single frontal position, there might be no reason for pirouettes. (1967, 58–59)

Cunningham's neoclassicism is rooted in a similar idea: that there is no fixed "front," or as he likes to put it (paraphrasing Einstein) "no fixed points in space." In actual practice, this means that bodies should be displayed to and from as many angles as possible. His 1994 "Ocean" (performed out-of-doors, in the round) often resembled a sculpture court in which the "body-as-object" rotated for the visual benefit of the seated spectator. (Single bodies slowly pivoted in place; lines of dancers rotated their way through the 360-degree perimeter of the space.) "Ocean" was as open, gracious, and "public" as anything Cunningham has ever choreographed; and it harked back to that most "classical" of Cunningham's dances, "Suite for Five" (1956). At the beginning of the famous pas de deux in "Suite . . . ," Cunningham sat on his knees with Carolyn Brown straddled across his shoulders in a delicate, horizontal balance. Cunningham then executed a 360-degree rotation—still on his knees—displaying Carolyn Brown from all sides. Similarly, Cunningham has spoken explicitly of the way in which Rauschenberg's design elements promote the goal of clarity or *visibility:* "For a dancer he does the maximum thing a designer can do—he allows the dancer to be seen" (1985, 173).

Clarity, clarity, clarity; that's the Cunningham/Cage mantra. In the words of Jasper Johns's: "Already it's a great deal to see anything *clearly,* for we don't see *anything* clearly." Recall Cage's program note from the 1968 season at BAM: "What comes through, though different for each observer, is *clear.*" The goal, in other words, is perceptual clarity, *not* the "flowing" sensation of physical freedom. One of Cage's favorite anecdotes reveals much about his attitude toward both freedom and nature:

> Artists talk a lot about freedom. So, recalling the expression "free as a bird," Morton Feldman went to a park one day and spent time watching our feathered friends. When he came back, he said, "You know, they're not free. They're fighting over bits of food" (Greenaway 1983).

Even more to the point, Susan Sontag, in a poem dedicated to Cunningham, Cage, and Johns, once wrote: "Dancing as the realm of freedom, that's less than half the story" (1989, 23).

6
Primitive Mysteries

"The word 'body,' its danger, how easily it gives one the illusory impression of being outside of meaning already, free from the contamination of consciousness-unconsciousness. Insidious return of the natural, of Nature."
—Maurice Blanchot (Jones 1998, 58)

"What is the beginning: Perhaps when we seek wholeness, when we embark on the journey toward wholeness."
—Martha Graham, *Notebooks* (1973, 305)

In Chapter 3 we looked at some of the ways in which both Graham and Pollock drew inspiration from a variety of "primitive" sources. We also examined the parallels between Cunningham's repudiation of Graham and Johns's and Rauschenberg's repudiation of Pollock. But primitivism plays a very different role in the dance world than it does in that of the visual arts. When Rauschenberg and Johns turn away from the primitivist aspects of abstract expressionism, they're breaking with one specific period in the history of painting. But when Cunningham rejects the primitive element in the choreography of Graham, he's parting ways with something that many people think of as fundamental to virtually all forms of dance. Consequently, this aspect of Cunningham's legacy deserves to be explored in greater detail.

Dance as the Most Primitive of Art Forms

Perhaps ironically, primitivism is a time-honored mode of modernism, an expression of deep discontent with modernity itself. The word "primitivism" (as opposed to "primitive") doesn't enter Webster's lexicon until 1934; and its definitions include "a return to nature" and "a belief in the *superiority* of primitive life." However, in the last few decades, the dismantling of the myth of exotic, "primitive otherness" has became a growth industry throughout the humanities. Principle targets of this demythologizing process include Gaughin's vision of Tahiti, Margaret Mead's ideas about coming of age in Samoa, Joseph Conrad's conception of Central Africa in *Heart of Darkness,* D. H. Lawrence's portrait of Mexican Indians in *The Plumed Serpent,* and Antonin Artaud's ideas about Balinese theater. But the single biggest bastion of contemporary primitivism merits barely a mention in any of this debunking literature. This primitivist "stronghold" is the world of dance— particularly the world of pre-Cunningham modern dance. Here, primitivism doesn't just linger in a vestigial way; it thrives—in part because so many people seem truly to believe that dance *is* the most primitive of art forms, the one most likely to offer a contemporary audience privileged access to the (otherwise discredited!) concept of "primitive" unity and vitality.

The title of this chapter is borrowed from one of Graham's most haunting and powerful early group works. But many of Graham's greatest dances— indeed many of the masterworks of pre-Cunningham modern dance— aspired to a state of primitive mystery. Thus, the master project that I've attributed to Merce Cunningham—"the modernizing of modern dance"— was predicated at least in part on the repudiation of its primitivist heritage. As outlined in the introduction, the dance world's conception of primitivism involves a dense constellation of interlocking and overlapping beliefs: the idea that dancing is the oldest and most Dionysian of the arts; physical gesture is more expressive and less duplicitous than verbal language; and, above all, dance is a "holistic" phenomenon; it helps heal metaphysical divisions and can serve to therapeutically restore a sense of health and wholeness increasingly rare in the contemporary world.

In Europe and America, the art of dance acquired unprecedented prestige during the 20th century; and it was the ethos of primitivism that helped pave the way for its acceptance. The literary critic Frank Kermode, in his well-known essay, "Poet and Dancer Before Diaghilev," attempts to account for the rhapsodic enthusiasm with which so many artists and intellectuals greeted the pioneer modern dancer, Löie Fuller, and the first Parisian performances of the Ballets Russes. Kermode attributes this love affair to a fascination with the "primitive" element in both modern dance and the early work of Diaghilev. Writing in 1961, he observed:

> The peculiar prestige of dancing over the past seventy or eighty years has, I think, much to do with the notion that it somehow represents art in an undissociated and unspecialized form—a notion made explicit by Yeats and hinted at by Valery.

> The notion is essentially primitivist; it depends upon the assumption that mind and body, form and matter, image and discourse have undergone a process of dissociation, which it is the business of art momentarily to mend. Consequently dancing is credited with a sacred priority over the other arts.... There is no fundamental disagreement that dance is the most primitive, non-discursive art, offering a pre-scientific image of life, an intuitive truth. Thus it is the emblem of the Romantic image. Dance belongs to a period before the self and the world were divided. (1983, 146)

Alas, the imagined satisfactions of "primitive" life often prove highly seductive to the 20th-century intellectual. Even as level-headed a writer as Eric Bentley can begin to sound like a raving Wilhelm Reich or Norman O. Brown when confronted with the primitive mysteries of Martha Graham:

> She is a priestess. A present-day priestess of an ancient cult. Notoriously, she is *the* dancer of the age of anxiety. But she is not content, like, say, Jerome Robbins in his ballet on this theme, to discourse *about* anxiety with the resources of top-drawer ingenuity. Nor is it enough to see neurosis from the vantage-point of neurosis as Robbins, in more earnest vein, occasionally may be said to have done. That is no vantage-point at all. We can only express neurosis in art by conquering it, if fragmentarily, if momentarily. The only vantage-point to view sickness from is health. And health is found at the very foundations or nowhere. Down through the cerebral nervosities to the primal energies, that is Martha Graham's journey. If we accompany her, even part of the way, must we not benefit? (1953, 183)

Cerebral nervosities? That's the sort of verbal infelicity one doesn't expect from a wonderful writer like Bentley. But we need to be tolerant: The man was obviously in love (or at least in heat). Clearly, for writers such as Bentley, part of the appeal of contemporary theatrical dance derives from its latently "primitive" character. Dance is envisioned as the last remaining link between the hypercivilized present and the otherwise vanishing vitality of an idealized primitive past.

Origins and Originality

Early modern dance was determined to flaunt its "originality." But paradoxically, before Cunningham, originality in modern dance was typically conceived of as a return to *origins*. (Note that the word "origin" is subsumed by the word "original.") This journey "back to the source" often took the form of a search for the most natural way of moving, an attempt to uncover the buried "essence" of all dancing. Consider John Martin's observations about the term "modern dance":

> Not only is the phrase non-descriptive, but it is markedly inaccurate, since there is absolutely nothing modern about modern dance. It is, as a matter of fact,

virtually basic dance, the oldest of all dance forms. The modern dancer, instead of employing the cumulative resources of academic tradition, cuts through directly to the source of all dancing. He utilizes the principle that every emotional state tends to express itself in movement, and that the movements thus created spontaneously, though they are not representational, reflect accurately in each case the character of the particular emotional state.... This principle is at least as old as man himself; primitive societies, as we have seen, have found it so potent that they have called it magic and based religious and social practices on it. But it had never been consciously utilized as the basis of art, so far as any record exists, until the turn of the present century when Isadora Duncan made it the very center and source of practices, and the so-called modern dance was born. (1983, 22–23)

Duncan's own words emphasize this sense of "eternal return": "If we seek the real source of the dance, if we go to nature, we find that the dance of the future is the dance of the past, the dance of eternity, and has been and will always be the same" (1977, 54). Duncan's admirers frequently invoked the language of "primitive origin" when describing her performances. Mary Fanton Roberts's hyperbolic prose exemplifies this temptation: "It is far back, deep down the centuries that one's spirit passes when Isadora Duncan dances; back to the very morning of the world" (Duncan 1927, 22). Pre-Cunningham modern dance often resembles an anthropological expedition in search of both the "natural" body and the "origin" or wellspring of all natural movement. Isadora Duncan, describing what sounds like an archaeological excavation of her own body, expounds on her discovery that the solar plexus constitutes the "central spring of all movement":

> I spent long days and nights in the studio seeking that dance which might be the divine expression of the human spirit through the medium of the body's movement. For hours I would stand quite still, my two hands folded between my breasts covering the solar plexus. My mother often became alarmed to see me remain for such long intervals quite motionless as if in a trance—but I was seeking and finally discovered the central spring of all movement, the crater of motor power, the unity from which all diversions of movements are born, the mirror of vision for the creation of the dance—it was from this discovery that was born the theory on which I founded my school. (1977, 92)

Graham attributed similar significance to "the contraction"; Humphrey and Weidman to the principle of "fall and recovery." Humphrey defined modern dance as "moving from the inside out"; Graham spoke of "making visible the interior landscape." Here we begin to sense the strong connection between primitivism and the "interior voyage" undertaken by so many early modern dance choreographers in the long tradition extending from Duncan through Graham. For all of these choreographers, "originality" meant one of two things: either the work "originated" wholly from within the "interior" of the choreographer or else it marked a return to primitive "origins." (Of course, these two "polar" extremes tend to meet around the bend: It's implied that if you probe deeply enough into the individual body and/or psyche, you land in the land of the collective unconscious.) Much the same can be said of the abstract expressionists, whose interior voyage was intended to put them in touch with those timeless Jungian archetypes that presumably reside in the depths of the unconscious. Adolf Gottlieb and Mark Rothko, in their famous joint manifesto, insisted that the only valid subject matter for abstract expressionism was that "which is tragic and timeless." Hence the significance of mythological archetypes. Myths, wrote Rothko, "are the eternal symbols of man's primitive fears and motivations, no matter in what land or what time, changing only in detail, never in substance" (Clearwater 1984, 23–24).

As Maurice Blanchot argues in one of the quotations that serves as an epigraph for this chapter, the primitivist cult of the body is the key to this quest for the natural and the uncorrupted—the search for all that (presumably) exists beyond time, history, and culture. "Nature," as Cezanne famously observed, "is on the inside." But the real treasure to be found therein, is not just Nature-with-a-capital "N," but Wholeness. Martha Graham, in the second epigraph to this chapter, poses what many pre-Cunningham modern dancers would have regarded as *the* fundamental question: "What is the beginning: Perhaps when we seek wholeness, when we embark on the journey toward wholeness" (1973, 305).

The Gesamtkunstwerk

The wholeness Graham seeks is presumed to be constitutive of the natural world. "In nature," Goethe observed, "we never see anything isolated, but everything in connection with something else which is before it, beside it, under it, and over it." Similarly, Wordsworth in "Prelude, I" attributes to nature:

> . . . a dark
> Inscrutable workmanship that reconciles
> Discordant elements, makes them cling together
> In one society.

If this is an accurate description of the natural world, then no aspect of Cunningham's work is more defiantly "unnatural" than the mutual autonomy of movement, sound, and décor in his dances. This isolation of the elements challenges what is probably the key concept in *all* primitivist thinking and writing about dance: the quest for wholeness, the idea that dance can help restore a sense of unity or cohesion otherwise missing from the contemporary world. All of the dualities that we accept as conditions of modernity—mind and body, subject and object, the distance between words and the things they signify—are presumably erased, or at least diminished, by the art of dance. One of the first great 20th-century primitivists, Havelock Ellis, makes the following observation in his rambunctiously rhapsodic ode to paganism, *The Dance of Life* (1923): "The participants in a dance, as all observers of savages have noted, exhibit a wonderful unison; they are, as it were, fused in a single being stirred by a single impulse" (1983, 492–93).

Not only does dance fuse its participants into an indivisible whole, it can serve as catalyst for the long dreamt-of "reunification" of the separate arts. Frank Kermode's essay, quoted earlier, focuses on the work of Diaghilev and Löie Fuller. What Fuller and Diaghilev had in common is that they were both committed to the integration of dance and the other arts. Kermode introduces Fuller as "the woman who seemed to be doing almost single-handed what Diaghilev was later to achieve only with the help of great painters, musicians, and dancers..." (1983, 151). In order to understand the broader significance of what Fuller and Diaghilev were attempting, we need first to examine the best known and most influential proposal for a reunification of the separate arts: Wagner's concept of the *Gesamtkunstwerk*. Invoking the unity of ancient Greek theater as the foundation for his "music drama," Wagner envisions dance as the powerful adhesive holding this Gesamtkunstwerk—his great synthesis of the arts—together:

> The arts of Dance, of Tone, and Poetry thus call themselves the three primeval sisters.... By their nature they are inseparable... for in the dance, which is the very cadence of Art itself, they are so wondrous closely interlaced with one another... when every barrier has thus fallen, then there are no more arts and no more boundaries, but only art, the universal, undivided. (1983, 191–92)

The poets and intellectuals that Frank Kermode discusses, the ones who genuflected at the feet of Loie Fuller and the early Ballets Russes, were all smitten with this Wagnerian dream of synthesis. Fuller, enveloped in billowing silks and bathed in brightly colored light, appeared to become "one" with her materials. "She blends with rapidly changing colours which vary their limelit phantasmagoria," wrote the awestruck Mallarmé. Yeats was also a great fan of hers; and it may well have been the memory of Fuller that inspired him to pose his famous question: "How can we know the dancer from the dance?"

Diaghilev, of course, was renowned for his ability to persuade the leading composers and painters of the day—Stravinsky, Picasso, Matisse, Derain—to devise music, decor, and costumes for the Ballets Russes. His success in these collaborative ventures led Camille Mauclair to announce that the early

Ballets Russes extravaganzas had out-Wagnered Wagner. Commenting on the collaboration among Fokine, Benois, and Bakst on *Schéhérazade,* he wrote:

> This dream-like spectacle, beside which the Wagnerian synthesis itself is but a clumsy barbarism, this spectacle where all sensations correspond and weave together by their continual interlacing... the collaboration of decor, lighting, costumes, and mime establishes unknown relationships in the mind. (Pridden 1952, 106)

That the artists of the Ballets Russes were themselves aware of Wagner and sought consciously to emulate (or even to surpass) him is evident in Benois's very definition of ballet: "a form of theater spectacle in which all the varied elements must blend into a whole to constitute what Wagner called Gesamtkunstwerk" (Hansen 1985, 14).

And why were the Russians able to out-Wagner Wagner? The answer has everything to do with the myth of primitivism. To the Parisian intellectuals typified by Mauclair, the Russians weren't Europeans. They were Slavs (which is to say, "primitives"). Lacking Western ego or personal individuation, they had (according to the myth of primitivism) not yet fallen from collective grace into the evil of competitive individualism. Consequently, they were thought better suited to "seamless" collaborations than their Western counterparts. As Henri Gheon wrote in 1910:

> To do true justice to the Russian Company, one should avoid making the slightest individual reference, for the collective result by far outweighs the sum of the individual talents which compose it. Its supreme quality is that of seeming indivisible, of being one with the work it represents, even to the point of seeming to issue from the very music itself before melting back into the colors of the settings. (Hansen 1985, 13)

From the vantage point of the Parisian intelligensia, the Russian artists were part child, part savage: both innocent and deeply instinctual—living, breathing embodiments of "l'âme slave." In the words of Joan Acocella, "Paris had imagined these Russians before they saw them. What they saw, consequently, answered their imaginings" (1984, 324). The Parisians projected their spiritual yearnings onto the Russians (in much the same way that a few years later, they would project their more purely erotic yearnings onto Josephine Baker). In 1909, Benois spoke of the unique way in which the Ballets Russes *conquered* the hearts and minds of the overly refined, neuraesthenic aesthetes who made up a good portion of its audience:

> The barbarians once again conquered Rome, and it is curious that contemporary Romans welcome this, their captivity, for they feel they will benefit from it, that

> the newcomers with their fresh blood and clear art will infuse new blood into
> their exhausted bodies. (Berg 1988, 15)

The Russians came to represent the triumph of body over mind—or, at least, the hope of healing the Cartesian split *between* body and mind—a "holistic" antidote to what Robert Desnos disparaged as "Logical Europe [that] crushes the mind endlessly between the hammers of two terms" (Nadeau 1965, 106).

In short, the Russians embodied the very essence of dance-world primitivism. This primitivism also was apparent in the "exotic" (i.e., "non-Western" or at least "archaic") movement sources prominently featured in many early works of the Ballet Russes: Fokine's 1910 solo for Nijinsky, "Les Orientales," echoed the mudralike use of the hands that its choreographer had witnessed in the work of the Siamese Court Dancers who had visited St. Petersberg a few years earlier. "Daphne and Chlöe," choreographed in 1912, drew on the "archaic" postures (e.g., Karsavina's bare feet arched to half-toe, one leg turned in) that Fokine had found in his studies of ancient Greek bas-reliefs. Nijinsky carried this "primitive" inversion of balletic "turn out" to its furthest extremes in his 1913 depiction of primitive sacrifice and renewal, "The Rite of Spring." (And of course, the forced two-dimensionality of his movement for "Faun" was yet another invocation of "archaic" source material.)

But there's an even more basic reason why the Ballets Russes was able to out-synthesize Wagner. Dance is presumed by the primitivists to be *the* natural catalyst for uniting the arts—regardless of whether the movement vocabulary in question is overtly "primitive." Kermode writes that dance "achieves naturally that 'organic unity' which... modern poetry can produce only by a great and exhausting effort of fusion" (1983, 148). Thus the body is thought to achieve—with relative ease—what words can only dream of.

The Anti-Gesamtkunstwerk: Cunningham, Brecht, and the Separation of the Elements

We often hear it said that Merce Cunningham is the postwar Diaghilev. Like Diaghilev, Cunningham commissioned decor, costumes, and music from the leading visual artists and composers of his era. But Cunningham's approach to collaboration is fundamentally different from (indeed, the very antithesis of) Diaghilev's. Serge Diaghilev—at least up until the time of "Parade" in 1917—was inspired by the Wagnerian (and primitivist) dream of synthesizing the separate arts into a unified whole. By contrast, Cunningham's approach to collaboration has much more in common with that of Wagner's most articulate intellectual adversary, Bertolt Brecht. It was Brecht, in his 1930 essay, "The Modern Theatre Is The Epic Theatre," who most clearly articulated (and anticipated) the approach to collaboration that would eventually triumph in Cunningham's work:

> So long as the expression "*Gesamtkunstwerk*" (or "integrated work of art") means that the integration is a muddle, so long as the arts are supposed to be "fused" together, the various elements will all be equally degraded, and each will act as a mere "feed" to the rest. The process of fusion extends to the spectator who gets thrown into the melting pot too and becomes a passive (suffering) part of the total work of art. Witchcraft of this sort must of course be fought against. Whatever is intended to produce hypnosis, is likely to induce sordid intoxication, or creates fog, [and] has got to be given up. *Words, Music, and setting must become more independent of one another.* [The emphasis is Brecht's.] (Brecht 1964, 37)

For Brecht, it was no coincidence that Wagner occupied such a privileged place in the cultural life of Nazi Germany. Brecht regarded Wagner's music as a massive "wall of sound" that forcibly subdues the listener. To Brecht, the Nuremberg rallies were one great Wagnerian opera: the masses mesmerized, the Fuhrer unified with his followers. (In Ray Muller's documentary film, *The Wonderful, Horrible Life of Leni Riefenstahl*, Muller and Riefenstahl are seen examining some of the more orgiastic moments in *Triumph of the Will*. Muller then comments to Riefenstahl: "Those crowd scenes are like something in a Wagner opera.") Brecht especially despised the way in which Nazi spectacle promoted Einfühlung, which we routinely translate into English as "empathy." But the Anglo-American conception of empathy (as an act of emotional identification) doesn't really do justice to the German connotation of deep and rather mystical unification—in short, a complete merging of spectator and spectacle. (The rhetoric of early modern dance, so rife with references to "kinesthetic empathy," brings us a bit closer to the true meaning of the German "einfühlung.") Brecht spoke disapprovingly of "this empathy on the part of the public... [this] being carried along, this transformation of all spectators into a unified mass" (Ewen 1969, 218). Hitler's public rallies, Brecht observed, were designed to make "the people, or better, his public, say that which he was saying or more accurately, feel that which he was feeling" (Ewen 1969, 218).

Rejecting Wagnerian wholeness, Brecht proposes intentional disunity, a separation of the elements which ultimately serves to keep the audience at a respectful distance—preventing them from being enveloped by the surrounding spectacle. In his best-known manifesto, "A Short Organum for the Theater" (1948), he wrote:

> So let us invite all the sister arts of the drama, not in order to create an "integrated" work of art in which they all offer themselves up and are lost, but so that with the drama they may further the common task in their different ways; and their relations with one another consist in this: that they lead to mutual alienation. (1964, 204)

("Alienation" or "estrangement" are common translations of Brecht's beloved word: Verfremdung.)

Ironically, Brecht's actual collaborative practices fell far short of his ideals. Where then do we look for concrete realizations of his concept of collaboration? The dance world may be the very last place one would expect to find instances of Brechtian influence, or even confluence. But the fact of the matter is that no one—including Brecht himself—has carried this principle of separation as far as Merce Cunningham has.

As we've already seen in a number of other contexts, every collaborative element in Cunningham's work maintains its autonomy. The choreography, the sound score, and the settings are all created independently and often don't encounter one another until the very first performance. This is an aesthetics of peaceful coexistence: sound, movement, and décor all inhabit the same space without fusing together into an organic whole. It's not uncommon for the various elements to function as a sort of obstacle course—in effect, running interference—for one another. Cunningham once said that his dancers maneuvered their way around Rauschenberg's ever-evolving "live decor" for "Story" (1963) "as one might with a fallen tree in the path, or a box suddenly there as you drive on the highway" (Sundell 1984, 11).

In proposing these connections between Cunningham, Cage, and Brecht, I don't mean to imply that Cunningham and Cage share Brecht's Marxist ideology; far from it. But that doesn't prevent their work from functioning in Brechtian ways. And, even though it would be preposterous to claim that Cunningham's work constitutes a conscious critique of fascism, his dances *do* provide a variety of counterintuitive perceptual training that is deeply resistant to most modes of sensory manipulation (the outright totalitarian as well as the more purely seductive strategies of capitalist consumerism). That qualification notwithstanding, references to Nazism may *still* seem ludicrously out of place in a book about Merce Cunningham. But, in Chapter 7, devoted to Cunningham's musical scores, we'll see that John Cage believes the Gesamtkunstwerk to be "a purely German idea . . . a fascist idea really." And even if we attempt to confine our attention to Cunningham's repudiation of primitivist wholeness, the topic of German fascism remains relevant because of the many disturbing similarities between Nazi ideology and the sort of primitivist rhetoric that animated so much of pre-Cunningham modern dance. (As we'll see momentarily, German modern dance was the one modernist art the Nazis didn't actively repress.)

Primitivism and Fascism

Needless to say, not all primitivists are fascists, but Hitler's fascism constituted a particularly virulent variety of 20th-century primitivism. Deep yearnings for the mythic, the instinctive, the essential, the pure—so basic to the primitivist agenda—are "core values" for the Third Reich. Peter Gay, in his study of Weimar culture, refers to the Germanic "hunger for wholeness." The swastika, with its mythic-archaic merger of male and female figures, is the symbolic embodiment of forced unity. As Kirk Varnedoe has written:

> Of all the primitive forms that have captured the imagination of twentieth-century man, certainly the swastika was among the most potent. This ancient cosmological symbol, on the banner of Hitler's Germany, testified to a frighteningly successful revivification of the power of archaic myth. (1984, 652)

Hitler's blatant appeal to the irrational ("Think with your blood") is a variation (albeit a pathological one) on the primitivist theme of decadent hypercivilization: that is, contemporary culture is thought to be impure, abstract, desiccated, estranged from its roots. Only by returning to its "primitive" folk origins can vitality (and Aryan purity) be restored.

When generalizing about the Nazi's official attitude toward artistic modernism, we often think of the infamous "degenerate art" exhibition of 1937; and we conclude (falsely) that all major modernists were—in one way or another—silenced by the government (intimidated, exiled, or deported to the death camps). But a great many modern dancers continued to work in Nazi Germany, and a good number were actively supported by the Reich's cultural ministry. Goebbels's enthusiasm for modern dance (and the dance community's willingness—sometimes eagerness—to place its talents at the service of the Reich) had a great deal to do with the ethos of primitivism. The Nazi ideology of body-mysticism, of Physik-Kultur, the insistent German desire to envision the bodies of their young people as a resurrected image of Greek Olympic athleticism—all these components of an otherwise abstract-sounding "purist" ideology—found their clearest, and most sensuous, embodiment in German modern dance. That the modern-dance community saw a reflection of its own ideals in Hitler's propaganda is made clear by Susan Manning:

> Many of the dancers heard in Nazi rhetoric an echo of their own beliefs. Had not they always believed that the body possessed a truth inaccessible to the mind? If so, then was it such a leap to embrace the cult of the irrational? Had not they always believed in dance as a way of creating community (Bemeinschaft)? If so, then was it such a leap to embrace the ideal of the Volksgemeinschaft? (Manning 1993, 173)

As a result, modern dance made a significant contribution to the Nazi's cultural agenda. For example, Rudolf von Laban's "movement choirs," which accommodated as many as 500 amateur participants, helped popularize the "Physik-Kultur" component of German fascism. Above all, German modern dance both understood and exploited the connection between kinetic empathy (so near and dear to a choreographer such as Mary Wigman) and the sort of einfuhlung so central to Nazi art and politics.

Theater and Ritual

Brecht wrote, "Theater may be said to derive from ritual. But that is only to say that it becomes theater once the two have parted" (1964, 204). He understood that one of the goals Nazi spectacle shared with Wagnerian opera was a desire to "return" theatrical performance to its presumed "roots" in ritual. As Rudolf von Laban argued in 1928, "The lay dance choir is a rediscovery of a much earlier artistic community in which mysterious ritual was the foundation of social unity and the spectator played a secondary role" (Toepfer 1997, 301). The enormous appeal that ritual held for the primitivists is easy enough to understand. Ritual—the primitivists liked to believe—is *sacred,* whereas theater is comparatively secular. Ritual was regarded as fully *participatory;* theater, by contrast, was an activity one "merely" watches. Einfuhlung—with its mystical breaking down of the separation between spectator and spectacle—was thereby associated with ritual rather than theater.

The rediscovery of the ritualistic roots of theater and dance was one of the great obsessions of early-20th-century anthropologists and literary critics such as Jane Harrison and James Frazer. And these very figures were required reading for the early pioneers of modern dance. Frank Kermode, in his essay on Fuller and Diaghilev, noted the connection between primitivism, ritual, and dance's newly acquired prominence in the early years of the 20th century:

> In view of this primitivizing, it is worth remembering that the increase of prestige was contemporaneous with a major effort by anthropologists, liturgiologists, and folklorists to discover the roots of the dance in ritual of all kinds. . . . We are all familiar with the interest shown by the generation of Valery and that of Eliot in these matters; and from Eliot, at the time, when he was busy with Jane Harrison and Frazer we can get some notion of how they struck the literary imagination. (1983, 146)

Jane Harrison's theory about the way in which Greek tragic theater evolved from Dionysian ritual was of central importance to the development of early modern dance. For example, the program for one of Isadora Duncan's concerts in 1900 lists Jane Harrison as "reader." We might go so far as to suggest that *early modern dance aspired to the condition of ritual* and if we take the time to examine some of the reasons the primitivists yearned to reritualize modern dance, we'll be better prepared to appreciate the ways in which (and the extent to which) Cunningham and company *retheatricalize* it.

From Doing to Seeing

In her classic discussion of the relationship between ritual and theatre in ancient Greece, Jane Harrison refers to Dionysian ritual as a "dromenon" or thing done. It is not (primarily) a "thing seen," something performed for the pleasure or edification of mortal spectators. According to Harrison, one doesn't just *watch* a ritual, one actively participates in it. There's no designated viewing space for a passive audience. Our English word "theater" by contrast derives from the Greek word "theatron" which means—literally— "*seeing* place" or the seating area for spectators. Harrison argues that the theatron evolved in ancient Greece as Dionysian rituals became secularized and lost their sense of magical potency. She describes this process in the following way: "Some day there will be a bad summer, things will go all wrong, and the chorus will sadly ask, 'Why should I dance my dance?' They will drift away or become mere spectators of a rite established by custom" (1983, 503).

For Harrison, the transformation is symbolized by changes in the physical architecture of the performance space. But it involves a transformation of mental architecture as well: An arena dominated by an orchestra (in Greek, literally "dancing place") is supplanted by a new space whose very name derives from the physical accommodations it makes for spectators:

> We have seen that the orchestra, with its dancing chorus, stands for ritual, for the stage in which all were worshippers, all joined in a rite of practical intent. We further saw that the theatre, the place for the spectators, stood for art. In the orchestra all is life and dancing; [but] the marble seats are the very symbol of rest, aloofness from action, contemplation. The seats for the spectators grow and grow in importance till at last they absorb, as it were, the whole spirit, and give their name theatre to the whole structure; action is swallowed up in contemplation. (1983, 505)

From the primitivist's perspective, the transformation of ritual into theater entails a virtual fall from grace, an expulsion from "the garden." Norman O. Brown explicitly contrasts what he calls "the abstraction of the visual" (the sensory practices encouraged by the "theatron" or "seeing place") with the fully tactile life of Eden:

> The garden is polymorphism of the senses, polymorphous perversity, active interplay; and the opposite of polymorphous perversity is the abstraction of the visual, obtained by putting to sleep the rest of the life of the body. The pure knowing subject of modern philosophy, winged cherub without a body.... Like the spectator in the traditional theater. (1966, 121)

This "critique of the visual" is an essential component of the primitivist ethos. "All great myths are dark," declared Antonin Artaud (1958, 87). "The darkness is well suited to devotion," insists Dionysus in Euripides *The Bacchae*. Wagner advocates the "invisible orchestra" and the "invisible theater." He is determined to shroud the conventions of the theatrical experience in *darkness* (the very antithesis of Brecht's "brightly lighted" approach to theatrical convention). We've already discussed those moments of "*blinding* revelation" in the work of Graham. "Night Journey" is only the most direct and literal example of the way in which Graham seeks to replace "sight" with "*in*sight." Recall Graham's hymn to

> She who is entranced by Vision
> Blinded by light . . . (1973, 26)

Nietzsche, the great resurrector of "the Dionysian," also conceives of Greek tragedy as a "night journey." In *The Birth of Tragedy*, he wrote:

> The language of Sophoclean heroes surprises us with its Apolline precison and lucidity; so that we immediately imagine we can see into the innermost core of their being. . . . (But) if we instead penetrate the myth projected in these bright reflections, we suddenly experience something that is the opposite of a familiar optical phenomenon. If we make a concerted effort to stare into the sun and turn away blinded, we have dark-coloured patches before our eyes as what we might call remedies. The light-image manifestations of the Sophoclean hero— the Apolline mask, in short—are the inevitable products of a glance into the terrible depths of nature: light-patches, we might say, to heal the gaze seared by terrible night. (1964, 541)

This is a prominent theme for the abstract expressionists as well. (In Adolph Gottlieb's "Troubled Eyes," an installment of his "Oedipus" series from the 1940s, a pair of human eyes is about to be devoured by a primordial creature). True "insight" is associated with bodily wisdom, with tactility rather than visual analysis.

The belief that the visual and the tactile are at odds with one another was conveniently summed up in the 1960s by Marshall McLuhan in books such as *The Gutenberg Galaxy:* " . . . touch is not so much a separate sense as the very interplay of the senses. That is why it recedes in significance as the visual faculty is given separate and abstract intensity" (1962, 83). Clearly, the primitivists sought to celebrate "the tactile" at the expense of the visual; Ortega y Gasset once suggested that "Primitive man is tactile man." Ritual is thus identified as a tactile experience, theater as a visual experience—one that promotes distance and detachment. Again, its very name is derived from "theatron" or "seeing place."

Here we see how dance begins to earn its reputation as the most "primitive" of the arts. Jane Harrison predicted that dance would play an increasingly vital role in the life of Western societies as the perception of *distance* between the observing self and the "natural" world intensified. Dance, she argued, would function as an antidote for this sort of "theatrical" mediation. Dance—especially modern dance—is endowed by the primitivists with a special sense of mission. It is envisioned as the art most fully capable of restoring a lost (or vanishing) sense of tactile connectedness. This is what John Martin means when he speaks of the "inherent contagion of bodily movement, which makes the onlooker feel sympathetically in his own musculature the exertions he sees in somebody else's musculature.... "This," he argues, "is the prime purpose of modern dance; it is not interested in spectacle… " (1983, 22). This "contagion of bodily movement" (the tactile) overcomes "spectacle" (the purely visual) by promoting a kinesthetic transference of physical sensation from dancer to spectator. Bolton Hall, describing Isadora Duncan's dancing in 1914, wrote that "it can only be perceived, not seen" (Daly 1995, 66). The very distinction between theatrical and ritualistic dance is eroded (in so far as tactility is thought to diminish the physical and psychological distance created by the "theatron"). The result is a closer bond—or at least the illusion of such—between performer and perceiver. John Martin is one of many 20th-century writers who subtly, but intentionally, blur the distinction between ritualistic and theatrical dancing, suggesting that the separation between spectator and spectacle (even in the most secular, aestheticized contexts) is somehow less distinct in the art of dance than in the other performing arts.

Edward Bullough, in his classic essay about the concept of aesthetic distance (which he calls "psychical distance"), argues that dance is the art that most effectively minimizes the sensation of distance between perceiver and thing perceived. According to Bullough, no other art form defies the "disinterestedness" of aesthetic distance quite as effectively as dance. Paul Valery, in his essay, "Philosophy of the Dance," writes that "part of our pleasure as spectators [of dance] consists in feeling ourselves possessed by the rhythms so that we ourselves are virtually dancing" (1983, 62). Havelock Ellis, in *The Dance of Life*, suggests that:

> Even if we are not ourselves dancers, but merely the spectators of dance, we are still, according to that Lippsian doctrine of Einfuhlung or "empathy" feeling ourselves in the dancer who is manifesting and expressing latent impulses of our own being. (1983, 494)

In other words, while watching dance, we are thought to "participate" to a greater extent than we do while watching the performance of a play or an opera. Dance is heralded as the most *participatory* of the arts, even if that participation remains virtual rather than actual. The art of dance is thereby entrusted with preserving that "participation mystique" which the anthropologist Levy-Bruhl identified as a prime characteristic of "primitive" life. "Their mental activity," Levy-Bruhl wrote of "primitive" peoples in 1910:

> is too little differentiated for it to be possible to consider ideas or images of objects by themselves apart from the emotions and passions which evoke these ideas or are evoked by them ... [thus] the difference between animate and inanimate things is not of the same interest to primitive mentality as it is to ours.... The mystic properties with which things and beings are imbued form an integral part of the idea to the primitive, who views it as a synthetic whole. (Rubin 1984, 335)

Norman O. Brown (writing more than 60 years later, in 1966) is quick to make a similar connection between participation and primitivism, and just as quick to distinguish this connectedness from the "purely visual" experience of theatrical perception. In *Loves's Body*, he wrote:

> "Primitive Mentality" involves participation; an extrasensory link between the percipient and the perceived; a telepathy which we have disowned. The spectator whose participation is restricted to seeing, who is passive, is held in passivity by that which he sees. (1966, 121)

This helps explain the deep desire on the part of the primitivists to associate dance with ritual rather than theater. No doubt, this is part of what motivated Martha Graham to declare that "Theater is a verb before it is a noun, an act before it is a place"—especially a "seeing" place! (This is another way of arguing that theater evolved from *ritual;* and theatrical dance must *return to ritual* if it hopes to regain authenticity.) The final section of Martha Graham's "Acts of Light" is particularly revealing. The dance is a barely theatricalized version of a Graham class, performed in practice clothes. But Graham titled it "Ritual to the Sun," suggesting that she viewed even the barebones of the technique itself in ritualistic terms.

From Duncan through Graham, modern dance committed itself to a reritualization of the theater, an impulse that may well have derived from the influence of Nietzsche's *The Birth of Tragedy* (a text that Duncan referred to as her "bible" and that Graham was intimately familiar with as well. Doris Humprhey's "Dionysiaques" [1932] was directly inspired by her reading of *The Birth of Tragedy* a year earlier.) In his monumental study of the ancient Greek theater, Nietzsche wrote, "The audience of spectators such as we know it was unknown to the Greeks" (1964, 520). Nietzsche believed that the Greeks of the 5th century B.C. had yet to evolve the mode of "detached" spectatorship that we associate with the proscenium theater. The tragedies of Aeschylus, Sophocles, and Euripides had not yet fully dissociated themselves from the Dionysian ritual (the choric dithyramb) out of which they were thought to have evolved. The living link between tragic theater and its ritualistic roots was of course, the chorus. For Nietzsche, "the chorus is a vision of the Dionysiac Mass"—and at the same time—"the chorus is the ideal spectator" (1964, 518).

This conception of the chorus is central to the "participation mystique" at the heart of pre-Cunningham modern dance. Duncan, for example, insisted "When I have danced, I have tried always to be the Chorus.... I never once danced a solo" (1977, 96). By conceiving of herself as a one-woman chorus, she connected her singular self to Nietzsche's "Dionysiac Mass." Graham, early in her career, danced a solo titled "Dithyrambic;" and Eric Bentley, upon encountering "Night Journey" in the mid 1940s wrote that "[it was] the first time I felt that I truly understood what the Greeks had meant by a chorus" (1953, 181). In *Time and the Dancing Image*, Deborah Jowitt concludes a lengthy consideration of Martha Graham by noting: "she construed herself as both celebrant and priestess, bringing Western theatrical dancing as close to ritual as it has ever come ... " (1988, 233).

This ritualistic desire for a diminishing of distance between the spectator and the art object is evident in the work of the abstract expressionists as well. Rothko wanted the spectator to be literally surrounded by his paintings, rather than allowing the viewer to experience them one at a time, from a disinterested vantage point. The Rothko Chapel in Houston totally envelopes the spectator in the sensory experience of the paintings. Much of Pollock's work also aspires to the condition of ritual. One of his paintings from 1953 is titled, simply, "Ritual." Kirk Varnedoe connects Pollock's work in the 1940s with the ritualistic nature of prehistoric cave painting:

> A painting such as "Wounded Animal" of 1943 already demonstrates Pollock's interest in primitive mark-making, in whatever format, as an activity of magic intent, bridging the gulf between representation and reality, between depicting and doing. The slashed marks and the arrow-form here echo similar marking on animal imagery in prehistoric caves like Altamira, markings thought to evidence prehistoric man's belief that strokes made against the image would be efficacious blows against the living creature, object of the hunt. (1984, 643)

Even more to the point, in his essay, "The Mythic Act," Harold Rosenberg imbues Pollock with an animistic aura of ritual magic. Note that Rosenberg refers to Pollock's brushes as "wands":

> With his paint-saturated wand, he will draw lines in the air, letting flecks of color fall on the canvas as traces of his occult gesticulations. His consciousness is directed not toward an effect determined by notions of good painting but toward the protraction and intensification of the doing itself, of the current that flows between the artist and his marked-out world and whose pauses, drifts, detours, and tides lift him into "pure harmony." From these apprehensions of presences and energies in nature Pollock passed into union with them through releasing paint in fluids that directly record his physical movements. (Jones 1998, 74)

Empathy

Rosenberg resorts to the language of mysticism when he describes Pollock's aspiration toward "union" with various animistic presences. This talk of union is reminiscent of Havelock Ellis's invocation of the German "Einfuhlung" and of the way in which it exemplifies the ritualistic aspirations of pre-Cunningham modern dance. Brecht's *separation* of the elements, his critique of Wagner's Gesamtkunstwerk, is designed with one principle end in view: to impede Einfuhlung. And as we've already seen, the ultimate goal of this "disunity" for Brecht is to preserve the spectator's perceptual freedom. Recall what he said about the spectator "getting thrown into the melting pot too."

Again, it's in the work of Cunningham that we find the most compelling examples of Brecht's proposals for separating the spectator from the spectacle. Consider the way decor and lighting function in many of Cunningham's most ambitious collaborations. They often impede the spectator's direct, "unmediated" perception of the choreography. We've encountered a number of the classic examples already: Quintessentially, Cunningham's "Tread" (1970) featured Bruce Nauman's row of standing industrial fans lined up downstage directly between the audience and the dance. In "Walkaround Time" (1968), Jasper Johns designed a series of movable plastic boxes that served a similar function. Frank Stella's brilliantly bright rectangles of colored cloth for Cunningham's "Scramble" (1967) were stretched over shiny aluminum frames of differing heights mounted on fast-moving casters. The result was an ever-shifting collage of "color-field" images (purple, blue, red, green, yellow, orange) that sometimes "cut off" the mid-sections or upper bodies of the dancers. Rauschenberg's lighting plot for "Winterbranch" (1964) contained chance elements that often left large areas of the stage in almost total darkness. And during "Canfield," (1969) the stage space was repeatedly dissected by a mobile, burningly bright beam of light designed by Robert Morris. "Summerspace" (1958), with decor and costumes by Rauschenberg, raised the issue of "visibility" in a more novel way: Both the dancers' costumes and the backdrop were painted with the same colorful patterns of tiny "pointillistic" dots. The idea—which never quite worked—was that the performers would appear to merge with the decor every time they stopped moving.

In some of Cunningham works, the dancers themselves function as visual obstacles or framing devices through which we view other performers. In "Scramble," Carolyn Brown would extend an arm or raise a leg just downstage of Cunningham; and he in turn would quickly duck—"or scramble"—underneath this human turnstile. In Cunningham's dance for video, "Points In Space" (1986), the camera often "peers through" the port de bras of other dancers, employing their arms as an architectural frame. In "Biped" (1999) computer-generated video projections of gridlike patterns on a downstage scrim mediate our relationship to the live dancers upstage of the scrim. These visual obstacles not only affirm the inevitable separation between dancer and spectator; they encourage us to view the dancing more actively (i.e., less passively) than we otherwise might. (As Cezanne once put it, "We see more clearly on a cloudy day.")

It's especially instructive to compare the visual obstacles in Cunningham works such as "Tread" or "Walkaround Time" with the setting for Alwin Nikolais's "Gallery" (1978). The décor in the Nikolais piece also constitutes a divider of sorts between the dancers and the audience. But the barrier in "Gallery" serves an illusionistic end; it promotes the trompe l'oeil from which the dance derives its magical effects. (Its function is to conceal the hidden dancers' manipulation of props that magically bob up and down from behind the barricade.) Cunningham's settings, on the other hand, promote an analytic scrutiny that is anti-illusionistic. Viewed in an analytical, anti-illusionistic way, many of Nikolais's works aren't much fun. In "Vaudeville of the Elements" (1965) for example, one occasionally glimpses the feet of the performers—even though they're supposed to remain concealed beneath the floor-length costumes. Thus, the natural temptation is to *squint* a bit—if only to help the illusion along. By contrast, Cunningham's décor tends to promote an active *scan* rather than a compensatory *squint*. This sort of perceptual scrutiny ultimately serves to remind us that what we're experiencing is a theatrical, rather than a ritualistic, event. The "inherent contagion of bodily movement" is deemphasized. There is no "participation mystique." And the kind of "seeing" involved is not only active, but self-conscious and reflective.

Is this a "Brechtian" mode of spectatorship? Technically speaking, yes and no. Brecht was primarily concerned with what he regarded as the undesirable consequences of emotional identification, illusionism, and the willing suspension of disbelief—conditions that rarely arise in the (inherently) less "realistic" world of dance. By contrast, the brand of empathy that most directly unites the dancer with his or her audience is kinetic responsiveness; and it's precisely this sort of empathy that is "interfered with" in much of Cunningham's work. The Russian Formalist Victor Shklovsky (a major influence on Brecht) sought to "remove the automatism of perception, to increase *the difficulty and length of perception*" (1965, 12). (Analogously, Duchamp once referred to "The Bride... " as "a *delay* in glass" [Charbonnier 1975, 82]). Similarly, in Cunningham's work, the interval between stimulus and response has been acknowledged and intensified, not ignored or diminished. In other words, no "automatic" responses.

In Brecht's theory (and Cunningham's practice), the ultimate consequence of this "separation of the elements" is to increase the spectator's perceptual freedom. Recall Brecht's concern that in the Wagnerian Gesamtkunstwerk: "The process of fusion extends to the spectator who gets thrown into the melting pot too and becomes a passive (suffering) part of the total work of art." Cunningham is equally eager to immunize his audience against this sort of perceptual manipulation:

> I like to think of the spectator as someone who comes to the theater, as was once said, to exercise his faculties. I like this idea much better than that the spectator comes after dinner on a full stomach and sits and goes to sleep, and expects to be awakened. I don't mind if people go to sleep, and I don't mind if they leave. But I would prefer to give the opportunity to people to exercise their individual faculties in the way that each one might choose to do. (1985, 71)

Note how very "Brechtian" Cunningham sounds when he says:

> We don't attempt to make the individual spectator think a certain way. I do think each spectator is individual, that it isn't *a public*. Each spectator as an individual can receive what we do in his own way and need not see the same thing, or hear the same thing, as the person next to him. (1985, 171–72)

Isolations

This individuation of the audience (so different from the sort of communal fusion that characterizes ritual) is mirrored in the way Cunningham isolates each performer on stage. Reviewing Cunningham's first solo concert in New York in 1944, Edwin Denby described the choreographer's style as "extreme elegance in isolation." Analogously, commenting on Cunningham's decentralization of bodies throughout the performance space, Carolyn Brown once suggested that everyone on stage in a Cunningham dance is always, ultimately, a *soloist*. (By contrast, Isadora Duncan, as we've seen, was so eager to associate herself with the spirit of the Dionysian chorus that she claimed never to have danced a solo!)

We can go a step further by observing that not only is everybody a "soloist" in Cunningham's choreography: Every section of every *body* can become a soloist as well—for Cunningham often sets the head, arms, torso, and legs moving in opposition to one another. As early as 1953, in "Untitled Solo," the movement for each of several subdivisions of the body was determined separately and by chance. Cunningham's atomization of the body was especially evident in a work like "Tread" (1970), where one often viewed the dancers' bodies through the spinning blades of a fan, thereby greatly intensifying the sense of fragmentation. The atomized body becomes a microcosm of the company-at-large, a mini-model of the way in which Cunningham decentralizes and fragments the entire space of the stage. The "isolation" (of one part of the body from another) is to Cunningham technique what the contraction, based on the more organic rhythm of breathing, is to Graham. (Graham's contraction also serves to generate an involuntary muscular response in the perceiver, thereby uniting the spectator and the dancer in a shared kinesthetic experience.)

Simone Forti, a dancer whose organic inclinations were fundamentally at odds with Cunningham's, makes this observation in her *Handbook in Motion:*

> I started going to the Merce Cunningham school. I remember watching my teachers, and feeling that I couldn't even perceive what they were doing, let alone do it.... An important element of the movement seemed to be the arbitrary isolation of the different parts of the body. I recall a statement I made in exasperation one day in the studio. I said that Merce Cunningham was a master of adult, isolated articulation. And that the thing I had to offer was still very close to the holistic and generalized response of infants. (1974, 45)

Wholeness and Holiness

Simone Forti contrasts Cunningham's "adult, isolated articulation" with the "*holistic* and generalized response of infants." When Cunningham rejects the "holistic," a word that conveniently sums up the primitivist aspiration toward "wholeness," he is also rejecting a closely related aspiration toward "holiness." (One of the many reasons the pre-Cunningham moderns aspired to the condition of ritual is that they sought to reimbue dance with a ritualistic sense of the holy.) The connection between wholeness and holiness is more than merely etymological. As M. H. Abrams argued in *The Mirror and the Lamp*, organicist theories of art are almost always, in essence, a substitute theology. This was especially true for the pioneers of modern dance whose rhetoric was often infused with religiosity, with the (primitivist) discovery that the soul is *in* the body: "My arms rose slowly toward the Temple... " wrote Duncan, "I knew then that I had found my dance, and it was a prayer" (Venza 1979, n.p.). Ruth St. Denis, in a 1919 journal entry writes, "My church is the theater. My pulpit my stage... the atmosphere of the institution is to be not only moral, but religious" (UCLA Dance Collection).

Cunningham by contrast, creates dances that are unabashedly secular in nature. Not only secular, but incompatible with the sort of "rootedness" that modern dance primitivism sought to reestablish.

From Roots to Routes

In *Gone Primitive*, Marianna Torgovnick has argued that modern primitivism is motivated by a sense of "transcendental homelessness," the desire to reestablish both physical and metaphysical roots. Note, by contrast, the "rootless" way Cunningham's dancers skim over every inch of stage space. We've already discussed the manner in which Cunningham dancers combine great speed with stop-on-a-dime reversibility of direction. (And as we saw in Chapter 5, this speed and reversibility was made possible in large part by Cunningham's rapprochement with ballet. Cunningham was also a great admirer of Fred Astaire; and nothing is more characteristic of Astaire than his sudden, unpredictable changes of direction.)

As a result, Cunningham's dancers, unlike earlier modern dancers, rarely appear "glued" to one spot; and they never treat the floor as a metaphorical substitute for "the earth." Cunningham has criticized the earlier modern dance choreographers' comparatively static treatment of space. "The modern American dance," he once wrote:

> stemming from German expressionism and the personal feelings of the various American pioneers, made space into a series of lumps, or often just static hills on the stage with actually no relation to the larger space of the stage area. (1992, 37)

More to the point, ritual and "primitive" dance are often performed in a single, sacred location. They're the antithesis of the movable feast we find in Cunningham's choreography where the stage space is entirely decentralized, where center stage no longer possesses any privileged pride of place. Note that for a modern dance choreographer such as Doris Humphrey, stage center *naturally* commands our attention in a way that stage left or right do not:

> I have often tried to estimate the number of forces operating on the center of a stage and never quite decided on the whole array. I should say there are at least eleven lines converging on it, plus the psychological security of the symmetrical design. This, commonly called by its misnomer, "dead center" is without doubt the most powerful single spot on the stage. (1959, 76)

But for Cunningham, no single spot is more sacred, powerful, central, or "rooted" than any other. The most extreme example of Cunningham's rejection of "roots" is one that we'll examine more fully in Chapter 8: his interest in what might be called "global village collages" (e.g., the 1982 performance in which Cunningham danced in his Westbeth Studio accompanied by a sound score of Jerry Hunt's being transmitted live over the phone lines from Texas). These collage performances proceed on the assumption that no one spot can ever constitute the "center" of the universe, that there are an infinite number of other locations and other perspectives—and that one can aspire to inhabit two or more such locations simultaneously.

The deep rootedness of the tribal village gives way to the relativism and simultaneity of the global village. Primitivist conceptions of wholeness are usually based on exclusion rather than inclusion. That is: one's experience *feels* "whole" precisely because it excludes large chunks of worldly experience that would fail to smoothly mesh with it. Cunningham and Cage by contrast, embrace a radical openness toward complexity and "difference."

Consider this famous exchange between Cage and the biologist C. H. Waddington:

> Waddington: I have a feeling that at present the world has lost a sense of unity at almost all scales, from the individual through these intermediate neighborhood groupings right up to the world scale. The question is, do you need to re-create the sense of unity?
>
> Cage: I would rather have "open-ness," not unity or wholeness but open-ness— and open-ness particularly to things with which I am unfamiliar. I think that in society the stranger has always had a great integrating effect. (Kostelanetz 1988, 258–59)

Let's conclude this chapter with an image of Cunningham-in-motion that exemplifies this global rootlessness. At the Museum of Modern Art in 1971, Cunningham danced his eccentric solo "Loops" in front of one of Jasper Johns's "Map" paintings, based on Buckminster Fuller's Dymaxion Airocean Projection of the Globe. Fuller divided the surface of the earth into 20 equilateral spherical triangles in order to produce the most "objective," least distorted, two-dimensional projection of the globe to date. And in much the same way that Fuller and Johns flatten out the earth with scrupulous objectivity, Cunningham danced in a rootless way that demonstrated no special preference for any one spot. In his 1998 book *Routes: Travel and Translation in the Late Twentieth Century,* the anthropologist James Clifford outlines a "decentered" conception of cultural interconnectedness in which the older concept of "roots" gives way to the newer concept of "routes"— visualized as a dense network of motion, collision, varying interaction, and above all, circulation. Back in 1971, Cunningham was "mapping" a vision of the earth that anticipates by almost 30 years the postmodern (and post-primitivist) anthropology of thinkers such as Clifford.

1. *Trackers* (1991) © Lawrence Ivy, courtesy of the Cunningham Dance Foundation. Dancers L to R: Michael Cole, Merce Cunningham, Jean Freebury (lifted), Carol Teitelbaum, Foofwa d'Imobilité

2. *Variations V* (1965) © Hervé Gloaguen, courtesy of the Cunningham Dance Foundation. Film projections by Stan VanDerBeek, video distortions by Nam June Paik, musicians and dancers, L to R, foreground to background: John Cage, David Tudor, Gordon Mumma, Carolyn Brown, Merce Cunningham, Barbara Dilley Lloyd

3. *Minutiae* (1954) © John Ross, courtesy of the Cunningham Dance Foundation. Decor by Robert Rauschenberg. Dancer in center: Remy Charlip

4. Cunningham with LifeForms figure on computer screen, © Edward Santalone, courtesy of the Cunningham Dance Foundation

5. *Tread* (1970) ⓒ James Klosty, courtesy of the Cunningham Dance Foundation. Decor by Bruce Nauman, dancers L to R: Merce Cunningham, Meg Harper, Mel Wong, Jeff Slayton, Carolyn Brown

6. *Rainforest* (1968) ⓒ James Klosty, courtesy of the Cunningham Dance Foundation. Decor by Andy Warhol, dancers: Merce Cunningham and Meg Harper

7. *Travelogue* (1977) © Jack Vartoogian. Dancers L to R: Merce Cunningham, Julie Roess-Smith, Ellen Cornfield, Robert Kovich, Karole Armitage, Meg Harper. Decor by Robert Rauschenberg.

8. *Fabrications* (1987) © Jack Vartoogian. Decor and costumes by Dove Bradshaw, dancers L to R: Alan Good, Chris Komar, Merce Cunningham

9. *BIPED* (1999) © Stephanie Berger. Digital imagery by Paul Kaiser and Shelley Eshkar. Dancers: Cheryl Therrien (right), Matthew Mohr (center), Jean Freebury (back)

10. *Suite for Five* (1956) © Marvin Silver, courtesy of the Cunningham Dance Foundation. Dancers L to R: Viola Farber, Carolyn Brown, Merce Cunningham, Barbara Dilley Lloyd

11. *Walkaround Time* (1968) © Oscar Bailey, courtesy of the Cunningham Dance Foundation. Decor by Jasper Johns ("after" Marcel Duchamp), dancers L to R: Carolyn Brown, Valda Setterfield, Meg Harper, Gus Solomons, Jr., Merce Cunningham

12. *Noctures* (1956) © Louis Stevenson, courtesy of the Cunningham Dance Foundation. Dancers L to R: Viola Farber, Bruce King, Remy Charlip, Carolyn Brown, Merce Cunningham

13. Jasper Johns's *Target* poster, 1968

14. *Root of an Unfocus* (1944) Merce Cunningham, © Barbara Morgan, Barbara Morgan Archive

15. *Grant Central Event* (October 9, 1987) © Tom Brazil, dancers L to R: Helen Barrow, Merce Cunningham, Dennis O'Connor

7
The Sound of Perceptual Freedom

If one feels protective about the word "music," protect it and find another word for all the rest that enters through the ears.
—John Cage (Quoted by Fisher, 1998, 167)

"I'm trying to fix it so we both can listen at once . . . Here, hold this phone to your ear. Do you hear anything?"
"Yes, static."
"Good."
—William S. Burroughs, *The Ticket That Exploded* (1987, 111)

The Germanic Context

Cage's critique of "wholeness" is also a critique of the specifically Germanic context in which the theory and practice of the Gestamtkunwerk first evolved. When Cage argues that "the stranger has always had a great integrating effect," he is explicitly criticizing the connection between the German "hunger for wholeness" and a craving for racial purity. Indeed, it often appeared as if Cage's self-appointed mission was to free the musical world from the influence of Germanic ideas about "unity" (even if he saves some of his strongest criticism for non-German practitioners of this "essentially" German idea):

> I think our teaching, and our ideas, particularly about music, have become controlled mostly by German ideas and you still see it. The other day, I picked up the lecture Stravinsky gave at Harvard University. . . . He said that the thing that interested him was unity in the situation of variety, and he wanted to find the single thing that brought together all the differences. And he recognized this

as an ideal which he believed. We all believe it until we begin to examine it. When we examine it, we see it is a purely German idea, it's a fascist idea really, which wants to find not the blackness in the black and the whiteness in the white, but wants to find the whiteness in the blacks too, and wants everything to be white. (Kostelanetz 1988, 280)

Cage was once asked the following question about his extraordinarily dense score for "Roaratorio": "Putting all these sounds together, aren't you afraid that you're going to get white noise?" His response: "I'm sure that it will be noise, but I doubt that it will be white."

Surely, Cage would have objected strenuously to much of the work created by German modern dance choreographers during the 1930s. Consider the 1930 collaboration between Mary Wigman and Albert Talhoff, a work called "Totenmal" ("Call of the Dead"). "Totenmal" was a Wagnerian exercise in "total" theater, combining the resources of a movement choir, speaking choir, and a light organ. Appropriately, it was hailed by a number of critics as the most complete realization to date of the Wagnerian Gesamtkunstwerk. Significantly, Talhoff, in his preface to the published text, claimed that he had consciously set out to create an alternative to "the political theater" of Bertolt Brecht. Listen to this description by an American journalist of the "emotional crescendo," which constituted the climax of the work:

> The light organ changed from dull to high, strong colors, the chanting grew in volume, the cymbals crashed, the organ blared red, and the mourners [the speaking choir] stood straight with their arms held high in token of victory and belief. An emotionally exhausted audience staggered to its feet. (Manning 1993, 157)

Obviously, the model for this sort of artistic fusion is the Wagnerian Gesamtkunstwerk.

Dalcroze and Eurhythmics

But when it comes to evaluating Cage's influence on the relation between music and dance, there's another figure we need to consider: Emile Jacques-Dalcroze, a Swiss-born, turn-of-the-century composer and theoretician who was instrumental in helping to translate Wagner's ideas about artistic synthesis into practice. Dalcroze founded a system of musical education called eurhythmics that exerted a profound influence on Mary Wigman and German modern dance more generally (as well as on the way in which Wagnerian opera was performed).

Dalcroze's eurhythmics—which sought to make the performer's body instantaneously responsive to musical stimuli—can be thought of as the very antithesis of Cunningham's and Cage's ideas about the relationship between music and dance. Originally intended for instrumentalists, eurhythmics combined gymnastics with the study of rhythm in the hope of physicalizing the student's understanding of music. Dalcroze believed that conventional musical training made a fundamental error in handing the student a musical instrument before he or she had physically internalized a concept of rhythm. For Dalcroze, the all-important first step in true musical education was a somatic experience of music involving the ear, the mind, and the entire body. The goal of the exercises he devised (which he called "rhythmic gymnastics") was to make the performer instantaneously and unselfconsciously responsive to musical rhythm. In his own words, "the aim was not to *interpret* music, but to *translate* it into direct physical embodiment." Eurhythmics thus seeks to minimize the interval between musical stimulus and physical response (the same interval, in other words, that both Brecht and Cunningham sought to strengthen and extend.)

Dalcroze, who later opened a school at Hellerau, quickly became a key figure in the history of dance pedagogy as well as music education. Indeed, his goal of *instantaneous responsiveness* to the beat served to further the aims of dance-world primitivism. Eurhythmics for example, played an important role in the rehearsal process for the mother of all primitivist works, the Nijinsky/Stravinsky "Le Sacre du Printemps" of 1913. Diaghilev hired Marie Rambert (who had studied under Dalcroze) to teach eurhythmics to the dancers who were struggling with the rhythmic complexity of Stravinsky's score. Rambert later observed that "Nijinsky wanted every note of the music interpreted"; and eurhythmics has often been pejoratively associated with excessively literal, step-for-note correspondences.

But, more important, Dalcroze's ideas exerted a considerable influence on productions of Wagner as well as on German modern dance. As Clark Rogers has argued, it was the *controlling discipline* of eurhythmics that enabled the director-designer Adolpe Appia (the artist whose name is most often mentioned in conjunction with Dalcroze) to solve the Wagnerian puzzle (i.e., how does one, *in practice*, achieve a seamless integration of the elements?). For Appia, the true Gesamtkunstwerk could only be achieved by insisting that every element of production surrender its autonomy to a single directorial "auteur." (This of course is the antithesis of the "separation of the elements" we find in Brecht—not to mention the genuine autonomy, the mutual coexistence, of collaborative activities we find in Cunningham's dances.) Note what Rogers says about the way in which Appia made eurhythmics central to his concept of Wagnerian wholeness: "All liberty is taken from the performer; music controls his every action, his every utterance" (1969, 22). And Appia—in a quote that would surely have pleased the Third Reich's rhetoricians—once argued that "... the life of the body tends to anarchy, then to ugliness; and it is music which must free it by imposing its discipline" (25–26).

Although it was actually designed by Heinrich Tessenow, Appia is generally regarded as the "spiritual father" of the large hall, the student festival space at Dalcroze's German school in Hellerau, which was dubbed by some observers "the Bayreuth of Modern Dance." (It was there that Wigman studied with Dalcroze.) Appia and Dalcroze collaborated on a number of productions including Gluck's *Orpheus and Eurydice* and Claudel's *Annunciation*, both of which were performed as part of the Hellerau Festival in 1913. (Wigman danced in the chorus of that production of *Orpheus*.) Selma Odom quotes a student who says of those years: "We were hearing and seeing how music, movement, and light melted into an harmonious whole." And in her next sentence, Odom observes, "Working in this innovative spatial environment must have been one of the most stimulating experiences of Mary Wigman's second year at the Bildungsanstalt Jacques-Dalcroze" (1986, 43). Susan Manning's description of the 1913 *Orpheus* emphasizes the word "integration":

> Integrating the performers and spectators within a single continuous space, Appia's novel theater design intended to involve the spectator in the production. . . . The integration of spectator and performer found an analog in the integration of formal elements: actor and chorus, music and movement, space and light. (1993, 75–76)

Behaviorism, Music, and Mediation

The connection that Dalcroze set out to forge between musical stimulus and muscular response is virtually Pavlovian. For Dalcroze, stimulus corresponds to music, and response to movement. Eurhythmics is the key to eliciting an involuntary response—a prereflective muscular reaction—from both the performer and the spectator. Dalcroze spoke of his desire "to play on this marvelous keyboard which is the muscular and nervous system" (Rogers 1969, 26). Behavioristic psychology and eurhythmics both radically devalue the role of consciousness as a mediating force between stimulus and response: As B. F. Skinner writes in *Beyond Freedom and Dignity:* "We can follow the path taken by physics and biology by turning directly to the relation between behavior and environment and neglecting supposed mediating states of mind" (1972, 15). But Cunningham insists that consciousness function as a *buffer* between musical stimuli and muscular response. He does not "follow the [Pavlovian-Skinnerian] path taken by biology . . . " (nor did Duchamp when he argued that "the direction in which art should turn is to an intellectual expression rather than an animal expression" [d'Harnoncourt 1973, 16)]. Here we return yet again to one of our central ideas: Those "mediating states of mind" that both dancers and audience-members cultivate during a Cunningham performance are another variation on the dandy's "unshakable determination not to be moved." Cage's unwillingness to be "pushed around" by other artists, to be cowed or wowed into submission, also exemplifies this attitude.

The necessity of cultivating a sensibility akin to dandified detachment is chillingly apparent in Carolyn Brown's recollection of what it was like to carefully rehearse Cunningham's choreography for many weeks in silence—and then suddenly (during dress rehearsal or first performance) find herself subjected to a relentless sensory assault from both sound and light:

> Usually we would hear the music and feel the lighting in the first performance. I will not pretend that this is not extremely difficult for the dancers. Loudness, especially unexpected loudness, affects the inner ear, the seat of balance, of equilibrium. Continual loudness can make one irritable, nauseous, even faint. Brilliant light which comes on suddenly can momentarily blind and disorient the dancer and that too affects the balance, and makes quick-moving exits hazardous; darkness cripples one's sense of space and therefore the fullness of the movement itself. (Klosty 1975, 28)

But the challenge of course, is to resist those external stimuli, to sustain an unshakable determination *not* to be moved. The contrast between Cunningham and Dalcroze could hardly be more pronounced in this regard. If Dalcroze sought to minimize the distance (and the difference) between musical stimuli and muscular response, then Cunningham seeks to maximize the physical and psychological space "in between."

Cunningham and Music

Again, it's instructive to compare Cunningham's attitude toward music with that of the pioneers of modern dance, beginning with Duncan, who conceived of choreography as the art of responding intuitively to musical inspiration: "Listen to the music with your souls," she told her students: "Now while listening do you not feel an inner self awakening deep within you—that it is by its strength that your head is lifted, that your arms are raised, that you are walking slowly toward the light?" (1927, 44).

But for Cunningham, it's not the force of musical inspiration that sets his dancers in motion; it's an act of conscious deliberation. Cunningham dancers are self-motivated movers. In a work like "Variations V" (1965), Cunningham explicitly calls our attention to the fact that the movement is in no way propelled or generated by sound. Here the stage is wired with photoelectric cells and 12 electronically sensitive pole-shaped (Thereminlike) antennae that produce sounds only when the dancers sweep past them. For "TV Rerun" in 1972, Gordon Mumma's score required that the dancers wear "telemetry belts" that transmitted movement-generated signals which he then further manipulated electronically. In Cunningham's solo "Loops" the previous year, Mumma had used FM Telemetry to amplify Cunningham's breathing and heartbeat as he danced. And in "10's With Shoes" in 1981, the sound designer Martin Kalve lined the stage with microphones that amplified the sound of the performer's jazz shoes brushing against the floor. David Tudor's score for "Polarity" (1990) bounced radar and ultrasonic frequencies off of metal strips attached to the dancer's costumes.

Regardless of where or how the sound originates in a Cunningham dance, it rarely, if ever, appears to *drive* the movement. In part, that's because the typical Cunningham sound score is anything but "propulsive" (distracting, to be sure; but rarely propulsive). One characteristic that much of the music of Cage, Brown, Wolff, and Feldman have in common is a tendency toward stillness, an absence of progressions that drive inexorably toward climax or completion. (This is especially true of Feldman's music. He's the unchallenged master of the "quiet" piece.) The result is a spatial field of calm, free-floating sound, interrupted occasionally by an abrupt, disruptive change of pitch or volume. (Often what we hear are "sustaining" sounds, initiated without attack, remaining constant in pitch.) Stockhausen became a great fan of Feldman's and once asked the composer for his "secret." Feldman's response was exemplary: "I don't push the sounds around" (Gann 1997, 145), he said, virtually paraphrasing Cage's famous desire to "let sounds be themselves." Cage's instructions to his musicians often specify "no vibrato, no attack," and he sometimes asks that sounds be "brushed" in and out of existence. As we'll see, the composer who exerted perhaps the greatest influence on Cage was Satie; and nothing is more characteristic of Satie's music than a similar indifference toward propulsion and drive.

Cunningham emphasizes the extent to which his dancers are propelled only by their own willpower and concentration: "When you do not work to music or to a pulse to push you, you must in a sense push yourself, you must be your own horse rather than have something outside of you be the horse . . . " (1985, 130). This is more than a matter of not performing *to* music. As attested to so poignantly by Carolyn Brown, Cunningham dancers must concentrate in such a way so as not to be literally or figuratively thrown off-balance by the sounds they hear. No doubt, this is part of what Brown meant when she said that Cunningham technique "is designed to develop flexibility in the mind as well as in the body" (Klosty 1975, 22). James Klosty elaborates on her point:

> Traditional ballet is a far more Dionysian enterprise, for the dancer can ride the musical pulse, using it as a kind of surrogate heartbeat on which bodily functions play without consciousness. Absence of metrical accompaniment only

intensifies the mental effort needed to establish the strict order that supports each dancer's part. Cunningham's dancing is a rigorously Apollonian activity: it is the dancer, not the music, who recreates the spatial and temporal structure that is each dance. To perform a work of several sections, each several minutes in duration, with one's muscular memory the only "clock," and to come within seconds of the required time at each performance, is a task no Dionysian would contemplate—nor attempt—nor accomplish. (1975, 12)

At least not as long as Cunningham is standing in the wings with a stop-watch! (In the 1994 "Ocean," the exact duration of the dance—90 minutes—was ticked off, second by second, on video monitors visible to the entire audience.) Referring to the seminal "Suite for Five in Space and Time" (1956), Cunningham has written, "This was one of the first dances where meter was completely abandoned, and we, the dancers had to rely on our own dance timing to guard the length of any phrase, and the timing of the complete dance" (Vaughan 1997, 91). No doubt the ultra-articulate look of Cunningham technique derives in part from the absolute clarity with which the dancers must accentuate the metrical values of each phrase, independent of ancillary, musical "punctuation."

Even in pre-Cunningham modern dance, where it's not uncommon for a musical score to be composed after the movement has been choreographed, the dancer in performance moves just as fully *to the music* as does the ballet dancer. And the goal for both is often to eliminate or minimize the length of the interval between musical stimulus and bodily response. This is where the contrast between Cunningham and Dalcroze becomes most fully apparent. What emerges is a fundamentally different attitude toward the relationship between music and the consciousness of the dancer.

There is one great exception to this rule, Cunningham's "Sounddance," created in 1975. But it's the sort of exception that *proves* the rule. Every-thing about this work, beginning with its title, is a deviation from the norm. The inspiration is Joyce's famous line from *Finnegan's Wake*, "In the be-ginning was the sounddance." Note the way it alludes—in true primitivist fashion—to the beginning, to a point in time when "sound" and "dance" were inextricably connected. (Indeed, in Joyce's typography, they *are* phys-ically connected.) And Tudor's score–appropriately titled "Toneburst"—is a relentlessly sustained *burst* of percussive tones, providing a machine-gun-like pulse that *appears* to animate the movement from beginning to end. The piece concludes with an image of the dancers caught up in a great whirl-wind that seems to suck them into the upstage canvas assemblage which constitutes the piece's decor.

Needless to say, melody is even harder to come by in the typical Cunningham sound score than rhythmic regularity. (If ever a composer was uninterested in melody, that composer is John Cage.) But ironically, the scores that most clearly highlight the autonomy of movement and sound are those that contain a distant echo or deeply buried "trace" of melody. For example, Cage's "Improvisation IV," the score for Cunningham's "Fielding Sixes" (1981), is a rerecorded arrangement—some might call it a derangement—of traditional Irish fiddle and bagpipe music. The moment we realize that what we're listening to began its auditory life as an Irish melody, the dancers' obliviousness to that melodic line, however faint, becomes all the more apparent. Much the same is true of Conlon Nancarrow's extraordinary score for "Crises" (1960) in which the composer uses three player pianos to distort (almost, but not quite, beyond recognition) a number of jazz and pop melodies. Similarly, a distant flavor of flamenco is audible in Takesha Kosugi's score ("Spectra") for Cunningham's "Cargo X" in 1989. Here, acoustic sound sources are fed into electronic processors. One source of "input" is a performer imitating an audio tape of flamenco singing. However, these three scores are—like "Sounddance"—anomalies in the Cunningham canon. But even when the Cunningham/Cage "separation of the elements" doesn't call attention to itself in this overt way, one still doesn't experience the sort of "closure"—the sense of organic unity—that results from a seamless, Wagnerian collaboration.

There is another, fundamental difference between a Cunningham/Cage collaboration and the musical structure of Wagnerian Gesamtkunstwerk: the absence of a structural principle similar to the Leitmotif. For Wagner, the "leading motive" or recurring musical theme is an important strategy for lending coherence and organic unity to a large-scale work that unfolds in time (in Wagner's case, extreme lengths of time). One thinks of the three-note death theme in *Tristan and Isolde* or the horn call in the second act of *Siegfried*, which transmutes from 6/8 to 4/4 time as it reappears in *The Twilight of the Gods*. Significantly when Berlioz utilized the rudiments of the leitmotif in his "Symphonie Fantastique," he referred to it as the "idée fixe." There is nothing more inimical to the spirit of Cunningham and Cage than the "fixed idea."

The Influence of Satie

By far the most revealing exceptions to the rule of complete-autonomy-between-sound-and movement in the Cunningham oeuvre are the many dances that Cunningham has choreographed over the years to the music of Satie. In each case, Cunningham was inspired by an already existing score, and he then choreographed a dance *to* it. (Between 1944 and 1953, Cunningham choreographed no fewer than seven works to music by Satie, a number exceeded during that period only by the sum total of his dances accompanied by the music of Cage.) Indeed, even after Cunningham and

Cage had formalized their ideas about the relationship between sound and movement, Cunningham was willing to make an exception when it came to the music of Satie: "Septet" (1953) and "Noctures" (1956) were both "set" to scores by Satie, although neither exhibited the sort of insistent step-per-note correspondence one associates with eurhythmics. (Still, many of those whose first experience of "Septet" was the White Oak revival of 1996 were startled by the number of light jumps that appeared to be directly propelled by individual notes in the score. The experience felt so uncharacteristic that for some audience members, it was no less strange than imagining a Balanchine ballet performed in silence.) "Septet" is choreographed to one of Satie's most innovative compositions, "Trois morceaux en forme de poire" ("Three Pieces in the Form of a Pear"), a work that bears no obvious relationship to either pears or the number three. (It's actually divided into seven parts and takes the form of a "collage" of already existing, shorter pieces.) Roger Shattuck, in his superb study of Satie (in *The Banquet Years*), suggests that "Insofar as it is possible in Western music, Satie was approaching a style of disjunction, of separation rather than unity of parts" (1968, 128).

Satie was also instrumental in encouraging Debussy and Ravel to extricate themselves from the (then) seemingly inescapable influence of Wagner. Satie is arguably the most anti-Wagnerian composer of all time. It's also worth noting that it was Satie's score for The Ballets Russes's "Parade" in 1917 that marked the end of Diaghilev's early infatuation with the concept of the Gesamtkunstwerk. As Lincoln Kirstein and others have pointed out, "Parade" also marked the end of the "first phase" of The Ballets Russes, the period characterized by exoticizing primitivism. According to Kirstein:

> L'ame slave, the Slavic soul—alien, quasi-barbaric, mystical—was effaced by l'originalité outrancière, outrageous, unprecedented novelty. "Parade's" originality also lay in its reduced, domestic, anti-opera house scale. (1970, 210)

Time-Length as Structure

For Cage, the great revelation to be found in the music of Satie was the idea that "time-length" can function as *the* fundamental ordering principle of musical structure. (And, of course, he and Cunningham would eventually decide that "time-length" is the only thing that movement and music need to share with one another.) In his notorious 1948 "Defense of Satie," Cage wrote:

> In the field of structure, the field of the definition of parts and their relation to a whole, there has been only one new idea since Beethoven. And that new idea can be perceived in the work of Anton Webern and Erik Satie. With Beethoven the parts of a composition were defined by means of harmony. With Satie and

> Webern they are defined by means of time-lengths . . . If you consider that sound
> is characterized by its pitch, its loudness, its timbre, and its duration, and that
> silence, which is the opposite and, therefore, the necessary partner of sound, is
> characterized only by its duration, you will be drawn to the conclusion that of
> the four characteristics of the material of music, duration, that is, time length,
> is the most fundamental. Silence cannot be heard in terms of pitch or harmony:
> It is heard in terms of time length. (Kostelanetz 1970, 81)

The idea of a "rhythmic structure based on the duration, not of notes, but
of spaces of time" was to Cage what the 12-tone method of composition
had been to his teacher, Schoenberg. Both composers were thus freed from
dependence on a harmonic system.

This concept had a profound influence on Cunningham as well. Speaking of his seminal 1944 performance at the Humphrey-Weidman studio in
New York, Cunningham has said, "I date my beginning from this concert."
He understood—even then, while he was still a member of the Graham
company—that his work on that program had more in common with the
objectivist time structures of Cage than with the emotion-drenched psychology of Graham:

> A lot of modern-dance people in the audience liked one of my dances on that
> program—the one called "Root of an Unfocus"—because it seemed to them to
> be tied to an emotional meaning. They thought it had to do with fear. It had
> nothing directly to do with fear as far as I was concerned. The main thing about
> it—and the thing everybody missed—was that its structure was based on time,
> in the same sense that a radio show is. It was divided into time units, and the
> dance and the music would come together at the beginning and the end of each
> unit, but in between they would be independent of each other. This was the
> beginning of the idea that music and dance could be dissociated, and from this
> point on the dissociation in our work just got wider and wider. (Tomkins 1968,
> 244–245)

Significantly, the "root" in "Root of an Unfocus" referred not to a
deep, inner core of emotion from which the dance evolved, but rather to
the numerical concept of "square roots" that governed its time structure.
"Root of an Unfocus," had three sections, with three different time lengths
(90 seconds, 180 seconds, 60 seconds). The tempo of each section varied
as well (starting from an original phrase of eight beats, ten beats, or six
beats). But the music and the dance "came together" only at key "structural
points." By the time of "Antic Meet" in 1958 (the music for which was Cage's
"Concert for Piano and Orchestra"), the only point of "agreement" between
Cunningham and Cage was the total time length of the piece (26 minutes).
There were no longer any predetermined points at which the music and the
dance coincided. In Cunningham's words, "The dancers' unsupported time
span was expanding" (Vaughan, 1997, 106).

Thus far, we've talked mostly about the *relationship* between sound and movement in Cunningham's dances. In the next section of this chapter, we'll examine the *quality* of the sound that accompanies Cunningham's choreography and the way in which that sound-quality contributes to the repudiation of primitivist wholeness.

Electronics, Noise, and Randomness

Let's begin by examining John Cage's relationship to the broader history of electronic music. The early 1950s was the period in which composers first began to make extensive use of audiotape. (Cage was first introduced to composition-on-tape by Pierre Schaeffer in Paris in the late 1940s.) The subsequent introduction of high-speed digital computers and synthesizers (most famously, Robert Moog's) appealed to composers who wanted to eliminate from performance the contingencies and variables inevitably introduced by human instrumentalists (i.e., they sought a higher degree of control over frequency, timbre, duration, amplitude, etc.).

But, Cage's employment of these technologies differed markedly from that of composers like Milton Babbitt or Karlheinz Stockhausen, for whom electronic technology functioned as a means by which the composer could assume ever increasing degrees of control over sound. (Although Stockhausen, under the influence of Cage, would eventually grant his performers a greater and greater role in determining certain key "parameters" of each piece.) For Babbitt and Stockhausen, the essential goal was to reconcile the new world of electronic sound with the discipline of strict serial structure, employing highly ordered groups of pitches and rhythms. In the 1950s, Stockhausen even coedited a journal call *Die Reihe* ("The Row"), which advocated a structure at least as rigorous as that employed by the 12-tone compositions of Schoenberg. (The "tone-row" consists of all 12 notes of the chromatic scale.) Stockhausen went considerably further than Schoenberg, who was focused primarily on the ordering of pitch; Stockhausen advocated a total serialism that applied to all musical paramenters. (One row would inform all the "variables" in each piece.) But Cage, despite his growing interest in electronics, never aspired to a comparable degree of control. Hence his growing commitment to *indeterminacy*—which deserves to be distinguished from his long-standing reliance on chance operations:

> I try to arrange my composing means so that I won't have any knowledge of what might happen. And that, by the way, is what you might call the technical difference between indeterminacy and chance operations. In the case of chance operations, one knows more or less the elements of the universe with which one is dealing, whereas in indeterminacy, I like to think ... that I'm outside the circle

> of a known universe and dealing with things I literally don't know anything
> about. (Kostelanetz 1970, 141)

And how does Cage accomplish this? For starters, the music he composed
or commissioned for the Cunningham company tends to feature *live*, rather
than prerecorded, electronic sound. (It was Cage and Tudor who inaugu-
rated the era of live electronic music in 1939 with their "Imaginary Landscape
No.1" during which they manipulated variable-speed phono turntables.) In
1951, Cage created "Imaginary Landscape No. 4," which utilizes 12 "live"
radios. (Each was operated by two performers, one of whom scanned the
wavelength, the second of whom varied the volume.) The radio became one
of Cage's favorite devices for infusing the performance space with "indeterminate" sounds that escaped his control. (Similiarly, Rauschenberg would
later incorporate radios into his mixed-media works like "Oracle" in the
1960s.)

Cut-Ups

Even Cage's fixed-tape works—which result in an "object" (independent of
site-specific, never-to-be-repeated, performative circumstances)—inhabit
a very different universe than those of a strict serialist composer such as
Babbitt. For example, in Babbitt's masterful "Ensembles for Synthesizer," the
values of frequency, amplitude, duration, and so on, are all determined in
advance of the recording. The completed tape required virtually no editing.
By contrast, Cage's use of tape is very different, more closely analogous
to William Burrough's "cut-ups" and "fold-ins." In other words, he utilizes
strategies for surrendering intention and for introducing "randomness" into
the system. (Randomness and "static" function in Cage's work as a means
of resisting control, habit, and conditioning.)

"Williams Mix," which Cage created in collaboration with Earle Brown,
Christian Wolff, and Morton Feldman in 1952–1953 (the same seminal time
period in which Cunningham founded his company) is one of the most elaborately "spliced" or "cut up" audiotape recordings ever composed. Cage and
his colleagues began with a vast library of recorded sounds that were divided
into various categories: city sounds, country sounds, electronic sounds,
wind-produced sounds, and so on. Using the *I Ching*, Cage experimented
with cutting and splicing the tapes at a variety of chance-dictated angles. In
one of Feldman's sections, 1,097 different sounds were spliced onto a mere
quarter inch of tape. In real time, that segment accounted for only one sixti-
eth of a second. (Cage's completed tape, which contains barely 4 minutes of
music, took almost a year to edit.) The sheer number of chance-generated
juxtapositions assures that the "original" sounds have been radically

recontextualized. Their "connotations"—even their "denotations"—are now totally dependent on their collagelike relationships with other, ever-so-tiny, tape splices. (Any "meaning" they may once have possessed is now lost in a labyrinth of reassemblage.)

It's instructive to compare "Williams Mix" with William S. Burroughs's use of the cut-up. In Burroughs's procedure, pages of text from magazines and books are cut and rearranged to form fresh combinations of word and image. (Similarly, in his later writings, Cage made a practice of fragment-ing already existing texts by Joyce, Thoreau, and others into what he calls "mesostic poems" composed largely of asyntactic phrases.) In the late 1950s and early 1960s, Burroughs also began to apply the cut-up method to au-diotape. The result was a terminally strange trilogy of "cut-up" novels: *The Soft Machine, The Ticket That Exploded,* and *The Nova Express.* The central theme of all three books is subliminal control; and Burroughs seized on the cut-up as a strategy for *resisting* control—as a method of introducing noise, randomness, and entropy into an otherwise closed and/or coercive system. (Anyone familiar with Burroughs's novels will no doubt remember Trak Enterprises, which makes an appearance as early as *Naked Lunch.* Trak's credo is "Invade, Damage, Occupy.") In retaliation against the "controllers," Burroughs utilizes the cut up in two related ways: as a compositional strategy for arranging the sequence of words on the page, and as a major thematic focus of the novels. The final section of *The Ticket That Exploded* contains the following instructions:

> record a sentence and speed it up
> now try imitating your accelerated voice
> play a sentence backwards and learn to unsay what you just said . . . such exercises
> bring you a liberation from old association locks

A few pages later he speaks of:

> the physiological liberation achieved as word lines of controlled association are
> cut . . . that gray veil was the prerecorded words of a control machine
> once that veil is removed you will see clearer and sharper than those who are
> behind the veil.

"A tape recorder," Burroughs writes:

> is an externalized section of the human nervous system. You can find out more
> about the nervous system and gain more control over your reaction by using a
> tape recorder than you could find out sitting twenty years in the lotus position.
> (Sobieszek, 21)

One can imagine how appealing this comparison must have been to Cage and Cunningham. Recall Cage's anecdote about Cunningham "changing his mind" after experiencing an unexplained surge of energy while sitting in the lotus position.

Burroughs's most ambitious employment of the cut-up philosophy is probably his concept of the "Writing Machine" that appears in *The Ticket That Exploded*. This is a contraption that produces cut-up texts without any human input:

> A writing machine that shifts one half one text and half the other through a page frame on conveyer belts—(The proportion of half one text half the other is important corresponding as it does to the two half's of the human organism) Shakespeare, Rimbaud, etc. permutating through page frames in constantly changing juxtaposition
> the machine spits out books and plays and poems.

Although their temperaments were very, very different (Burroughs's work is hallucinatory, phantasmagoric, overtly homoerotic, and apocalyptic), I believe that Burroughs is the figure who comes closest to articulating the way noise and randomness function in Cage and Cunningham's work. Burroughs, like Cage and Cunningham, is well aware of the fact that what "feels" spontaneous may well be culturally conditioned. "You record, say, ten minutes on the recorder," he once observed:

> Then you spin the reel backwards or forwards without recording. Stop at random and cut-in a phrase. How random is random? We know so much that we don't consciously know we know, that perhaps the cut-in was *not* random.

But ironically, the chance methods he utilizes for generating random-ness are much less rigorous and painstaking than those devised by Cage. (It sometimes appeared that Burroughs, unlike Cage, still believed in the liberating possibilities of surrealist-style automatism.) Here, theory and practice don't entirely coincide. On the one hand, Burroughs articulates more thoroughly than Cage a theory for explaining the ways in which randomness can subvert a variety of "control" mechanisms. But on the other hand, Cage remains the artist who really practices what Burroughs preaches. This becomes especially clear when we consider the *quality* of the sound in a typical Cage/Cunningham dance. Anyone who thinks that Cage's principle innovation was to have liberated dance music from the strait-jacket of A–B–A is missing a much more important accomplishment. Often the sound for a Cunningham dance resembles nothing so much as static, the "noise" that lies between clear signals. These are impure, not "clean" sounds, the very opposite of today's digitally mastered CD sound. Audio-feedback for example, is often "welcomed" (with open ears) into the perfor-mance. Similarly, Burroughs "signals" his approval of such practices in the passage from *The Ticket That Exploded* that serves as an epigraph for this chapter:

> "I'm trying to fix it so we both can listen at once . . . Here, hold this phone to your ear. Do you hear anything?"
> "Yes, static."
> "Good."

Why is static good? Because it disrupts "the system." It breaks down the distinction between inside and outside, information and noise, between "wanted" and "unwanted" sound.

Many members of the Cunningham circle have acknowledged their aesthetic kinship with Burroughs. For example, Cage and Burroughs worked together on three different LPs (from the "Dial-A-Poem" series) in the 1970s; and Cunningham was the only choreographer to perform at the Nova Convention, held in honor of Burroughs in New York City in 1978. Rauschenberg embedded fragments of texts by Burroughs in the photomontages he produced for "American Pewter with Burroughs" in 1981.

What Cage and Cunningham most clearly share with artists like Burroughs is the desire to resist control—whether it's the all-too-obvious police state coerciveness of German fascism or the much less obvious, subliminal and perceptual seductiveness exercised by today's multinational corporate empires (and their propaganda wing made up of advertising and popular culture). For Burroughs, there was little or no distinction between the two. To his mind, *1984* and *Brave New World* were part and parcel of the same control mechanism. In a 1963 interview, he declared: "The Luce magazines are nothing but control mechanisms. They're about as human as a computer. Henry Luce, himself, has no control over the thing now, it's grown so large" (Sobieszek 1996, 21).

Of course, Burroughs was certifiably paranoid, a conspiracy theorist who makes Oliver Stone seem like a model of sweet reasonableness. Cunningham and Cage, to the best of my knowledge, never indulged in the sort of the sci-fi fantasies that led Burroughs to associate Big Government with Big Brother, extraterrestrials, and interplanetary conspiracies. At the very least, we need to distinguish between the genuinely totalitarian conditions Burrough's envisioned in his most paranoid fantasies and the rather different political circumstances that Cunningham and Cage actually found themselves in (where coercion is replaced by seduction). We'll explore these distinctions more fully in the final section of this book.

Sound versus Musicality

Before concluding this chapter, we need to acknowledge some important distinctions between Cunningham and Cage as well. One consequence of titling this chapter "The Sound of Perceptual Freedom" has been to limit our frame of reference to the way in which Cunningham's sound scores function as a mode of perceptual training. And throughout this section, I've employed the terms "sound score" and "music" more or less interchangeably. Thus, to some extent, I've been dodging the question that now comes unavoidably into focus: Does this "sound of perceptual freedom" have anything whatsoever to do with "musicality"? And more importantly, if the answer to that question is "no," can we still talk about the *musicality* of Cunningham's choreography? Here we need to recognize some fundamental differences between Cunningham and Cage (and this applies as well to the other composers who've worked with Cunningham over the years).

There have, of course, always been skeptics (or cynics) who've argued that Cage's most radical innovations were motivated more by a lack of conventional musical talent than by an overabundance of it. Remy Charlip, a member of the original Cunningham company, once suggested that "John couldn't keep the beat or follow the phrasing of the dancing. And that's how indeterminacy began" (Brown, Charlip, et al. 1992, 52). Even among self-professed Cage enthusiasts, there are—if the truth be told—many individuals who would greatly prefer to write or talk about his music than to actually sit down and *listen* to it. Indeed, some of Cage's most fervent admirers would probably agree with Arnold Schoenberg's estimation of his "most interesting" American pupil: "He's not a composer," argued Schoenberg, "but he's an inventor—of genius" (Tomkins 1968, 85). Perhaps we should say of Cage—as Mark Twain said of Wagner—"His music is better than it sounds." To my mind, the fairest assessment of Cage's ultimate place in the musical firmament comes from Richard Kostelanetz. Writing in 1969, Kostelanetz emphasized the importance of evaluating Cage's work in the context of other performative elements:

> Rather than, as some antagonists would have it, abandoning inept musical composition for "stunts," Cage became the true master of mixed-means musical theater, perhaps the most valid American species of "opera." ... To my sensibility, these recent pieces are far more interesting and valid as theater of mixed means ... than as purely aural art; compared with Milton Babbitt's or Elliott Carter's music, they seem feeble indeed. For that reason, not only are records of certain recent Cage works, such as "Variations IV" invariably embarrassing; but, in confronting a live experience of these pieces, one quickly discovers that purely musical values and categories do not provide satisfactory and/or relevant perceptual expectations or critical standards. (1970, 204)

I agree, but I would also add that even Cage's severest detractors would be hard pressed to deny the beauty (and inherent musicality) of say, "The Perilous Night" (1943–44; one of his finest early works for the prepared piano), "Music for Marcel Duchamp" (1947), "Sonatas and Interludes" (1946–48), or his "String Quartet in Four Parts" (1949–50). This list could continue on for quite some time. These works are all conventionally notated. Structural principles—rhythms, dynamics, harmonic images—are easily identified. The form is often "micro-macrocosmic," (e.g., in the "Sonatas and Interludes" each movement can be divided into rhythmic units whose structure is duplicated by the larger work that contains it). But following Cage's discovery of chance operations and indeterminacy in the 1950s, his scores gradually abandoned all audibly discernable forms of musical structure. And herein we begin to encounter a major difference between Cunningham's choreography and Cage's scores: The eradicating of the distinction between "music" and "noise" has no exact equivalent in the vast majority of Cunningham's dances. Cunningham's movement vocabulary remains, for the most part, highly technical and virtuosic—immediately recognizable in other words, as "dancerly." With the exception of the "found movement" sequences in "Collage," "Walkaround Time," and a handful of other works, Cunningham rarely opens the floodgates of movement in the same way that Cage so eagerly opened the floodgates of sound.

True, Cunningham "subjects" his movement phrases to a whole arsenal of impersonal, chance dictated-operations; but the phrases remain recognizably *his*. Chance for Cunningham is a strategy for transcending the limitations of his own taste, not a recipe for completely abandoning his likes and dislikes. Thus, when considering the way Cunningham uses chance-operations, we should always bear in mind the implications of Louis Pasteur's famous aphorism: "Chance favors the prepared mind." Cage, by contrast, *did* eventually attempt to completely suspend his desires (as well as his aversions); and the result was often sound with no recognizable signature. In *For the Birds*, Cage tells of the following experience he once had at a party: "As I was coming into the house, I noticed that some very interesting music was being played. After one or two drinks, I asked my hostess what music it was. She said, 'You can't be serious?'" (Hyde 1998, 146). Needless to say, the music was his. By contrast, it's difficult to imagine Cunningham catching a glimpse of his own work on television and failing to recognize it.

But there exists an even more fundamental difference between Cunningham's and Cage's approach to "musicality," and it can be summed up in a single word: rhythm. Cunningham's choreography is—in and of itself—inherently (indeed, *unfailingly)* rhythmic. Cunningham has always insisted that musicality in dance is not dependent on musical accompaniment in the conventional sense. Speaking of a performance that took place in 1951, Cunningham recalls:

> Years ago I gave two or three dances one evening in some small place on Martha's Vineyard. There was no music at all. Afterward, a lady in the audience came up and asked how could I possibly do this dancing without music, because there was no rhythm. At that particular moment, in this funny, dark little place, a gorgeous moth flew in and began moving in the most spectacular way around the one light. And I just pointed. (Tomkins 1994, 74)

Cunningham is undoubtedly the only major (i.e., world-class) choreographer who doesn't rely on music as a primary inspiration. But, as Don Daniels once observed,

> Dance metrics govern Cunningham's work, aid in its production, sometimes even become the preponderant expressive element out of several (attack, dynamics, plastique, etc.) I know trained dancers (with no background in Cunningham classroom training) who say they can "count" a Cunningham dance while watching it being performed. (1992, 160)

Valda Setterfield recalls that "The rhythms were always so incredibly strong. The audience may not have heard anything, but the rhythms were pounding in our blood" (Brown 1992, 107). Nancy Dalva offers an intriguing theory about the source of this inherent musicality:

> Always—on stage, on film, in videos, and in rehearsal—the dancers seem to be dancing to something—keeping up with it, slowing down to it—their phrasing exquisite and driven. By what? By the sound—or the memory—of Cunningham's own snapping and clapping. Merce Cunningham works with a stopwatch. He is the White Rabbit (I'm late! I'm late!) of choreographers, and in his own way the most musical of all. One could see this when he revived "Septet," made in 1953 to Erik Satie's Trois Morceaux en Forme de Poire. To see "Septet" is to realize that for Cunningham, working to music must be like turning on the radio when the record player is already on. It interferes with music he already hears. (Dalva 1992, 182)

Even when the auditory accompaniment falls into the category of nonmusical sound, the movement itself is likely to supply its own dynamic musical pulse. Then again, in some Cunningham dances, the very *absence* of a direct connection between music and movement can produce effects that sound both remarkably musical and dramatic. Listen to the composer Earle Brown discussing the use Cunningham made of his score for "Springweather and People" in 1955:

> When I first experienced the music and dance together, I was astonished at how effective the lack of synchronization was, dramatically—if you let yourself be taken by the drama that wasn't put into it but was there, anyway, intrinsically. An extraordinary moment in it was Merce coming out of the wings in a leap at a

point in the music when there was only one note being played on a violin. Merce flew on the one held note. A dancer other than Merce—a composer other than myself—would have supported that leap with a dramatic musical flourish. But I've always disliked what's termed Mickey Mousing the music, as in animated cartoons, where Mickey imitates the music, has a jiggly relationship with it. Merce's leap was stunning dramatically the way it joined that one violin note, much more astonishing than it would have been to anything else I could have written in order to support it. (Brown, Charlip, et al. 1992, 56)

One of the most original aspects of Cunningham's musicality is the way it relates rhythm not to music, but to changes of weight within the structure of each phrase. Note what Cunningham says about the phrasing in "Torse" (1976):

There are sixty-four phrases, because that's the number of hexagrams in the *I Ching.* The phrases are formed like the numbers themselves. For example, one has one part in it, two has two, three has three, up to sixty-four. But I didn't make it as though one were one rhythmic beat, and so forth, metrically. Let us take the second phrase, it will be clearer. The counts are related to *weight changes.* That is, if you stand on your foot, that's one; if you bend your knee, that's a weight change, so that's two. Now that could be done slowly or quickly. At sixty-four, you have sixty-four weight changes. (1985, 20–21)

Don Daniels, in the course of discussing American Ballet Theatre's production of Cunningham's "Duets" (1980), illustrates the way this approach to musicality functions in performance:

Take, for example, the perception of the metrical weight of Cunningham's dance style. By "weight" I am not referring to a physical weight used by performers in the production of Cunningham dance on stage. (Cunningham's dancers are asked to use their ballon with more variety, and more regularity, than the ballet-trained ABT dancers.) I mean something like the viewer's awareness that the dance has an insistent metrical order. (1992, 160)

In considering Cunningham's musicality, it's also worth remembering that one of the reasons he turned away from the Graham vocabulary and toward ballet was his hunger for greater rhythmic clarity and musicality. In Chapter 5, we noted that John Cage, in his seminal essay "Grace and Clarity," praised ballet for its structural clarity. But that, of course, was the John Cage of 1944, the Cage who had yet to declare, "Let us say 'Yes' to our presence together in chaos" (Retallak 1994, 255). Cage, I think it's fair to say, grew increasingly less determined to "find a form that accommodates the mess." Or, more properly, the form is so complex, *so* nonlinear and chaotic, that it eludes the human sensorium's capacity for pattern-recognition. Cunningham by contrast has never abandoned his commitment to clarity of rhythmic structure; and thus, no matter how dense and complex his "movement information" becomes, no matter how distracting or disruptive the accompanying sound score may be, the overall experience never slides down that slippery slope into utter and incomprehensible randomness. (Or: no matter how much "mess" Cage generates, Cunningham invariably finds a form to accommodate it.)

But in the final analysis, it's the distinctive combination of Cunningham's highly refined movement vocabulary, the innate musicality of his phrasing, *and* Cage's (or Tudor's or Mumma's . . .) sound scores that produce a peculiarly contemporary classicism. In Chapter 13, we'll examine the way in which the "purity" of Cunningham's movement and the "impurity" of Cage's sound scores compliment one another in the course of performance. And (despite the very real differences between them) what ultimately lends aesthetic coherence to a Cage/Cunningham collaboration is, above all, the shared sensibility we've already examined at length: a sensibility that, *mutatis mutandis,* unites not just Cunningham and Cage but also every member of "the Cunningham circle." As Cage once said of his relationship to Rauschenberg, "There was from the beginning a sense of absolute identification, or utter agreement, between us" (Tomkins 1980, 70).

8
Cunningham, Cage, and Collage

The principle of collage is the central principle of all art in the
20th century in all media.

—Donald Barthelme (1997, 58)

In sum, the collage is an awkward amalgam of three unresolved elements (1) purely worldly elements, especially such fragments of
dailiness as newspapers; (2) purely artistic elements such as line,
color, and shape—the typical constituents of form; and (3) mixed
or impure elements, or residual images of an imitated nature, ranging from the famous imitation wood grain and chair caning to traces
of such domestic objects as clay pipes and such studio props as gui-
tars. . . . The elements are already "relative" by reason of their dis-
placement from the life-world into the "art world," and by reason
of their fragmentary state. . . . They are an experiment in time and
space—which shows that the old idea of Modern art as an experiment concerned with articulating the fourth dimension has, for all
its charming naivete, a certain truth to it.

—Donald Kuspit, "Collage: The Organizing Principle of Art in the
Age of the Relativity of Art" (1989, 55–56)

A piece of string, a sunset, each acts

—John Cage, *Silence* (1961, x)

Chapter 7 explored a number of affinities between Cage's scores for magnetic
tape in the 1950s and William Burroughs's experiments with "cut-ups." But
the deeper connection between Cage and Burroughs is that both practiced
the aesthetic of *collage*. In 20th-century art, collage was arguably the chief

alternative to—indeed the very antithesis of—the Gesamtkunstwerk. And even though collage is a practice we tend to associate primarily with the visual arts (where it originated), its modus operandi is readily observable in the performing arts as well. Collage is a principle organizing strategy in the work of Elizabeth LeCompte and The Wooster Group, the plays of Heiner Mueller, the theater pieces of Robert Wilson, the choreography of Pina Bausch, the music of John Zorn, and the films of Godard, Kubrick, and Makavejev. But the earliest—and arguably, still most influential—practitioner of collage in performance is Merce Cunningham. Collage has been central to the work of Cunningham and his collaborators—to both their process and their product—from the very beginning.

In 1952, when Cunningham choreographed a new work to excerpts from Schaeffer and Henry's "Symphonie Pour un Homme Seul," he became the first choreographer to utilize musique concrète as the score for a dance. (Indeed, this performance at Brandeis marked the first time musique concrète was heard publicly in the United States) Schaeffer and Henry's concept of "musique-concrète" was derived directly from the example of collage in the visual arts. In their work, concrete (i.e., "real" or preexisting) sounds were recorded on magnetic tape, which was then elaborately edited in a cut-and-paste, collagelike fashion. Significantly, a year later, when Cunningham formed his company and added this dance to its emerging repertory, he retitled it "Collage." Reportedly, Cunningham's movement vocabulary in "Collage" was unpredecentedly diverse. It juxtaposed his usual modifications of ballet with utterly pedestrian movement (hair combing, nail filing) as well as steps drawn from ballroom and social dance. In other words, varieties of "found" movement existed alongside varieties of "found" sound. In order to appreciate the significance of this expanded field of movement possibilities—this side-by-side juxtaposition of the vernacular and the virtuosic—we need to examine the etymology (both linguistic and "art historical") of the word "collage."

Borrowed from the French, "collage" is adapted from the verb "coller"; translated literally, it connotes "pasting, sticking, or gluing" onto a surface. The most famous early example of collage comes from the visual arts: Picasso's cubist collage, "Still Life With Chair Caining" (1911–12). Here, a section of printed oilcloth emblazoned with a chair-caning design was pasted onto a stretch of canvas whose outer edge was lined with real rope. (The rope and the chair-caning design function as intruders from the world of "real things.") Picasso's still life combines three distinct levels of representation: painted illusionism, pasted paper (i.e., printed oilcloth that simulates chair caning), and actual rope. These differences demonstrate the way in which collage can complicate the boundaries of "the frame," conflating traditional distinctions between inside and outside, art and nonart, abstract and representational. Similarly, many of Johns's and Rauschenberg's innovations were informed by the aesthetic of collage. Rauschenberg's combines such as "Monogram" (1959) and Johns's juxtapositions of painted targets and plaster casts conflate the distinction between painting and sculpture. Johns also utilizes elements of simulation that recall Picasso's use of the chair-caning design. For example, his Ballantine Ale cans (1960)—despite their deceptively "realistic" appearance—are actually cast in bronze.

Often analogized to the art of "assemblage," collage has come to imply the sort of "couplings and uncouplings" we now routinely associate with many different aspects of the work of Cunningham and Cage. Unlike the Gesamtkunstwerk, which exemplifies a hunger for wholeness, collage appeals to an age that has come to distrust claims of closure, "unity," and fixed boundaries. As Donald Barthelme once confessed: "Fragments are the only forms I trust" (1997, 5). The chance operations that Merce Cunningham utilizes for linking together disparate fragments of movement, produce— almost by definition—a performative version of collage. But almost every aspect of Cunningham's work is informed in some way by the collage aesthetic: the autonomy of sound, movement, and décor in his dances, the decentralized way bodies are distributed throughout the performance space; and even the spectator's choices about where and when to focus his or her visual and auditory attention. Cunningham is well aware of the way these collagelike procedures mirror the increasingly fragmented nature of urban life. Interviewed for the *New York Times* in 1987, he drew an analogy between "the way we [the company] work[s]" and "the way that society exists now. . . . Being able to take fragments, long and short, and put them together in different ways—we have to, in a sense, do that in our lives all the time, although we don't think about it" (Hutera 1987, sec. 2, 8). Cunningham has admitted that one of the things that appealed to him about the title for "Scramble" (1967) was its connotation of "scrambling" and "unscrambling" both signals and words. Frank Stella's mobile décor for that dance also worked to scramble and unscramble the stage space, slicing up the planes of the stage in a collagelike, multilayered fashion.

If the Wagnerian ideal of artistic synthesis models itself on the presumed unity of the natural world, then collage corresponds to the deep disjunctive structures of the contemporary city. This is not to imply that the art of collage is only practiced in urban settings. Certainly, if we conceive of collage as nothing more than an exercise in pasting, gluing, and juxtaposition, then we can find examples of it in virtually every culture , time-period, and context (e.g., 12th-century Japanese collage-books featuring pen and ink paintings on pasted paper; delicate butterfly wing collages that exemplify 1890s aestheticism at its most rarified; the seashell, coral, bead, and pressed-flower collages one finds in tourist bazaars all over the globe; family photo album collages, etc.). But in the context of modernism, collage and its three-dimensional counterpart, assemblage, are both closely associated with the sharp disjunctions and peculiar juxtapositions of 20th-century urban experience. As William Seitz notes, "...from cubism and futurism, Duchamp and Schwitters, to the present, the tradition of assemblage has been predominantly urban in emphasis" (1961, 73).

The modern newspaper is a privileged icon in the world of 20th-century collage. Fragments of newsprint are often one element of the collage mix. But at an even more fundamental level, the newspaper provides a model for the collagelike disjunctiveness of modernity itself. Apollinaire was one of the first 20th-century artists to recognize this dimension of the newspaper, "which"—as he put it—"on a single sheet, treats the most diverse matters and ranges over distant countries" (Seitz 1961, 76). Similarly, Susan Sontag has referred to

> a kind of involuntary collage-principle in many of the artifacts of the modern city: the brutal disharmony of buildings in size and style, the wild juxtaposition of store signs, the clamorous layout of the modern newspaper, etc. (1966, 270)

This in turn recalls Cunningham's description of the collagelike structure of his own work: "each thing can be and is separate from each and every other, viz: the continuity of the newspaper headlines" (Rose 1968, 280).

The surrealist Max Ernst defined collage as "the meeting of two distant realities on a plane foreign to them both" (Rubin 1968, 68). Collage, however, borrows only one-half of the surrealists' agenda (their interest in radical juxtaposition), while discarding their equally strong fascination with automatism. Many surrealists were particularly fond of Lautreamont's haunting phrase, "the chance meeting of an umbrella and a sewing machine on a dissecting table" (Lippard 1970, 6). The unrelatedness of the two objects, the paradoxical tension between "meeting" and "dissecting," and the role that chance plays in the encounter, all anticipate the way collage functions in the work of Cunningham. For example, in "Doubletoss" (1993), one of Cunningham's most complicated explorations of the collage aesthetic, a sense of radical juxtaposition was accomplished by dividing every aspect of the dance—costumes, choreography, even stage space—into unmatched pairs. Two autonomous dances were conceived and choreographed; but all fourteen dancers performed in (or more precisely, alternated between) both dances. To emphasize the principle of duality, the dancers also alternated between tights and leotards and garments sewn out of black net. A scrim hung a few feet downstage of the backdrop creating a discreet "second space" clearly divided from the rest of the stage. And the juxtaposition of spaces corresponded to the juxtaposition of costumes. (The only dancers who performed upstage of the scrim were those dressed in the black net outer garments, contrasting with the downstage dancers costumed in practice clothes.)

Within the universe of collage, seemingly unrelated elements begin to "resonate" off one another—across gaps of both space and time—resulting in protean, unstable, and wholly provisional relationships. If the Gesamtkunstwerk celebrates the "eternal" love of Tristan and Isolda, then collage is the art of the one-night stand. (In French slang, "collage" sometimes connotes extramarital sex.) The way in which the discreet fragments of collage "resonate" in the eye and mind of the viewer is not unlike the effect of op art: a perceptual/intellectual "flicker" that draws one's attention in conflicting directions (although, in collage, these relationships aren't dependent on an optical illusion). The poster that Jasper Johns designed for the Cunningham company in 1968 is based on the artist's "Target With Four Faces." Leo Steinberg's observations about the way the collage principle functions in this work are equally applicable to the relationship among separate elements in almost any Cunningham dance: "Johns puts two flinty things in a picture and makes them work against one another so hard that the mind is sparked. Seeing then becomes thinking" (1972, 14). The gaps or spaces—sometimes physical, sometimes merely perceptual and psychological—between the disparate components are essential to this "resonating" effect.

The Temporal Dimension

Without a doubt, the most famous examples of collage and assemblage come from the visual arts . A short list would surely include Picasso's and Braque's papier collés, Schwitters's Merz constructions, Max Ernst's collage book, *La Femme 100 Têtes,* the photomontages of Moholy-Nagy, Joseph Cornell's boxes, Dubuffet's assemblages, and John Chamberlain's junk sculptures. But it's my belief that the "collage principle" has been carried to its furthest extreme in the more fully *temporal* realm of performance. There are two reasons for this: in performance, all of the elements are potentially dynamic (i.e., set in motion); and the gaps of space and time that separate these disparate components can be more highly accentuated—in some cases, *much* more highly accentuated.

Long before the arrival of the Internet, Cunningham was experimenting with the juxtaposition of simultaneous activities across widely separated locations. In 1982, for example, Cunningham danced in his Westbeth Studio in Lower Manhattan, accompanied by electronic music being played "live" in Texas by the composer Jerry Hunt and transmitted via the telephone lines. Cunningham has also participated over the years in a number of Nam June Paik's global video linkups that feature simultaneous collaborations between artists on different continents: "Good Morning, Mr. Orwell," linking Paris and New York, was Paik's and Cunningham's way of greeting the arrival of 1984. (The telecast took place on January 1 of that year.) In 1988, Paik's "Transpacific Duet" linked Cunningham and the composer David Tudor across the "gap" of the Pacific Ocean. Paik was arguably the first artist to recognize the connection between the collage aesthetic and McLuhan's concept of the "global village." In 1967, he contributed a video installation called "McLuhan Caged," to the Museum of Modern Art's exhibition titled "The Machine." The video images included a tight closeup of Marshall McLuhan's face undergoing a series of severe distortions ("outside interference" run wild) in the spirit of Paik's "prepared televisions." Paik's 1973 "Global Groove," which includes performances by Cunningham and Cage, is probably his most straightforward homage to McLuhan's concept of electronic simultaneity. Paik has described his globe-shrinking collaborations with Cunningham, Cage, Tudor, and others as "multitemporal, multispatial symphonies." Even more to the point, it was Paik who predicted that "As collage technic [sic] replaced oil paint, the cathode ray tube will replace the canvas" (Hanhardt 1982, 36). "Random Access/Paper TV," an ongoing project created between 1978 and 1981, is one of Paik's most ingenious explorations of the relationship between collage in the visual arts and collage on video. Here, two sets of playing cards were printed with silk-screened images reproduced from videotape footage of Cunningham and Cage. Like any conventional set of playing cards, they can be shuffled and reshuffled in an infinite variety of orders; and when they're randomly dealt out on a flat surface, the result is a striking collage made up of fragmentary glimpses of Cage and Cunningham.

In Chapter 6, we discussed James Clifford's distinction between "roots" and "routes." Paik's global village/collage performances are the ultimate example of the way in which "roots" have been displaced by "routes," a system of circulation, fluctuation, and interaction "at a distance." Collage performances that foster collaboration across vast gaps of space and time mark a radical break with the heritage of primitivism because they proceed on the implicit assumption that one's own community is *not* the center of the universe, that there are an infinite number of "other places," other perspectives, other "points in space."

The Events

Cunningham's 1982 collaboration with the Texas-based composer Jerry Hunt was one example from a broader category of dances that Cunningham refers to simply as "events." Cunningham's "events" may well constitute the single best example of collage in the history of contemporary performance. In the dances Cunningham refers to as events, fragments are dissected from already existing works and then spliced together into new combinations. "Splicing" strikes me as a useful (if not altogether accurate) way of describing Cunningham's relationship to the raw material of the events. In other words, he approaches his older works much in the way a film or video editor manipulates his daily rushes: cutting, assembling, and reassembling the fragments at will (although in Cunningham's case, it's not "will," but chance-operations that often determine the new order of the fragments). A little later in this chapter, we'll examine the ways in which Cunningham's investigation of collage carries over into his work with film and video—media in which "splicing" becomes a literal rather than a metaphorical activity.

The events are performed without an intermission and tend to last about 90 minutes. Almost invariably, the "spliced"-together movement sequences in the events are accompanied by new or different sound scores and decor. Nam June Paik, for example, composed and performed new sound scores for two of Cunningham's events in 1974. Andy Warhol's silver-mylar pillows, originally conceived as the decor for "Rainforest" (1968), reemerged in an "Event" staged in the ruins of Persepolis in 1972. Jasper Johns's setting for "Walkaround Time" (1968) was reutilized in a series of events at BAM in 1997. Sometimes, in the course of a live event, sequences of movement appropriated from totally different works will unfold simultaneously on different parts of the stage. And there are also a number of Cunningham dances whose highly malleable, "modular" structure is itself modeled on the protean nature of the events. "Changing Steps" (1973) for example, is a series of solos, duets, trios, quartets, and quintets that are linked together "indeterminately" from one incarnation to another. When all of the individual sections are performed separately—which is to say, one at a time—the work lasts more than forty minutes. But in other configurations—with the maximum degree of simultaneity—the dance can be completed in a little over 12 minutes.

One of the most distinctive aspects of the Events is the way they illustrate the idea that "meaning" or "interpretation" is always dependent on perceptual context. Recall that in Cage's "William's Mix," more than 1,000 different sounds were spliced onto a mere quarter inch of tape. The sheer number of chance-generated juxtapositions assured that the "original" sounds were all radically recontextualized in juxtapositions determined entirely by chance-operations. The meaning (i.e., the "connotations") of these sounds was now dependent on their collagelike relationships with one other. Granted, in most instances, Cunningham's dances don't cry out for psychological or thematic "interpretations." But that is not to imply that his works aren't imbued with a distinct emotional texture. Indeed, as Cunningham himself once put it, "I don't think that what I do is nonexpressive. It's just that I don't try to inflict it on anyone" (1985, 106).

The events, though, demonstrate that "expressiveness" is by no means inherent in (or "natural" to) specific bodily movements. The "meaning" of movement—even Merce Cunningham's movement—is largely a function of the context in which that movement is performed. For example, when segments of "Winterbranch" (1964) were incorporated into subsequent events, the emotional tone of the work was no longer nightmarish or apocalyptic. Stripped of Rauschenberg's disorienting lighting and LaMonte Young's aggressive, high decibel-level sound score, what the audience saw was (merely) the act of dancers *falling*. Without other factors to color the emotional texture, this basic movement motif came to resemble a series of vaudevillian pratfalls; hence, the spectators tended to laugh rather than recoil in horror. I suspect that a similar sort of transformation would overtake the movement in Cunningham's "Fabrications" (1987), if the dance were ever performed without Dove Bradshaw's costumes. "Fabrications" is one of the very few Cunningham works in which the women wear dresses and the men wear shirts and trousers. The costumes—more than any quality inherent in the movement itself—lead audiences to associate "Fabrications" with the narrative ballets of Tudor and Ashton.

Collage, Cunningham, and The Museum

This concern with perceptual context illustrates yet another connection between Cunningham and Duchamp, one that derives from their shared fascination with the aesthetic of collage. It was of course Duchamp's ready-mades (the urinal, the bottle rack, the bicycle wheel, etc.) that established the idea that any object can be transformed into a work of art simply by virtue of its context. And the concept of "the art context" is germane to the origin of the events. It's neither coincidental nor insignificant that Cunningham's earliest "events" were performed in art museums ("Museum Event No. 1" took place in Vienna's Museum of the 20th Century in 1964; Events No. 2 and No. 3 took place later that year in the Moderna Musset in Stockholm). One of the architectural peculiarities of the Vienna museum made it necessary for Cunningham to perform in front of a large glass wall (a real-life Duchampian "Large Glass"), a symbolic reminder that "the art context" is always a matter of perceptual "framing." As Cage once put it "Whenever there is a concert *situation,* there is a concert" (Corrigan 1981, 336).

The Duchampian/Cageian idea that *any* object (or groupings of sound or movement) can constitute a work of art (if "framed" in the requisite way) is often regarded as a threat to the sort of connoisseurship associated with the museum. But ironically, the idea of the ready-made, the found object or found movement—indeed, the idea of the "art context" itself—is possible *only* in the age of the museum. No institution has done more to promote the concept of collage, not only as a space for *displaying* actual collages or assemblages; but the museum *itself* can be viewed as a "collage space" in which works of art—even pre-20th-century works—constantly find themselves rearranged in fresh and revealing juxtapositions. The clean white walls of the museum constitute a "cling-free space"—where nothing is permanent, where every relationship is provisional. This marks the major difference between "the museum" (where values are constantly in flux) and the older concept of the art "academy" (where values are governed by tradition). The museum, in effect, institutionalizes the concept of the "art context." And conversely, Duchamp and Cage transfer this "museumized" mode of perception into daily life, reconceiving the art context as a moveable feast. (Duchamp's "Boite-en-Valise" is a "portable museum" containing miniaturized copies of many of his works.) How very wrong Gertrude Stein turned out to be when she declared, "A museum can either be a museum or it can be modern, but it cannot be both." It may well be that in the age of collage, MOMA (The Museum of Modern Art) is the prototype of *all* museums. (In Chapter 10, we'll examine the additional significance of the fact that so many of Cunningham's early supporters came from the art world rather than the dance world. Clearly, his work is "at home" in the ambience of the contemporary museum in a way that the work of earlier modern dance choreographers was not.)

Collage, Montage, Video, and Film

The first of the events was performed in 1964. A decade later, the sort of "splicing" that is metaphorically exemplified by collage found its real-world equivalent in Cunningham's growing involvement with filmakers and videographers such as Charles Atlas and Elliot Caplan. Cunningham's first serious exploration of video-as-a-unique medium was "Westbeth," his groundbreaking collaboration with Charles Atlas in 1974. Each of its six sections explores a distinct set of questions and problems about the relationship between dance and video; e.g.: What becomes of the integrity of "stage space" when the dancers are filmed exclusively in close up? By contrast, how does the illusion of depth created by "deep focus" photography compare with the actual depth of a proscenium stage? When multiple cameras record the same movements from different perspectives, what sort of editing is required—what sort of "cutting on motion" is necessary—in order to preserve an illusion of rhythmic continuity? But it was in the final section of "Westbeth" that Cunningham first began to examine the connection between video, the editing room, and collage. Here, Atlas and Cunningham explored the possibilities of *montage:* editing together short, disjunct movement phrases, creating entirely new continuities and discontinuities.

Traditionally, montage (ála its great master and most important theoretician, Sergei Eisenstein), has been regarded as a first cousin to collage. But collage is actually different from (albeit related to) cinematic montage. One can think of it as a first cousin, once removed. In film and video editing, the direct, end-to-end juxtaposition of two seemingly unrelated images coalesces in the mind's eye of the viewer to generate a third distinct entity. For example, in Lev Kuleshov's famous editing experiment involving the actor Mozhukhin, a closeup of an impassive expression on the actor's face was juxtaposed with a variety of objects including a bowl of soup and a dead woman in a coffin. The effect of these edited juxtapositions was to convince the viewer that the actor's facial expression was changing radically from shot to shot. Different audiences responded in much the same way: "How hungry Mozhukin looks when staring at the soup. How mournful when viewing the coffin," and so on. But in fact, the actor's expression never changed; what changed was the perceptual context. Cinematic montage, unlike the inherently less manipulative aesthetic of collage, fuses its separate components into a single entity; and the resulting juxtaposition of the two is imposed upon the viewer, often quite didactically. (Think of Kerensky and the peacock in Eisenstein's "October" [1928].) However, when the juxtaposition is separated by a gap of space and time, then we begin to enter the world of collage. (And of course, there are many filmmakers—Godard, Kubrick, Makavejev, even Griffith in *Intolerance* [1916]—who freely borrow from the principles of collage as well as montage.)

In Cunningham's subsequent video and film explorations, a variety of strategies are utilized to increase the distance (or at least, the perception of distance) between background and foreground as well as between individual components of each frame. For example, in 1975, Cunningham and Charles Atlas contributed a segment to Nam June Paik's "Blue Studio: Five Segments." The title, "Blue Studio" refers to the chromakey process by which images are "collaged" into the blue sector of a video projection. Here, Cunningham and Atlas relied on "chromakeying" to juxtapose images of Cunningham's dancing against shifting, ever-changing backgrounds. As in "Collage," Cunningham incorporated a wide range of pedestrian movement (for example, simple walking) as well as "realistic" gesture.

Nam June Paik is probably best known for his video installations involving vast banks of multiple screens broadcasting asynchronous images. And it may well have been Paik's example and influence that led Cunningham and Atlas to employ multiple monitors in "Fractions," a work for video they created two years later in 1977. In it, Cunningham and Atlas devised an especially ingenious method for emphasizing the spatial separateness of individual bodies within the frame. Sharing the floor space with the eight performers were four video monitors whose images alternated between close up details of the dancers already visible within the frame and images of dancers positioned just *outside* the frame of the camera's viewfinder. The resulting sense of fluctuation between presence and absence, inside and outside, whole bodies and body-fragments was an especially striking example of the "resonance-effect" peculiar to collage.

But Cunningham's most sophisticated exploration of collage (as opposed to montage) on either video or film was probably "Channels/Inserts," a 1981 film shot and edited by Atlas. Alternating between footage filmed in Cunningham's main Westbeth Studio and sequences photographed in the smaller studio, hallway, and office space, this film attempted to create the sense that one was watching a series of actions taking place simultaneously in different locations. In addition to extensive cross-cutting, Atlas employed animated traveling mattes or "wipes" as a means of switching from image to image. Initially, the effect suggests a series of quick "inserts" or intrusions from the "subsidiary" spaces into the "main" space. But by the end of the film, it's no longer clear which is the "*main* channel" and which is a cross-cutting *insert*. (Again, we encounter the most radical function of collage: its capacity for conflating the distinction between foreground/background, inside/outside.)

Illusion and the Space of the Stage

This blurring of boundaries between back and front, inner and outer, results in a "flattening" out of perspectival space; and this, in turn, leads to an important connection we have yet to explore between the collage aesthetic, pictorial anti-illusionism, and Cunningham's "decentralizing" of stage space. Collage abandons the illusion of depth we associate with single-point perspective. This is not to imply that collage never takes three-dimensional forms ("Assemblage" is the most familiar example of collage in three dimensions.) But in the assemblages of an artist such as Johns or in the "combines" of Rauschenberg, the depth is literal, not illusionistic. Picasso was quick to recognize the anti-illusionistic implications of the collage aesthetic:

> The purpose of the papier collé was to give the idea that different textures can enter into a composition to become the reality in the paintings that competes with the reality in nature. We tried to get rid of "trompe l'oeil" to find a "trompe l'esprit." ... And this strangeness was what we wanted to make people think about because we were quite aware that our world was becoming very strange and not exactly reassuring. (Hoffman 1989, 7)

Note the connection that Picasso makes between radical juxtaposition and a sense of unease. He realizes that collage is another attempt "to find a form to accommodate the mess," implicitly acknowledging that 20th-century urban environments are not classically "well-made" spaces and that there is no single, ideal vantage point from which to view these disturbing urban spaces. Single-point perspective by contrast, is comfortably adjusted to the perceptual field of the spectator. It creates the illusion of a space that he or she can physically "enter" in a familiar way.

Of course, the challenge to perspectival illusion in the visual arts predates modernist collage by half a century. The rejection of trompe l'oeil can be traced back at least as far as Manet, who acknowledges and emphasizes the actual two-dimensionality of the canvas (Collage thus becomes another step along the path toward literal "objecthood.") But, significantly, Leo Steinberg attributes the final stage in the repudiation of pictorial illusion to Jasper Johns. Commenting once again on the artist's collage, "Target With Four Faces," Steinberg contrasts Johns' rigorous anti-illusionism with *all* previous painting, even that of the abstract expressionists:

> The pictures of De Kooning and Kline, it seemed to me, were suddenly tossed into one pot with Rembrandt and Giotto. All alike suddenly became painters of illusion. After all, when Franz Kline lays down a swatch of black paint, that paint is transfigured. You may not know what it represents, but it is at least the path of an energy or part of an object moving in or against a white space. Paint and canvas stand for more than themselves. Pigment is still the medium by which something seen, thought, or felt, something other than pigment itself, is made visible. But here, in this picture by Jasper Johns, one felt the end of illusion. No more manipulation of paint as a medium of transformation. This man, if he wants something three-dimensional, resorts to a plaster cast and builds a box to contain it.... There is no more metamorphosis, no more magic of medium. (1972, 12–13)

Not only is there no more "manipulation of paint." Manipulation of the eye of the spectator is abandoned as well. In perspectival space, by contrast, the artist relies on what the Renaissance art critic Georgio Vasari called "magnets to the eye" (Steinberg 1972, 7). The spectator's attention is drawn involuntarily toward a series of vanishing points.

Cunningham treats proscenium stage space in a similar way. He deemphasizes its traditional tendency to kidnap the spectator's visual focus and force it toward a vanishing point located upstage center in deep space. The proscenium, it's important to remember, evolved in Italy in the late 16th century as a direct corollary to the development of single-point perspective in painting. Note what Cunningham has said about the connection between his decentralized, "open field" organization of stage space and the width of today's proscenium stages:

> Stages that are on the eighteenth century model are all deeper than they are wide, like that of the Paris Opera. The reason for this is probably that decor was important, as well as the idea of perspective.... We have a different idea about space now and a different use of it.... Recent stage spaces are almost always

wider than they are deep. Your eye can jump from one point to another, you don't have to be led any longer from one point to another. (1985, 173)

Ironically, even when choreographing for the Paris Opera, Cunningham disregards the traditional imperatives of deep space and single-point perspective. "Width" replaces "depth" in his work just as surely as it does in most examples of collage. The eye of the spectator is not automatically guided upstage center. One's attention—auditory as well as visual—moves in a "collagelike" fashion between shifting points in space. Cunningham frequently cites Einstein's declaration that "There are no fixed points in space." (Hence the title of Cunningham's 1986 work for video, which we'll discuss later in this chapter, "Points in Space.")

It may well be that the shifting perspective of the camera, so basic to Cunningham's work with video and film, is simply a further exploration of the spatial decentering that he's been utilizing in live performance since the early 1950s. The camera merely institutionalizes the multiplicity of perspectives that has fascinated Cunningham all along. "TV Rerun" (1972), for example, was a piece for the stage; but Jasper Johns's "decor" consisted of a cinematographer with handheld camera. The camera-operator's vantage-point was usually different from that of any member of the audience, thereby suggesting the absence of a single fixed focus or "front." Similarly, the film version of "Torse" (1978) employs a collage of two synchronous 55-minute films designed to be projected side-by-side on adjacent screens. The multiple perspectives emphasize Cunningham's asymmetrical approach to space as well as his rejection of the idea that there exists a single, ideal vantage point from which to view the stage version of "Torse" (e.g., "12th row center"). In the film "Locale" (1979), Cunningham's cinematographer Charles Atlas began to actively explore the shifting focus of camera movement; and he alternated between cameras-on-dollies, cameras-on-cranes, and Steadicams. (At one point, the camera travels "full circle" around Cunningham's Westbeth studio). By contrast, "In the theater," notes Cunningham:

> the spectator and the stage are fixed. Most stage work, particularly classical dancing, is based on perspective, a center point to and from which everything radiates. But we don't do that anymore—I don't mean in art, but in general. Ever since Einstein and now astronauts, we've realized something wholly different about space—that everything is moving. Well, I apply that to dancing. (1985, 172)

Deemphasizing the perspectival illusion of deep space also affects (i.e., complicates) the spectator's sense of one-directional, linear time. According to Joseph Frank: "When depth disappears and objects are presented in one plane, their simultaneous apprehension as part of a timeless unity is obviously made easier" (1958, 391). The collapsing of distinctions between foreground/background, inside /outside also results in a conflating of "before" and "after." Nam June Paik's 1978 video, "Merce by Merce by Paik," is an explicit exploration of the relationship between the collage aesthetic and time. Paik's videotape juxtaposes two distinct components: a series of Cunningham dances adapted for video by Charles Atlas and a section called "Merce and Marcel," which explores the affinities between Cunningham and Duchamp. At one point, while Cunningham occupies the frame, an "offscreen" voice asks him, "Can art kill time or occupy it?" Cunningham responds to this ambiguous question with an equally ambiguous answer: "No," he replies, "It's the other way around."

The Emotional Values of Stage Space

To fully appreciate how radically Cunningham breaks with his predecessors in the world of modern dance, we need to compare his collage-inspired organization of stage space with Doris Humphrey's enormously influential practice of assigning particular emotive and thematic values to different areas of the stage. Pre-Cunningham modern dance tended not only to treat space illusionistically, but to animate—indeed, anthropomorphize—the space of the stage. Consider the way Humphrey describes a dancer walking—simply walking—on a diagonal from "dead center" to downstage left:

> The glory of the climax begins to fade. We see him moving toward the downstage corner and oblivion. We know he must traverse another dangerous place, the weak spot between the center and the corner, but we do not fear the menace of it because the end is so near. He reaches the proscenium. Its vertical is reminiscent of the original departure. Is it perhaps another home, not so strong but familiar, or is it the entrance to a tomb? The figure vanishes, cut off like a knife thrust by the final engulfing vertical. Just a simple walk, but how dramatic and pulsating in all its implications! One other thing: On his journey, as he comes near to the downstage exit, this human being changes from someone impersonal, remote, whom we do not know, to a friend, someone we care about. As he reaches the exit, where he is close to us, we are concerned about him. He is no longer an abstraction but a fellow human being.... Stand a dancer in any of the four corners and note what happens. The upper two make the figure seem important with a remoteness which suggests, if there is no other specific mood, a heroic beginning. The powerful verticals energize the body; it seems to be upheld by walls of both physical and spiritual strength. (1959, 76–77)

But Cunningham does more than challenge the choreographic principles that had hardened into dogma in the teachings of early modern dance pioneers such as Doris Humphrey. He undermines theatrical conceptions of space that have dominated proscenium staging in all of the performing arts since the Italian Renaissance. A classic guide for theater directors such as Alexander Dean's *Fundamentals of Play Directing* (1962) shows how common it once was (and in some quarters, still is) to conceive of stage space in ways that are strikingly similar to Doris Humphrey's teachings. Consider the following chart from Dean's (once influential) book.

Mood values of areas in terms of tone qualities and suggestive scenes:

TONAL QUALITIES IN EACH AREA	SCENES SUGGESTED
a. Down center: hard, intense, harsh, strong, climactic, great formality	Quarrels, fights, crises, climaxes
b. Up center: regal, aloof, noble, superiority, stability	Formal and romanticized love scenes, scenes of domination and Judiciary nature, Royalty
c. Down right: warm, informal, close intimacy	Intimate love scenes, informal calls, confessions, gossip . . .
d. Down left; not so warm as down right; distant intimacy	Conspiracies, casual formality, introspection, love scenes, soliloquies, formal calls, business matters

These anthropomorphized "tonal qualities" derive from the proscenium tradition that begins in the Italian Renaissance. And, as we've seen, there's a close parallel between Cunningham's rejection of those perspective conventions that exaggerate the depth of the stage and Johns's and Rauschenberg's rejection of trompe l'oeil in the visual arts. Cunningham in fact has been so deeply influenced by the contemporary art world's antiperspectival, antiillusionistic way of seeing that he tends to regard the very concept of Renaissance "deep space" as illusionistic.

It's not that Cunningham conceives of space in a two-dimensional way or that he regularly "flattens out" his dancers in the manner of Nijinsky's "Faun," where the performer's bodies often confine their movement to a single left/right plane, and the dancer's arms are held tightly alongside their torsos (although he does seem to allude to "Faun" in a number of dances, including "Way Station" [2001]). But the only occasion on which Cunningham really explores (or exploits) the concept of *deep* space is, paradoxically, on film and video—where what he's experimenting with is clearly *the illusion* of deep space.

For example, in the film of "Coast Zone" from 1983, Cunningham and Charles Atlas continued the exploration of spatial depth they began with the fourth section of "Westbeth" in 1975. In "Coast Zone," they tested the "outer limits" of the sort of "deep focus" photography one finds in the films of Orson Welles. Here, dancers whose faces are virtually pressed against the camera in the foreground contrast markedly with dancers in the distance who appear to be disproportionately far away. ("Coast Zone" was filmed in the "literally" deep space of the Cathedral of St. John the Divine in New York.) In subsequent dance videos such as "Points in Space" (1986), co-directed by Elliot Caplan, Cunningham frequently "layers" his dancers as they recede into deep space away from the camera, much like the multiplying 17th-century wing-units that created the illusion of vast vistas on Italianate proscenium stages.

On stage, Cunningham's most compelling experiments with depth have less to do with "deep space" than with the *actual*, sculptural, three-dimensionality of the dancer. This is especially evident in a work like "Pictures" from 1984. Here, groups of dancers assemble themselves into complex, multibody, sculptural formations that tease the eye of the viewer in conflicting ways: One can trace the outline of the group architecture *or* one can just as easily focus on the "negative space" within (or behind?) the external outline. The duality is strikingly similar to that which we experience in Edgar Ruben's famous visual conundrum, "Vase/Profile" (1915); and it's akin to the "resonance-effect" created by collage. In the original production of "Pictures," Cunningham utilized silhouetted lighting to highlight the frozen tableaus. But the complex alternation between negative and positive space is even more effective when excerpts from "Pictures" are performed in the Events format, without the original—and to my mind, overly didactic—silhouetted lighting. (Cunningham's sculptural effects are nonillusionistic; there's no need to "enhance" them theatrically.)

Univocal versus Polyvocal Works

In Chapter 7, we examined Adolphe Appia's belief that Wagner's theory of the Gesamtkunstwerk can only be translated into practice when every element of production surrenders its autonomy to a single directorial "auteur." But the collage aesthetic resists this sort of "centralized" control. Collage is an excellent example of what the poststructuralists call a polyvocal, rather than a univocal, work of art. This is another way of saying that the component parts of any successful collage speak with separate, often disunified voices. It's no coincidence that collage was a "collaborative"—or at least, simultaneous—discovery by both Picasso *and* Braque, and cannot be definitively attributed to either artist. Cage's "Williams Mix," as we've seen, was also a collaboration (with Wolff, Brown, and Feldman). The "mix" generated Feldman's "Intersection" and Wolff's "Suite by Chance" as well as Brown's "Octet," which was devised from "out takes" from the other pieces. By contrast, the quintessential example of a univocal text might well be Wagnerian music-drama, where all of the elements were conceived by the same artist (Wagner himself) and unified in an organic way. (Wagner-as-control-freak is central to his image as crypto-fascist.) It follows that Brecht, the ultimate anti-Wagnerian, was also a great proponent of collage/montage; and he too conceived of his texts in a "polyvocal" way. Brecht once described himself as follows: "He thought in the heads of others; and in his own, others than he were thinking" (Barthes 1985, 195). (*The New Yorker's* 1992 obituary for John Cage read in part, "A suitable epitaph might be: He composed music in others minds.")

The single most compelling model of the polyvocal work may well be those Cunningham collaborations in which the choreographer's "voice" vies with the separate voices of the composer and the designer. By contrast, Alwin Nikolais—who provides such a striking contrast to Cunningham in so many different ways—was responsible for *all* aspects of his productions: choreography, costumes, decor, lighting—even, in most instances, the sound scores. Invariably, in Nikolais's work these elements tend to blend seamlessly into a sort of techno-Gesamtkunstwerk (dancers bodies often function as mobile projection screens; and it's often difficult to tell where the dense slide projected patterns leave off and the body begins). By contrast, on those rare occasions that Cunningham utilizes projections, they never meld organically into (or onto) the dancers. In "Biped" (1999), which we'll discuss more fully in the next two chapters, digitized video images projected on a downstage scrim often seem to float outward toward the audience, thereby *increasing* the sense of separation between these virtual images and the live dancers upstage of the scrim curtain. Perhaps it's no coincidence that Nikolais's lineage leads back to German expressionism. (He was a student of Hanya Holm's, and she in turn was a disciple of Mary Wigman's.)

Barthes's S/Z

The most profound and searching examination of the polyvocal principle in art is probably Roland Barthes's *S/Z*, his deconstructive reading of Balzac's *Sarrasine*. The very title of Barthes's book is an alphabetic collage in which the letter "S" is juxtaposed against the letter "Z"—but not physically merged with it (the very opposite of the *forced* union between male and female icons that we find in an archaic primitivist image like the Nazi swastika.) It's instructive to compare Barthes's spatial reorganization of Balzac's text with the decentralization of the elements in a performance by Cunningham and company. Barthes's professed goal is to "deoriginate the utterance" (in other words: to make it impossible for us to trace the utterance back to a single originating consciousness). Barthes situates his deconstruction of Balzac in a three-dimensional theatrical space: "Nowadays, the representational codes are shattered to make room for a multiple space no longer based on painting (the 'picture') but rather on the theater (the stage)" (1974, 56). This "multiple space" is remarkably similar to the decentered stage space of a Cunningham performance—a space in which movement, sound, and décor have no single authorial "origin." Each "speaks" in a voice of its own. Correspondingly, Barthes's "opens up" Balzac's text in the following, collagelike way:

> We shall therefore star the text, separating, in the manner of a minor earthquake, the blocks of signification of which reading grasps only the smooth surface, imperceptibly soldered by the movement of sentences, the flowing discourse of narration, the "naturalness" of ordinary language. The tutor signifier will be cut up into a series of brief, contiguous fragments, which we shall call lexias. (1974, 13)

A few pages later, he adds: "This is the place for multivalence and for reversibility; the main task is always to demonstrate that this field can be entered from any number of points" (19).

Is there a better description anywhere of Cunningham's "open field" with its "lexias" of fragmented movement, its multiple entrances and exits, its resonating, reversible relationships between image, sound, and decor? And if Barthes's description of this "open field" also seems to uncannily anticipate the space of the computer screen, then so much the better. For, as we'll see in Chapter 9, many of the most radical implications of the collage aesthetic find their fullest realization in the collaborations between Merce Cunningham and digital technology that begin in the 1990s.

9
Dancing for the Digital Age

If you don't accept technology you better go to another place because no place here is safe.... Nobody wants to paint rotten oranges anymore.

> —Robert Rauschenberg, 1967 (Quoted by Rogers-Lafferty, 1998, 11)

It is not a question of what the artist *should* do with technology, but what he *will* do with technology.

> —Billy Kluver, "Theater and Engineering: An Experiment (Notes by an Engineer)" (Quoted by Kren, 1997, 59)

John Cage to Richard Kostelanetz: "People are terribly presumptuous. They call me at midnight—total strangers—just to hear my voice. They have nothing on their minds, nothing." Kostelanetz: "Why do you keep your name in the phone book?" Cage: "I consider it a part of twentieth-century ethics."

> —"Conversation with John Cage," Richard Kostelanetz, 1970 (Kostelanetz, 1970, 6)

In 1989, as he approached the age of 70, Merce Cunningham began experimenting with LifeForms, a computer animation program that represents the dancer's body as a series of concentric circles. Seated at the computer, Cunningham can dictate—and simultaneously record—a wide variety of choreographic variables (everything from the flexing of a joint to the height and/or length of a jump, the location of each dancer on stage, the transition from one phrase to the next, and so on). By the early 1990s, Cunningham had became the first choreographer of international renown who routinely utilized the computer as a choreographic tool. (So much for the popular belief that the digital revolution is exclusively a young person's game.)

The earliest dance Cunningham choreographed with the assistance of LifeForms was "Trackers" in 1991. And significantly, when Cunningham appeared on stage in this work, he did so with the assistance of a portable barre that also seemed to function as a "walker." Was there a connection between these two, seemingly unrelated, facts? Perhaps. The upright posture after all, had always been central to Cunningham's choreographic identity. But by 1991, severe arthritis had made it increasingly difficult for Merce Cunningham to stand—let alone walk or dance—in an upright position for any extended length of time. The portable barre in "Trackers" poignantly illustrated his determination to remain vertical. But it also intimated that he would not be able to continue—at least, not indefinitely—choreographing from the standing position that had constituted both his starting point and his center of gravity for the previous 50 years. It's therefore tempting to conclude that the LifeForms software became available at the very moment Cunningham most needed it (i.e., LifeForms made it possible for Cunningham to choreograph from a seated, rather than a standing, position).

Still, it would be a mistake to assume that Cunningham's increasing reliance on LifeForms as a choreographic tool was dictated primarily by orthopedic necessity. It's my contention that Cunningham would have been attracted to the idea of choreographing at the computer in any event—independent of considerations prompted by advanced age and advancing arthritis. Cunningham's own words bear this out: In 1994, he wrote a short essay entitled, "Four Events That Have Led To Large Discoveries." The four events, listed chronologically, are (a) the decision "to separate the music and the dance"; (b) the decision "to use chance operations in the choreography"; (c) "the work we have done with video and film"; and (d) "the use of a dance computer, LifeForms" (Vaughan 1997, 276). It seems to me that the journey from event "a" to event "d" was all but inevitable, that each discovery laid the groundwork for its successor. In other words, "the four events that led to large discoveries" have also led—like a chain of dominos—from the one to the other. For example, Cunningham's initial dissociation of sound and image in the late 1940s (the decision "to separate the music and the dance") finds its anatomical equivalent in chance-generated compositional processes.

We can see this occurring as early as 1953 in "Untitled Solo" (which we've already discussed in a number of other contexts). Recall that Cunningham's movement choices for the arms, legs, head, and torso were all developed separately and ultimately linked together by chance operations. This collagelike conception of the body (the body as an inorganic "assemblage" of parts) anticipates the way a film or videotape editor arranges and rearranges individual shots and splices. (Hence the transition from discovery

[b] to discovery [c].) There's a significant precedent that links cinematic montage to the "reconfiguring" of the human form. In 1923, the filmmaker Dziga Vertov, inspired by the utopian rhetoric of Soviet Constructivism, wrote:

> You are walking on a Chicago street today in 1923, but I make you nod to comrade Volodarsky, who is, in 1918 walking down a street in Petrograd; he acknowledges your greeting. . . . I have created a man more perfect than Adam. . . . I take the most agile hands of one, the fastest and most graceful legs of another, from a third person I take the handsomest and the most expressive head, and by editing, I create an entirely new, perfect man. (Rhode 1976, 105)

Note, too, that in my original reference to Cunningham's "Untitled Solo" from 1953, I suggested that his head, arms, and legs appeared so oblivious to one another that they could have been grafted together from three *different* bodies, moving at three different speeds. By the 1990s—the decade in which Cunningham began to choreograph at the computer—this "cut and paste" vision of human identity found its real-life equivalent in the emerging concept of the technobody, a "machine organism" whose component parts—limbs, organs, even genes—seem increasingly alterable, exchangeable, spliceable, ultimately . . . cloneable. (This after all was the decade in which corporate CEOs living in Latin America began to have microchips implanted in their bodies, miniature transmitters that were capable of wirelessly communicating with Global Positioning Systems, thereby alerting law-enforcement officials to the executive's whereabouts in the case of a kidnapping.)

Cunningham had actually begun to utilize computer terminology—and to draw analogies between his ways of working and the operations of the computer—as early as 1968. "Walkaround Time," choreographed that year, took its title from computer jargon; and in his book *Changes,* also published that same year, Cunningham wrote " . . . the use of chance methods demanded some form of visual notation. . . . A crude computer in hieroglyphics" (1968, n.p.). Similarly, John Cage had long conceived of the computer as little more than a high(er)-tech version of the *I Ching,* which he and Cunningham had employed since the 1950s as a principal tool for chance-dictated decision making. (The computer program Cage eventually had designed for generating random variations of pitch, timbre, amplitude, and duration was called *ic.*)

In Chapter 2, I drew a number of parallels between Cunningham's work and Thomas Pynchon's *The Crying of Lot 49,* a novel infused with the jargon of thermodynamics, information theory, entropy studies, and references to James Clerk Maxwell's famous conundrum known as "Maxwell's Demon." In 1970, Stephen Smoliar, who was then a student in applied mathematics at

MIT, wrote an essay about Cunningham for *Ballet Review*. In the course of discussing "Canfield," which had recently been performed at the Brooklyn Academy of Music, Smoliar wrote:

> After the stage became more occupied, a standing dancer would be set in motion as another dancer walked by, and would then proceed to another location and again come to rest—sort of like a thermodynamic system of Maxwell's demons. Admittedly, it is somewhat unconventional to view dance in terms of thermodynamics or information theory; however, in the case of Merce Cunningham, such an approach is not that far off base. (1992, 78)

Smoliar makes no mention of Pynchon; but my point is simply that Cunningham, like Pynchon, is the sort of artist whose work is both informed by—and "at home" with—the languages of science and technology.

Cunningham's new reliance on the LifeForms computer program—which enables him to manipulate the component parts of the human body on screen—seems less like a quantum leap and more like a logical, perhaps even inevitable, *next step*. Furthermore, many aspects of Cunningham's work anticipate the spatial and temporal dimensions of the digital world. Most obviously: his "decentered" organization of stage space that has long provided a model for the sort of "liquid architecture" one now finds in the world of "hypertext" and the CD-ROM—where multiple "windows" of information can be opened simultaneously in an overlapping collage of interactive choices. Hypertext provides the ultimate example of the fluctuation between background/foreground, inside/outside we discussed in the context of the collage aesthetic. No matter how many windows one has opened simultaneously, they all seem to inhabit the same shallow plane and they can displace one another with the click of a mouse. In addition, the process by which the "user" actively selects these choices closely parallels the process by which the Cunningham spectator freely chooses how and where to focus his or her attention.

Cunningham has presided over a number of important marriages between dance and technology: the use of electroacoustic sound; electronic tape splicing and *musique-concrète*; video synthesizers; FM telemetry; radar and ultrasonic transmissions; sound scores produced by the dancers in performance as they sweep past photoelectric cells—not to mention more recent digital developments such as LifeForms and a very different computer/video process known as "motion capture." But, the *deeper*, more significant, connection between the work of Cunningham and Cage and that of other artists who have been similarly influenced by technology is their shared commitment to the impersonal *methods* of scientific inquiry—even when the dance in question doesn't incorporate some easily recognizable form of advanced "technology." (When Cunningham and Cage speak of "chance methods," their emphasis lies as much or more on the rigor of the methods as on the randomness of the chance.)

In *Literature and Technology* (1968), Wylie Sypher discusses a wide variety of aesthetic phenomena that aspire to the rigor and impersonality of the sciences. Although he doesn't specifically mention Cage and Cunningham (his focus is poetry and the novel), he accurately sums-up the precise attitude toward scientific objectivity that pervades so much of their work:

> The heavy investment in method suggests that the artist was subject to the same imperatives as the scientist and that the fissure between art and science was not so wide as is alleged, or the kind of fissure one might think, since both were highly specialized executions or procedures (xvi).

Sypher goes on to draw analogies between artistic method and

> a mentality expressing itself in its sparest and most impersonal form in engineering, the choice of methods that most economically yield the designed results. A law of parsimony worked in aestheticism as it did in science. Such privative or puritan discipline is associated with the notion of distance, the detachment that makes the artist or scientist a neutral spectator, isolating him from the realm of Nature. (xvi–xvii)

This is an excellent description of the underlying sensibility that has informed Cunningham's work from the very beginning. In 1967, a significant crossection of the "Cunningham circle"—Cage, Rauschenberg, and Tudor, as well as former Cunningham dancers Steve Paxton and Deborah Hay— participated in an event titled "Nine Evenings: Theatre and Engineering," held at the 69th Street Regimental Armory in Manhattan (the site of the infamous "Armory Show" of 1913, where Duchamp unveiled his "Nude Descending a Staircase"). During the previous 10 months, the artists worked with a group of 30 engineers assembled for the occasion by Billy Kluver, a physicist at Bell Laboratories who had collaborated previously with Cage, Rauschenberg, and Johns.

Rauschenberg's contribution to the "Theatre and Engineering" evenings, a piece called "Open Score," proved remarkably prescient. It began with a tennis match between Frank Stella and Mimi Kanarek. Their rackets were electronically wired so that whenever either of them made contact with the tennis ball, one of the overhead lights automatically switched off. The progressive darkening of the space served as prelude to the real heart of the piece. The moment total darkness was achieved, a large group of volunteers executed 10 simple movements devised by Rauschenberg. These group movements were monitored by infrared cameras and projected via closed circuit television onto three large overhead screens. As a result, activity being performed live, in the very same space, was visible to the audience only in the "mediated" form of projected images. "Open Score" anticipated one of the central facts of contemporary life: our increasingly mediated relationship to the human body and to other human beings. Cunningham, as we've seen, also utilizes a wide variety of strategies that mediate the relationship between spectator and spectacle.

The Influence of Technology on Movement

More than anything else, what attracts Cunningham to new technologies is his fascination with the effect they exert on human movement. This interest is simultaneously sociological and aesthetic. Cunningham is curious about the extent to which our daily rhythms have been influenced by technology; but he also wants to learn about the ways in which new technologies can facilitate movement invention when they function as an active partner in the choreographic process. For example, Cunningham has spoken explicitly about the way in which television has affected the tempos of his work: "The speed with which one catches an image on the television made me introduce into our class work different elements concerned with tempos which added a new dimension to our general class work behavior" (Vaughan, 276). (Here he seems to illustrate the truth of a prediction Alvin Langdon Coburn made in 1918: that the camera would help bring about the advent of "fast seeing.") Not only have tempos accelerated under the influence of film and video. Stage space has been arranged and subdivided in new ways as well. The spatial organization of "Five Stone Wind" (1988), for example, was based on Cunningham's recollection of five different camera positions that he had utilized in earlier video and film projects.

Even the most superficial overview of the way Cunningham's movement vocabulary has evolved over the past 50 years leads to the following conclusion: After Cunningham began to work on a regular basis with film, video, and the LifeForms computer software, his choreography began to change in ways that show the unmistakable influence of these technologies. This is reflected by the sheer number of Cunningham dances whose titles have been inspired by technological terminology: As I mentioned earlier, in 1968, the title "Walkaround Time" was borrowed from computer jargon. It refers to those intervals when the computer is operating autonomously of its human programmer—who is thereby free to "walkaround" for a time. "Enter" (1992)—created just after Cunningham had begun to utilize LifeForms on a routine basis—is named after one of the most prominent control keys on the computer. The title "CRWDSPCR" (1993) is one of Cunningham's most insightful references to the affect of the microchip on our conceptions of space and time. "CRWDSPCR" can be read as a condensation of the words "crowd spacer" or "crowds pacer," a twin reference to the way in which technology has both crowded space and quickened pace. What computer science knows as Moore's Law, formulated in the mid-1960s by Gordon Moore, former chair of Intel, argues that the size of each transistor on an integrated circuit will be reduced by 50% with each passing year. Computational power thus expands exponentially. In the sheer speed and density of its movement, "CRWDSPCR" offers us the choreographic equivalent of Moore's Law.

But more significantly, throughout the last 15 years, Cunningham's basic movement vocabulary has changed in fundamental ways that reflect his work with LifeForms computer animation. In "Trackers," (1991), the unusual walking rhythms resulted from experimenting with the spacings between walking step patterns that already existed on the LifeForms "menu." (To be more specific: changes in rhythm resulted from manipulating the spatial proportions between shapes.) Even earlier, in "Polarity" (1990), Cunningham began to employ unprecedentedly complex counterrhythms for the arms and legs. It's probably no coincidence that "Polarity" was one of the first dances Cunningham choreographed after he began his experiments with LifeForms. Typically, he used the computer to devise movements for the legs, arms, and torso that were totally autonomous of one another. Cunningham's long-standing tendency to conceive of the body as an assemblage of separate parts is facilitated immeasurably by the computer which obeys no innately "organic" preferences. In the choreography devised with the assistance of LifeForms, it's not uncommon for the dancers to move stage left in a series of successive hop-turns on one leg while their heads circle in the opposite direction.

The single most noticeable change in Cunningham's movement vocabulary since he began to work with LifeForms is surely the attention he now pays to the arms (particularly arms raised above the head). This may be related to the fact that Cunningham (who is now in his eighties) no longer works from the starting point of his own two feet. Rather than standing upright, with weight distributed equally on both legs, he now *sits* in front of the screen. (This may also help to explain why one sees so many more "off-balance" positions in Cunningham choreography of the 1990s.) Given that the computer is incapable of either consciously or unconsciously "favoring" the legs, all body parts become inherently equal in the world of LifeForms; and the arms can be manipulated with the same ease as any other subdivision of the body. Of course, the raison d'être of chance operations was *always* to free the artist from his innate "preferences." Therefore, LifeForms may have accomplished something that even the *I Ching* was unable to do: liberate Cunningham from his, perhaps unexamined, inclination to favor the legs and the feet. But, Cunningham himself offers a rather different explanation for this newly developed interest in upraised arms. Cunningham argues that the space above the LifeForms figure on the computer screen looks underutilized unless the arms are raised above the head and brought actively into play (Copeland 2001, 5–6).

Another significant development in the era of LifeForms is that Cunningham's overall phrasing has gotten longer, tending to counterbalance the "cut-and-paste" style of fragmentation that the computer implicitly encourages. Perhaps it's easier—certainly it's less physically taxing—to choreograph long phrases on digital figures than on the human body. Furthermore, by the time "CRWDSPCR" was choreographed in 1993, movement motifs began to appear in Cunningham's choreography that looked as if they'd been directly influenced by—indeed virtually "modeled on"—the inwardly curved shapes of the LifeForms wire-frame figures themselves. One example is the solo in "CRWDSPCR," in which Frederic Gafner jumped up and down while sharply twisting his torso as he moved downstage toward the audience. The staccato rhythm of the solo also may allude to the transition from one "key frame" to the next in the LifeForms software. Similarly, in "Ground Level Overlay" (1995), Gafner performed a tortuous series of jumps and reversed turns in a tightly held second position. There were also a number of agonizingly tricky jumps with the legs bent at the knees throughout the entire phrase.

Partnering was especially difficult to devise on the earliest versions of LifeForms; and perhaps as a result, duets became infrequent in Cunningham's work during the 1990s. Or else, when they did appear, as in "Rondo" (1996), they seemed to pose for themselves the question: how can I partner someone while maintaining the maximum amount of *distance* between our two bodies? During the first duet in "Rondo," the male and female dancers' hands are clasped together, but their mid-sections are forced as far from one another as possible. Eventually they each rotate 180 degrees. Their hands are still touching, but they no longer face one another, as if to say: "The body is a totally *objective* entity," no front, no back, no sense that it's more or less "appropriate" to face or not to face one another while dancing a "duet." This is partnering conceived by—or at least "on"—a computer.

Another recent evolution in Cunningham's choreography is the unprecedented degree of deformation, a tendency to twist and gnarl the body in ways that appear not so much mechanical as "deformed." "Scenario" (1997) with costumes by the fashion designer Rei Kawakubo of "Comme des Garcons," seemed to carry this tendency to its logical (or illogical) extreme. Here was one of those exceedingly rare occasions when Cunningham allowed a designer to conceal the dancer's silhouette with costumes that altered the fundamental shape of the human body. Based on her notorious Spring 1996 collection, which some members of the fashion press dubbed the "Quasimodo" line, Kawakubo "de-formed" the dancer's body shape with comically grotesque humps and bulges. (It was as if Alwin Nikolais had designed costumes for a dance adaptation of *Richard III.*) Perhaps Cunningham was implicitly declaring in this piece, "I fear that I've reached the outer limits of the human bodies' distortability; and in order to carry this impulse any further, I need the assistance of prosthetic appendages."

Many choreographers who work with LifeForms speak of the extent to which they begin to think and see in terms of the VRML body, the prototypical "wire-frame" body of computer animation. (VRML stands for Virtual Reality Modeling Language). Perhaps coincidentally (perhaps not), this wire-frame body-prototype looks remarkably like some of the more robotic designs from Oscar Schlemmer's 1922 "Triadic Ballet." VRML by the way, is pronounced "virmul." It sounds—and this is not altogether inappropriate—like some flesh-eating virus unleashed in a David Cronenberg sci-fi film.

Motion Capture and Cyberspace

Computer technology, almost by definition, offers a number of methods for confronting (and transcending) the "limitations" of the human body. In recent years, Cunningham has also been experimenting with the technology of "motion capture," which serves to "liberate" movement from the actual, human bodies in which it originates—subsequently propelling their skeletal or ghostly residues into virtual space. This is a complicated process, the sheer mechanics of which will require a bit a explanation. For the sake of clarity, rather than generalizing about motion-capture, I've chosen to describe the way this process functions in specific works.

Cunningham's first experiment with "motion capture" was "Hand Drawn Spaces" (1998), a collaboration with multimedia computer artists Paul Kaiser and Shelley Eshkar. In the initial stage of the process, two live, flesh-and-blood Cunningham dancers (Jared Philips and Jeannie Steele) performed in front of a digital video camera while wearing light-sensitive disks called "motion capture sensors" attached to key joints of their bodies. The movement of these sensors was optically recorded as "points in space" and then converted into digital 3D files. These data files capture the position and rotation of the body-in-motion without preserving its mass or musculature. Movement is thereby "extracted" (i.e., captured)—some might go so far as to say, "liberated"—from the performer's body. In a quite literal sense, motion capture aspires to reverse the import of Yeats's famous question "How can we know the dancer from the dance?" Motion capture aspires to give us the dance *minus* the dancer. This explains why many of its more enthusiastic proponents believe that motion-capture has a bright future ahead of it as a new tool for dance documentation and preservation. The completed version of "Hand-Drawn Spaces—which was projected on large-scale, multiple video screens—existed solely in virtual space. To be sure, the ultra-articulated limbs we saw in the projected images of "Hand-Drawn Spaces" were performing a vocabulary that was unmistakably Merce Cunningham's. But the arms and legs of the dancers appeared to have been X-rayed through-to-the-bone. These were performers divested of flesh and blood, virtual dancing skeletons.

The notion of extracting or "capturing" movement from actual bodies would seem to lead us into the world of William Gibson's 1984 novel, *Neuromancer*—the book that popularized the term "cyberspace." Case, the book's protagonist, is the original prototype of the cyberpunk, a "keyboard jockey" who escapes the physical, geographical limitations of his body by plugging himself into "the matrix."

> Case was twenty-four. At twenty-two, he'd been a cowboy, a rustler, one of the best in the Sprawl . . . He'd operated on an almost permanent adrenaline high, a byproduct of youth and proficiency, jacked into a custom cyberspace deck that projected his disembodied consciousness into the consensual hallucination that was the matrix. A thief, he'd worked for other, wealthier thieves, employers who provided the exotic software required to penetrate the bright walls of corporate systems, opening windows into rich fields of data. (1984, 5)

But Case gets caught stealing from his employers; and as retribution, they impair his nervous system in ways that make it impossible for him to plug back into the matrix. Case is thus en*cased* in "the prison of his own flesh." And in this cyber-universe, to be subject(ed) to the limitations of one's body is to fall from grace:

> For Case, who'd lived for the bodiless exultation of cyberspace, it was the Fall. In the bars he'd frequented as a cowboy hotshot, the elite stance involved a certain relaxed contempt for the flesh. The body was meat. Case fell into the prison of his own flesh. (1984, 5)

Here we begin to edge toward the dark, dystopian side (although some of William Gibson's characters might consider this the bright, utopian side) of cyberpunk culture where the "techno-body" becomes the only body. Or at least the only desirable alternative to life as lived in an old fashioned "organic" body (or what Gibson refers to as a "meat puppet").

Cunningham and his digital collaborators may view the body as an "assemblage," but they can hardly be said to share the cyberpunk's "contempt for the flesh." "Hand-Drawn Spaces" is indeed a work for virtual reality; but as its title suggests, it never completely severs its ties to the human hand or body. More to the point, Shelley Eshkar is a very talented graphic artist who embellishes the motion-captured skeletal shapes with a digital equivalent of *hand-drawn* lines and squiggles that resemble elegant charcoal drawings. Furthermore, the skeletal dancing figures in "Hand-Drawn

Spaces" never completely soar into the weightless world of cyberspace. They remain firmly planted on the floor. The fact that these phantom figures have more in common with human skeletons than with robots or cyborbs is also surely significant. Merce Cunningham was 79 years old when "Hand-Drawn Spaces" premiered; and thus, on an existential level, it's difficult not to see the movement of these skeletal traces as a dance macabre, a glimpse of the skull beneath the face, an intimation of mortality, ultimately a melancholy reminder of human limitation (rather than a glimpse of immortality in the bodiless world of cyberspace). There's a dynamic give-and-take in this work between Kaiser and Eshkar—who begin in the digital world and then work their way back toward the realm of the "hand-drawn"—and Cunningham, who begins in the world of the body, but then replaces its flesh and blood with the digital mapping of movement implicit in "motion capture." As a result, the choreographer and his digital collaborators meet "mid-way" between the realm of the flesh and the realm of the virtual.

The movement vocabulary that the motion-captured figures perform in "Hand-Drawn Spaces" strongly suggests that it was first choreographed with the assistance of LifeForms. This makes sense in part because there's a marvelous complimentarity between these two systems: To work with LifeForms is to begin in the world of computer animation, but with the intention (at least in Cunningham's case) of devising movement for human beings who will eventually perform live on stage. The process of motion capture, by contrast, begins with the live dancer—but ultimately leaves his or her actual, physical, body behind: solid joints become digital points (in space). If Cunningham's "Hand-Drawn Spaces," is an example of "dot-com dance," then it's motion capture that puts the dots in the dot-com.

This sort of reciprocity between the physical and the virtual was explored even more fully in Cunningham's next collaboration with Kaiser and Eshkar, "Biped" (1999), a work conceived for the stage, juxtaposing live dancing with virtual imagery. Disembodied ("motion-captured") images of Cunningham dancers were projected on a downstage scrim curtain that covered the entire width of the proscenium. Kaiser and Eshkar generated approximately 25 minutes of motion-captured animation, slightly more than half the length of the dance. This material was subdivided into a series of discontinuous sequences, ranging from about 15 seconds to 4 minutes in length. The order in which these sequences were projected on the scrim was determined by chance operations. Cunningham's 14 dancers wore silver-blue jumpsuits designed by Suzanne Gallo. The costumes were coated with an iridescent metallic sheen that reflected both the projected light of the motion-capture sequences (as it penetrated the scrim) and beams from more conventional lighting instruments positioned overhead and in the wings. Gavin Bryars's lush musical score interwove deep rumbling electronic tones with the acoustical sounds of cello, double bass, electric guitar, and keyboard. The balance between acoustic and electronic sound was a perfect auditory compliment to imagery that juxtaposed the live and the virtual.

"Biped" utilizes much of the fiendishly difficult movement vocabulary Cunningham has been devising for the past several years with the assistance of LifeForms. Feet planted firmly on the floor provide the foundation for almost impossibly "torqued" bending and twisting of the back and neck. In other words, the upper body tends to work in disjointed counterpoint to the legs. Both arms frequently stretch up and over the head, but then curl back down toward the shoulder blades in a jagged arc. Necks often tilt upward, directing the dancer's gaze toward the ceiling. As with much of Cunningham's recent choreography, the arms now seem at least as active— and often more prominent—than the legs. But this is work that makes extreme demands on the lower body as well. For example, the dancers often execute low, rapid jumps on one foot, while the other leg is raised and tilted at a 45-degree angle. Occasionally, as both arms rise to frame the head symmetrically, both feet perform a bent-legged jump that finishes in first position.

All of the (actual) movement takes places upstage of the scrim. But what distinguishes "Biped" from the earlier dances composed with LifeForms is the fact that we often view this live movement in juxtaposition with mutating motion-captured images of virtual movement projected onto the downstage surface of the scrim curtain. The result is a complex interplay of flesh and image that begins to challenge our conventional notions of animate and inanimate, interior and exterior. For example, it sometimes looked as if the dancers were wearing their skeletons on the *outside* of their bodies. Paul Kaiser, commenting on the dance's first performance at Berkeley in 1999, wrote, "By a miracle of chance operations, one of the first dancers on stage [Jeannie Steele] was haloed in a projection of her own motion-capture—'as if I were dancing inside myself,'" she said afterward (2000). The projected image of Jeannie Steele that Kaiser refers to was similar to the skeletal imagery from "Hand-Drawn Spaces." But, unlike "Hand-Drawn Spaces," where the virtual figures maintained their anthropomorphic outlines throughout the dance, here they metamorphosed—or simply "morphed"—into a variety of other shapes. For example, on some occasions, the projected images consisted solely of the actual motion-captured "points in space" (which we might think of as the initial building blocks in the transformation of live dancer into "virtual" dancer.) Imagine a lighted Christmas tree, but then erase the tree, leaving only the lights (glowing dots that roughly approximate an organic form).

Once we understand the basic technology behind motion-capture, we soon begin to realize that these virtual dots have been extracted (or "captured") from the joints of actual bodies. Subsequently, in the course of "Biped," these image-traces transmute into a variety of other shapes. Diagonal lines fan out in a kaleidoscopic way recalling the photo-montage-like replicating edges in Duchamp's "Nude Descending a Staircase." Kaiser refers to these forms as "stick bodies" and acknowledges that they were inspired by the yarrow sticks sometimes tossed by Cunningham and Cage as they utilize the *I Ching* to generate compositional choices. According to Kaiser:

> Having motion-captured about five minutes of the "Biped" choreography, we now used it to animate our figures much more freely than in "*Hand-Drawn Spaces*." Freely, but still truly: we took care never to lose the underlying perception of real and plausible human movement. A case in point: when our stick figure leaped, its various lines were flung upward in the air, then gathered back together again on landing. While no human body could do this, you could still feel the human motion underlying the abstraction. (2000)

Kaiser alludes to one of the most intriguing and distinctive possibilities afforded by motion capture technology: the fact that the motion "captured" from a live dancer can be easily transformed into (or superimposed onto) a variety of inanimate shapes which then begin to move in ways that incorporate key choreographic qualities of the original, "human" dance. These techniques have become commonplace in film, television commercials, and computer games (e.g., the dancing baby in "Ally McBeal" and *Tomb Raider*'s Lara Croft). Not only is motion-capture a technique that graphic designers have used to create images of cyborgs (as in *Terminator II*), but the technique itself exemplifies the ever-increasing fusion of "organic" and "inorganic" forms in the age of the technobody.

Liquid Architecture and the Computer Screen

"Biped" also was Cunningham's most extensive exploration of the relationship between proscenium space and the collagelike, "liquid architecture" of cyberspace. "You stop thinking of space as being one set construction, but rather as a myriad of possibilities," says Shelley Eshkar (Hamilton 1999, 90). The porous, spatially indeterminate nature of computer space, its absence of fixed boundaries and fixed "centers," the way in which fragments of hypertext can be "linked" to a seemingly infinite number of other "sites" are all alluded to one way or another in the course of this dance. (Indeed, I'm almost tempted to say that these concepts were "illustrated" in a number of ways by "Biped.") For example, the dancers both entered and exited through an upstage wall—a dimensionless, black abyss—that gave the impression of bodies alternately materializing and dematerializing (as opposed to the impression of bodies moving "toward" or "away" from the audience in the manner of more conventional entrances and exits). In actuality, this upstage wall was a black velvet curtain lined with narrow slits through which the dancers made their magical-looking entrances and exits. The floor of the stage was divided into a grid pattern of white-and-blue squares of light that cross-faded in ways making it difficult to determine which squares were solid floor and which were mere projections of light from overhead. The result was a collagelike blurring of the distinction between "negative" and "positive" space.

Although never a literal representation of a computer screen, the cross-fading patterns on the floor poetically evoked the image of multiple "windows" displacing one another in the same plane. When all of these elements began to resonate off of one another, the entire performance space—upstage wall, downstage scrim, and "window-patterned" floor—pulsated with the sort of "collage effect" we discussed in Chapter 8. The resulting visual collage was unlike anything ever witnessed in the "natural" world.

Against Nature

Cunningham's long-standing fascination with "impersonal" and techno-logical processes helps to both illuminate and dispel one of the greatest misconceptions about his work: the idea that he models his dances on the processes and structures of nature. This belief, repeated like a mantra, has hardened into a kernel of "received" wisdom. James Klosty's remarks are typical: "It is hardly chance that—next to dancing—plants, animals, and the workings of nature fascinate him most; and his theater echoes that pre-occupation by imitating nature in its manner of operation" (1975, 14). It may well be that Cunningham himself would subscribe to this view. If so, I would proceed to invoke D. H. Lawrence's wise advice, "Never trust the teller, trust the tale." Because the "tale" to my mind (to my eyes and ears) is a distinctly *urban,* nonnatural tale, one that reflects the sights, sounds, rhythms, and collagelike disjunctiveness of the modern, digitally depen-dent, city. Examining those densely packed exercises in simultaneity that Cage calls "Musicircus," Charles Junkerman argues that "the Musicircus is an urban genre—crowded, noisy, and insubordinate..." and describing a particular Musicircus that Cage organized at Stanford in 1991, Junkerman cites a spectator who shouted "I feel like I'm in New York" (1994, 40). Furthermore—to cite Wylie Sypher once again—the impersonal, chance operations at the heart of Cunningham's and Cage's work invariably in-voke "the notion of distance, the detachment that makes the artist or scientist a neutral spectator, isolating him from the realm of Nature..." (1968, xvii).

One could of course counter by citing Cage's oft-quoted maxim (bor-rowed from Ananda Coomaraswamy), which argues that "the function of art is to imitate Nature in her manner of operation" (Junkerman 1994, 41). (Hence James Klosty's appropriation of this phrase a few sentences back.) But the Cage quote needs to be read closely. Cage isn't defining art as an imitation of nature but, rather, the imitation of nature's *manner of operation*. And what rarely if ever gets quoted in this context is the *next* sentence in Cage's essay, which reads, "Our understanding of her 'manner of operation' changes according to advances in the sciences" (1967, 31). (After all, botany and zoology—indeed all of biology—is a branch of science.) Thus, even for John Cage, the focus of art is not so much the things of nature but, rather, the nature of things. My aim is not to establish a false dichtomy between "science" and "nature," but rather, to emphasize, yet again, the extent to which Cunningham and Cage have created an essentially *urban* experience.

Those who continue to think of Cunningham's work as an extension of the processes of nature are also apt to associate Cage and Cunningham with the "holistic" worldview of "Eastern philosophies." But consider the way Cunningham and Cage actually utilize a classic "Eastern" text like the *I Ching*. They don't employ the ancient Chinese Book of Changes in the "conventional" way: as a source of "divination." Given Cage's utter openness to the unforeseen and the chaotic, it's difficult to imagine him agreeing with the claims John Blofeld makes in the introduction to his 1963 translation of the *I Ching*:

> ... it enables any reasonably unselfish person who is capable of fulfilling a few simple conditions both to foresee and to CONTROL the course of future events! By rightly interpreting and strictly following the I Ching's interpretation of universal laws, we can make ourselves as farsighted as the lesser Gods! (1965, 14)

It's equally difficult to imagine Cage agreeing with the conception of the *I Ching* that Carl Jung proposes in his preface to the English edition of Richard Wilhelm's earlier translation of the book. For Jung, the *I Ching* was another means of "exploring the unconscious," an interpretation that Cage would surely dispute. As Cage himself has argued, "I wanted rather to open my mind to what was outside my mind" (Kostelanetz 1970, 141). Granted, there's no denying Cage's deep interest in Zen Buddhism. (Cage became friendly with Nancy Wilson Ross, who was probably the first person to draw analogies between Zen and Dada; and it was the same Nancy Wilson Ross who would go on to edit the *Notebooks* of Martha Graham.) More importantly, Cage became a virtual disciple of Daisetz T. Suzuki in the late 1940s. But when Cage told Suzuki that he was determined to live and work in the *city*, the Zen philosopher expressed his severe reservations. "I took that as a challenge," Cage told me in the course of an interview in 1986.

Thus, in the final analysis, the dissociation of sound and image in a Cunningham/Cage collaboration is difficult to reconcile with *any* "holistic" philosophy. Their way of working has infinitely more to do with the fragmentation of the modern city than with any Zen-based theory of "multiple perspectives." Or—another way of thinking about this—the meditative forms of "selective inattention" one masters by studying Zen can become an invaluable means of *coping with* the fragmentation of the modern metropolis.

Nature as Seen through an Urban Temperament

Does this mean that Cunningham's works are never sunny, buoyant, open, or in any way evocative of the natural world? Of course not. *Summerspace* and *Field Dances* are but two of the works that fall into this category. But even here, the result is nature seen through an urban temperament. This is a restorative weekend in the Hamptons, not a permanent relocation to the backwoods of Vermont. It's a temporary reprieve from the world of works like "Aeon" (1961) with its flares and strobe-pulses or the blindingly bright lights and ear-splitting decibel levels of "Winterbranch" (1964). Consider the uncharacteristically explicit suggestions Cunningham gave Rauschenberg with regard to the sort of lighting he wanted for "Winterbranch":

> I asked Robert Rauschenberg to think of the light as though it were night instead of day. I don't mean night as referred to in romantic pieces, but night as it is in our time with automobiles on highways, and flashlights in faces, and the eyes being deceived about shapes the way light hits them. (1968, n.p.)

Even when a Cunningham work incorporates an element from the natural world, it's invariably transformed in ways that make it virtually unrecognizable. Cage's score for "Inlets II" (1983), for example, amplifies the "natural" sound of dripping water. But the amplification results in distortion that produces a sound unlikely to remind anyone of "nature."

Much the same is true of the work of Johns and Rauschenberg. Cage once described Rauschenberg's white paintings as "airports for lights, shadows, and particles." Certainly, there are remnants of the "natural" world in Rauschenberg's art—the famous stuffed Angora Goat in "Monogram," for example—but these elements are usually juxtaposed against something incongruously "unnatural" (the automobile tire the goat wears around its waist). And in Johns's oeuvre, the natural "landscape" is generally replaced by the map. (See, for example, his "Map" painting based on Buckminster Fuller's Dymaxion Airocean Projection of the Globe, first discussed in Chapter 6.)

There are of course, Cunningham works whose titles make us think of nature. But subsequently what we actually see on stage does little to support our preconceptions. (I defy anyone to point out a single visual image in "Ocean" [1994] that is evocative of either water or waves.) David Tudor's score for "Rainforest" (1968) utilized urban junk sculptures as sound sources (bicycle rims, lawn sprinklers, car windshields), all made to audibly "vibrate" with the help of transducers. Even the already mentioned "Field Dances" and "Summerspace" utilize compositional principles that have little to do with the operations of the natural world. Cunningham has admitted in interviews that the title of "Field Dances" is intended to evoke not only outdoor fields, but *optical* fields as well. And Rauschenberg's costumes and decor for "Summerspace" owe more to the highly studied, mathematically dictated pointillism of Seurat (executed in the studio) than to the impressionist landscapes of Monet (painted out of doors). This is nature viewed through the lenses of science. Indeed, as early as 1955, a Cunningham Company program note for a performance of "Fragments" describes the work as: "The sounds and sights of this dance occur in the contemporary world of magnetic tape, fables of science, and atomic research" (Vaughan 1997, 81).

Of course, there are also occasions when Cunningham's movement seems unmistakably "animal-like." Alastair Macaulay for example, refers to "Inlets II" as

> one of Cunningham's most hushed nature studies . . . those flat rhythms of Cunningham dance can catch the very essence of animal life. I see birds floating, taking wing, hovering, resettling; rodents scuttling and then freezing. (1992, 175)

One think, too, of Cunningham's famous "cat" solo (from "Solo Suite in Space and Time," 1953), or—to my mind—the single best such example, "Beach Birds" (1991), with its port de bras that evokes swooping wings (accented by dark stripes on the arms of the leotards). The illusion of wings was furthered by the fact that the dancer's fingers—very uncharacteristically— were concealed by black gloves. Yet, to my mind, Cunningham rarely "represents" animals in so straightforward a way. What he *does* sometimes do is emulate their heightened powers of sensory alertness. But the perceptual dexterity he invokes is infinitely more useful to the inhabitants of the city than to those who live in the country.

I don't deny that Cunningham displays a continuing interest in nature; but again, this is nature perceived through a distinctly urban temperament. Cunningham's fondness for a remark by Nell Rice from his Black Mountain College years in the early 1950s reveals a great deal about the attitude toward nature that informs his work. Martin Duberman first reported the anecdote in his book *Black Mountain:*

> Cunningham was charmed by Nell Rice's stylish comment as she gazed out at the distant trees: "I've been looking at this landscape for twenty years, and I've come to the conclusion that there's only one tree that's out of place." (1972, 279)

The insistence on linking Cunningham with the natural world turns up even in writing about dances whose basic look, sound, and feel are utterly, inescapably, urban. Arlene Croce, for example, discussed Cunningham's "idea of nature in the theater" in the course of reviewing a concert that featured "Squaregame" (1976). Here the designer, Mark Lancaster, flooded the stage with bright, white, light. The back wall of the theater was fully exposed and the white floor cloth and duffel bags fairly shimmered in the blaze of (clearly) artificial lighting. Lancaster's décor looked more like a cool, clean, minimalist art installation erected in a white museum space than any sort of picnic-on-the-grass (its white floor cloth notwithstanding).

"Variations V" (1965) ended with Cunningham riding a bicycle on stage in a relaxed and leisurely rhythm. But the "fields" he glided through were anything-but-Elysian. They were *electromagnetic* fields that Cunningham "broke" and activated as he navigated his way between Theremin-like, sound-producing antennae. "Canfield" (1969), with its blazing beam of search-light, intermittently illuminating dancers in gray leotards against a white cyc, looked more like a prison break than a pastoral retreat.

In "Place" (1966), the dancers wore sheets of transparent plastic over their leotards. And plastic—as fans of Dustin Hoffman in "The Graduate" (1967) will fondly recall—was the 1960's favorite symbol for the "unnatural." "Place"—in which the dancers also manipulated geodesic lights—concluded, as we've already seen, with Cunningham thrashing along the surface of the floor, half encased in what looked like a plastic garbage bag.

"Place" was arguably the most urban and violent dance Cunningham has ever created: Gordon Mumma, who composed its score, has suggested a possible link to mental illness: "Some people have seen 'Place' as a clinical panorama of the schizophrenic experience, the narrative of a degenerative syndrome which culminates in stark, outright withdrawal" (1967, 14). But one could also argue that "Place" merely intensified one of the distinguishing characteristics of the Cunningham body: its dissociated, inorganic quality, its sense of being "alienated" from both its surroundings and from itself. Cunningham's description of Viola Farber, applies—in one degree or another—to almost all of his best dancers: "Her body often had the look of one part being in balance, and the rest extremely off. Now and again it was like two persons, another just ahead or behind the first" (1968, n.p.).

As much as one may strive to avoid psychological interpretations of Cunningham's choreography, some of his dances—especially the solos—often create an inescapable impression of dementia. In "Loops" (1971), for example, Cunningham's hands and fingers twitch absentmindedly above his head in a manner that suggests a severely deranged street person. During a key moment in "Tango" (1978), Cunningham gazes obsessively at the audience, rather like the paranoid Travis Bickle in Martin Scorsese's *Taxi Driver* (1976); De Niro's legendary character is best known for the scene in which he stares at his own reflection in the mirror and inquires, over and over again, "Are You Talking to Me?" Cunningham's performance in "Tango" is no less disturbing. At another point in the dance, Cunningham finds an abandoned raincoat, but he can only manage to slide one arm into one sleeve. Obviously, dementia is not a peculiarly urban phenomenon, but the fleeting fragments of "characterization" that sometimes creep into Cunningham's solos evoke the sort of anomie and anonymity we're much more likely to associate with urban, rather than rural, life.

And while it's true that Cunningham embraces many aspects of the city that his predecessors in modern dance were apt to condemn, his work is by no means an uncomplicated celebration or denunciation of urban life. He shows us figures who appear to be both isolated and deracinated, but he does this objectively and dispassionately—without any sense of pity or didactic moralizing (which helps to explain Moira Roth's accusation of indifference).

Mechanical Ballets

The distance between Cunningham and the natural world also can be measured by the sheer number of overt machine images in his work. Indeed, long before he began to work with film, video, or the computer, the image of the machine—sometimes mobile and robotic—had become central to Cunningham's dances. "Walkaround Time" (1968) alludes on several occasions to the allegory about the mechanization of sex we find in Duchamp's "The Bride Stripped Bare By Her Bachelors, Even." The partnering in "Walkaround Time" often suggests a "machine game" in which body parts emulate smoothly meshing gears, pistons, and rods. Furthermore, David Behrman's musical score incorporates the "found" sounds of engines alternately roaring into action and sputtering to a halt. (We might also recall those "primitive computers," the art-making machines in Roussel's *Impressions of Africa*, which exerted such a profound impact on the young Duchamp.) For "Aeon" (1961) Rauschenberg designed a moving, smoke-belching contraption with an exposed battery and a light, over which hovered what looked like an antenna (actually it was the stripped metal insides of an umbrella). Similarly, "Winterbranch" (1964) featured a blinking red light (affectionately dubbed, "the monster"), which was dragged across the stage.

These "inanimate movers" in Cunningham's work may well have been inspired by Nam June Paik's growing interest in robotics during this same period of time. In 1960, Paik became fascinated with wireless remote-control devices such as children's cars and model airplanes. Four years later, in 1964, Paik presented a public performance featuring his Robot K-456, a human-sized automaton constructed from metal and wire. But Robot K-456, unlike the robots in much of science fiction and Hollywood fantasy, is no lean, clean, fighting machine. K-456 was a rather vulnerable-looking, sticklike creature who resembled an ordinary human more than a Robo-Cop style cyborg. (On occasion, K-456 even "defecated" a trail of dried beans.) The robot's fragility was most poignantly dramatized nearly two decades later, in 1982, as part of The Whitney Museum's Nam June Paik retrospective. Outside the museum, at the intersection of Madison Avenue and 75th Street, Paik staged what he called "The First Catastrophe of the 21st Century." As he guided K-456 across the avenue via remote control, the robot was hit—and mangled—by a car. The driver was the visual artist William Anastasi, who began to serve as one of Cunningham's artistic advisors in 1984, and who subsequently went on to design settings and/or costumes for "Phrases," "Points in Space," "Shards," "Eleven," "Polarity," and other works choreographed by Cunningham.

"The First Catastrophe of the 21st Century" recalls Cage's comment about Rauschenberg: "Now that Rauschenberg has made a painting with radios in it, does that mean that even without radios, I must go on listening even while I'm looking, everything at once in order not to be run over?" (1961, 101).

The Machine and the Garden

It would be difficult to overestimate the fundamental differences between Cunningham and his major predecessors in the long tradition of modern dance that extends from Duncan through Graham. Cunningham's rapprochement with the lightness, uprightness, and speed of classical ballet (André Levinson's "machine" for manufacturing beauty) is only the most obvious. But the technological dimension of Cunningham's work marks another significant divide between his dances and those of his modern dance predecessors. It's virtually (no pun intended) impossible to imagine the aging Martha Graham working with LifeForms or motion capture technology. Either technique would have struck her as blasphemous—abstract and unbodily—whereas for Cunningham, these recent utilizations of the computer are merely the latest installment in an ongoing series of collaborations with technology that began half a century ago.

And—to return to an example we've already considered—one can only imagine what Graham would have thought of the idea of Cunningham dancing in 1982 in his Westbeth Studio, accompanied by electronic music being played live in Texas and transmitted over the telephone lines. Perhaps it's no coincidence that before Cunningham acquired it, the Westbeth space that serves as "home" to his company was an experimental laboratory run by Bell Telephone. Thus, as long ago as the early 1980s, Cunningham understood the world we will soon inhabit, where "home" is redefined as anyplace on the planet where one has access to a laptop, a cellular phone, and a global positioning system. That is not the sort of "home"—the sort of deeply "rooted" relationship to mother earth—that Graham and the pioneers of modern dance wished to cultivate. In that time-honored American tension between "the machine" and "the garden," Cunningham represents the machine and Graham represents the garden.

10
Rethinking the Thinking Body
The Gaze of Upright Posture

Thus Murphy felt himself split in two, a body and a mind. They
had intercourse apparently, otherwise he could not have known that
they had anything in common. But he felt his mind to be bodytight
and did not understand through what channel the intercourse was
effected nor how the two experiences came to overlap. He was satis-
fied that neither followed from the other. He neither thought a kick
because he felt one nor felt a kick because he thought one.
> —Samuel Beckett, *Murphy* (Robinson, 1969, 88)

The artificial construction people make is that painting is not intellectual, and does not involve much thinking, but involves psychic or
subconscious pressures which are released through the act of painting. But I think painting like mine shows obvious kinds of hesitation
and reworking which people associate with thought.
> —Jasper Johns, 1978 interview (Francis, 1984, 48)

Could a machine think?—Could it be in pain?—Well, is the human
body to be called such a machine? It surely comes as close as possible
to being such a machine.

But a machine surely cannot think! Is that an empirical statement?
No. We only say of a human being and what is like one that it thinks.
We also say it of dolls and no doubt of ghosts too. Look at the word
"to think" as a tool.
> —Ludwig Wittgenstein, *Philosophical Investigations*
> (Francis, 1984, 50)

Recall that in her attack on Duchamp and the "indifferent" gang of four (Johns, Rauschenberg, Cage, and Cunningham), Moira Roth wrote:

> Coolness and intelligence were the hallmarks of The Aesthetic of Indifference and, as a concomitant, there was among the new group a widespread disdain for traditional artistic manual skills and the artist's personal touch. (1977, 50).

Duchamp's ready-mades had already raised a fundamental question about what it means to *make* a work of art. Must the artist's hands and/or body play a necessary role in that process? Can the "work" that goes into a work of art be primarily or exclusively a labor of the intelligence? Can the artist—and this question is particularly vexing with regard to choreographers—function principally as a Cartesian mind pried loose from a body? And an even more basic question: Can a work of art (most poignantly, a work of choreographic art) exist as a purely "conceptual" experience? Duchamp, the father of so much of what we now describe as conceptual art, once confessed:

> I was interested in ideas, not merely in visual products. I wanted to put painting once again at the service of the mind.... This is the direction in which art should turn: to an intellectual expression rather than to an animal expression. (d'Harnoncourt 1973, 16)

This emphasis on mind-over-instinct helps explain Duchamp's penchant for equating the painter's hand with the animal's "paw":

> In French there is an old expression, la patte, meaning the artist's touch, his personal style, his "paw." I wanted to get away from la patte.... The only man in the past whom I really respected was Seurat.... He didn't let his hand interfere with his mind. (Tomkins 1968, 16)

Joseph Kossuth once argued that "After Duchamp, all art is conceptual" (Meyer 1972, x). Does Kossuth's maxim apply to dance as well as to the visual arts? Much of what follows in this chapter grapples with that question.

Of course, Cunningham—unlike some of his younger Judson-era, legatees—never abandons the physical body in favor of purely "conceptual" experience. But Cunningham is the first choreographer whose work begins to raise these potentially heretical issues. One of the many differences between pre-Cunningham and post-Cunningham modern dance is the attitude that each displays toward *intelligence:* the value of possessing it, the strategies for displaying it—above all, the manner of defining it. In the rhetoric of pre-Cunningham modern dance, we hear references galore to the "thinking body" and the "whole" person. But, in practice, this holistic philosophy all too often translates into the triumph of body *over* mind. Alas, if the mind/body ethos of pre-Cunningham modern dance were to be summed up in a single bumper-sticker-style slogan, it might well read: "Man cannot live by head alone." Perhaps this helps explain why Doris Humphrey wasn't the least bit embarrassed to suggest that:

> The person drawn to dance as a profession is notoriously unintellectual. He thinks with his muscles; delights in expression with body, not words; finds analysis painful and boring; and is a creature of physical ebullience. (1959, 17)

Pre-Cunningham modern dance proved only too willing to volunteer its services as a therapeutic antidote for the supposed cerebral excesses of technocratic civilization and its Cartesian habits of thought. "Bodily think-ing" was defined in a manner generically different from verbally expressible modes of intelligence. Edwin Denby sums up the conventional wisdom on this subject when he argues that:

> Dancing is physical motion. It dosen't involve words at all. And so it is an error to suppose that dance intelligence is the same as other sorts of intelligence which involve, on the contrary, words only and no physical movement whatever. (1949, 31)

Denby is talking about dance-in-general. He doesn't distinguish between modern dance and ballet. (The anti-intellectualism of the ballet world is a different matter entirely.)

By contrast, one can argue that the guiding spirits of pre-Cunningham modern dance practice a sophisticated brand of anti-intellectualism that is peculiar to artists and intellectuals: a *distrust* of intellect rather than a *lack* of intellect. (Humphrey, in fact, was reported to have posted a recommended reading list for her dancers. But what matters here is the recommended reading: Havelock Ellis, Adolphe Appia, and Nietzsche-intellectuals to be sure, but the sort of intellectuals who argued *against* the tyranny of intellect.)

Susan Sontag has written about the differences between a viscerally charged painter like Francis Bacon and more cerebral artists such as Duchamp and Jasper Johns. What she says about them is equally applicable to the contrast between pre-Cunningham and post-Cunningham modern dance:

> It is obvious from Bacon's work that he is extremely intelligent. But Bacon's work (unlike Duchamp's or say, Jasper Johns's) is not "about" being intelligent. It is "about" being in pain. (1975, 136)

Much the same can be said of Doris Humphrey—as well as of Duncan, Fuller, and Graham: It is obvious that they are *intelligent;* and, yet, their work is not "about" being intelligent. For example, one would be reluctant to describe most pre-Cunningham modern dance as "brainy." (To be sure, "brainy" is an adjective rarely applied to modern dance before the advent of Cunningham and the Judson era.) Deborah Jowitt recently referred to the Cunningham company's "high IQ limbs." It's difficult to imagine her praising Graham's dancers in the same way—even though their bodies are just as technically high-powered.

Many of the dancers who have performed with Cunningham first gravitated toward his work (at least in part) because it struck them as "brainy." Braininess in this context includes—but is hardly limited to—what Denby referred to as the verbal dimension of intelligence. Cunningham himself, who danced with Martha Graham between 1939 and 1945, has confessed that one source of his growing dissatisfaction with the dance community was its intellectual narrowness and indifference—if not outright hostility—toward ideas:

> It was difficult for me at the time . . . to talk with dancers. Not that I don't like them. They would mainly talk about the way somebody did something: they didn't like this or did like that, it always had to do with personalities. It's like gossip. That's entertaining and I like it too, but I also want to talk about ideas and there wasn't anybody I could talk with, except John [Cage]. I couldn't talk with dancers. (1985, 42–43)

Recalling his first experience with Cage in a composition class (way back in 1939), Cunningham has said that

> [it was] a revelation—suddenly there was something very precise and very strict to work with. He simply made us make things—you had to think about it, not just have some feeling about what you were going to do next, but *think* about it, and that was an extraordinary experience. (Vaughan 1997, 17)

Clearly, what distressed him about modern dance at the time was even more of a problem on Broadway and in the world of ballet. Calvin Tomkins tells the following story about Cunningham in his book, *The Bride and The Bachelors:*

> In 1943 [Agnes] de Mille offered Cunningham a dancing role in *Oklahoma!* for which she was doing the choreography. Cunningham turned it down. Six months later though, he did accept a solo dancing part in another show that Miss de Mille choreographed, *One Touch of Venus*. He rehearsed and performed with the show for a week in Boston, and felt so ridiculous that he withdrew before the opening in New York. (1968, 255)

It may well be that the very idea of a "Broadway musical"—or, for that matter, the utter absence of ideas in the average Broadway musical—simply insulted his intelligence. Cunningham subsequently acknowledged that "probably a lot of dancers who have worked with me may have wanted to study with me originally because of the ideas, not just my ideas—the rapport with contemporary music and art" (1985, 71). This rapport between Cunningham and the art world was nowhere more evident than with respect to theatrical pretense and role-playing, the very idea of which was viewed by many visual artists as an insult to the intelligence. Twyla Tharp was one of many post-Cunningham choreographers who lived in close personal and professional proximity to the art world, where a fierce anti-illusionism was very much the order of the day. Note what she has to say about the radically differing attitude toward impersonation in the work of Graham and Cunningham:

> [Graham's] dances were narratives, requiring her dancers to play roles. This involved an element of pretend with which I was uncomfortable. I could not begin imagining myself a Fury or, for that matter, even the star of the piece herself, Clytemnestra. I could not picture myself other than what I was—an Indiana farm girl to whom seeds meant plants, not metaphors. Merce Cunningham must have had similar feelings when he left Martha's company in the late Forties. Martha's dancers approached ideals in their roles, portraying gods and goddesses, but Merce's company became a blend of individuals who stamped their dancing with their own personal characteristics; no one in the Cunningham company danced in roles with names other than their own. (Jefferson 1992, 13)

To most New York painters and sculptors in the late 1960s, *every* variety of theatrical role playing appeared childish and unsophisticated. Many Cunningham dancers take a comparably dim view of "pretense" or the slightest semblance of "make-believe." Douglas Dunn, who danced with the company from 1969 to 1973, tells the following story about an exceedingly unrepresentative moment in Cunningham's "Objects":

> When Merce made a piece called "Objects" in 1970, there was a section in which about four of us had to sit down on the floor and mime playing jacks; and for the first and perhaps only time in my stint with the company, I was really offended and turned off. . . . I came here to dance; and [Cunningham] has all this mythology about the steps, and I'm doing it and that's great. And all of a sudden I'm asked to be a *mime*—something I wasn't comfortable with at all. I don't like that attitude about movement. (Brown 1992, 112)

The "attitude about movement" that Dunn refers to is another index of intelligence. Especially in the late 1960s and early 1970s, certain dancers gravitated away from other companies and toward Cunningham precisely because his work struck them (above all) as "intelligent." Albert Reid, for example, who danced with Cunningham between 1964 and 1968, left his previous venue, Alwin Nikolais's company, largely because he found the work there so "simpleminded." But it would be misleading to equate Cunningham's conception of "the thinking body" with the intellectual "buzz" his dances generate in the form of conversation. The "intelligence" of his movement is, first and foremost, a quality inherent in the movement itself. And yet—I hasten to add—Cunningham's mode of bodily intelligence remains comfortable with (rather than suspicious of) the verbal dimensions of thought. In an essay about Cunningham and Duchamp, Noël Carroll and Sally Banes provide a beautiful description of the difference between the *image* of the human mind we derive from both Graham and Cunningham:

> Whereas the image of human thought in Graham was heavy, organic, brooding, and altogether nineteenth century, in Cunningham, it is permutational, correlational, strategic, exact, rarefied, and airy. This is not to say that Cunningham presents a pantomime of the mind, but that he presents the body as intelligent in a specifically contemporary way. (1983, 73)

What accounts for these differences? In what ways does the movement of the body serve to generate images of the mind? (After all, it's not as if Cunningham's dancers announce their intelligence by reciting passages from the works of Descartes, Wittgenstein, or Bertrand Russell.) Presumably, the difference between "organic" and "brooding," on the one hand, and "permutational" or "correlational," on the other, is (literally) *embodied* in two different movement vocabularies.

It's helpful to recall Simone Forti's observation about Cunningham that we first noted in Chapter 6. Forti is a dancer/choreographer whose organic inclinations are fundamentally at odds with Cunningham's. In her own choreography, she frequently attempted to emulate the movement patterns of infants and young children. Two of her earliest works, "See-Saw" and "Rollers" (1960), were derived almost entirely from observation of children on teeter-totters and other forms of playground equipment. The goal was to coax the adult bodies of her performers back into patterns of movement that children exhibit unselfconsciously. Forti also choreographed a series of dances that she called "the animal studies" where the sources of movement inspiration came primarily from four-legged creatures. (In 1974, she performed a solo titled "Crawling" in which her principle method of traversing space was—as the title implies—crawling across the floor.) In her devastating assessment of Cunningham's movement style, she criticizes "the arbitrary isolation of the different parts of the body." The heart of her critique is the contrast she draws between Cunningham's "adult isolated articulation" and her own fondness for the "holistic and generalized response of infants." This comparison is very revealing. The word infant derives from the Latin root "infans," which means, literally "unable to speak." Infants are, by definition, preverbal; and their movements presumably have not yet been inflected (or infected) by language. Thus, Forti's notion of "adult, isolated *articulation*" takes on a double meaning: linguistic as well as physical. Is it purely coincidental that the word "articulate" usually connotes verbal proficiency? And is there a connection between the "adult" isolations of Cunningham's movement and its *articulateness*? Lewis Hyde, in the course of exploring the etymology and varied meanings of the Latin "articulus," notes

> "Articulate" nowadays usually has to do with speech, but it also means joining bones together, as in this description from an old anatomy book: "[The body's] most movable joints are those in which the adjacent bones are articulated on the principle either of a pivot or of a hinge.".
>
> When these words describe joints in language, they again connote clarity and precision. "Jointed" speech has clear divisions to it, just as a masonry wall has clear lines between the bricks; these divisions turn the sounds that any animal can make into intelligible human language.... To break an uninterrupted flow of letters into words, sentences, paragraphs, and chapters (or the older "articles"), to divide it with spaces, commas, periods, indentations and so on, is to articulate it, to make evident the places where thought itself has joints or points of demarcation. (1998, 24)

This emphasis on spaces, interruptions, and joints also helps explain why we routinely describe Cunningham's style of dancing as "highly articulate." The jointedness of his movement—the attention his choreography calls to the clean flexing and unflexing of the joints—is one key to this articulate clarity.

What Banes and Carroll call the "permutational" and "correlational" image of the mind embodied in Cunningham's movement is reflected in the way his choreography "articulates" the body, assembling and reassembling its component parts in a manner that mirrors the analytical nature of verbally expressed intelligence (making "evident the places where thought itself has joints or points of demarcation"). Taking another hint from Simone Forti's observation about Cunningham, we can advance the argument a step further by exploring the contrast between linguistic articulation (a "thoroughly adult" activity) and the "holistic and generalized response of infants."

A great deal of sophisticated art (Forti's included) is designed to illustrate Baudelaire's maxim that creativity is "childhood recaptured at will." The return to innocence—seeing the world once again through the eyes of the child—is a time-honored modernist practice. But the art of a choreographer such as Cunningham moves in the opposite direction, toward a distinctively "adult" conception of intelligence. We see this in the emphasis that Cunningham, his collaborators, and his legatees all place on *complexity.* They conceive of their art as a thoroughly "adult" activity, inaccessible to the mind and/or sensorium of the child. As Cage wrote of Duchamp: "He requires that we know that being an artist isn't child's play: equivalent in difficulty—surely—to playing chess." (1975, 68). Cage added:

> Duchamp showed the usefulness of addition (mustache). Rauschenberg showed the function of subtraction (de Kooning). Well, we look forward to

> multiplication and division. It is safe to assume that someone will learn trigonometry. Johns...(67)

And Johns rose eagerly to the challenge: "Generally, I am opposed to painting which is concerned with conceptions of simplicity. Everything looks very busy to me" (Bernstein 1985, 219). Likewise, Johns is quick to acknowledge a connection between complexity, hesitation, and thought. ("... painting like mine shows obvious kinds of hesitation and reworking which people associate with thought [Francis 1984, 48].")

Upright Posture

The unashamedly "adult" nature of Merce Cunningham's choreography is evident not only in the "articulate" nature of the Cunningham body but in its upright orientation as well. Unlike the infant—who neither talks nor walks—the Cunningham dancer is both articulate and squarely planted on two feet. Indeed, nothing marks Cunningham's break with Graham and early modern dance quite so dramatically as the emphasis his choreography places on upright posture. As Cunningham once declared, "A man is a two-legged creature—more basically and more intimately than he is anything else" (Vaughan 1997, 86). Reviewing Cunningham's very first solo concert in New York in 1944, Edwin Denby noted that:

> his instep and his knees are extraordinarily elastic and quick; his steps, runs, knee bends and leaps are brilliant in lightness and speed. His torso can turn on its vertical axis with great sensitivity; his shoulders are held lightly free and his head poises intelligently. The arms are light and long, they float. (1949, 291)

Lightness; uprightness; the head poised "intelligently." Not the sort of qualities one associates with the typical Graham dancer (certainly not in the 1940s). But Cunningham's verticality, the importance his technique places on the back rather than the torso, the speed and complexity of his footwork—all of these elements are more than just knee-jerk repudiations of that "love-affair-with-the-floor" which virtually defined modern dance at the time. Graham emphasized the tension between spine and pelvis; but Cunningham emphasizes the verticality of the spine. His dancers maintain the essence of their verticality even when they lean against one another. They tend to tilt without bending at the waist.

In a 1996 interview, Cunningham told of a remarkable encounter he once had with Helen Keller. The year was 1941. The place was Martha Graham's studio, where Cunningham—then a member of Graham's company—was immersed in her afternoon technique class:

> At the end of the class, Miss Keller apparently asked if she could touch a dancer. Miss Graham asked me to stand at the barre. Miss Keller and her companion

came to my side. I was facing the barre, could not see her, but felt the two hands around my waist, like bird wings, so soft. I began to do small jumps. Her fingers, still around my waist, moved slightly as though fluttering. I stopped, and was able to understand what she said to her companion. "So light, like the mind." (Vaughan 1997, 24)

There's something remarkably poignant about Helen Keller—whose tactile sense was, no doubt, highly evolved—analogizing Cunningham's verticality and lightness to the workings of the mind. The "upward" journey from body to mind is the traditional path of Freudian sublimation. In Cunningham's choreography, we find an art firmly rooted in the body that nevertheless celebrates (rather than vilifies) the analytical propensities of the intellect. But at the same time, this partial sublimation of libidinal and bodily energy constitutes another major repudiation of the ethos of primitivism. Cage makes no secret of his distaste for art that exploits the power of raw sexuality. He has openly criticized the way Nam June Paik sometimes employs overtly sexual content (indeed conduct) in performance:

> Paik's involvement with sex, introducing it into his music, does not conduce toward sounds being sounds. It only confuses matters. I am sure that his performance with Charlotte Moorman of my 26'1.499 for a String Player is not faithful to the notation, that the liberties taken are in favor of actions rather than sound events in time. I am thinking of the point where Paik, stripped to the waist, imitates a cello, his back being bowed by Charlotte Moorman. (1993, 24)

In 1986, I interviewed Cage about his score for "Roaratorio." Just as I was about to leave his apartment, he volunteered a quite extraordinary confession: "You know," he remarked, "I've never really liked dance."

"What do you mean?" I asked in utter bewilderment: "Why not?" Adopting an expression of mock disgust, he shook he head and said simply, "All those faces, all those (and he paused again for special emphasis) . . . *bodies!*"

My motive for repeating this story is not to suggest that Cage's lifelong involvement with dance was fundamentally disingenuous. Quite the contrary. It's precisely this touch of puritanism in Cage that has lent a chastened rigor to the Cunningham/Cage aesthetic. He and Cunningham know how easily the body can seduce, how effortlessly it can push an audience's hot buttons; and they're eager to circumvent that sort of facile manipulation. This also helps explain why so many Cunningham aficionados were appalled by the sexy, flesh-revealing costumes that James Hall designed for "Way Station" in 2001. Cunningham, of course, is philosophically committed to accepting—and finding a way of working with—whatever his designers give him. Whether or not he was privately dismayed by these glitzy costumes we may never know, but those who cherish his refusal to exploit his dancers' sexuality would like to believe so.

This implicit critique of the connection between dance and sexuality marks a major break with the Graham aesthetic, ever eager to situate itself in what Graham once called the "the house of pelvic truth." I'm not only referring to the shameless, Halston-designed costumes that Graham's dancers wore as her choreographic powers declined precipitously during the 1980s. Much of the 20th-century fascination with "the primitive" can be attributed to a growing loss of faith in the great Freudian project of sublimation (the activity Stephen Spender set out to celebrate when he argued that "Writing poetry is a spiritual activity which makes one completely forget, for the time being, that one has a body" [Brown 1959, 157].) But in the century of D. H. Lawrence and Isadora Duncan, artists became more and more convinced that the soul is *in* the body. Thus *de*sublimation became the great project of high culture throughout much of the 20th century. The status of dance immediately began to rise, because dance seemed inherently the least *sublimated* of the arts. Given that its raw material (its physical medium) is the human body itself, dance actively resists the impulse toward sublimation even when the performer's body is crafted into the most exquisitely wrought formal structures. To quote Havelock Ellis once again, "Dance is no mere translation or abstraction from life, it is life itself." A rather more succinct formulation of this credo appeared in a popular T-shirt slogan of the late 1960s: "Fuck Art, Let's Dance." Of course, the project of desublimation, once initiated, is difficult to arrest. In a British punk club in the late 1970s, I came across a T-shirt emblazoned with the slogan "Fuck dance, let's fuck."

Theories of Evolution

But Cunningham's "uprightness" is more than a model of sublimation, more than a reproach to those who regard dance as inherently erotic. His dances also pay implicit tribute to the role that upright posture has played in the evolution of human intelligence. By contrast, Rudolf Arnheim has argued that modern dance—or at least the tradition that culminates in the work of Graham—implies an evolutionary *regression*. He once spoke of:

> the modern dancer's assertion that movements should issue from the center of the body, the torso.... If one asks observers to compare movements issuing from the head or limbs with those springing from the torso, they describe the former as conveying intellectual, conscious action whereas the latter suggest nonconscious, largely emotional behavior. (1966, 264)

Arnheim then poses this question:

> Does this mean then, that in the [modern] dance the conception of man is reduced to a biologically lower, precerebral stage? The dancer seems to be faced with the dilemma that functionally the highest, specifically human powers of the

nervous system control the organism from the head, while the visible structure of the body suggests as the center an area that typically produces non-reflective action, such as in fear, sex, or the lazy stretching of the muscles.... On this plane, the phylogenetically late developments of the organism lose weight. (265)

Viewed in this light, Cunningham's balletic verticality takes modern dance in a very different direction—one that reaffirms our evolutionary mandate (which is to say, our upright posture). Verticality, of course, also serves to distinguish "adult, isolated articulation" from "the holistic and generalized response of infants." Uprightness in fact, helps to establish an essential division between nature and culture. In an essay titled "The Vertical: The Fundamental Principle of Classic Dance," the Russian balletomane A. K. Volinsky wrote: "With the vertical begins the history of human culture and the gradual conquest of heaven and earth.... Standing upright is an act of the spirit that overcomes the natural state and raises man above nature" (1983, 256).

Of course, one can adopt an upright posture without automatically availing oneself of the intellectual and perceptual advances that such posture makes possible. Otherwise, the average ballet would automatically exude a greater degree of bodily intelligence than do more earthbound forms of modern dance. Possessing such potential and actually *utilizing* it are two very different things. And, needless to say, the tribal peoples that early-20th-century anthropologists identified as "primitive" did not walk on all fours. Still, the contrast between Cunningham and Graham couldn't be greater in this regard. Cunningham technique pays scant attention to the sort of "floor work" that figures so prominently in a daily Graham class. As Cunningham once noted "I start from a standing position because that's mostly the way we move. We don't really move sitting down much ..." (1985, 60). In other words, Cunningham's movement is based (to a much greater extent than traditional modern dance) on who we are as a species, on where we *stand* (literally!) in relation to the rest of the animal kingdom.

No aspect of Cunningham's legacy has become more poignant in recent years than his unflagging commitment to upright posture. Arthritis has made it visibly painful for Cunningham to walk, let alone dance. In "Trackers" (1991), he travels, as we've seen, with a portable barre—which also doubles as a walker. Alternately sad and heroic, Cunningham emerges as a performer determined to remain vertical despite the debilitations of age. In 1999, when Cunningham appeared on stage with Mikhail Baryshnikov in "Occasion Piece," a series of makeshift barres were constructed as hand-holds behind the separate boxes of Jasper Johns's décor for "Walkaround Time" (which was recycled, "event style," as the setting for this piece). Note again Denby's observation that Cunningham's "head poises intelligently." Even in

1999, the "intelligent poise" of Cunningham's head remained readily apparent. But as early as 1943, in the course of writing about Cunningham's dancing for Martha Graham, Denby had already noticed that: "Among the dancers in the company, Merce Cunningham's lightness, and his constantly intelligent head are very fine" (1986, 187). Is there any other choreographer for whom the flexibility of the head (and the independence of the head from the rest of the body) is more essential? Discussing the principle aim of his technique class, Cunningham once said "My point always was to make people strong and resilient in the head..." (1985, 54). This strength and resilience is more than merely anatomical. It's part of what the great Cunningham dancer, Carolyn Brown, alluded to when she argued that Cunningham technique is "designed to develop flexibility in the mind as well as in the body" (Klosty 1975, 22). This dual emphasis on the head and the mind often makes itself immediately apparent in the eyes of the Cunningham dancer which tend to radiate an alert intelligence.

In fact, there's an important connection between the evolution of upright posture and the increasing prominence of the visual sense. In *Civilization and its Discontents*, Freud speaks of "the new form of life that began with the erect posture" (1930, 78). What he means is that on all fours, the sense of sight is no more important than the senses of smell and touch. But the moment the organism becomes bipedal and stands upright, the sense of sight is literally raised up from the ground, disengaging it from earthier, olfactory and tactile sensations. (The skull of Homo Erectus reveals eyes that are larger and more widely spaced than those of its primate predecessors; its vision is becoming increasingly stereoscopic.) The result is a distinctively new mode of perception that the psychologist Erwin Straus calls "the *gaze* of upright posture." Straus defines this mode of perception as the ability "to look at things straight ahead and withstand their thrust" (1963, 340). This is a very apt description of the perceptual conditions that prevail during a Cunningham performance. Rather than "riding" a musical pulse, the dancers must concentrate so as not to be distracted by the accompanying sounds. And the spectator must constantly, actively make decisions about where to focus his or her visual and auditory attention.

Cunningham's dances demand an unprecedented degree of alertness and mental agility on the part of those who perceive them as well as those who perform them. In the terminology of "effort/shape," Cunningham style is referred to as "the alert style." One index of this alertness is the effect that the gaze of upright posture has on the head. Whether watching a Cunningham dance or performing a Cunningham dance, the head tends to swivel, to scan. Charles Atlas filmed a short documentary about the making of "Locale," his 1979 video collaboration with Cunningham. Its title is very revealing: "Roamin 'I'" (which can, of course, also be pronounced as "roaming *eye*").

This equating of "I" and "Eye"—the self as an essentially visual (rather than tactile) entity—is an essential theme in Erwin Straus's argument about "the gaze of upright posture." According to Straus:

> With the acquisition of upright posture, a characteristic change in language occurs. In the early years, when speaking of himself, a child uses his given name. However, when he has reached the age when he can stand firmly on his own feet, he begins to use the pronoun "I" for himself. This change marks a first gaining of independence. (1963, 171)

Straus also proposes a connection between the gaze of upright posture and the cultivation of various varieties of "distance" (e.g., "upright posture removes us from the ground, keeps us away from things, and holds us aloof from our fellow-men" [170]). He also proposes a connection between upright posture and the organism's evolving ability to oppose "automatic" responses and instinctual "drives." "Evolution," he writes, "is a passage from . . . the most automatic to the most voluntary (183)":

> Upright posture characterizes the human species. Nevertheless, each individual has to struggle in order to make it really his own. . . . While the heart continues to beat, from its fetal beginning to death, without our active intervention, and while breathing neither demands nor tolerates our voluntary interference beyond narrow limits, upright posture remains a task throughout our lives. . . . In getting up, in reaching the upright posture, man must oppose the forces of gravity. It seems to be his nature to oppose, with natural means, nature in its impersonal, fundamental aspects. However, gravity is never fully overcome; upright posture always maintains its character of counteraction. It calls for our activity and attention. . . . Much as we are part of nature with every breath, with every bite, with every step, we first become our true selves in waking opposition to nature. (168)

"Waking opposition to nature": It's difficult to conceive of another phrase that conveys the essence of Cunningham's "alert style" more succinctly.

The Theatron and Theory

In Chapter 6, I proposed some distinctions between ritual and theater, characterizing the former as a primarily "tactile experience" and the latter as primarily "visual." I also pointed out that the root of our English word "theater" is the Greek "theatron," which translates as "seeing place"—and that signifies, in practice, the creation of a distinct architectural space for detached spectators. The special kind of "seeing" that we practice in the theatron is made possible by "the gaze of upright posture." This kind of seeing also promotes a special kind of thinking; it is seeing *informed* by thinking. Michael Goldman makes the connection:

> "Theory" and "Theater" derive from the same source. The theater is a theatron, a seeing place, but the kind of seeing involved is legitimately *theorin* as opposed to other seeing—an inspection, a looking at with a distinctive intensity, as a traveler or ambassador looks at things. (1975, 113)

What Goldman describes is remarkably similar to the relationship between seeing and thinking that Leo Steinberg associates with a work such as Johns's "Target With Four Faces": "Johns puts two flinty things in a picture and makes them work against one another so hard that the mind is sparked. Seeing then becomes thinking" (1972, 14).

In their current English incarnations, the words theatre and theory seem unlikely companions. But if, as Goldman suggests, we trace them back to their etymological roots, it becomes evident that they share a common ancestry. Eric Partridge, in his *Short Etymological Dictionary of Modern English*, writes that the root words for "theatre" include not only "theatron" ("a thing compelling the gaze"), but also theorein ("a sight, an object of study, a speculation, hence a theorem"). Turn to the word "theory" on the very next page, and you are referred back to "theatre." Thus, at least etymologically, the two words are blood brothers. And in practice, both make similar demands on us: both require that we detach ourselves from the "thing seen," that we stand apart from it, and examine it from a distance, from multiple perspectives.

Thus, the primitivist's desire to reritualize even the most *theatrical* forms of dance reveals another, related aspect of dance-world primitivism: not just an aversion to the concept of distance or a preference (clearly related) for the tactile over the visual, but an implicit anti-intellectualism—a visceral distaste for art that appears to possess a theoretical component. Recall Arlene Croce's 1968 comment about Cunningham: "I thought, watching Merce's dances, that I was being subjected to a theory about dancing. I was too worried about the theory to look at the dancing…"(1968, 24). Straus and Goldman would see this as a false dichotomy. One watches a choreographer like Cunningham, they might well suggest, in a spirit that is both informed and enhanced by theory. To cite Michael Goldman once again: "The kind of seeing involved is legitimately *theorin* as opposed to other seeing."

"Biped," Mutation, and Thinking Machines

Around the time that Merce Cunningham's "Biped" had its first New York performances in 1999, a television documentary about the dance appeared on cable's Sci-Fi channel. This was not altogether inappropriate. If ever a Cunningham dance appeared to have been inspired by the writings of Arthur C. Clarke, it was "Biped." I'm well aware of the dangers of interpreting Cunningham's dances in allegorical ways (a practice that in most other contexts, I've actively resisted). But here was a work whose very title evokes an evolutionary landmark: the emergence of upright posture, that dividing line between human beings and most other primates. In addition, "Biped" juxtaposed live, upright bodies with motion-captured outlines of forms— both animate and inanimate—that existed only in "virtual" space. Paul Kaiser suggests that the title "Biped" has a dual connotation: technological as well as anatomical. Discussing the genesis of the dance—and the multiple meanings that he associates with its title—Kaiser wrote:

> Merce had started choreographing a new full-length dance, which he had decided to call "Biped," a name of special significance to us. "Biped" had been the working title for the alpha and beta releases of the figure animation software we had used to choreograph the virtual dance of "Hand-Drawn Spaces." Biped was as apt a term for Cunningham's choreography as it was for the software, for Merce's lifelong interest has been to figure out all that a body on two legs can do. (2000, n.p.).

Erwin Straus, building on Freud's ideas, develops the argument that upright posture fundamentally alters the relationship between human beings and the ground. Cunningham's "Biped" seemed to imply that the *next* great evolutionary transformation beyond the "gaze of upright posture" may well involve the transcendence of the "grounded" body. Virtual reality and cyberspace promote precisely that sort of transcendence.

The LifeForms-influenced movement motifs in recent Cunningham choreography—the lifted neck that directs the dancer's gaze up and away from the ground—may signify an anticipation of this process. The motion-captured imagery that's projected on the scrim in "Biped" seems to take us alternately backward and forward in evolutionary time, with the emergence of bipedal, upright posture as the dividing line. On occasion, we see wafting wisps of smoke that slowly congeal into suggestions of living forms. Analogously, the partnering of the live dancers upstage of the projections sometimes takes the form of bodies back-to-front, with two performers facing the same direction, thereby hinting at the possibility that a single body is replicating or perhaps cloning itself.

There are many images in "Biped" that suggest either division or multiplication of forms, both actual and virtual. "Biped" begins with a series of solos, in which each dancer seems not so much to exit as to dissolve into a fathomless black abyss at the rear of the stage. When one dancer reenters and stands opposite four additional bodies, it's as if her image had suddenly been multiplied by mirrors. One could even suggest an allegory in which images of recombinant DNA illustrate evolutionary growth at the genomic level. But the bulk of the dance suggests a more futuristic vision: the emergence of cybernetic organisms that can transcend the usual anatomical limitations of the human biped. Earlier I mentioned the motion-captured "stick bodies" in "Biped" that seem to suggest an animated version of Duchamp's "Nude Descending A Staircase." Paul Kaiser specifically cites these "cubist/chronophotographic bodies" as "our nod towards Duchamp." Cunningham has long been fascinated with the allegory about the mechanization of sex that informs Duchamp's "Bride Stripped Bare By Her Bachelors, Even." And Jasper Johns' setting for "Walkaround Time," which appropriates the iconography from Duchamp's "Bride . . . ," was incorporated into a new, one-time-only work called "Occasion Piece" that accompanied the New York premiere of "Biped." If the iconography in the Johns/Duchamp setting for "Walkaround Time" refers to a futuristic fusion of machines and human sexuality, then the title of that 1968 work evokes a sort of pas de deux between a human programmer and his computer (i.e., he "walks around" for a time while the machine is on autopilot). And the juxtaposition of live dancers and motion-captured projections that Cunningham utilizes in "Biped" exemplifies the ever-increasing fusion of "organic" and "inorganic" forms in an age increasingly dominated by the technobody.

But digital motion-capture technology constitutes merely the latest example of Cunningham's ongoing interest in the relationship between the animate and the inanimate. In Chapter 9, we discussed the mobile robotic devices that appeared in dances such as "Winterbranch" and "Aeon" in the early 1960s, inanimate movers that may have been inspired by Nam June Paik's Robot K-456. Paik—it's worth mentioning—was insistent that his robot emulate the upright posture of human beings; and his reasons were rooted in theories about the evolution of intelligence. According to Wulf Herzogenrath, a leading historian of video art:

> Paik wanted to build an anthropomorphic robot, because he was fascinated by the scientist's discovery that the human brain had begun to grow after man stopped walking on all fours and had to figure out what to do with his two "free" hands. (1993, 98)

(It's entirely possible that the writer Paik had been reading was Erwin Straus.) Clearly, Paik wanted to endow Robot K-456 with essential human qualities such as upright posture.

Fredric Jameson, in his classic study of postmodernism, wrote of Paik:

> I believe that the most striking emblem of this new mode of thinking relationships can be found in the work of Nam June Paik, whose stacked or scattered television screens, positioned at intervals within lush vegetation, or winking down at us from a ceiling of strange new video stars, recapitulate over and over again prearranged sequences or loops of images which return at dysynchronous moments on the various screens. . . . [Paik's viewer] is called upon to do the impossible, namely, to see all the screens at once in their radical and random difference; such a viewer is asked to follow the evolutionary mutation of David

> Bowie in *The Man Who Fell to Earth* (who watches fifty-seven television screens simultaneously) and to rise somehow to a level at which the vivid perception of radical difference is in and of itself a new mode of grasping what used to be called relationship: something for which the word *collage* is still only a very feeble name. (1991, 224)

Jameson connects a number of themes that recur throughout this book: the collage aesthetic; the increasing interpenetration of the organic and the technological; and, most important—at least for the purposes of this section—the idea of the evolution (or mutation) of new modes of perceptual intelligence. He elaborates on this idea when he discusses the perceptual difficulties encountered when we attempt to orient ourselves in what he calls postmodern "hyperspace":

> We do not yet possess the perceptual equipment to match this new hyperspace, as I will call it, in part because our perceptual habits were formed in that older kind of space I have called the space of high modernism. The newer architecture therefore...stands as something like an imperative to grow new organs, to expand our sensorium and our body to some new, yet unimaginable, perhaps ultimately impossible, dimensions. (38–39)

In an intriguing historical coincidence, Jameson's essay appeared in—of all years—1984. That same Orwellian year also marked the publication of William Gibson's novelistic envisioning of cyberspace, *Neuromancer*. Since then, a vast literature has come into being—both fiction and nonfiction—devoted to cybernetic organisms (e.g., cyborgs). The underlying premise of much of this writing is that the next great evolutionary leap for the human (or, more properly, posthuman) being will be driven by the convergence of neurophysiology, robotic hardware, and "virtual (computer-enhanced) reality."

A few weeks after seeing Cunningham's "Biped" for the first time (during the summer of 1999), I learned of a recently completed experiment at the San Diego Institute for Non-Linear Science. Utilizing a process known as reverse engineering, a mathematical model was produced that "mapped" the neural circuits in a spiny lobster. Clusters of biological neurons were replaced with electronic substitutes; and the creature—now a true cyborg—continued to function "normally." Analogously, the Media Lab at MIT has been experimenting for some years now with "wearable computation." Steven Mann, one of the pioneers of this technology, has devised a pair of ultra-enhanced sunglasses that contain a miniaturized computer screen and video camera enabling the wearer to transmit what he sees directly onto his Web page. Mann's computer files thus become an immediate extension of his visual memory; and the special features on his mini-cam, when set on say, the freeze-frame setting, allow him to read the writing on the rotating wheels of a car or to, in effect, zoom-in on the individual blades of a fast moving airplane propeller. Clearly, it's only a matter of time before neuron-transistors implanted in the human brain will be able to communicate wirelessly with the Internet. Indeed, Ray Kurzweil, also of MIT, predicts that within 50 years, microscopic "nanobots" will carry these neuron-transistors to the individual nerve fibers that control the five senses. The result will be "virtual reality from within"—computer-enhanced experience that is perceptually indistinguishable from externally generated sensory stimuli.

It's difficult to imagine a scenario more inimical to the underlying ethos of "primitivism." Not only does the body lose all claim to "naturalness." But, perhaps more to the point, the idea of the "primitive other"—once the very emblem of authenticity—can now be as easily "simulated" as any other virtual reality. And if the sensorium of a 21st-century Gaughin is unable to distinguish the actual Tahiti that exists outside his mind from the virtual Tahiti simulated within his mind, then technological evolution will have driven the final nail into the coffin of modernist "primitivism." Stelarc, the contemporary performance artist who often implants various sorts of transmitters in his own body, has written a much-quoted essay called "Obsolete Body." In it, he argues that:

> It is time to question whether a bipedal, breathing body with binocular vision and a 1400cc brain is an adequate biological form. It cannot cope with the quantity, complexity and quality of information it has accumulated; it is intimidated by the precision, speed and power of technology and it is biologically ill-equipped to cope with its new extraterrestrial environment.
> ... It might be the height of technological folly to consider the body obsolete in form and function , yet it might (also) be the height of human realisations. For it is only when the body becomes aware of its present position that it can map its post-evolutionary strategies. ... THE BODY IS OBSOLETE. (2001)

Of course, it's more than a bit of a leap from Cunningham's tentative work with the computer to that sort of cybernetic future. But one of Cunningham's most distinguished—and distinctive—legatees, the choreographer and dancer Kenneth King (who first came to prominence in the mid-1960s), has long been fascinated by the relationship(s) between the dancer's body and the science of artificial intelligence. King's prose—reader be warned— often borders on incomprehensible technobabble. But for all of its daunting difficulties, his extended tribute to Cunningham (written in 1991) is worth quoting, because it associates the latter's technique with a tendency toward both robotics and artificial intelligence. King characterizes Cunningham as:

> the most advanced choreographer on the planet. ... Merce's body was the first to systemically synthesize ballet and modern dance to find all the multiplex ways the contracting and rotating spine could work with and against the mechanics of the

legs to create planar shifts and axial transformations, and the first to register the digital pulse, coincidentally around 1950, at the time when TV's were entering every household. The digital pulse links three contracting spinal and thoracic zones in the lower, middle, and upper spine. And: when you pulse, contract, and rotate the spine's "geomimetric" facings, you get the metatheoremics of robotics! Merce's dance is already a kind of futuristic Artificial Intelligence. (1992, 187, 188)

I haven't the faintest idea what "geomimetric" facings or "metatheoremics" are; clearly, we've left the realm of anatomy and entered the realm of science fiction. And yet, what other choreographer would inspire such flights of futuristic fancy? From the very beginning, the chief distinction between Cunningham and his predecessors in modern dance has always centered on the idea of what it means to be "human." Jill Johnston, discussing the consternation that Cunningham's choreography generated among the modern dance community in the early 1950s, wrote "One of the key words was HUMAN. There was much discussion about what it meant to be human . . . they did feel, I guess, that Merce threatened the concept they had of what it meant to be human" (1968, 21). Cunningham was the first choreographer to unleash the potential inherent in the gaze of upright posture; and once one's gaze is no longer directed toward the ground, the horizon of possibility becomes (virtually) limitless.

Abstract Expressionism and the Horizontal Plane

We've already discussed the special significance of the floor and the ground for both Jackson Pollock and Martha Graham. I even suggested that the practice of displaying Pollock's paintings in an upright position can obscure an essential aspect of their identity. In her book *The Optical Unconscious*, Rosalind Krauss writes:

This, I think, is the process of sublimating Pollock. Of raising him up from the dissolute squat, in his James Dean dungarees and black tee-shirt, slouched over his paintings in the disarray of his studio or hunkered down on the running board of his old Ford. This is the posture, in all its lowness, projected by so many famous photographs, images recording the athletic abandon of the painting gesture but also the dark brooding silence of the stilled body, with its determined isolation from everything urban, everything "cultured." The photographs had placed him on the road, like Kerouac, clenching his face into the tight fist of beat refusal, making an art of violence, of "howl." Clem's [Clement Greenberg's] mission was to lift him above those pictures, just as it was to lift the paintings Pollock made off from the ground where he'd made them, and onto the wall. Because it was only on the wall that they joined themselves to tradition, to culture, to convention. It was in that location and at that angle to gravity that they became "painting." (1993, 244)

A few paragraphs later, she connects this upward move to "the look," "the *act* of looking" (which she describes in terms that sound remarkably similar to Erwin Straus's "gaze of upright posture"):

> the raising of the work off its knees and onto the grace of the wall in one unbroken benediction, the denial of wild heedlessness in order to clear a space for the look, the look that will (in its very act of looking) create order, and thus create painting—"sophisticated" painting.... It was a vertical bounded plane, an object that stood before the viewer's own vertical body, facing off against it. (245)

This "facing off against it" is very similar to what Straus calls "the ability to look at things straight ahead and withstand their thrust." Krauss elaborates: "The vertical is not, then, just a neutral axis, a dimension.... To stand upright is to attain to a peculiar form of vision: the optical; and to gain this vision is to sublimate, to raise up, to purify" (246).

Primitivism rejects the vertical plane. It emphasizes the "dissolute squat," the downward motion, the *buried* treasure. It's domain is the tactile (the "*Dark* Meadow," the "*Cave* of the Heart") not the optical space of the "eye." "Primitive man," Ortega y Gasset reminds us, "is tactile man." Verticality requires resistance to gravity; horizontality encourages a surrender to gravity. The horizontal plane is also the space of sleep (the eyes are closed) and sex—the most somatic of human experiences. By contrast, "The Look" is an act of "pure" isolated vision—increasingly cut off from the earthbound senses of touch and smell.

And this helps to explain why so many abstract expressionists—not just Jackson Pollock—cultivated an especially intimate relationship with the ground. Rothko, for example, insisted that his canvases be hung low to the ground, in part because he wanted them to exist in a one-to-one correspondence with the spectator's lower body. But even though the spectator then experienced his paintings "straight on," the mode of vision they promote is *not* "the gaze of upright posture." Rothko's signature bands of color diffuse in a way that extends the viewer's field of vision *peripherally*, invoking the sensation that Freud called "the oceanic," a limitless, totally enveloping sense of the sublime. Also, Rothko wanted his canvases to remain unframed. Color wraps itself around the very edge of the canvas—and metaphorically at least, beyond. In addition, Rothko wanted his paintings displayed panoramically—in serial groupings—so that the spectator would be literally surrounded by them. The sensation of the "oceanic"—as Freud describes it—is a multisensory experience, not exclusively or primarily a visual experience. It reconnects seeing with the olfactory and the tactile senses.

This is also the realm of "ritual," not the sort of optical experience one has in "the theatron." John Cage has contrasted ritual and theater in precisely this way:

> theater involves primarily the two sense perceptions of seeing and hearing. I don't think that tasting, smelling, and touching, the other senses, are as much involved in theater as seeing and hearing. If you add tasting, smelling, and touching to theater, you get ritual. (Kostelanetz 1988, 194–95)

Similarly, we might recall the way Duchamp anticipated Johns's and Rauschenberg's repudiation of abstract expressionism when he expressed his distaste for "olfactory" artists.

If, as Rosalind Krauss suggests, a deep connection exists between Pollock and the ground, then Rauschenberg issued a direct challenge to the earthly plane of abstract expressionism when he displayed a work called "Bed" in 1955. Beds not only invite us onto the horizontal plane; they are also the objects we associate most directly with night, sleep, and sex (perhaps even, psychoanalysis). But what Rauschenberg does in this "combine" is to take a bed, cover it with paint, and then turn it fully *upright*, exhibiting it vertically on the wall of the museum.

Abstract Expressionism and Anti-Intellectualism

Pollock, like Graham, would not have considered the adjective "brainy" much of a compliment. For Pollock, the experience of drip painting was all about flow and unimpeded impulse. ("It is only when I lose contact with a painting that the result is a mess" [Karmel 1998, 112]) For Johns—as we saw at the beginning of this chapter—painting is more an act of "hesitation," a physical embodiment of "thought." Encaustic—a medium Johns worked with quite often—is painstakingly slow, at least when compared with the sort of oil paint the abstract expressionists preferred. (The process by which the wax colors in encaustic are "fixed" is highly exacting. The temperature, for example, needs to be precisely controlled.) In this sense, Johns's work with encaustic is as far removed as any medium could possibly be from the spontaneous drip and splatter of action painting. Another contrast between Johns and the abstract expressionists: The history of oil paint is inextricably connected to painterly depictions—as well as more abstract evocations—of the human body. "Flesh is the reason that oil paint was invented," declared De Kooning (Butler 2002, 8).

We might think of the transition from De Kooning and Pollock to Johns and Rauschenberg as a journey from "action painting" to "*in*action painting." In Rauschenberg's "Trophy 1" a combine from 1959, two images stand out: a photograph of Cunningham performing an arabesque in the right-hand side of the canvas and a street sign on the left that reads "Caution: Watch Your Step." "Caution" is the antithesis of the "existential leap" encouraged by the ethos of abstract expressionism. Similarly, it's difficult to imagine the abstract expressionists incorporating words into their work (as did Duchamp, Rauschenberg, and Johns), or for that matter, taking much pride or satisfaction in their ability to speak and write eloquently about the creative process. Emulating the mumbled monosyllables of Brando and Dean, they wore inarticulateness on their sleeves and flaunted it like a badge of honor. (Which is not to imply that they weren't intelligent, but rather that they chose to conceal their verbal intelligence.) George Segal, speaking of the defiantly macho, anti-intellectualism of the Cedar Bar, once observed, "If you had an education, you had to hide it and sound like a New York cab driver" (Roth 1977, 49). Or—as Barnett Newman defiantly declared—"Aesthetics is to the artist as ornithology is to the birds" (Friedman 1972, 110).

By contrast, Duchamp was impatient with (indeed, embarrassed by) this sort of willed inarticulateness. He seemed to suffer from an intellectual inferiority complex—or at least a fear that the visual arts were perceived to be less "mentally demanding" than the verbal arts. In a remarkable burst of candor, he once admitted, "The painter was considered stupid, but the poet and writer were intelligent. I wanted to be intelligent." He singled out the expression "bête comme un peintre"—"stupid as a painter"—as evidence of a widespread belief that painters are often un- or anti-intellectual.

Irony

The heroic, self-sacrificing dimension of modern dance and abstract expressionism can be attributed in large part to an absence of irony. Nothing promotes intellectual detachment more readily than a highly developed sense of irony. When Moira Roth accuses the Cunningham circle of indifference, she's really longing for art of "total commitment" (both emotional and moral) that is uncorrupted by irony. The cool intelligence of Cunningham's work often takes ironic forms, most notably its impatience with the aura of "suffering" that suffused both Graham and abstract expressionism. Those who gravitated toward Cunningham, Cage, Johns, and Rauschenberg usually preferred the sly, wry smile to the agonized grimace. As Cage argued in 1966:

> [the] smile is largely missing from abstract expressionism. I remember hearing Harold Rosenberg say, after the exhibition of Pop and Op art a year and a half ago, "Where is all the suffering?" And I continually made it clear in my discussions of art that I prefer laughter to tears. (Kostelanetz 1970, 176)

This is yet another reason that Cage never demonstrated much enthusiasm for the work of Martha Graham, who repeatedly described both herself and her protagonists as "doom eager" (a phrase she borrowed from Ibsen, by way of Robert Edmund Jones). Yvonne Rainer has spoken explicitly of the way in which Rauschenberg's sense of humor helped to liberate her from both the spirit of Graham (whose technique she was then studying) *and* abstract expressionism:

> The year I came to New York, immersed as I was in the abstract expressionist ethos, Rauschenberg's "Monogram" opened a window on the future of my own funny-bone. I all but rolled on the floor in a convulsion of laughter when I saw it. (1974, 9)

The Thinking Body

Cunningham's conception of cool intelligence differs markedly from the attitude toward bodily thinking that dominated modern dance between the time of Duncan and Graham. Ironically, the now familiar phrase "the thinking body" was first introduced into dance world discourse by Mabel Ellsworth Todd's 1937 book of that name. (I say "ironic" because *The Thinking Body*, a classic work about body alignment for modern dancers, is—first and foremost—a critique of upright posture, the very evolutionary advance that Freud associates with the development of intellectual detachment and its perceptual first cousin: a visually based method of surveying the world, i.e., "the gaze of upright posture.") For the edition of *The Thinking Body*, published in 1968, Lula Sweigard wrote a new preface that began: "In his quest for physical fitness, man unfortunately labors under the basic handicap of moving in an upright position" (Todd 1968, ix). One of the book's central arguments is explicitly focussed on upright posture:

> Structural balance as we know it became a problem with the slow evolution of a biped whose structural arrangements had been functioning on all fours. . . . One author, W. C. Mackenzie, is quoted to the effect that "if generalizations were to be made about the causes of human diseases, it would be along the line of failure of accommodation to the erect posture." (45–6)

My point is not to argue with Todd about the anatomically problematic nature of the human back. But I find it curious, to say the least, that a book whose title promises a discussion of bodily intelligence winds up criticizing the very evolutionary transformations that distinguish human beings from the rest of the animal kingdom.

Modern dance may view itself as an advanced or progressive development in the history of choreographic art; but prior to Cunningham, its major practitioners all strove to take us *back* to that point in pre-history "before the atrophy of civilization set in." Of course, it was also the author of that phrase (Doris Humphrey) who argued that "The person drawn to dance as a profession is notoriously unintellectual." But, unlike Humphrey and so many of his predecessors in modern dance, Merce Cunningham has never associated "braininess" with "the atrophy of civilization."

Erwin Straus's classic meditation on upright posture ends with a paragraph that addresses—with wonderful directness—the distinctiveness of *human* nature.

> Upright posture, which dominates human existence in its entirety, makes us see that no right exists for claiming any kind of priority for the drives. The "rational" is as genuine a part of human nature as the "animal." (1963, 192)

By resisting the "holistic" rhetoric of Mabel Todd and her legions of devotees, by paying as much attention to the head and the mind as to the rest of the body (even if this means acknowledging the inevitability of a Cartesian split between the two), Merce Cunningham gives us a much more complete and convincing image of "*human* nature" than do his predecessors in the world of modern dance.

11
Modernism, Postmodernism, and Cunningham

The term modern dance is obviously an inadequate one. It is not synonymous with contemporary dance, for it is by no means that inclusive. It is only of temporary accuracy in so far as it is accurate at all, for tomorrow, when a more advanced type of dance shall have arisen, it will be impossible to refer to the dancing of today as modern.
—John Martin, *The Modern Dance*, 1933 (1972, 3)

Allan Ulrich once suggested that all American modern dance choreographers are the children of Martha Graham; and that all postmodern choreographers are the *rebellious* children of Martha. No former Graham dancer was more rebellious than Merce Cunningham; and therefore, if Ulrich's formulation is correct, Cunningham should probably be categorized as a postmodern choreographer. But throughout this book I've referred to Cunningham as the major "modernizer" of modern dance. Even a brief foray into the realm of classification-by-genre illustrates how quickly such exercises can degenerate into the sort of convoluted word games that Shakespeare parodies in *Hamlet* when he has the pedantic Polonius speak of "tragedy, comedy, history, pastoral, pastoral-comical, historical-pastoral, tragical-historical, tragical-comical, historical-pastoral, tragical-historical, tragical-comical-historical-pastoral," and so on. But—for better or for worse—I've already begun to play this semantic game, by suggesting that Cunningham, Cage, Johns, and Rauschenberg are the single most important pioneers of one of the great paradigm shifts in the arts of the late 20th century: the transition from modernism to postmodernism. So perhaps the time has come to officially

229

"situate" Merce Cunningham in relation to the problematic landscape of modernism versus postmodernism.

I embark on this task with some reluctance because it requires that we take up residence—at least temporarily—in the misty highlands of contemporary theoretical "discourse," a land inhabited for the most part by the sorts of abstruse theory-mongers whose prose would benefit from nothing so much as a radical jargon-ectomy. For the sake of clarity, I'll do my best both to minimize the jargon and to observe the strict dictates of Occam's razor, which implores us not to multiple verbal entities (i.e., new categories and/or terminologies) unnecessarily. As Robert Benchley once quipped, "There are two categories of people: those who believe that people can be divided into two categories and those who don't." Finally, by way of introduction to this chapter, I should state flat out that I don't believe Cunningham to be the sort of choreographer whose achievements can't be fully appreciated unless they've been "illuminated" by the bright glare of poststructuralist, deconstructive theory. In fact, contemporary theory needs Cunningham more than Cunningham "needs" contemporary theory. That is: Cunningham's dances offer a working model that can illustrate— indeed embody—some otherwise, pretty obscure-sounding theoretical constructs.

Let's begin on terra firma by posing the single most straightforward question about genre classification: How should Merce Cunningham be categorized? Is he modern, postmodern, somewhere in between, or neither of the above? Conventional thinking tends to place Cunningham "somewhere in between" these two genres—too cool and objective for modern dance, too virtuosic and technically accomplished for Judson-era postmodernism. This view is not so much wrong as incomplete—insufficiently nuanced; but in order to address this issue responsibly, we'll need to examine some of the differences between the way the dance world uses the term "postmodern" and the way the other arts—especially architecture—employ this phrase. Cunningham *does* occupy a position between modern and postmodern, but in ways that are considerably more complicated than received wisdom would lead us to believe.

No one denies that Cunningham and Cage were a major—probably *the* major—influence on the Judson generation. But despite the pervasiveness of Cunningham's influence, the official histories of Judson and postmodern dance maintain that Cunningham's continuing dependence on technically trained dancers should effectively bar his admission to the postmodern club. David Vaughan for example, argues: "The Judson group, in the true tradition of the modern dance, consciously repudiated the aesthetic of the preceding generation—that is, of Cunningham himself" (1978, 44). But is the issue of "technique" really so decisive as to be divisive? Granted, what

Yvonne Rainer called "found movement" is vital to the Judson aesthetic. But the actual number of Judson works that were performed by genuinely untrained dancers or that consisted exclusively (or even predominately) of pedestrian movements is rather miniscule. What really distinguished most Judson works was their willingness to freely incorporate elements of pedestrian movement—something that Cunningham had done as early as "Collage" in 1953. More to the point, the fact that technically trained movement was given no special pride of place in the Judson Dance Theater doesn't mean that the average Judson work could have been executed by untrained performers.

Ironically, many of the choreographers with the strongest commitment to pedestrian movement were actually among the most technically accomplished of the Judson dancers. (Deborah Hay, for example, had previously performed with both Limón and Cunningham; and Steve Paxton was a member of the Cunningham company between the years of 1961 and 1964, the last two of which were probably the most significant for Judson pedestrianism.) It could be argued that Judson provided them the opportunity to "unlearn" their theatrical training; but Cunningham's practice of subjecting his compositional process to the impersonal dictates of chance operations serves a similar (if not identical) function. Conversely, a number of Cunningham works—the "intermission" section as well as the final moments of "Walkaround Time" (1968), for example—incorporate found and pedestrian movements (and do so without theatrically "enhancing" the movement in the manner of Paul Taylor's "Esplanade" [1975] or his "Lost, Found, and Lost" [1982]).

In the book *Merce Cunningham: Fifty Years,* David Vaughan notes that Robert Ellis Dunn (then married to Cunningham dancer Judith Dunn) taught a series of Cage-inspired composition classes in Cunningham's 14th Street studio between 1960 and 1962 that "led to the concerts of experimental dance at the Judson Memorial Church in Washington Square, out of which grew the 'post-modern' phase of contemporary dance" (Vaughan 1997, 125). But what Vaughan fails to mention—perhaps because it isn't widely known—is that in July 1962 (the month of the first Judson Dance Theater concert) Cunningham himself taught a composition class to Dunn's students based on the strategies he had employed for generating the movement sequences in his seminal "Suite by Chance" from 1953.

Specific examples of Cunningham and Cage's influence on particular Judson dances are almost too numerous to mention. Lucinda Childs's "Three Piece" (1963) was danced "alongside" a score by Malcolm Goldstein. The dancers counted their phrases independent of any metrical support from the music. Jill Johnston, reviewing the dance for *The Village Voice,* wrote that " 'Three Piece' is a short, neat, clean, concise dance, well done, in the

Cunningham style" (Banes 1983, 258). Deborah Hay's similarly titled "Three Here" (1964) was accompanied by Cage's spliced-tape score, "Williams Mix #5." In "Word Words," a 1963 collaboration between Steve Paxton and Yvonne Rainer, Paxton (who was still dancing with Cunningham at the time) devised movement that was unmistakably Cunninghamesque (and no less technically demanding than Cunningham's choreography); Rainer, in fact, found it tremendously difficult to execute. Paxton also composed the musical score—but decided to carry the principle of separation between sound and movement even further than Cunningham and Cage typically did. His composition, "Music for Word Words," was not only autonomous of the dancing. It was separated from the choreography in *time* as well as space. (Which is to say: it was performed as an independent piece of music on a subsequent concert.) This list of Judson-era works that are "deeply indebted" to Cunningham and Cage could go on indefinitely.

Postmodern Architecture

The real complications emerge when we begin to look at the definitions of postmodernism utilized by artists in virtually every other medium. Consider, for example, Robert Stern's classic definition of postmodernism in architecture:

> This condition, frequently labeled as post-modernist, seeks to recuperate traditional form in order to go beyond the impasse of late Modernization with its belligerently anti-symbolic stance, extreme abstraction, and reductionism. (1977, 34)

This is hardly a description of the early work of Rainer, Childs, or Brown. If anything, their choreography typified the antisymbolic stance, the extreme abstraction, and very reductionism that Stern is rejecting. Exemplary instances of this pared-down, purist tendency would surely include Rainer's various versions of "Trio A" (beginning in 1966), many of Brown's "Accumulation" pieces (1971–73), and Lucinda Childs's "Calico Mingling" (1973). To an architect, the term "postmodern" connotes a rejection of the very austerity and reductivism that characterized so many early postmodern dances. Yvonne Rainer's manifesto of renunciation ("No to spectacle no to virtuosity no to ... magic and make-believe. . . . No to moving or being moved," and so on [1974, 51]) sounds very much like the holier-than-thou Puritanism of the orthodox *modern* architects (against whom the postmodernists rebelled). Granted, Cunningham shares some of these qualities as well (especially the antisymbolic stance). But in numerous other ways, he has considerably more in common with what architects mean when they speak of postmodernism than do almost any of the early Judson choreographers. If we look beyond the issue of technique versus pedestrianism, we find some even deeper connections between Cunningham's way of working—especially his collage aesthetic—and the broader cultural landscape of postmodernism as defined by critics in the other arts.

The most striking parallel between Cunningham's work and postmodern culture more generally is undoubtedly his rejection of "wholeness," anticipating by many years Robert Venturi's landmark manifesto of 1966, *Complexity and Contradiction in Architecture.* In this seminal postmodern document, Venturi first announced his opposition to the cool, austere impersonality—the glass and steel formalism—of the "International Style," the architectural wing of high modernism. "Architects," he wrote:

> can no longer afford to be intimidated by the puritanically moral language of orthodox modern architecture. I like elements which are hybrid rather than "pure," compromising rather than "clean"...perverse as well as impersonal, boring as well as "interesting"... accommodating rather than excluding, redundant rather than simple, vestigial as well as innovating.... *I am for messy vitality over obvious unity. I include the non-sequitur and proclaim the duality.* (Venturi 1966, 16 [my emphasis])

Many postmodernists challenge that long-standing tradition in almost all of the modernist arts that sought to transcend dualities in the name of wholeness—a tradition that extends from Nerval and Nietzsche through D. H. Lawrence and Artaud. (Jean Laplanche for example, speaks of a "synthesis compulsion" at the heart of modernism.) If we're looking for a specific analogy between Cunningham and an influential contemporary architect who eschews an overly centralized notion of "unity," then we might compare his "separation of the elements" with the dense network of public spaces that constitutes Rem Koolhaas's Euralille (in the French city of Lille). Writing about such "complex structures," Koolhaas notes:

> Beyond a certain critical mass, a building becomes a Big Building. Such a mass can no longer be controlled by a single architectural gesture, or even by any combination of architectural gestures. This impossibility triggers the autonomy of its parts. (1995, 59)

John Cage made no secret of his profound disagreement with many aspects of high modernism; he pithily criticized a building by the great modernist architect Le Corbusier in four words: "Its shape is tyranny" (Kostelanetz 1970, 206) (and this comment presumably applied to all practitioners of the "International Style"). Cage also had a major philosophical falling out with the high-modernist composer Pierre Boulez over the issue of authorial "control." (This also may help explain why Cage never particularly liked the word "aleatoric"—which he associated with Boulez's theoretical writings.) Consider, too, his attack on the "purely German idea, a fascist idea really" of unity in the arts, that he associates not just with Wagner, but with the modernism of Stravinsky (because of his emphasis on overall "unity").

The Body Without Organ(ization)

This critique of unity and wholeness is also evident in Cunningham's conception of the individual dancer's body. The Cunningham body provides a vivid illustration of the central ideas in a highly influential work of poststructuralist criticism, Gilles Deleuze's and Felix Guattari's two-volume tome, *Anti-Oedipus: Capitalism and Schizophrenia*. The heart of their theory lies in the phrase "body without organs"—which, in practice, means a body without organ-ization. This can sound at first like Norman O. Brown's conception of the polymorphously perverse Dionysian body, in which libido is no longer "centered" in the genitals. And it's true that Deleuze and Guattari provide us with an image of a body without "hot spots," a decentered body that might be said to correspond to a larger "decentered" space in the work of Cunningham, where no specific location (e.g., stage center) assumes special pride of place. But the connections go deeper because the terminology Deleuze and Guattari employ is much less organic than Norman O. Brown's. They conceive of the body as a "schizo-subject," a "nomadic desiring-*machine*"; and thus, their imagery has more in common with Cunningham's and Duchamp's conception of the mechanical bride, the body-as-a-machine whose component parts can be fragmented and randomly rearranged. And in much the same way that the "isolations" of the Cunningham body provide a microcosm of the wider, decentralized space through which it moves, Deleuze and Guattari emphasize the "rootlessness" of the individual body in a "deterritorialized" world. Thus, the transition from Graham to Cunningham, as we've seen, can be conceived of as a transition from a world of "roots" to a world of "routes."

The nomadic and machinelike conception of the body in *Capitalism and Schizophrenia* ultimately takes the form of an attack on what it's authors call the "*arborescent* model of thought," the idea that experience is organized into "branches" of knowledge "grounded" in firm foundations (literally "roots"). Their mission is to *uproot* the individual, to undermine foundations, and create a sense of the body as a dynamic, nomadic machine. Desire manifests itself in what they call "break-flows"; the body is resolutely "nonrepresentational" in character; and "liberation" for Deleuze and Guattari arrives when "human beings are able to behave as intentionless phenomenon" (Best & Kellner 1991, 98)—a notion that John Cage undoubtedly would have applauded.

When summarized in this way, Deleuze and Guattari's celebration of the "schizo-subject" can begin to sound suspiciously like a contemporary variation on an older primitivist theme, one that played an essential role in the surrealist movement: the romanticizing of mental illness (which the surrealists were inclined to view as a permanent externalizing of the unconscious.) One thinks, quintessentially of Dali's "paranoiac-critical method." (The "innocent eye" of the child, the mad person, and "the primitive" often constituted a holy trinity for the surrealists.) But for Deleuze and Guattari, "schizophrenia" is a *process* rather than an illness, one that bears a striking resemblance to the Dostoevskian variety of "self-contradiction" that we've already attributed to Cunningham, Cage, Johns, and Rauschenberg. In a fascinating gloss on Deleuze and Guattari's writings about the "schizo-subject," François Peraldi, asks:

> Shall we say that schizophrenia is a process? And if so then, what kind of process? I'd venture to say that it appears to me as an affirmative process in the negative. Something like "I am and I remain whatever you do not want me to be." Let's understand it as an affirmation against.

But what precisely does he mean by an "affirmation against"? He means—and this dovetails with one of our recurring themes—resistance to any and all forms of Pavlovian conditioning:

> It keeps us at least from entering into this horrifying world of the behavioral sciences which, to us, is nothing but the most extraordinarily powerful and dangerous system of repression ever invented, because it has never been able to state clearly the political, economic, and ideological grounds on which it has built its Skinnerian boxes of torture. (1978, 20)

For writers such as Peraldi, Deleuze, and Guattari, the "exemplary" case history, the Ur-schizophrenic, was surely Antonin Artaud. Thus, it's no coincidence that Deleuze and Guattari's key phrase "body without organs" is adapted from a radio play by Artaud (*To Have Done with the Judgment of God*, 1947). Therein, one encounters Artaud's terror that he will be involuntarily manipulated by sexual desire:

> When you have made him a body without organs,
> then you will have delivered him from all his automatic reactions
> and restored him to his true freedom.
> Then you will teach him again to dance wrong side out. (1976, 571)

Cunningham, it seems to me, offers us an image of someone who has learned to dance "wrong side out," who has taught himself to avoid "automatic [i.e., conditioned] reactions." Recall Gordon Mumma's suggestion that Cunningham's own dancing in "Place" offered a "clinical panorama of the schizophrenic experience." This view of sexuality, freedom, and the body is strikingly at odds with the sort of primitivism that animates so much of pre-Cunningham modern dance. Furthermore, Artaud suffered from an excruciatingly acute separation of mind and body, a pathologically divided self. He was, in a very real sense, perpetually uprooted from himself. Of course—and we'll examine this notion further in just a moment—Artaud wanted to reritualize the theater in a manner that is fully consistent with the modern dancer's primitivist romanticizing of ritual. But Deleuze and Guattari aren't interested in the organicist ideas associated with the Artaud best-known for the essays collected in *The Theatre and Its Double*. For Deleuze and Guattari, Artaud becomes the exemplary schizophrenic "case history," the quintessentially "divided self."

In the final analysis, the "nonarboreal" rootlessness that Deleuze and Guattari associate with schizophrenia poses a stark alternative to modernist primitivism. The primitivist believes in the possibility of returning to "the source," to his "roots," the promise of "going home again." As Marianna Torgovnick writes in *Gone Primitive:*

> The metaphor of finding a home or being at home recurs over and over as a structuring pattern within Western primitivism. Going primitive is trying to "go home" to a place that feels comfortable and well balanced . . . "going home" like "going primitive" is inescapably a metaphor for the return to origins. (1990, 185)

The ways in which Cunningham's collage technique—his avoidance of wholeness and unity—undermines (or at least complicates) the "synthesis compulsion" that unites so many different kinds of modernist art first became evident in the late 1960s. By the end of that decade, two very different conceptions of modernist performance had emerged: purity of media (or what Grotowski called "poor theater") on the one hand, and "total theater" (a sort of neo-Wagnerian synthesis) on the other. Cunningham's practice of collage performance provided a stark contrast to both. In addition, each of these apparent opposites shared, in their very different ways, an underlying conception of unity, wholeness, and fidelity to the "the natural" which Cunningham's work resists.

The Modernist Striptease

The 1960s was the decade in which nudity often functioned as a symbol of unmediated truth: a peeling away not just of clothing, but of all social traps and trappings. The naked (or barely clothed) body figured prominently in work as diverse as Allan Kaprow's "18 Happenings in 6 Parts" (1959), Peter Brook's production of *Marat/Sade* (1964), Carolee Schneemann's "Meat Joy" (1964), Yvonne Rainer's and Robert Morris's "Waterman Switch" (1965), Anna Halprin's "Parades and Changes" (1967), and of course, The Living Theatre's *Paradise Now* (1968)—not to mention an even wider range of fundamentally unserious work (*Hair, Che, Oh Calcutta!*). In retrospect, it may strike us as naive to have believed that a body minus clothing is any more "natural" (any less culturally conditioned) than a body sashaying about in the latest Halston or Oscar de la Renta. But if nothing else, the cult of nudity reminds us how essential the notion of "underlying nature" was to all modes of 1960s modernism. We can characterize this impulse as "the modernist striptease" (stripping down to essentials, to essences, to some "authentic" inner core that lay buried within—or below—the world of social masks and cultural conventions).

Even Clement Greenberg's more purely aesthetic concept of minimalist self-purification proceeds on the assumption that one is stripping away everything extraneous to the underlying *nature* of the medium. Greenberg's most frequently quoted position paper, "Modernist Painting" (the definitive draft of which was published in 1965) gives us a version—and a vision—of modernism *as* striptease: "The task of self-criticism became to eliminate from the effects of each art any and every effect that might be borrowed from or by the medium of any other art. Thereby each art would be rendered pure" (1973, 68). Jerzy Grotowski's manifesto of 1965, *Towards A Poor Theatre* (which could just as accurately have been titled "Towards a *Pure* Theatre") provides the clearest example of the way in which this Greenbergian modernist mandate was being applied to the performing arts:

> What is the theatre? What is unique about it? What can it do that film and television cannot? ... By gradually eliminating whatever proved superfluous, we found that theatre can exist without makeup, without autonomic costume and scenography, without a separate performance area (stage), without lighting and sound effects, etc. It cannot exist without the actor-spectator relationship of perceptual, direct, "live" communion.... The poor theatre challenges the notion of theatre as a synthesis of disparate creative disciplines—literature, sculpture, painting, architecture, lighting, acting. (1969, 19)

There were many well-known theater pieces in the late 1960s and early 1970s that proceeded in this unembellished fashion: Grotowski's own work as well as productions such as The Living Theatre's *Antigone* (1967) and The Open Theatre's *The Serpent* (1968). And, as we've already seen, many of Yvonne Rainer's manifesto-like proclamations from the same period (as well as many Judson-era performances) apply this purist thinking to dance.

Total Theater

But what are we to make of all those neo-Wagnerian attempts to create some sort of Mixed-Media Theater or Total Theater, such as The Living Theater's *Frankenstein* (1965–67), Ronconci's *Orlando Furioso* (1969), Brook's *Marat/Sade* (1964), Mnouchkine's *1789* (1970), or Meredith Monk's *Vessel*

(1971). This work, it seems to me, constitutes the *other* side of the modernist coin, the side that Clement Greenberg disparaged as well. Yet, when all is said and done, this "other" side of modernism has more in common with Greenberg's conception of purity than Greenberg himself would ever have been willing to admit. For all of the manifest differences, the fact is that the quest for "naturalness" (of one sort or another) is the point at which minimalist and maximalist versions of modernism meet. In other words, Total Theater and Poor Theater were complimentarities, the sort of opposites that "meet around the bend." The model for both is the presumed *wholeness* of the natural world.

The Gesamtkunstwerk is an exercise in organic synthesis: (". . . . no more boundaries . . . only art, the universal, undivided.") In all such forms of "total theater," wholeness or unity is achieved by inclusion. By contrast, Greenbergian purity is achieved by *exclusion,* by stripping away anything and everything at odds with the underlying "nature" of the medium.

But Cunningham provides us with a complicated middle ground between these two extremes. His movement, music, and décor (in and of themselves) might easily qualify as examples of Greenbergian self-purification. But they are mixed-and-matched ("collaged" we might say) into a new sort of Gesamtkunstwerk that allows pockets of purity to coexist side by side without ever being stirred into an organic Wagnerian broth. This results in what Roland Barthes would call a "chattering" of separate voices, a "polyvocal" performance that has much in common with the worldview of postmodernism as it is understood in architecture and most of the other contemporary arts.

Modernism, Postmodernism, and Primitivism

This postmodern perspective on Cunningham can also shed fresh and valuable light on our previous discussions of modernist primitivism. Modernism, broadly construed, was predicated on the absolute, irreconcilable distinction between "culture" and "nature." Culture was defined as the "man-made" part of the environment: language, tool making, the conscious regulation of sex, and so on, implicitly suggesting that nature is the "God-made" part or that which defies and escapes the conscious control of human beings. The natural was presumed to be . . . well . . . *natural,* with all the accompanying connotations of moral goodness. And the cultural, by contrast was, at best, inauthentic, and, at worst, something that ensnares, enslaves, and diminishes us.

High modernism also assumed an innate adversarialness between art and the dominant culture. As Carl Andre put it, "Culture is something that is done to us. Art is something that we do to culture" (Schjeldahl 1984, 49). This is a relatively new idea, one that is coextensive with the concept of a modernist avant-garde. Modern art, in other words, is thought to resist the forces of enculturation. According to this scenario, "Culture" (especially the popular, industrialized, mass-produced variety) threatens to do to its victims what Jarry's Ubu does to his: "disembrain" them. The process by which the prevailing culture was thought to condition its inhabitants resembled the plots of Grade B, 1950s science fiction films (*Invasion of the Body Snatchers, The Blob*). The underlying fear was of creeping homogenization, conformism, mechanization, suburbanization—all those concepts that gained currency in the gray-flannel suited decade of the 1950s—each of which was thought to contribute to a cumulative deadening of the spirit. The modernist view of the concept of "culture" receives what is perhaps its classic formulation in an essay written just a few years after Cunningham formed his company in 1953, Lionel Trilling's "Freud: Within and Beyond Culture" (first delivered as a lecture in 1955):

> At some point in the history of the West—let us say, for convenience, at the time of Rousseau—men began to think of their fates as being lived out in relation not to God or to the individual persons who are their neighbors, or to material circumstance but to the ideas and assumption and manners of a large social totality. The evidence of this is to be found in our literature, in its preoccupation with newly discovered alien cultures which, in one regard or another, serve to criticize our own. Walter Scott could not have delighted the world with his representation in *Waverly* of the loyalty, sincerity, and simplicity of the Highland clans had not the world learned to think of life in terms of culture, had it not learned to wonder whether some inscrutable bad principle in its present culture was not making it impossible for all men to be as loyal and sincere and simple as they should be. (1968, 104–5)

Clearly, this is the view of culture that underscores modernist primitivism. Indeed, what Trilling goes on to say about Freud can function as a casebook introduction to the ethos of primitivism:

> [Freud] made it apparent to us how entirely implicated in culture we all are ... he made plain how the culture suffuses the remotest parts of the individual mind, being taken in almost literally with the mother's milk. ... But he also sees the self as set against the culture, struggling against it, having been from the first reluctant to enter it. ... He needed to believe that there was some point at which it was possible to stand beyond the reach of culture. Perhaps his formulation of the death-instinct is to be interpreted as the expression of this need. "Death destroys a man," says E. M. Forster, "but the idea of death saves him." Save him from what? From the entire submission of himself—of his self—to life in culture. (105, 108)

For Trilling, as for Freud, the possibility of an *escape from culture* was inextricably tied to the biological component of the self (which is another way of saying, the buried "primitive" core of our being):

> We can begin to see why we may think of Freud's emphasis on biology as being
> a liberating idea. It is a resistance to and a modification of the cultural omnipo-
> tence. We reflect that somewhere in the child, somewhere in the adult, there is
> a hard, irreducible, stubborn core of biological urgency... that culture cannot
> reach. (114–15)

The adversarial modernist assumes that an escape hatch still exists, that it
is still possible to propel oneself (in Trilling's own phrase) "beyond culture." The traditional sanctuaries, the unconscious and/or the "primitive"
(for Trilling and Freud: the biological) were presumed to be preverbal,
pristine, and unacculturated. This is the assumption we find embodied—
quintessentially!—in the work of Graham and Pollock.

But this is also where we begin to encounter the first glimmer of a distinction between modernism and postmodernism. The moment that culture
(especially in the form disseminated by mass media) is believed to have en-
croached on and infiltrated these safe houses, the modernist project comes
to an end. In the words of Clement Greenberg: "The arts then, have been
hunted back to their mediums, and there they have been isolated, concen-
trated and defined" (1985, 42). Hunted back! What a revealing phrase. It
resonates with all the defensiveness and self-proclaimed martyrdom of a
high-modernist avant-garde seeking to protect itself from the encroach-
ments of an omnivorous popular culture. But Greenberg still believes in
the possibilities of escape. His image of the modernist artist being "hunted
back" to his medium exemplifies this adversarial relationship between the
prevailing culture and the modernist avant-garde.

By contrast, the lesson that the postmodernist teaches the modernist
is: you can run, but you can't hide. The postmodern era begins with the
realization that *some* degree of cultural accommodation is unavoidable. As
Robert Rauschenberg once said, "I really feel sorry for people who think
things like soap dishes or mirrors or Coke bottles are ugly, because they're
surrounded by things like that all day long, and it must make them miserable"
(Umland 1988, 82). Andy Warhol, in defense of Pop Art, said that he wanted
to "celebrate all the great things the abstract expressionists overlooked."
The primitivism of a Graham or a Pollock, by contrast, proceeds on the
assumption that modern dance and abstract expressionism are two of the
things that *don't* go better with Coke.

Postmodernism and Primitivism

By contrast, the postmodern era can be said to begin when artists no longer
consider it possible to return to a "purer," more authentically primitive mode
of existence. Marianna Torgovnick, in her book *Gone Primitive*, speaks of

"the peculiar value 'the primitive' holds for the postmodern." (288) I would revise that statement so as to read: "the peculiar value that the *repudiation* of primitivism holds for the postmodern." Consider the fate of poor Claude Lévi-Strauss. To my mind, no one has done more than Lévi-Strauss to refine and revise turn-of-the-century anthropological notions that regard the "savage mind" as magical, superstitious, and prelogical. Above all, he challenged Levy-Bruhl's influential primitivist notion about the "participation mystique," the idea that the divisions between animate and inanimate were less distinct for the primitive than for the rest of us. In *Structural Anthropology,* Lévi-Strauss wrote that:

> the kind of logic in mythical thought is as rigorous as that of modern science, and that the difference lies, not in the quality of the intellectual process, but in the nature of things to which it is applied . . . man has always been thinking equally well; the improvement lies, not in an alleged progress of man's mind, but in the discovery of new areas to which it may apply its unchanged and unchanging powers. (1963, 230)

But postmodern gurus such as Jacques Derrida seem determined to repudiate every last vestige of primitivism from contemporary anthropology. Thus, even Lévi-Strauss can't escape accusations of residual primitivizing. (Needless to say, he doesn't demonize or condescend to "the primitive." But he's accused of making the mistake of idealizing the nonliterate culture of the Nambikwara and of lamenting the intrusion of literacy into their previously oral culture.) Consider this passage from Derrida's famous attack on him:

> One already suspects—and all Lévi-Strauss's writings would confirm it—that the critique of ethnocentrism, a theme so dear to the author of *Tristes Tropiques,* has most often the sole function of constituting the other as a model of original and natural goodness, of accusing and humiliating oneself, of exhibiting its being-unacceptable in an anti-ethnocentric mirror. . . . Non-European peoples were not only studied as the index to a hidden good Nature, as a native soil recovered, of a "zero degree" with reference to which one could outline the structure, the growth, and above all the degradation of our society and our culture. As always, this archaeology is also a teleology and an eschatology; the dream of a full and immediate presence closing history . . . the suppression of contradiction and difference. (1976, 114–15)

Thus, for Derrida, Lévi-Strauss is guilty of vestigial primitivizing, of associating the primitive with wholeness ("the suppression of contradiction and difference") and of taking us back to origins: "a native soil recovered." Of course, any form of "essentialism," any theory of "origin" is anathema to postmodern dogma.

Here we encounter the most important connection between Merce Cunningham and the "discourses" of postmodernism. Cunningham, as we saw in Chapter 6, abandoned the modern dance choreographer's quest for the primitive origin of movement (as well as the search for the most "natural" way of moving).

Cunningham repudiates the same tendencies in modern dance that have been the subject of so much recent criticism of modernist art. Consider, for example, the continuing controversy over The Museum of Modern Art's 1984 exhibition "Primitivism in 20th Century Art: Affinity of the Tribal and the Modern." In a devastating critique of the exhibition, Thomas McEvilley attacks the idea that Gaughin, Picasso, Brancusi, and other "modern primitivists" had in fact rediscovered the timeless and transcendent values that modern art shared with primitive art. McEvilley argues that William Rubin, chief curator of the exhibition, was motivated by a desire to validate a besieged formalist modernism by illustrating its affinities with the "timeless" qualities of primitive art:

> The collection of the Museum of Modern Art is predominantly based on the idea that formalist Modernism will never pass, will never lose its self-validating power. Not a relative, conditioned thing, subject to transient causes and effects, it is to be above the web of natural and cultural change; this is its supposed essence. ... By demonstrating that the "innocent" creativity of primitives naturally expresses a Modernist esthetic feeling, one may seem to have demonstrated once again that Modernism itself is both innocent and universal (1984, 55).

Recall John Martin's similar-sounding definition (and defense) of pre-Cunningham modern dance:

> ... there is absolutely nothing modern about modern dance. It is, as a matter of fact, virtually basic dance, the oldest of all dance forms. The modern dancer ... cuts through directly to the source of all dancing ...

But the Cunningham body, as we've seen repeatedly, makes no such claims, no pretense of having returned to the natural "source." In fact, in Chapter 1, I suggested that the body in Cunningham's choreography often looks as if it had been *assembled* by a practitioner of cubist collage. And although it doesn't advertise itself as the sort of *social* construction that postmodernists claim the human body to be, it nonetheless anticipated by many years the deconstruction of the "primitive" and/or "natural" body we find in so much postmodern discourse. Consider the anthropologist James Clifford's analysis of Josephine's Baker's "primitivist" appeal:

> The black body in Paris of the 20's was an ideological artifact. Archaic Africa (which came to Paris by way of the future—that is, America) was sexed, gendered, and invested with "magic" in specific ways. Standard poses adopted by "La Bakaire," like Léger's designs and costumes, evoked a recognizable "Africanicity"—the naked form emphasizing pelvis and buttocks, a segmented stylization suggesting a strangely mechanical vitality. (1988, 197–98)

Ann Daly brings a similar deconstructive logic to bear on Isadora Duncan's fabrications of naturalness:

> Far from being a tabula rasa, beyond the contingencies of culture and history, this "Natural" body was an artistic invention as well as a rhetorical strategy—a conceptual cipher for an ideal of harmony that embraced the Greeks and rejected "African Savages." "Nature" was Duncan's metaphorical shorthand for a loose package of aesthetic and social ideals: nudity, childhood, the idyllic past, flowing lines, health, nobility, ease, freedom, simplicity, order, and harmony. (1995, 89)

Between Modern and Postmodern

I began this chapter by asking how Cunningham should be "categorized" in relation to both modern and postmodern dance as well as the broader, cultural categories of modernism and postmodernism. It may appear that I'm eager to situate him squarely in the postmodern camp. But in fact, nothing could be further from the truth. As Christopher Hitchens once put it, "The truth rarely lies, but when it does, it lies between." And so, in this instance, does Cunningham: *between* modernism and postmodernism.

Granted, Cunningham has more than a little in common with a postmodernist like Thomas McEvilley who challenges the idea that modernist primitivism has rediscovered the original "source" of all true creativity. But McEvilley, it's important to remember, is one of those postmodern ideologues eager to demonize the aesthetic of formalism. To politically engaged (and politically correct) postmodernists such as McEvilley, Cunningham's brand of formalism is hopelessly insulated and apolitical, an example of what Moira Roth calls "the aesthetic of indifference." But, Cunningham's work *does* possess a distinctly political dimension. It offers us a variety of strategies for resisting environmental conditioning, for dancing "wrong side out." And far from holding the real world at bay, it repudiates the "timeless," ahistorical primitivism of Graham. In so doing, Cunningham acknowledges the contemporary urban world in a way that Graham never did. But Cunningham does so on his own terms—terms that are rather different from those that a postmodernist such as McEvilley would endorse.

Now we can begin to clarify Cunningham's complicated relationship to both modernism and postmodernism, broadly construed. Cunningham allows much of the "noise," "static," and even some of the visual detritus of contemporary urban life into his collaborations with Cage, Rauschenberg, and Johns. Collectively, they seem to acknowledge that Coca Cola and television have become an inescapable part of our lives. But at the same time, they don't (or at least, Cunningham doesn't) *embrace* these things in the undiscriminating manner of a postmodernist. Cunningham's basic movement vocabulary remains for the most part classical and abstract.

His dancers are technical virtuosos. There's no blurring of the differences between the professional dancer and the average mover. When Cunningham incorporates pedestrian movement into his work, it's not because he wishes to declare that "everyone is a dancer." He remains an "elitist"—in the best sense of that word—when it comes to the definition of dance. Even Cage—whose approach to sound can often appear utterly democratic and antihierarchical—never really forsakes the idea of quality. As he once admitted in an interview:

> I am actually an elitist. I always have been. I didn't study music with just anybody; I studied with Schoenberg. I didn't study Zen with just anybody; I studied with Suzuki. I've always gone, insofar as I could, to the president of the company. (Gann 1997, 138)

By contrast, many postmodernists are so eager to blur the distinction between "high" and "low"—and so eager to avoid the charge of "elitism"—that they welcome the leveling of all value distinctions. Indeed, in the realm of contemporary Cultural Studies, it's even become unfashionable to criticize the consumer culture of Coca Cola and MTV (i.e., "How dare you elitists criticize and condescend to the taste of the average consumer?," etc.). Andreas Huyssen typifies this now pervasive position: "The boundaries between high art and mass culture have become increasingly blurred, and we should begin to see that process as one of opportunity rather than lamenting loss of quality and failure of nerve" (1986, 44–45). My own attitude is much closer to that of Martha Bayles, who complains about:

> the postmodernist embrace of popular culture as a battering ram against the very idea of artistic standards. For every gray-haired highbrow who denied that art can exist in the schlock swollen flood of popular culture, there is a wet-behind-the-ears postmodernist who insists that every morsel of schlock belongs in an art gallery or a concert hall. One side says that artistic standards cannot be applied to popular culture, the other that they should not. The two sides claim to be in opposition, but if you ask me, they're in cahoots. (1994, 7)

In other words, it's one thing to avoid knee-jerk dismissals of popular culture, to argue (as Susan Sontag did during the late 1960s) that it's all right to like both The Supremes *and* Jasper Johns. But it's something else again to maintain that the *very distinction* between high and popular culture is nonexistent or undesirable and that everything can be leveled into the same "pluralistic," crazy quilt collage. For all of their supposed opposition to synthesis, wholeness, totalizing, and so on, postmodernists often blur otherwise valuable distinctions of the sort that an artist like Cunningham is careful to maintain.

I would be among the first to concede that Clement Greenberg's monolithic conception of modernism was unnecessarily narrow and restrictive.

But the reaction against his brand of impassioned purism has resulted in a mix-and-match culture whose true inspiration is the Cuisinart. The sort of indiscriminate homogenization encouraged by postmodernists is actually the hallmark of television. It's here—in Cunningham's (fundamentally antagonistic) relationship to the perceptual habits inculcated by television—that we can observe the way his dances work to immunize us against "automatic responses" that come to feel like "second nature." In this sense, Cunningham remains an adversarial *modernist*—but one who realizes just how deeply television and mass media have infiltrated the traditional modernist safe houses of "the primitive" and "the unconscious."

High modernists proceeded on the assumption that it was possible to erect a protective frame between one's art and the corruptions of contemporary culture. Postmodernists realize that this is no longer possible; but, all too often, they welcome the weakening of these barricades and celebrate the resultant merging of nature, culture, avant-garde, and kitsch. Cunningham realizes that all frames are now porous, but he provides us with a variety of strategies that can help to filter or "reframe"—and on some occasions, "filter out"—much of the noise and sensory stimuli that have become an inescapable part of contemporary urban life. The final two chapters of this book examine the *political* dimension of these strategies.

12

Fatal Abstraction: Merce Cunningham in the Age of Identity Politics

It was one of those "I-Have-Seen-The-Future-And-It-Works" declarations. In the mid-1980s, a choreographer of my acquaintance, fresh from his first, revelation-filled encounter with the work of Pina Bausch, triumphantly announced that she had shown him the way: the shining path toward dance *theater*. "Finally," he declared, "we have a real alternative to the escapist formalism of choreographers like Merce Cunningham."

I was taken aback. Formalism was a charge I could stomach—even savor. But *escapist*? That's a fighting word in my lexicon—especially when it's applied to an artist like Cunningham. Of course, I wasn't about to deny the distinction between watching dancers in tights and leotards execute chaîné turns, traveling pas de chats, and arabesques (to cite but some of the academic vocabulary that Cunningham has always favored) and the experience of entering into the world of Bausch's Tanztheatre—with its ballrooms and ballgowns, stiletto heels, and in-your-face sexual politics. But it wasn't entirely clear to me why the embrace of Bausch should necessarily entail the vilification of Cunningham. And so I inquired, "Why do you call Cunningham an escapist?" "Oh, you know," came the reply . . . "all that movement for its own sake . . . line, shape, patterns." Cunningham, he seemed to be saying, was guilty of fatal abstraction.

Perhaps he sensed my growing distress and was eager to taunt me a bit—for he then upped the rhetorical ante: "Worse than escapist. Autistic. . . . A closed system!" he said decisively. "Cunningham's movement is only about itself. It doesn't engage the real world in a recognizable way, let alone a politically useful way. Whereas Bausch . . . " Who could argue with the claim that Bausch's work is *about* something? It's plain for all to see that her dances are about many things other than the purely "formal" architecture of bodies arranged in space and time. I'd even concede that her dances are "socially situated" (thanks to realistic costume and decor) in a much more specific and easily recognizable way than Cunningham's work will ever be.

But does that mean that Bausch and her disciples exercise some sort of monopoly over the ways in which dances can create images of the social order? Does the fact that Cunningham's view of the world is embodied in variations on a basically abstract and formal vocabulary mean that his work is necessarily "escapist," that it unfolds in a parallel universe: aesthetically rarefied, hermetically sealed, and light years away from life as lived by real people? Have we become so literal-minded, so incapable of appreciating and deciphering abstract modes of representation that only the most transparent, instantly legible images are thought to reflect the world around us? And what exactly, in this context, do we *mean* by political? Can an art like modern dance ever *really* function in any meaningful way as an agent of social reform? Is there still a place for works of art whose ambition—whether or not we define it as "political"—is simply to elucidate (with great formal precision) *the way things are* rather than actively aspiring to change things for the better?

Those were some of the thoughts and questions that raced though my mind as I prepared to defend Cunningham against charges of "escapism." But given the fact that I was up against a true believer—a recent convert to the presumably superior virtues of dance theater—I began to sink into a defeatist funk. It dawned on me that my adversary was no lone voice in the wilderness—but, rather, someone who, for better or for worse, probably *had* seen the immediate future of American dance in the last quarter of the 20th century. He was only articulating what our old acquaintance, the art critic Moira Roth, had said more eloquently in print a few years earlier. In her view, the art of Cunningham and company amounted to a species of moral cowardice, yet another legacy of the chilling effect that McCarthyism had exerted upon American artists who dared to deal with overtly political themes. But ironically (and anomalously), the aesthetic of indifference reached fruition in the "activist" decade of the 1960s. This resulted, according to Roth, in a total disconnect between art and politics that bordered on schizophrenia.

Roth is hardly alone in her conviction that the art world (i.e., the world of painting, sculpture, conceptual art) in the 1960s was dominated by sensibilities of coolness and "indifference." In 1967, the critics Barbara Rose and Irving Sandler asked a number of their artist friends to answer a questionnaire designed to pinpoint the dominant spirit of the age. The key words that recur again and again in the responses they elicited include "cool," "impersonal," and "hard-edged." Gene Davis wrote that: "Coolness, passivity, and emotional detachment seemed to be in the air. Pop, op, hard-edge, minimal art and color painting share it in some degree." The abstract expressionist Jack Tworkov sounded even more like Moira Roth, arguing that: "The emphasis is on thingness, polish, smoothness, brightness on the one hand—uninvolvement, indifference and heartlessness on the other" (both Sundell 1988, 7). Curiously, though, when it came to their politics (and here I mean *real*, i.e., *practical* politics—as manifested in the ideologies they espoused, the causes they contributed time and money to, the candidates they voted for, etc.), even Roth readily acknowledges that many of these same painters and sculptors were anything but disengaged (let alone reactionary):

> ...many of the Pop and Minimal artists were actually sympathetic to radical causes, such as anti-war or Black Panther support demonstrations and the like. Why did they forget this when they went back to their studios to make art? Why this denial of commitment and feeling in art? Much of this bizarre discrepancy between life and art can be ascribed to the legacy of the Aesthetic of Indifference, together with Formalist theories (which were stamped with their own brand of "indifference") .... Formalism and the Aesthetic of Indifference together provided a powerfully persuasive counsel to artists of the 1960's: play it cool .... Formalism at least, only advocated coolness of form; but the Aesthetic of Indifference was a more potent and dangerous model for the 1960's: It advocated neutrality of feeling and denial of commitment in a period that otherwise might have produced an art of passion and commitment. (1977, 53)

But if radical politics is alive and well, why must art be conscripted into battle (especially the sort of battle it's not well equipped to fight)? Only someone who fails to appreciate the real and necessary *differences* between art and life would ask painters and sculptors to symbolically reenact or redundantly reannounce the storming of various real-life barricades. In 1948, Clement Greenberg (chief spokesperson for those "formalist" theories Roth disparages) argued:

> As a person, the writer ought indeed to involve himself...to the "point of commitment." Why should we ask less of him than of any other adult interested in the survival of the common decencies and authentic culture? However, he is under no moral—or aesthetic—obligation whatsoever to involve himself in this struggle as a writer.... Qua writer he is only interested necessarily in what he can write about successfully. (Hughes 1993, 43)

Greenberg asserts that there's no necessary incompatibility between a formalist art and an activist life. Greenberg was typical of those intellectuals who wrote for *Partisan Review* in the 1930s and 1940s, many of whom combined an instinctive leftishness in politics with a taste for the most difficult varieties of "high modernism" in art. (T. J. Clark has referred to this political and aesthetic balancing act as "Eliotic Trotskyism" [1985, 50].) Roth, it would appear, can't even conceive of art and politics engaging in this sort of dialogue. (Furthermore, it apparently never dawns on her that when daily life turns as hot, convulsive, and politically engaged as it did in the 1960s, a truly adversarial art might be inclined to emphasize distance and coolness.)

Appearing in the late 1970s, Roth's polemic was an early example of the growing backlash against artists such as Cunningham and Cage, for whom formal and perceptual concerns took precedence over verbally paraphraseable, socially engaged "content." What accounts for this change in the aesthetic weather? Was it just another swing of the art-historical pendulum away from the severity and austerity of formalist purity? If so, this pendulum-swing is in part a reaction against that excessively monolithic view of modernism we discussed in the Chapter 11 (Clement Greenberg's attempt to disenfranchise those avant-garde movements—surrealism, expressionism, collage—which don't operate comfortably within the claustrophobic confines of a single medium). But the backlash against formalist purity cannot be explained in purely aesthetic terms. Its deeper motivations are political. Roth's misreading of the 1960s (and of the complicated transactions between aesthetic and political radicalism which characterized that era) was probably inevitable given the transformed climate in which she formulated her argument. By the late 1970s, a viable political "left"—committed to strengthening and expanding society's public sector—had all but disappeared in the United States. Any impulse toward activism would soon find itself channeled into a highly Balkanized "identity politics" according to which sexual, racial, and ethnic minorities were expected to affirm their own cultural identities and differences.

In an age of steadily increasing multiculturalism, talk of purity (no matter how ardently one attempts to confine the discussion to the aesthetic realm) invariably leaves a bad taste in one's mouth, evoking as it does unsavory notions of racial and ethnic purity. Much recent scholarship sets out to demonstrate that genre distinctions are not unrelated to gender distinctions, or that preferences for "pure" genres (those that don't mix otherwise separate mediums or conflate distinctions between the verbal and the visual, the spatial and the temporal) are rooted in a repressed fear of miscegenation, gender-bending, or homosexuality. W. J. T. Mitchell has written about what he believes to be the disguised gender agenda at the heart of Lessing's *Laocoon*. This remarkable 18th-century tract is the great grandparent of all high modernist attempts to delineate the "natural" boundaries between aesthetic mediums. (Clement Greenberg admitted his close kinship with Lessing when [in 1940] he wrote an article advocating purity of medium titled "Towards A Newer Laocoon.") Mitchell concludes that:

> Lessing has disclosed what is probably the most fundamental ideological basis for his laws of genre, namely the laws of gender. The decorum of the arts at bottom has to do with proper sex roles. (1984, 115)

Clearly, the rise of "identity politics"—which we'll address at greater length later in this chapter—plays a significant role in the backlash against formalist ideas of "purity."

But in recent decades, the most sustained intellectual challenge to the formalist tradition comes from another branch of postmodern discourse: "deconstructionist" ideas about the central role that language plays in *all* forms of human experience. In the tradition that stretches from Jacques Lacan to Jacques Derrida and on to Frederic Jameson, even the unconscious is thought to be structured like a language and, to a great extent, *formulated* by language. "Il n'est structure que de language"—"There is no structure, without language"—insists Lacan (cited in Culler 1982, 86).

It follows that for the practitioners of deconstruction, all of the arts—even the most visual and least verbal—were thought to be trapped in the "prison house of language" or ensnared in the web of textuality, and were thus to be regarded as "texts to be read." One consequence of this linguistic strategy was that considerations of *content* become primary. (Verbally paraphraseable content—which a formalist art like Cunningham's sought to eliminate or deemphasize—always boils down to a matter of language: of one's ability to "say" what the work of art is about.) By contrast, in the age of high modernism, the "mute" nature of much formalist art, its resistance to verbal paraphrase, was taken as proof of its integrity and inviolability. The formalist painter Ad Reinhardt declared that "The frame must isolate and protect the painting from its surroundings" (1973, 169). But from the vantage point of Derrida-style deconstruction, that sort of "pure" isolation is neither possible nor desirable. The "frame" is now declared to be porous, penetrated and permeated by language (in much the same way that the unconscious was no longer to be regarded as a preverbal bastion of purity). Language serves as the principle link—the chief route of transmission—between the artwork and the world beyond its formal boundaries.

This idea meshed smoothly with the "anti-elitism" of identity politics. Any impulse toward abstraction or formal experimentation—anything not verbally paraphraseable—could now be dismissed as "elitist" on the assumption that it would be less accessible to a mass audience. Didactic content of the "racism is bad," "sexism is wrong" variety began to displace formal and perceptual concerns. MFA programs in studio art promoted a sort of postmodern update of 1930s agitprop, with race and gender replacing class as the principle arena of concern. Peter Plagens summarized the increasingly formulaic nature of this art: "You just assemble found objects into an installation, say the word 'gender' and you're done" (Solomon 1999, 39).

Politics, too, was reconceived as an essentially verbal activity, as if society was so thoroughly structured by language that linguistic reform would automatically promote social reform. This led to some of the more easily parodied excesses of political correctness in the 1980s (e.g., the feminist seminars that were retitled "ovulars"). Whereas an earlier generation of leftists might have proposed a Marshall Plan for the inner cities or the nationalizing of health insurance, the practitioners of deconstructive identity politics placed a high social priority on changing the spelling of woman to "womyn" and history to "herstory." Of course, it would be foolish to deny the role that language—especially public discourse—plays in shaping generalized perceptions of the real world, but that's very different from claiming that the real world is essentially a "linguistic construction."

Ironically, neoconservatives began to complain about the politicizing of academia, but the *real* problem (from the vantage point of an older left preoccupied with the public sector) was the academicizing of politics, the sublimation of concrete political activism into theoretical "discourse." In 1987, the journal *October* published a special issue devoted to AIDS activism, and many of the essays came dangerously close to declaring the disease an essentially "linguistic" phenomena. Paula A. Treichler for example, stated:

> . . . the very nature of AIDS is constructed through language . . . . The name AIDS in part *constructs* the disease and helps make it intelligible. We cannot therefore look "through" language to determine what AIDS really is. Rather we must explore the site where such determinations *really* occur and intervene at the point where meaning is created: in language. (1987, 31)

By the late 1980s, the AIDS pandemic, coupled with the Reagan and Bush administrations' concerted effort to dismantle the nation's (already) slender social safety net, had begun to produce a widespread impatience with art that doesn't wear its social conscience on its sleeve, that doesn't "spell out"—in capital letters—its political sympathies.

Saying versus Doing

Thus, it's easy to understand why, amid such a climate, Cunningham and Cage might be accused of "escapism." As Cage admitted:

> We are not, in these dances and music, saying something. We are simple-minded enough to think that if we were saying something we would use words. We are rather doing something. (Smith 1981, 117)

Yet the fact that Cunningham's dances aren't "saying" something that could just as easily have been expressed in words doesn't mean that his choreography is purely self-referential (let alone "escapist"). However satisfying his dances are on a "purely" formal level, they are also about many things other than the beauty and complexity of their own architecture. Yes, Cunningham *is* a formalist; but it's difficult to think of another choreographer whose work provides a more vivid representation of what might be called the *deep structure* of contemporary urban life (e.g., simultaneous occurrences, decentralized action, the dissociation of what we hear from what we see, sudden reversals of direction, unpredictable entrances and exits).

Cunningham and the Choreographic Medium

In an ideal world, it would come as news to no one that "abstract" form can function in ways that are both representational and deeply expressive. As Doris Humphrey wrote: "Four abstract themes, all moving equally and harmoniously together like a fugue would convey the significance of democracy far better than would one woman dressed in red, white and blue, with stars in her hair" (Cohen 1972, 252). This is an ancient truth, but one that we're in imminent danger of forgetting in this "content-obsessed" period. Indeed, one of the refrains we hear most often these days from young, Bausch-inspired choreographers is: "I have things to say that cannot be expressed by movement alone. I need spoken text and (quite possibly) slide projections, decor and props to convey my (often political) message." That may well be true. And if so, it tells us one of two things: that many of today's choreographers have chosen the wrong medium for what they need to "say," or else they greatly underestimate the expressive and communicative powers of movement.

So perhaps we should turn this talk about "escapism" on its head. Maybe the real problem is that so many of today's "choreographers" want to escape from the constraints (otherwise known as conventions) of the very medium in which they work. The result—and it's one way of describing the current Zeitgeist in which choreographers rely on virtually everything *but* movement to "say" what they need to "say"—is Dance For People Who Don't Like Dance. Cunningham, by contrast, creates dances for people who not only like dance, but who want dance to *do* something unique to its own medium: to provide them with experiences that can be obtained in no other way. (And in that sense, he remains much more of a "modernist" than a "postmodernist.") Of course, the forms of expression that are unique to the dance medium may not be as immediately accessible to a broad public as those which lend themselves to verbal paraphrase (or what Cleanth Brooks once called "the *heresy* of paraphrase").

But today, the danger exists that almost any work of art that isn't immediately comprehensible to a mass audience will be accused of "elitism" and dismissed by the cultural left as either apolitical or downright reactionary. Thus there's more at stake here than concerns about "purity of medium" or the virtues of subtlety. This is also a debate about what it means to call a work of art "political."

Hitting Them over the Head

Throughout this book, I've argued that Cunningham's and Cage's work promotes perceptual freedom by challenging many sorts of cultural conditioning. This sort of perceptual reeducation can and *should* be regarded as serving a "political" end. Cage consistently maintained that he wanted his art to prove "useful" to people who are engaged in varieties of social activism. For example, he once wrote: "We could make a piece of music in which we would be willing to live, a piece of music as a representation of a society in which you would be willing to live..." (Retallack 1994, 260). Indeed, Cunningham's and Cage's work is incomparably more "radical"—both aesthetically and *politically*—than most of today's manipulative, "content-based" art that proselytizes on behalf of specific causes.

We need only compare Cunningham's and Cage's attitude toward their audiences with that of artists such as Karen Finley or Holly Hughes. Finley and Hughes are both decorated veterans of the 1990's Culture Wars; both are members of the "NEA Four" (whose federal arts funding was withdrawn retroactively amid the "decency" campaign waged by Jesse Helms and other paleoconservatives). Helms, needless to say, was not attacking Finley or Hughes for their "formal strategies," but rather for "content-related" offenses—more specifically their respective gender agendas. In a 1991 interview, Finley declared her distaste for abstract and formalist art:

> Real art is supposed to embrace current political and social issues.... So when I see a huge red cube or some abstract-shaped public sculpture—well, that doesn't give me anything. Something like that is the least threatening it can be. (Schlossman 2002, 225)

Holly Hughes goes even further. Her monologue *World Without End* (1990) is a no-holds-barred attack on the formalist enterprise. The author's alter-ego discusses an epiphany she experienced in art school:

> Oh I tried to learn how to lie, in art school, and I learned to believe in the universality of art, that art transcends the grubby artless ghettos of gender and race and sexual preference, that art is abstract and never gets blood on his clothes

even when witnessing a murder, oh no! Art turns the other way and looks out the window.

A few pages later, her character adds:

> Oh, I know the difference between politics and art! I went to art school...and the first thing they said when they saw me coming through the door was: "Holly, don't hit them over the head. Art is not supposed to hit them over the head." Well, neither are fathers. And when Joel Steinberg hit his daughter so hard she died I read in the paper the next day a columnist, Pete Hammil, saying it was worse morally for Hedda Nussbaum to not intervene than it was for Joel Steinberg to kill her in the first place. That's when I gave up on my macrame career.

Unlike Cunningham and Cage, Hughes and Finley are willing—indeed, eager—to "hit them over the head."

This also explains why, in part, Finley and Hughes are sometimes referred to (by critics like Arlene Croce and Robert Hughes) as practitioners of "victim art." In the emotionally manipulative world of victim art, it's simply taken for granted that certain sorts of content (e.g., the victimization of Joel Steinberg's daughter) will *automatically* engage the audience's sympathy. James Joyce once defined sentimentality as "unearned emotion"; and, in this sense, victim art is always an exercise in sentimentality (however "unsentimental" its subject matter may seem). Thus, one big problem with this sort of work—from the vantage point of artists like Cunningham and Cage—is that it almost invariably relies on emotional manipulation. It elicits precisely the sort of "automatic response" that Cunningham, Cage, Johns, and Rauschenberg seek not only to avoid, but to actively immunize their audiences against. In Cunningham's words:

> I don't think political art is useful. I think it ends up being like all politics—about greed and power. You get into politics, and it's always about somebody who wants to control somebody else. (Joyce 1999, n.p.).

To state the problem a bit more aphoristically: Art that "hits you over the head" almost always winds up inadvertently shooting itself in the foot. And I mean that as an axiomatic principle: As long as we live in a society dominated by the ethos and practice of advertising, morally didactic and emotionally manipulative art will simply add to the din. It will constitute yet another ad campaign (even if we approve of the products it's pushing); its "ends" will always be invalidated by its "means." Its victories are pyrrhic, in so far as every additional act of sensory and emotional manipulation ultimately diminishes our capacity for free choice. You don't have to be John Cage to realize this. That venerable old socialist Eugene Debs once warned, "If someone can lead you into the promised land, someone else can lead you out." Without a degree of distance and a dose of disinterestedness, there can be no true choice and thus no true freedom.

An art like Cunningham's and Cage's—which chooses not to "hit you over the head"—isn't *necessarily* any more convincingly or effectively "political" than one that does. But at the very least, it avoids what we might call the original sin of all such art: emotional manipulativeness and moral didacticism. An art that "disengages" its audience from the prevailing perceptual orthodoxies can be just as radical as an art that seeks to "engage" its audience on behalf of specific causes. As Brecht wrote, "Disbelief can move mountains" (Munk 1988, 119), and, furthermore, as D. H. Lawrence observed, "The world doesn't fear a new idea. It can pigeonhole any idea. What it fears is a new experience" (Trilling 1968, xvii). Didactic, content-centered, verbally paraphraseable art rarely amounts to more than a new idea (a new "whine" in an old bottle). It proceeds on the assumption that accessibility (the effort to reach the largest possible audience) is—in and of itself—politically progressive. And that results in the tendency to package or "bottle" the content in a familiar, user-friendly form (alas, the very form least likely to challenge existing patterns of perception). As a recipe for preaching to the choir, such strategies may well have merit; as a prescription for social change, they amount to self-delusion.

The Politics of Difference

It's highly ironic that many of those who complain about the push-button sentimentality of victim art and other such work blame these practices on the 1960s, the decade that Moira Roth associates with "the aesthetic of indifference." Arlene Croce's legendary "nonreview" of Bill T. Jones' *Still/Here* (1994) is a prime example of this revisionist misreading of the 1960s:

> From the moment that Bill T. Jones declared himself H.I.V. positive and began making AIDS focused pieces for himself and members of his company—from that moment it was obvious that the permissive thinking of the sixties was back, and in the most pernicious form. (1995, 58)

How peculiar: Croce accuses the art of the 1960s of being too political, whereas Moira Roth dismisses the art of that decade as not political enough! Clearly, what passes *today* for political art (the work of Finley and Hughes for example) has much more in common with the message-laden sentimentality of the 1930s than with art works created during the 1960s (although issues of class are now subordinated to those of gender and race). The attack on Cunningham as an "escapist formalist" is eerily reminiscent of the broadside against "art for art's sake" that we find in a work of 1930s agit-prop like Marc

Blitzstein's *The Cradle Will Rock*. In his own parody of "escapist formalism," Blitzstein has his rarified aesthetes sing:

> Be blind for Art's sake
> And Deaf for Art's sake
> And dumb for Art's sake
> Until for Art's sake
> They kill for Art's sake.
> All the Art for Art's sake!

Then again, if the truth be told, I'd sit through a good revival of Blitzstein's witty, if didactic, satire much more eagerly than I'd endure another act of Bill T. Jones's lugubrious *Still/Here*. Indeed, from the vantage point of the early 21st century, the politics (if not the art) of the 1930s can begin to look strangely appealing. During the years of the Great Depression, leftist politics was understood to transcend the boundaries of personal identity. It was assumed to be about the shared, public good (the ties that bind, rather than the differences that separate). Not so today. Identity politics proceeds on the assumption that we cannot, as individuals, transcend the defining characteristics of race, class, and gender. We seem to care about every difference but one: the all-important difference that separates the artist's "art" from the artist's "life." Nothing sounds quite so quaint or foreign to our ears as T. S. Eliot's wise counsel: "The more perfect the artist, the more completely separate in him will be the man who suffers and the mind which creates" (1963, 143).

Cunningham would be quick to concur with that sentiment. In 1989, during a panel discussion of his work, someone (perhaps a gay activist who was into "outing") tried to put Cunningham and Cage on the spot. Smugly (and no doubt, accusingly) the audience member inquired about the "true nature" of their partnership. Cage chimed in with an exemplary response: "It's very simple," he said, "I do the cooking and Merce Cunningham does the dishes." That, it seems to me, is more than one needs to know about Cunningham's private life in order to fully appreciate his work; Cunningham's life—to a very considerable extent—*is* his work. My approach to Cunningham's choreography—which I believe to be in keeping with the spirit of the work itself—is the absolute antithesis of today's "identity" politics, where one's art is expected to noisily and didactically affirm some aspect of one's ethnicity, sexual orientation, or history of personal victimhood. Cunningham's work is about the beauty and pleasure of *escaping* one's identity and personality. As Cunningham himself once wrote, "If one's concern is self-expression, then the proper area is psychoanalysis" (1957, 22).

But perhaps the term "escapism" will come back to haunt us yet; for one could argue that in devising strategies for circumventing his own tastes and desires, Cunningham is seeking to flee some aspect of himself that he would rather not publicly acknowledge. A "sexual/political" reading of this sort might tell us something of interest about Merce Cunningham, but it would do little to illuminate his art. Nevertheless, Susan Foster, the doyen of contemporary gender studies, pursues this very line of argument:

> [Cunningham's] dances focused especially on the spatial and temporal characteristics of bodies in motion. It was this focus that eventually prevailed as the epistemological grounding for his entire choreographic vision. Rather than characters and stories, his dances would present bodies in motion. Meaning would be located, not in the psychological implications of bodily gesture, but in the physical characteristics of movement itself.... In this focus on movement and on the individual response and interpretation to that movement, Cunningham found protection for his homosexual identity. (1997, 20–21)

Similarly, Jill Johnston sets out to

> ... make a case for Cage's inventions as a "homosexual aesthetic"—a muted, but potent version of such overt epiphanies as Allen Ginsberg's *Howl* of 1956.... Cage was a role model for that very repression, having sworn himself to silence (the name of his first book!) on the subject of his difference.... Silence as a key facet of his music can be construed as an exemplary cover, a "speech act" from the closet, the expression of a homosexual who is "empowered to speak, but unable to say." (1996, 123)

Jonathan Katz approaches Rauschenberg's work in much the same way:

> He became famous for a series of all-white canvases consisting of flat white paint on a flat white surface: no incident, no brushstrokes, no detail. These paintings are the absolute inverse of Abstract Expressionism in mood, surface, color, expression ... they are so without autographic or gestural content of any kind that Rauschenberg decreed they were to be painted by others, using a roller. There is an overwhelming feeling of silence in these paintings, a sense that there is nothing to say, or better, that there is nothing to say that can be said. (1993, 194–95)

This is the 1990s update of Moira Roth's 1970s accusation that Cunningham and Cage practice an aesthetics of indifference. For Roth, Cunningham and company evade the (presumed) obligations of political engagement; and for Foster, Johnston, and Katz, they evade the new obligations of identity politics. ("All gays and lesbians—no matter what generation you are—out of the closet ... Now!" Furthermore, "If your art isn't overtly 'about' your sexual orientation, you've evaded your responsibility to 'the movement.'") Susan Foster compares Cunningham's "choreographic closet" with the one she claims Ted Shawn constructed for himself a generation earlier:

> Shawn's protective closet had disguised the individual sexual orientations of his dancers within the hypermasculinity of their performance personas.

Cunningham's closet, in contrast, fractured bodies into parts of equal significance and value so that individuality could only be defined by the activities, all
of equal value, in which the dancer was at each moment engaged. Where Shawn
had exaggerated his dancer's masculine capabilities, Cunningham neutralized
all masculine, feminine, and sexual connotations by focusing on space, time,
and motion. (1977, 21–22)

In actual practice, it seems to me that Ted Shawn's hypermasculine beef-
cake hid his homosexuality about as effectively as the Macho Man costumes
worn by The Village People. If Cunningham had really been determined to
hide his homosexuality, why would he have entered the dance profession
in the first place? And why would he have lived openly with Cage for over
forty years? Why not enter instead into a sham marriage and go to work as
an insurance salesman? (Would a compulsive gambler attempt to conceal
his compulsion by moving to Las Vegas?) In an interview published in 2000,
Cunningham undefensively addressed this issue:

I don't think I was guarded about my personal life. It is quite true I didn't speak
about it very much but I didn't see any reason to speak about it. John and I were
together. We did our work together. We traveled together. What more was there
to say? (O'Mahony, n.p.)

Only a sexual/political ideologue would assume that the principle reason
for choosing an aesthetic of objectivity over subjectivity is the attempt to conceal (or "escape") one's sexual orientation. Those who make such assumptions appear to know little about the history of modernism. Indeed, ever
since the early 19th century, when the romantic movement first legitimized
the notion of an artwork rooted in personal experience, the art-historical
pendulum has swung back and forth at regular intervals between extremes
of objectivity and subjectivity. (Jonathan Katz virtually acknowledges this
when he observes—correctly—that Rauschenberg's white paintings are a
repudiation of the practices of abstract expressionism.) What the Germans
call *Die Neue Sachlichkeit*—The New Objectivity—is an aesthetic impulse
that surfaces quite often in the 20th century as an antidote to extremes of
inwardness, spontaneity, self-expression, and the cult of personality. Were
the Bauhaus artists who rejected the Sturm and Drang of German expressionism all closeted homosexuals? Was T. S. Eliot concealing "a love that dare
not speak its name" when he argued that "Poetry is not a turning loose of
emotion, but an escape from emotion; it is not the expression of personality,
but an escape from personality" (1963, 145).

In this regard, it's instructive to compare Cunningham with Ashton or
Balanchine. As Julie Kavanagh makes clear in her recent book *Secret Muses:
The Life of Frederick Ashton*, the great British choreographer's dances were
often inspired by his (frequently) unrequited pursuit of attractive young

men (i.e., his "muses"). Similarly an account of the choreography that Balanchine created for Suzanne Farrell in the mid-1960s would be incomplete without at least *some* acknowledgment of the role that his unrequited lust for Farrell played in the creative process. By contrast, there is no reason to believe that Cunningham's work was animated by any similar sort of sublimation. If Cunningham has a "muse," it's probably the *I Ching*. And yet, for the race/class/gender fanatics like Susan Foster, it's not enough to accuse Cunningham of sexual cowardice. Academic fashion compels her to play the race card as well:

> Cunningham's approach presumed an absolute equivalence of male and female bodies, and also black and white bodies. Living in the kind of world constructed by his dances, homosexual conduct or Afro-American identity would carry valences no different from those of white, heterosexual behavior.

Castigating "its inherent racism," she alludes to "the whiteness of Cunningham's approach":

> The very project of locating identity in a physicality that denied racial difference could only be supported by a tradition that presumed its own universality. His particular version of chaste dancing, even as it deflected inquiries into his sexual orientation, denied the racial inequalities embodied in modern dance and its cultural surround. Focusing on the problematic of race in Cunningham's work thus brings into sharp relief the precise structure of the closet he crafted. (1977, 22–23)

Perhaps Foster should specify which "racial differences" she wants to see highlighted. Is she implying that Cunningham's "chaste dancing" represses the raging libido of the black man? Or that the "natural rhythm" of the black dancer is disguised by Cunningham's unpredictable weight changes? Maybe she believes that all African American men have large penises—and that their costumes should emphasize this anatomical difference. And why, in the final analysis, does she settle for only two out of three of today's most fashionable topics (gender and race)? Why not go all the way and reproach Cunningham for his utter indifference to issues of *class* as well? I, for one, have always prayed that his choreography would somehow, someday, differentiate between those dancers who grew up in blue-collar neighborhoods and those who were raised in posh middle-class suburbs.

The Complexities of "Story"

John Cage once defined the artist's task as the effort to "preserve us from all the logical minimalizations that we are at each instant tempted to apply to the flux of events." No contemporary choreographer has done more to honor the *complexity* of contemporary experience than Merce Cunningham; and that's why it makes so little sense to me when I hear him accused of "escapist formalism."

Consider a complex and ambiguous work such as Rauschenberg's combine titled "Story" (currently owned by the Toronto Museum of Art). As detailed in Chapter 3, "Story" was constructed "live on stage" during a series of performances of Cunningham's dance—also called "Story"—in London in 1964. (The design concept for "Story" required that Rauschenberg devise a new object in the course of each performance, drawing entirely from materials found in the vicinity of the theater that same day.) Some of the more prominent icons and objects that Rauschenberg "cut and pasted" into this combine-collage include an image of the Ace of Spades, faded ads for Harp Lager and Outspan Oranges, as well as an actual wheel from a child's scooter. Imagine the sorts of "readings" this work might elicit from ideologues of different generations such as Moira Roth and Jonathan Katz. (In 1998 Roth and Katz collaborated on a collection of essays called *Difference/ Indifference* that set out to compare and contrast their respective approaches to activism.)

Let's zero-in on a key detail of Rauschenberg's work: the fact that the Harp Lager ad is layered over the image of the Outspan Orange label, and as a result, only the word "out" remains visible on the surface of the orange. In Great Britain during the 1970s, Outspan Oranges—which were harvested entirely in South Africa—had become a controversial symbol of apartheid and a flash point for issues of divestment and corporate complicity. Thus a critic like Moira Roth, in her avowed hostility to the "aesthetic of indifference" and her desire to promote issue-oriented activism, might well interpret the image to read "out of South Africa." Jonathan Katz, by contrast, interpreting through the prism of gay activism and identity politics, might just as easily read those three letters as a partially disguised cri de cour on Rauschenberg's part, an expression of his repressed desire to get "out" of his homosexual closet. But *any* single reading along these lines would invariably reduce the ambiguity and complexity of the images. Indeed, if we're going to engage in literal-minded readings of this sort, why not suggest that "out" refers to Rauschenberg's desire to get "out" of the Cunningham company (for which he still served as artistic director.) The company's 1964 World Tour, during which "Story" was created, was—by all accounts—a dismaying experience for Rauschenberg; and he resigned his company post immediately following its conclusion.

My point is not to rule "out" *any* of these interpretations, but to keep multiple possibilities resonating simultaneously. As Theodore Adorno argued time and again, art reveals what ideology conceals. A nonideological art like Cunningham's or Rauschenberg's embraces the very sort of complexities and contradictions that political ideologies tend to iron-out or gloss over.

Joan Retallack elaborates on Adorno's argument in a stunning meditation about John Cage's "Lecture on the Weather" (1989). The heart of Retallack's essay is summed up in this question:

> Does ideology conceal weather? It certainly attempts to conceal "whether," i.e. alternatives, and they usually come only in twos. In considering anything beyond that—complexities of three and more . . . not to say the infinite possibilities of "weather," ideology becomes simply an engine of obscurantism and denial. (1994, 247)

In what is surely the single best record of a performance of "Story"—a film version shot for Helsinki television during the 1964 tour—Rauschenberg and Cunningham make use of a revolving stage that keeps revealing the action from an ever-shifting variety of perspectives. It's a reminder, however inadvertent, that Cage's interest in the indeterminate nature of "weather" was also an interest in "whether" (or not), a strategy for keeping matters open rather than closed, a means of suspending—perhaps indefinitely—the moment of "not yet decided."

13
Dancing in the Aftermath of 9/11

Never lie. Never say that something has moved you if you are still in
the same place. You can pick up a book, but a book can throw you
across the room. A book can move you from a comfortable armchair
to a rocky place where the sea is. A book can separate you from your
husband, your wife, your children, all that you are. It can heal you
out of a lifetime of pain. Books are kinetic, and like all huge forces,
need to be handled with care.
  —Jeanette Winterson, *Art Objects: Essays on Ecstasy and Effrontery*
                                                                  (1996)

And what good will it do you
to go home and put on the Mozart Requiem?
Read Keats? How will culture cure you?
                    —Adrienne Rich, "In Memoriam: D.K." (1986)

Gather 10 people at random from the streets of New York City, line them up in
a row, and (to borrow a phrase from Holly Hughes) "hit them over the head."
Not with a didactic monologue excerpted from a blunt exercise in victim art,
but with a blunt object of some sort; in other words, literally—rather than
metaphorically—hit them over the head. They will all react. Then, expose
the same randomly selected focus group to a performance of Cunningham's
"Summerspace" or "Rainforest." In this case, the results will be much less
predictable, uniform, and immediate. Surely, some members of this captive
audience will be bored or indifferent, others baffled and irritated, a few may
be mildly intrigued, and one or two may be awestruck and conclude that
the encounter "changed their lives." These predictions are highly speculative,
but one thing is certain: the effect of the Cunningham performance on those

who attend it will not be a matter of Newtonian action/reaction or Pavlovian stimulus/response; both the short and long-term result will be something more closely analogous to a dawning of awareness or the planting of a seed, which may or may not blossom at a later date.

Writing in 1997, the art critic Peter Schjeldahl recalled the profound effect that a Cunningham performance had exerted on him years earlier: "I caught a Rauschenberg-Cunningham-Cage-Tudor evening in Minneapolis in 1963. I think it altered my genetic code" (1997, n.p.). In 1968, when I first encountered works like "Walkaround Time," and "Rainforest," I felt similarly transformed. My way of seeing and thinking about dance—not to mention my ideas about the relationship between dance the other arts—began to change in a fundamental way. Both Schjeldahl and I are describing moments of personal enlightenment; neither of us make any claims for the way in which our favorite Cunningham collaborations may have reconfigured the genetic hardwiring of the entire audience. And here we encounter one of the fundamental differences between a great work of art like "Summerspace" or "Rainforest" and the brute force of a hurricane, an airborne epidemic, a power blackout, or (to cite an especially timely example) a terrorist attack, which indiscriminately effects everyone in its path. When Jeanette Winterson (in one of the quotes that prefaces this chapter) analogizes works of art to "huge forces" that need to be "handled with care," she presumably is not referring to the sorts of huge forces that toppled the Twin Towers on September 11, 2001.

This is a particularly poignant moment to be comparing the efficacy of an art like Merce Cunningham's with various forms of "direct" action. As sad coincidence has it, I find myself writing the conclusion to this book in the immediate aftermath of 9/11, a time when the arts in general—and the less socially engaged of the arts in particular—are finding it harder than ever to articulate a reason-for-being. Chapter 12 amounted to a defense of Cunningham's work in response to the currently fashionable accusation that choreographic formalists are guilty of fatal abstraction—that their work, in other words, is too insulated from the concerns of the real world. But at this melancholy moment, it's no longer even a question of socially engaged art versus formalist art. In the immediate aftermath of 9/11, anyone who isn't either a firefighter or a policeman can easily be made to feel as useless as Oblomov, that most superfluous of superfluous men. What is there to *do*—aesthetically speaking—other than light a candle and listen to Samuel Barber's plangent "Adagio for Strings," hoping that it functions as a much-needed exercise in the therapeutic management of collective grief? We don't dare fall back on the usual irony that (in less traumatic circumstances) would lead us to resist the numbingly habitual way this particular piece of music gets automatically pressed into service as the official cultural signifier of "Grief."

But the feelings of futility and self-doubt that have overtaken the arts community go beyond the question of whether or not art can "do" anything of practical value to help the victims, their families, or the nation's sense of security and well-being. Many artists—even if they don't dare admit to it— find themselves *envying* the sheer power, sensory impact, and global reach of what the terrorists accomplished on September 11. What else might have possessed the composer Karlheinz Stockhausen to declare, a mere 5 days after the attacks, that the events in New York and Washington amounted to "the greatest work of art for the whole cosmos." Just a few months earlier, Stockhausen had been awarded the 2001 German Music Publishers Society Prize for his *Helicopter String Quartet*. In that high-tech (and high-decibel-level) multimedia work, members of the Arditti String Quartet played their instruments while aloft in four helicopters that hovered over the concert hall. Cameras and microphones transmitted both sounds and images of the live performers to four towers of video screens and amplifiers strategically dispersed throughout the performance space. An auditory engineer at a central console mixed and modulated the deafening sounds of the helicopters' turbines and rotors with the more lyrical sounds produced by the string instruments. The result was a "wall of sound" that both Wagner and Phil Spector might have envied. Its sheer power proved difficult for any listener to resist, let alone ignore. But measured in terms of audience size as well as in terms of the ultimate emotional and intellectual impact it exerted on that audience, Stockhausen's piece could hardly compete with the sounds and images of 9/11. It's my guess that Stockhausen's unfortunate comments were occasioned less by knee-jerk anti-Americanism than by the dilemma that serious artists almost always face when confronted with a real-life event as horrific and far-reaching as the terrorist attacks of 9/11. Many years ago, Jean Paul Sartre referred to what he called "the crisis of the imaginary" (Brook 1968, 198), the manifold ways in which fact has put fiction on the defensive in a century of unprecedented horror (then the 20th, now the 21st). Allen Ginsberg once phrased the whole matter more aphoristically, in a line that inspired the title of William Burroughs's most famous book: "A naked lunch is natural to us. We eat reality sandwiches. But allegories are so much lettuce" (Burroughs 1959, xxxiv).

In the first issue of *The New Yorker* published after September 11, the novelist Jonathan Franzen wrote: "Somewhere—you can be absolutely sure of this—the death artists who planned the attack were rejoicing over the terrible beauty of the tower's collapse" (2001, 29). A phrase like "death artists" makes us cringe at first, but it seems to me that Franzen is simply marveling at—without in any sense condoning—the sheer leap of imagination that engendered the attacks on 9/11. Granted, there's something undeniably repulsive about the equating of terrorism and art. (Indeed, Stockhausen began to back pedal and apologize for his comments almost immediately.) But in another sense, both Stockhausen and Franzen were merely acknowledging one of the most extraordinary things about the attacks of 9/11: that they were not just unexpected, but unimagined—and perhaps unimaginable. One can hardly fault an artist for consciously or unconsciously envying a leap of imagination, but does it really make sense for artists to ever attempt to *compete* with the sheer sensory impact of an event like the attacks of 9/11, or to imagine that art can prove as useful as the actions of a first responder? Perhaps one legacy of September 11 will be a renewed realization that art is inherently different from all forms of direct action (both benign and malign)—and that any attempt by artists to metaphorically "hit people over the head" or to comfort those who really *have been* hit over the head will always prove either aesthetically unsuccessful or politically unproductive.

Cage once titled an installment of his Diary, "How to Improve the World (You Will Only Make Matters Worse)" (1969, 3), a sentiment that seems difficult to reconcile with his belief, professed elsewhere, that his and Cunningham's art can prove politically "useful." But this particular diary entry concludes with a paradoxical set of questions: "How can you believe this when you believe that? How can I not?" (1969, 20). For Cage, the power of contradiction and paradox far exceeds the power of (raw) power. No doubt, his lifelong study of Zen Buddhism has much to do with this. Recall his insistence that art change his way of seeing, not his way of feeling. And Cage's oft-expressed distaste for art that "pushes you around" is a quintessential example of this sentiment. It didn't matter if the work was a sledgehammer exercise in political didacticism (Frederic Rzewski's "Attica") or the "Hallelujah Chorus." Cage resisted even the most artful varieties of emotional manipulation:

> It has precisely in it what government has in it: the desire to control, and it leaves no freedom for me. It pushes me towards its conclusion, and I'd rather be a sheep, which I'm not, than be pushed along by a piece of music. I'm just as angry with . . . the "Hallelujah Chorus" as I am with "Attica." The moment I hear that kind of music I go in the opposite direction. (Kostelanetz 1996, 295)

Cage was notoriously uncooperative whenever he found himself in attendance at an Allan Kaprow-style "Happening" where audience members were expected to follow instructions for "actively" participating on cue (e.g., "when the bell rings, move to the seat opposite you and take your shirt off"). One can easily imagine Cage declaring, "I'd rather be one of Pavlov's dog's, which I'm not." Cage's music may sometimes be hard on the ears, but it's never organized in such a way that it "forces" a particular response. Similarly, Cunningham's collaborations with Cage—unlike so many earlier examples of modern dance—rarely create even the *illusion* that the dancer is being moved involuntarily by huge "forces." As Deborah Jowitt argued, "... you never feel the presence of a force in the center of [Cunningham's] body, pulling the limbs awry, knocking him off-balance ... the debilitating whirlwinds—external or internal—that were so much a part of the modernist aesthetic—did not apparently preoccupy him" (1988, 281).

In repudiating primitivism, Cunningham also repudiated the idea—most often associated with an aesthetician like Susanne Langer—that movement doesn't become "dance" unless and until it creates the illusion that the body is being propelled by invisible forces or powers, a vestigial legacy of the medium's "primitive" origins. In *Feeling and Form,* Langer wrote, "The substance of such dance creation is the same Power that enchanted ancient caves and forests, but today we invoke it with full knowledge of its illusory status ... " (1983, 45). Langer's book was published in 1953, the same year that Cunningham formed his company. If her theory of dance seems a bit quaint and old-fashioned to us today, it's largely because of the success that Cunningham has had in modernizing modern dance.

Why Cunningham Matters

In time, this post-9/11 obsession with direct action—this Stockhausian hunger for an art that aspires to compete with "huge forces"—will surely pass, as will the pressure to evaluate all of one's actions solely in terms of their socially beneficial consequences. But when the dust settles—both literally and figuratively—we will be left with a different sort of urgency: a heightened sense that life is both fleeting and precious. And the most urgent question we can then ask ourselves is simply "What matters now?" For me, the question becomes: Why do Cunningham and Cage (and Johns and Rauschenberg) *matter* enough to devote a book of this length to them? Obviously, they don't matter in the same way that the work of the NYPD and the FDNY matter. But surely there must be art that will continue to matter even if it *doesn't* bear in any direct way on the world we find ourselves in, post-9/11. Many of my favorite dances—Balanchine's "Agon," Taylor's "Esplanade," Tudor's "Pillar of Fire," Ashton's "Enigma Variations," Tharp's "The Bix Pieces," Morris's "Gloria" (to cite just a few)—will, one assumes, continue to offer the same pleasure and edification they've always offered.

I have no desire to preside over a shotgun marriage between dance and politics or between dance and social utility. The idea that all works of art are in some sense political—the notion that every dance either reinforces or resists the political status quo—strikes me as both simpleminded and wrong. This idea is too similar to George W. Bush's post-9/11 declaration that the rest of the world is either "with us or against us." Indeed, it's only in totalitarian countries that *all* works of art are evaluated according to their political leanings. And let's face it: the most consciously politicized forms of art usually amount to one variety or another of agit-prop, which ultimately does a disservice to both art *and* politics. And yet, I can't help but acknowledge that Cunningham's work matters for me in a different way than say, Balanchine's or Tharp's work—not necessarily a better way, just a different way: It seems to embody aspects of this strange post-9/11 world I'm trying my best to understand. Perhaps it will assist—in some small way—my efforts to both comprehend this world and to navigate my way through it.

Primitivism and Globalization

What *are* the most distinctive features of the world we inhabit, post-9/11; and what is the relationship between that world and Cunningham's dances? To my mind, the best analysis of the competing forces and values that ultimately culminated in the attacks of 9/11 appears in Benjamin Barber's brilliant 1995 study *Jihad vs. McWorld*. Barber's book is a frightening projection of a future (now a present) in which the planet is caught in a tug of war between two equally undesireable forces: corporate globalization (which he dubs "McWorld") and militant tribalization (which he designates as "Jihad"). The former homogenizes while the latter balkanizes.

The most subtle and insightful aspect of Barber's analysis is the emphasis he places on the interdependence of these two tendencies, the way they inadvertently reinforce one another: The more rapidly a country such as Indonesia is colonized by McDonald's and Kentucky Fried Chicken, the more militant the opposition from anti-modernist Islamic fundamentalist groups such as Jemaah Islamiah, an organization with demonstrated ties to al-Qaeda.

For Barber, the meaning of "Jihad" is by no means confined to Islamic fundamentalism. Jihad for Barber is a blanket term that refers to

> the grim prospect of a retribalization of large swaths of humankind by war and bloodshed: a threatened balkanization of nation-states in which culture is pitted against culture, people against people, tribe against tribe, a jihad in the name of a hundred narrowly conceived faiths against every kind of inter-dependence . . . against technology, against pop culture, and against integrated markets; against modernity itself. (1995, 4)

Thus Jihad connotes not only al-Qaeda's brand of Islamic fundamentalism (Wahabbism); it applies equally to *all* forms of antimodern fundamentalism: the Protestant fundamentalists such as Jerry Falwell and Pat Robertson in the United States, Hindi fundamentalists in India, and Jewish fundamentalists in Israel who insist on referring to the West Bank and Gaza as Judea and

Samaria, thereby implying a Biblical mandate to occupy and annex these territories.

By contrast, "McWorld":

> paints that future in shimmering pastels, a busy portrait of onrushing economic, technological, and ecological forces that demand integration and uniformity and that mesmerize peoples everywhere with fast music, fast computers, and fast food—MTV, Macintosh, and McDonald's—pressing nations into one homogenous global theme park, one McWorld tied together by communications, information, entertainment, and commerce. Caught between Babel and Disneyland, the planet is falling precipitously apart and coming reluctantly together at the very same moment. (4)

Barber's great insight is to emphasize the way these two impulses feed on one another and the way in which *both* imperil genuine democracy:

> Jihad not only revolts against but abets McWorld, while McWorld not only imperils but re-recreates and reinforces Jihad. They produce their contraries and need one another. . . . Jihad and McWorld have this in common: they both make war on the sovereign nation state and thus undermine the nation-state's democratic institutions. Their common thread is indifference to civil liberty. (5)

Jihad would replace democracy with totalitarian theocracy; and McWorld undermines democracy by refusing to make any significant distinction between "citizens" and "consumers."

"Jihad," he notes glumly "pursues a bloody politics of identity, McWorld a bloodless economics of profit. Belonging by default to McWorld, everyone is a consumer; seeking a repository for identity, everyone belongs to some tribe. But no one is a citizen. Without citizens, how can there be democracy?" (1995, 8)

Is there a connection between Barber's vision of the 21st century and Merce Cunningham's dances? Needless to say, it would be exceedingly naive as well as presumptuous to claim that Merce Cunningham has ever consciously set out to choreograph dances that relate in any way to Barber's (or anyone else's) thesis. But, at the same time, it's difficult to deny the way in which the basic philosophy of Cunningham's work relates to Barber's argument. Just for starters: in modernizing modern dance, Merce Cunningham repudiates the primitivist desire to take dance back to a time "before the atrophy of civilization set in." This idealizing of a primitive point of origin is fundamental to all forms of religious fundamentalism. Bin Laden's brand of Wahabbism is animated by a desire to return to the presumed purity of 7th century Islamic life. By contrast, in Cunningham's work, there is no yearning for a return to an imagined state of unity and purity. But, it's essential to emphasize that, by embracing modernity, Cunningham is by no means embracing McWorld. Roland Barthes—in a quote first cited in Chapter 4—was, in effect, talking about "McWorld" when he spoke of "the mystification which transforms petit-bourgeois culture into a universal nature" (1970, 9). Throughout this book I've sought to demonstrate the many ways in which Cunningham's and Cage's use of "chance operations" serves to short-circuit precisely the sort of cultural conditioning that Barthes refers to as "mystification" (i.e., the increasingly sophisticated manner in which multinational "hidden persuaders" condition us to confuse culturally manufactured desires with instinctual "needs").

In defending Cunningham's work against charges of "escapist formalism," I've referred on several occasions to Cage's conviction that his (and Cunningham's) work is politically "useful." Cage speaks again and again of "musical situations which are analogous to desirable social circumstances" (Junkerman 1994, 39–40); and it's in that spirit—the conviction that Cunningham's and Cage's work can be viewed as a map or a model of social relations—that I want to propose three specific ways in which their collaborations can be meaningfully described as "political" in the post-9/11 world. The Cunningham-Cage approach to collaboration and the work it produced:

1. serves as a model of benign globalization, one that avoids both the homogenizing forces of McWorld and the balkanizing dangers of Jihad.
2. redirects our interest away from ourselves and the competing subjectivities of cultural "difference" and back toward the shared, *public* space of the "outside," objective world, providing a much-needed antidote to the balkanizing effects of today's identity politics.
3. formulates and refines the perceptual tools we need to survive in what might be called the global city, the increasingly urbanized world of the 21st century.

Collaboration At A Distance

To some readers, the very idea that the Cunningham/Cage approach to collaboration might be viewed as a model of a progressive politics for the 21st century will seem patently absurd. Cynics have long complained that Cunningham's concept of "collaboration" hardly constitutes collaboration at all. At the very least, we need to acknowledge that this sort of collaboration "at a distance" has little to do with what most people have in mind when they talk about the great artistic collaborations of the past (e.g., the total merging of sensibilities we find in the great jazz collaborations of say, Charlie Parker and Dizzy Gillespie or Duke Ellington and Billy Strayhorn, artists who seem to anticipate and reciprocate one another's every move in the manner of great lovers). Some would even argue that simple pragmatism and expediency are the principle motivation for this peculiar practice of "collaboration at a distance." Put bluntly, if you want artists of the stature of Johns, Warhol, or Stella to design settings and costumes for the dance, you'd better allow them a degree of freedom approximating that which they enjoy in the privacy of their studios. One of Cunningham's favorite anecdotes seems to confirm this view. Cunningham is describing the way the separate components of "Summerspace" were conceived and executed:

> Morton Feldman who did the music was in New York. Bob [Rauschenberg] must have been in South Carolina, and I was in Connecticut. Somebody asked Morty here in New York what he was doing. . . . He said he was writing a piece for me, that Bob was doing the decor and so on. This person said to Morty, "How is it that Merce can be up there, Bob down there, and you're here doing this?" Morty said, "Suppose your daughter's getting married, and suppose I tell you her wedding dress won't be ready until the morning of the wedding, but that it's by Dior." (1985, 97)

But at the same time, when Cunningham and Cage talk about the *origin* of their concept of collaboration, politics often enters into the discussion. As Cage noted in the documentary introduction to the film *Points in Space:*

> The modern dancers wanted the dance to be finished first and then the music to be written to fit it. Formerly, the ballet had taken a piece of music which was already finished and they made the dance fit the music. Neither situation struck me as being politically good.

Cunningham both echoed and elaborated upon that idea in a recent interview: "It's really a political move that says things are equal—and that in the case of music and dance they are equal in that they both utilize time." (Copeland 2001, 4). On an earlier occasion, when Cunningham was specifically asked about his "politics," he responded by making reference to his collaborations with composers and visual artists, citing them as a new model of social interaction: ". . . we are dealing with a different idea about how people can exist together. How you can get along in life, so to speak, and do what you need to do, and at the same time not kick somebody else down in order to do it" (1985, 163–64). This recalls Cage's belief that: "We could make a piece of music . . . as a representation of a society in which you would be willing to live . . . " (Retallack 1994, 270).

How then does the Cage-Cunningham representation of the social order compare to the vision of a *globalized* world that emerges from Benjamin Barber's *Jihad vs. McWorld?* We might begin by considering the most obviously "globalized" of the Cunningham/Cage collaborations: the events that Nam June Paik refers to as "multitemporal, multispatial symphonies" (long-distance collaborations in which say, the sound that accompanies the dance originates in a different time zone; yet the audience experiences the movement and the sound simultaneously). Granted, these high-tech, globe-trotting collaborations are "special" events, but its equally true that *every* Cunningham performance provides a model of "collaboration at a *distance*": not only are the contributions of each collaborator conceived and executed independently, but each maintains its "autonomy" in performance. This is another way of saying that the spaces—both physical and perceptual—that separate the movement, the sound, and the décor are an absolutely essential element of the collaboration. Cage once praised Buckminster Fuller for representing the world in a way that emphasized the necessary spaces between things: "[Fuller] describes the world to us as an ensemble of spheres between which there is a void, a necessary space. We have a tendency to forget that space" (Junkerman 1994, 58).

When viewed as a collective body of work, the Cunningham/Cage collaborations offer a map and model of global relationships that provide a radical alternative to Jihad *and* McWorld, both of which attempt to erode the "spaces" that are essential to political freedom. To crowd those spaces out of existence is to impose an artificial (and politically dangerous) "unity" on the globe. In the case of McWorld, this undesirable unity takes the form of corporate homogenization: the world becomes a giant theme park advertising multinational brand names (alas, Disney *World*). For Jihad, this hunger for wholeness manifests itself in the effort to erode (in fact, to annihilate) many of the checks and balances—the internal divisions of power—that are essential to a modern democracy (most notably the separation between Church and State.)

Recall my discussion of the original 1971 production of "Loops," in which Cunningham danced in front of Johns's "Map" painting based on Buckminster Fuller's projection of the globe. I made note of the "rootless" way he traversed the space around it, recalling the anthropologist James Clifford's distinction between a traditional world of "roots" and a contemporary world of "routes." Jihad seeks to reestablish roots, whereas the globalized world of the 21st century is a dense, interconnected network of routes: a criss-crossing circulatory system of goods, global capital, and information exchange. The spatial patterns connoted by a phrase such as "circulatory system" are especially relevant to "Loops" because Gordon Mumma (who composed the score for the piece) used FM Telemetry to amplify the live sounds of Cunningham's heart beat and breathing. If a dance like "Loops" can be said to offer us a picture of the contemporary world, then the world it pictures is one of *circulating* routes (or loops) rather than roots. But not the sort of "one-way" routes that increasingly characterize globalization in the age of McWorld, in which these trajectories are controlled by increasingly powerful corporate conglomerates. A more progressive (genuinely multidirectional) system of global exchange would more closely resemble the collagelike nature of a Cunningham/Cage collaboration where widely dispersed elements resonate off of one another in a variety of directions, criss-crossing the *gaps* of space and time that physically separate them.

The rootless nature of Cunningham's dancing in "Loops" was especially evident in the way his hands and fingers often flickered frenetically above his head, rather like an agitated butterfly that refused to settle down in any one spot. (Consistent with his determination to decentralize the space of performance, Cunningham's twitching fingers never seemed to point in any one direction or favor any particular part of the world represented by Johns's map painting immediately behind him.) Viewed from the vantage point of the 21st century, it's difficult to envision Cunningham's fingers "fluttering" in front of Jasper Johns's map-of-the-world without also thinking of Edward Lorenz's now legendary concept of "the butterfly effect." In 1972, one year after Cunningham first performed "Loops," Lorenz posed his famous question: "Does the flap of a butterfly's wings in Brazil set off a tornado in Texas?" (2000, 91). Post-9/11, the butterfly effect has come to represent much more than complex systems such as "the weather." A recent ad for *The Economist* juxtaposes Lorenz's famous question with the heading "America and the Arabs." We might even argue that "the butterfly effect" has become the most potent and popular metaphor for the way in which global relations have come to resemble a Cunningham/Cage collage.

In the summer of 2000, Paul Kaiser and Shelley Eshkar (the same artists responsible for the digital imagery in "Biped") convinced Cunningham to allow them to motion-capture his hand movements from "Loops." The result was a 21st-century reincarnation of "Loops" even more evocative of the true complexity of "the butterfly effect" than the original version in 1971. In collaboration with Marc Downie of MIT, Kaiser and Eshkar transformed Cunningham's image into a flickering collage of constantly moving points in three-dimensional space. According to Kaiser (2003), their goal was to treat these motion-captured dots as "nodes in a variable visual network. The nodes seek to connect with each other, sending out lines in the direction of other nodes. Sometimes the interconnections mirror the structure of the hands, while at other times they join corresponding points on the opposing hands, creating a kind of variable cat's cradle." The digital version of "Loops" not only evoked the ever-varying visual complexity of a game like cat's cradle; it also utilized a soundtrack that "collaged" two additional elements: Cunningham reading diary entries about his first encounter with the distinctive spaces of New York City and electronic music composed and performed by Takehisa Kosugi. These two auditory components were "looped" independently of each other so that fresh combinations of image, word, and electronic sound were continually emerging.

As we've seen, the resonating "flicker-effect" created by collage provides a radical alternative to the forced unity of Wagner's Gesamtkunstwerk; and it's helpful in this context to recall Bertolt Brecht's main objection to Wagner's integration of the arts: the way this imposed synthesis imposes itself on the spectator as well: "The process of fusion extends to the spectator who gets thrown into the melting pot too and becomes a passive (suffering) part of the total work of art" (1964, 37–38). Cage and Cunningham are no less eager than Brecht to resist this sort of fusion; and they decentralize the performance space in a manner that refuses to direct the spectator's attention toward particular images and sounds. But this doesn't mean that the movement, the sound, and the décor never "intermingle," "run interference" for one another, or in any way effect one another. Quite the contrary. Having been guaranteed his or her perceptual freedom, the spectator can freely choose to "make connections" between otherwise autonomous parts. In an interview with Richard Francis, Cage asked:

> Why do you always ask about the relationship or connection between us? Let me put it to you this way. Don't you see that the fan is here and that the Norfolk pine is there? How in Heaven's name are they related? . . . Well, they are in the same space and the same time and they're not interfering with one another. In Zen this is called non-obstruction. But they interpenetrate; I can look at both at the same time and in me they become an experience which may not be the same as comes to someone else. (1989, 25)

Toward A Restoration of Objectivity

Initially, it may appear that Cage is encouraging the perceiver to wallow promiscuously in his or her subjectivity, but nothing could be further from the truth. Recall my anecdote about John Cage's adamant opposition to the idea of audience members donning Walkmans so as to provide their own, alternative auditory accompaniment during Cunningham performances. It's easy to imagine a proponent of today's race-and-gender identity politics endorsing a scenario in which some audience members are listening to Dr. Dre and others to Ani de Franco or Bronski Beat (rather than insisting that everyone share the experience of listening to a score by Cage or Takehisa Kosugi). But for Cage it was essential—for *political* reasons—that each audience member be exposed to the same sensory stimuli. Each of them will of course proceed to process that information in their own subjective ways. But—at a minimum—Cage insisted that the individuals who make up his audience get out of their own heads long enough to respond to something they experience in common. Cage was particularly fond of the following quotation by composer Joe Byrd

> ... the obligation—the morality, if you wish—of all the arts today is to intensify, to alter, perceptual awareness and, hence, consciousness. Awareness and consciousness of what? Of the real material world. Of the things we see and hear and taste and touch. (Kostelanetz 1970, 23)

In this regard, the formalist impulse in Cage and Cunningham's work proves to be anything but "escapist." When Cunningham declares that "The body shooting into space is not an idea of man's freedom, but is the body shooting into space" (1955, 72), he focuses our attention on the material reality of the dance, not on our subjective emotional responses to it or our ideas about it. In this sense, Cunningham and Cage have a great deal in common with Alain Robbe-Grillet when he argues that:

> Even the least conditioned observer is unable to see the world around him through entirely unprejudiced eyes. Not, of course, that I have in mind the naïve concern for objectivity which the analysts of the (subjective) soul find it so easy to smile at. Objectivity in the ordinary sense of the word—total impersonality of observation—is all too obviously an illusion. But *freedom* of observation should be possible, and yet it is not. At every moment, a continuous fringe of culture (psychology, ethics, metaphysics, etc.) is added to things, giving them a less alien aspect, one that is more comprehensible, more reassuring. Sometimes the camouflage is complete: a gesture vanishes from our mind, supplanted by the emotions which supposedly produced it, and we remember a landscape as austere or calm without being able to evoke a single outline, a single determining element. (1967, 274–75)

Robbe-Grillet, Cunningham, and Cage remind us that, despite our subjectivities, there is indeed a "there there." Without some sense of a shared objective world, it is difficult to talk about "politics" in any meaningful way. But objectivity is a much-maligned concept these days. The practitioners of identity politics proceed on the assumption that any claim to "objectivity" is merely someone's hidden agenda, some disguised and despised *centrism* (euro-, logo-, phallo-, etc.) posing as universal truth. And thus, in its own way, identity politics often turns out to be as balkanizing as Benjamin Barber's terrifying vision of Jihad. The philosopher Stanley Cavell, in his book *The World Viewed,* writes beautifully about the way in which the formalist nature of an art like Cunningham's and Cage's (an art that serves to focus our attention on what Robbe-Grillet calls the "être-la des choses" or the "being there of things") can help coax us out of the protective cocoon of our own subjectivity:

> Attracted from distraction by abstraction. Not catching our attention yet again, but forming it again. Giving us the capacity for appeal and for protest, for

contemplation and for knowledge and praise, by drawing us back from private and empty assertion. (1971, 117–18)

"Abstraction" in Stanley Cavell's sense, is anything but "fatal." It helps to reconnect us with the world outside our own minds. My claim is not that abstraction in the work of Cunningham and Cage can fully restore our belief in an objective world, only that it can help, as Cavell asserts, to hold subjectivity "in check." And that, politically speaking, constitutes a step in the right direction.

Robbe-Grillet makes a similar argument:

> Around us, defying the noisy pack of our animistic or protective adjectives, things are *there*. . . . Let it be first of all by their presence that objects and gestures establish themselves, and let this presence continue to prevail over whatever explanatory theory that may try to enclose them in a system of references, whether emotional, sociological, Freudian, or metaphysical. (1967, 275)

His reference to "animistic" adjectives (e.g. a "calm" landscape or a "pitiless" sun) is especially relevant to our on-going discussion of primitivism. Why does Robbe-Grillet refer to such adjectives as "animistic?" Because, they perpetuate a primitivist sense of the "animistic" interconnectedness between things that is largely *un*characteristic of the world we inhabit in the 20th and 21st Centuries. Recall Levy-Bruhl's description of the "participation mystique" (which he believed to be an important characteristic of the thought process of "primitive" tribes.)

When the literary critic, Peter Brooks, argues that Robbe-Grillet has repudiated metaphorical and allegorical modes of perception, he is (in effect) arguing that Robbe-Grillet has also repudiated Levy-Bruhl's conception of the primitive "participation mystique":

> Robbe-Grillet contends that metaphor is treacherous because it entertains the notion of a link between consciousness and the phenomenal world which is illusory. To talk of a pitiless sun or a house nestled in the valley is to assume that human consciousness is at home in the world, that it has appropriated things to the states of the soul—which then leads to alienation and tragedy when man discovers the world to be other. (1979, 439)

At Home in the Global City

Cunningham and Cage insist that we live today without the sustaining illusion of this "link," this sense that everything is connected in a direct and causal way. In the increasingly urbanized world of the 21st century, only religious fundamentalists and paranoid conspiracy theorists continue to argue for this sort of deep connectedness between otherwise separate events. The "nonlinear," collagelike structures that result from Cunningham's and

Cage's use of chance operations pose a fundamental challenge to the sort of "neoprimitivist" logic practiced by Jerry Fallwell and Pat Robertson when they attempt to attribute the events of 9/11 to God's dissatisfaction with decadent American secularization. "Primitive" notions of causality often take the form of "post hoc ergo propter hoc" (after this therefore *because* of this). In Cunningham's work, events coexist and/or succeed one another directly without establishing any sort of "causal" linkages. Cunningham acknowledges the inevitable rift between spectator and spectacle, but makes no attempt to "heal it" by providing us with pseudo rituals. He doesn't hark back to some distant, preindustrial point of origin or wholeness (a "womb-with-a-view"). Perhaps we will never feel fully "at home" in our world to the extent that so-called primitive peoples felt at home in theirs (at least in the manner imagined by anthropologists like Levy-Bruhl). But the work of artists such as Cunningham and Cage can help us to develop the perceptual tools we need to navigate our way around and through the world we *actually* inhabit.

One of the best descriptions of this postprimitivist world appears in Roland Barthes's essay "Objective Literature." Barthes's description of the way in which one's eyes scan the surface of things in the novels of Robbe-Grillet could just as easily have been a description of the way one experiences a dance by Cunningham:

> [Robbe-Grillet] seeks to establish the novel on the surface: interiority is put in parenthesis; objects, spaces and man's circulation among them are promoted to the rank of subjects. The novel becomes a direct experience of man's surroundings, without this man's being able to fall back on a psychology, a metaphysics, or a psychoanalysis in order to approach the objective milieu he discovers. The novel, here, is no longer of a chthonic, infernal order, it is terrestrial: it teaches us to look at the world no longer with eyes of a confessor, a physician, or of God . . . but with the eyes of a man walking in his city with no other horizon but the spectacle before him, no other power than that of his own eyes. (1972, 23–24)

The "chthonic" in this context is another name for the primitive.

Barthes provides us with a superb description of the way one's eyes function *after* the repudiation of primitivism. By contrast, in pre-Cunningham modern dance, people don't just "walk," they move in ways that appear to be animated by mysterious and dramatic "powers." Consider again Doris Humphrey's description of a dancer who (in *objective* terms) is walking—simply walking—on a diagonal from stage center to downstage left:

> The glory of the climax begins to fade. We see him moving toward the downstage corner and oblivion. We know he must traverse another dangerous place, the weak spot between the center and the corner, but we do not fear the menace of

it because the end is so near.... The figure vanishes, cut off like a knife thrust by the final engulfing vertical. Just a simple walk, but how dramatic and pulsating in all its implications! (1959, 77)

Letting the (Urban) World In Again

One of the most important ways in which Cunningham breaks with Humphrey's and Graham's primitivism is by allowing aspects of the contemporary urban world to enter his work. Consider what Leo Steinberg has said of Rauschenberg:

> What he invented above all was ... a pictorial surface that let the world in again. Not the world of the renaissance man who looked for his weather clues out of the window; but the world of men who turn knobs to hear a taped message, "precipitation probability ten percent tonight," electronically transmitted from some windowless booth. Rauschenberg's picture plane is for the consciousness immersed in the brain of the city. (1972, 90)

Rauschenberg and Cunningham are more fully immersed in this urban sensibility—the sheer sensory onslaught of city life—than Steinberg recognizes. In addition to acknowledging the world of electronic transmissions that both emanate from and penetrate various "windowless booths," they let in other varieties of urban noise that threaten to "disturb the peace" of even the most soundproof sanctuaries. In his book *The Responsive Chord*, Tony Schwartz discusses the modern city dweller's attempts to insulate himself from the sounds of the street:

> Thirty years ago it would have been impossible to imagine an apartment house with sealed windows. Today, it is common for new windows to be sealed and old windows to be closed, draped, and forgotten. It used to be of considerable importance whether windows were exposed to morning or afternoon sun. This affected lighting, temperature, and the *mood* of different rooms. Today, light and heat are controlled electronically, and if someone wants to affect the *mood* of an apartment, he usually tunes to a different radio station.
>
> In the past people were primarily influenced by sounds *of* the street—sounds generated by persons or objects on a block and carried through the air to the listener's ear. Today, we are primarily influenced by sounds that come *to* our street—sounds generated by persons or objects anywhere in the world and carried over radio waves or cables to the listener's ear. (1972, 136)

A few pages later, Schwartz addresses our contemporary obsession with "noise pollution":

> The present concern about noise pollution is based on a shift in the location of sounds we want to hear. We want to hear sounds generated within our controlled electronic environment. Outdoor sounds therefore become noise since they interfere with sounds coming into our homes via electronic media.

> I have collected seventy-three articles on noise pollution. Without exception, all are concerned with outdoor sounds. A paragraph or two may decry teenager's music; and how it may cause deafness, but the main suggestion is that noise pollution originates outdoors. Yet there is no hard evidence that a typical urban street environment today is significantly louder than the typical street environment thirty years ago. . . . A sound is not noise because it is loud. It is noise because it disturbs us or interferes with our activity. Noise is *unwanted sound.* (141)

Recall our survey in Chapter 1 of the objections routinely raised by the dance community to the "intrusive" nature of John Cage's musical scores, the way in which they distract attention from what presumably *really matters:* Cunningham's movement. Alaistair Macaulay's comments about the sound score for Cunningham's "Eleven" (1988) are especially revealing in this regard: "Fending off the wretched music, as I tried to do at a second performance, I isolated several new aspects of movement information" (1992, 177). His priorities are all-too-clear. Cunningham's movement constitutes "information"; but the intrusive musical score is mere "noise" (indeed not just noise, but noise *pollution*). Cage addressed the relationship between "information" and "noise" in countless anecdotes. In the film *Four American Composers,* for example, he discusses a piano performance by Christian Wolff that took place in an urban apartment located on a noisy street:

> One day when the windows were open, Christian Wolff played one of his pieces at the piano. The sounds of traffic and boat horns were heard not only during the silences in the music, but also [during] the piano sounds themselves. Afterwards, someone asked Christian Wolff to play the piece again with the windows closed. Christian Wolff said he'd be glad to, but that it wasn't really necessary, since the sounds of the environment were in no sense an interruption of those of the music.

The window remains open—just a crack—in many Cunningham/ Cage/Rauschenberg/Johns collaborations. Speaking of his highly indeterminate score for "Field Dances" in 1963 ("Variations IV"), Cage maintains it "could consist solely of opening and shutting the doors that lead out to the streets" (Vaughan 1997, 130). In "Travelogue" (1977), Cage's score incorporates phone recordings about the time, the weather, and so on that were dialed live during the performance and amplified throughout the auditorium. Sometimes the world beyond "the window" intrudes purely by chance. Conceptually, Cage's score for "Inlets" (1977) was supposed to have been limited to "natural" sounds involving air, fire, and water. But when Cage attempted to record the crackle of burning pinecones, the microphones picked up the sound of an airplane flying overhead (which Cage, of course, left in).

One of Cunningham's "Events," created for the Brooklyn Academy of Music in October of 1997, incorporated four sections from what—for me at least—is the most exquisitely classical of all Cunningham works, the 1956 "Suite for Five." (The BAM Event however, recontextualized "Suite's" ultra-classical movement in a quite radical way.) The excerpts from "Suite" began with Thomas Caley dancing Cunningham's solo "Stillness." Gently rising from a sitting position, the upward motion of Caley's body was extended into a slow developé, the end point of which was delicately punctuated by a black-out. The middle section consisted of that extraordinary duet, "Suspended Moment"—a bona-fide classical pas de deux—originally performed by Cunningham and Carolyn Brown. Reconstructed here on Caley and Banu Ogan, it contains one of those paradigmatic Cunningham moments: Caley kneels, with the outstretched Banu Ogan balanced atop his shoulders, and turns a full 360 degrees, displaying his partner from all four sides.

Given the level of classical ballet technique that every Cunningham dancer now possesses as a matter of course, the choreography may well have looked even "purer" and more classical in 1997 than it did originally. But this was a collage-style "Event," in which *context* is all-important. And on this occasion, the accompanying musical score was no longer Cage's "Music for Piano (4-84)," the gentle, pointillistic, Satie-like composition composed for the 1956 version. Instead, the sound consisted of a clamorous collage of electronic bleeps, blurts, and scratchy static composed by Takehisa Kosugi, with the assistance of Thurston Moore and Jim O'Rourke. Classically pure movement images unfolded in an environment that refused to filter out distraction, that refused to let us forget what century we inhabit.

Carolyn Brown, participating in a symposium about Cunningham at BAM the following afternoon, complained bitterly about the "intrusive" nature of the music. "To have this clutter of sound with the purist of dances is just terrible," she maintained. But was it really so terrible? Why can't the two co-mingle? Perhaps this uneasy, incongruous coexistence of sound and image is the truest form of "*contemporary* classicism," the closest we can come to "purity" as the 20th century gives way to the 21st. This attitude toward "purity" was equally evident in the work that preceded the "BAM Event," a new dance titled "Rondo" (1996). Approximately 10 minutes into that particular performance of "Rondo," the sound of a ringing cell phone was clearly audible. From my vantage point, it was impossible to determine whether this sound was part of the score or a chance eruption (courtesy of a discourteous cellular phone-carrying member of the audience.) The ringing only occurred once; and thus there was no way of confirming whether the pulsing sound originated from "within" or "without" the porous frame that separated "art" from "life" in "Rondo." (John Cage, whose score was being used posthumously, might well have been pleased.)

This openness to "impurity" is no less important a concept for the visual artists who Cunningham collaborates with. For example, Jasper Johns, in his decor and costume design for "Exchange" (1978), choose what he himself called "polluted" colors: dark, grungy, *sooty*. And David Tudor's sound score for "Exchange" evoked industrial noise—not so very far removed from the postpunk world of death metal and grindcore (combative riffing, thrashing drum patterns). Johns's costume design for "Second Hand" (1970) utilized what might be thought of as a "bleed-through" color scheme: Each set of tights and leotards were dyed in a single color, except for the edges, which exhibited just a trace of one of the other color choices. The interconnectedness of the color patterns didn't become apparent until the curtain call when the dancers lined up in a way that illustrated the flow of color—the blurring of boundaries—from one leotard to another. Purity of the sort that Graham and Pollock yearned for is no longer feasible. Post 9/11, it's not even a matter of *deciding* "to let the world in again"; the world cannot be kept "out." This is the principal lesson of globalization; and 9/11 was proof positive that America has become fully globalized. No longer protected by two vast oceans to its east and west, the United States is no longer immune to the global reach of terrorism.

But even in the wake of 9/11, McWorld still poses a greater and more fundamental threat to American democracy. This is due in part to McWorld's remarkable success at concealing its own anti-democratic tendencies. With regard to the much-touted idea that the international dissemination of American-made music videos promotes political liberty, Benjamin Barber writes that

> MTV succors liberty...of a kind. It is certainly good for the kind of choice entailed by consumption, but whether it is of any use to civil liberty is quite another question. (1995, 108–109)

Furthermore, there remains a fundamental form of freedom that mass media culture does little to encourage: The freedom to say no to *it*, the freedom not to be surrounded by it and immersed in it. Try—just try—*not* listening to the saturation coverage of the O.J. trial, the death of Princess Di, MonicaGate, or any of the recent "mediathons." Of course, in the age of McWorld, this state of affairs is often perceived as pleasurable rather than coercive. The all encompassing, world-devouring, inescapable omnipresence of these "stories" illustrate the sad fact that Americans are never happier than when a single narrative dominates the mass media.

But every time a single story controls the air waves, crowding so much else out, the result—whether it "feels" that way or not—is a little taste of totalitarianism (which can be defined in this context as a system in which a single, easily followed narrative precludes other, more complex, competing narratives).

Cunningham and Television

Television is McWorld's medium of choice. Certainly, no aspect of contemporary life has blurred more boundaries, penetrated more barriers, ironed out and smoothed over more differences than the medium of television. No other force has infiltrated the traditional modernist safe houses of "the primitive" and "the unconscious" more deeply or effectively. Television is not only the principle tool for global advertising; it's also the central metaphor for the larger process by which McWorld blurs the essential distinctions between nature and culture that high modernists such as Graham and Pollock were so determined to preserve.

Jerzy Kosinski masterfully depicted television's homogenizing sense of flow—its ability to erode once-firm distinctions between the natural and the cultural—in his short novel *Being There:*

> Chance went inside and turned on the TV. The set created its own light, its own color, its own time. It did not follow the law of gravity that forever bent all plants downward. Everything on TV was tangled and mixed and yet smoothed out: night and day, big and small, tough and brittle, soft and rough, hot and cold, far and near.

Nature and culture have become hopelessly comingled:

> He sank into the screen. Like sunlight and fresh air and mild rain, the world from outside the garden entered Chance, and Chance, like a TV image, floated into the world, buoyed up by a force he did not see and could not name.

This is the very same world that Cunningham collaborator Nam June Paik depicted in some of his best-known works, "TV Garden" and "TV Fish," in which the distinctive glow of the television screen illuminates flora, fauna, and the fish swimming in an aquarium. The result is the interpenetration of plants, television commercials, and aquatic life, all equally present to us: "live at five."

One of the great popular misconceptions about television is that the medium is characterized by one "interruption" after another. For example, we routinely complain about the way commercials *interrupt* the programs they advertise. But, as the sociologist Raymond Williams was among the first to observe, the characteristic rhythm of the television medium is really a variety of *flow* (the sort of flow—as in lava flow—that breaks down and absorbs everything in its path.) Television commercials don't so much interrupt the programs they advertise as flow into them, ultimately blurring essential distinctions between fiction and nonfiction, news and entertainment, the serious and the frivolous.

Received wisdom continues to view Merce Cunningham's work as a direct outgrowth of the perceptual habits encouraged by television rather than as an alternative (or even an antidote) to them. And it's true that the process of choosing how to distribute one's attention while experiencing a Cunningham work is superficially similar to the practice of channel surfing with a remote control. But the differences between these two activities greatly outweigh the similarities; Cunningham—both literally and figuratively—refuses to go with the flow. His distrust of boundary-blurring, his determination to preserve the *separation* of the elements, avoids creating not only the feeling of flow but also the illusion of wholeness and unity.

One possible antidote to the dominance of the "single narrative" so often created by mass media in the age of McWorld is the sort of "polyvocal" work we encounter in a Cunningham/Cage collaborative collage: the chattering of *separate* voices, the periodic (and unpredictable) interruptions (*genuine* interruptions) of static and noise that regularly jolt us into a state of renewed attentiveness. Similarly, Cunningham's commitment to an aesthetic of collage prevents his work from arriving at any final, unified sense of closure. There's a sentence in E. L. Doctorow's 1975 "collage" novel *Ragtime* that perfectly captures this anti-utopian conception of openness and flux: "The world composed and recomposed itself constantly in an endless process of dissatisfaction."

Accordingly, any sense of "wholeness" one experiences in the contemporary world is probably nothing more than an illusion. And in the realm of realpolitik, the hunger for wholeness is demonstrably dangerous. Wholeness, like innocence, cannot be regained, except perhaps through the most ruthless and dictatorial means imaginable. China's Great Proletarian Cultural Revolution, Pol Pot's genocidal effort to create a "pure" egalitarian peasant culture in Cambodia, the Taliban's effort to return Afghanistan to the imagined purity of 7th Century Islamic life during the age of Mohammed are but three of the more lamentable recent efforts to forcibly "recreate" an ideology of wholeness, a political utopia.

The exemplary modernist (Graham, Pollock) believed in the possibility of escaping the prevailing culture, of returning to and reestablishing contact with, The Natural. (In fact, Pollock, as we've seen, once boasted "I am nature.") Perhaps today, Michael Eisner and the other philosopher-kings of the Disney and McDonalds Empires could boast "I am *Second* Nature," a vast network of cultural commodities so omnipresent, so tightly interwoven, so ... "synergistic" (to use the multi-national's favorite buzz word) that they come to seem perfectly ... Natural: (e.g. the endless spin-offs and tie-ins, the pervasive replication of the same images and ideas across all forms of media:

As Benjamin Barber is quick to point out, Disney Microsoft, Nike and other gargantuan multi-nationals exert infinitely more influence worldwide than do the vast majority of nation-states. Thus, the global city of the 21st century is threatened by both balkanization *and* homogenization. In Barber's words, the globe is "falling precipitously apart and coming reluctantly together at the very same moment" (1995, 4).

Cunningham and Cage's strategy for dealing with these dilemmas is twofold: unlike the high modernists (Graham, Pollock), they "let the world in again." But, unlike the postmodernists, they don't indiscriminately embrace what they "let in." As Cage once put it (in bold, all capital letters), "PERMISSION GRANTED. BUT NOT TO DO WHATEVER YOU WANT" (1969, 28). The world their work "lets in" is "immersed in the brain of the city." It's a world of information overload, scrambled signals, and collagelike juxtapositions that make competing—and often irreconcilable—claims on our attention. But Cunningham and Cage provide us with the tools we need (chance metholdologies, perceptual filters) to "reframe," deflect, and otherwise circumvent varieties of sensory input that might overwhelm us—or at the very least, diminish our perceptual freedom. Recall the question posed by John Cage after first encountering one of Rauschenberg's mixed-media works: "Now that Rauschenberg has made a painting with radios in it, does that mean that even without radios, I must go on listening even while I'm looking, everything at once in order not to be run over?" (1961, 101). The best answer to that question comes from Brian O'Doherty who has written with special brilliance about the way Rauchenberg's art can help sharpen one's perceptual reflexes. Writing about a Rauschenberg exhibition in 1963, O'Doherty observed that

> His art encouraged what could be called the city dweller's rapid scan rather than the art audience's stare.... Looking at these [Rauschenberg] works ... gave you the feeling of crossing the street. You wanted to look over your shoulder to see if you were going to be run over. The work wouldn't let me settle down, and I remember feeling uncomfortable that I'd brought my street reflexes in with me. Rauschenberg had introduced into the museum and its high-art ambience not just the vernacular object but something much more important, the *vernacular glance.*
>
> The vernacular glance is what carries us through the city every day, a mode of ... divided attention. Since we usually are moving, it tags the unexpected and quickly makes it familiar, filing surplus information into safe categories.... This is the opposite of the pastoral nineteenth-century "walk," where habitual curiosity evoked wonder, but found nothing except ugliness in the city. The vernacular glance doesn't recognize categories of the beautiful and the ugly. It's just interested in what's there.... Its directions are multiple. Up and down (elevators, bridges, tunnels, overpasses, activity above the street and below it) are as much a habit as side to side. The one direction it doesn't have is distance, or the

perspective distance gives. Everything is close-up, in transit.... [The vernacular glance] can tolerate everything but meaning (the attempt to understand instead of recognize) and sensory deprivation.... It is very appropriate for looking at Rauschenberg's work. (1973, 197–98)

And, we might add, for looking at Cunningham's work as well.

O'Doherty emphasizes the way his street-smart reflexes followed him into the museum; but I would argue that, for Cunningham and Cage, the traffic moves in the other direction as well. The perceptual reeducation their work offers us proves indispensable on the urban street. We might even say that Cunningham and Cage provide us with a do-it-yourself survival kit for maintaining our sanity—or at least our perceptual clarity—in the global city. The vernacular glance is nimble; it's a mode of perceptual cruising—it "takes in" diverse stimuli without becoming absorbed or captivated by them. It combines aspects of Baudelaire's "unshakable determination not to be moved," Erwin Straus's "gaze of upright posture" (the ability "to look at things straight ahead and withstand their thrust"), and Brecht's Verfremdungs-effekt. It can assume a variety of forms. It balances "selective innattention" against what Cage calls "polyattentiveness." During a Cunningham/Cage performance we are free to "background" or "turn off" a sound so as to focus more intently on the movement. "Tango" (1978) was—among other things—a model for this sort of selective inattention. Here Cunningham danced alongside a television set broadcasting a live image, but with the sound turned alternately on and off. By contrast, in a work such as "Variations V" (which incorporated multiple film and video projections), we need to divide our attention so as to simultaneously apprehend two or more unrelated phenomena. This is a prime example of what Cage called "polyattentiveness," and he proposed this mode of attention as a discipline to be practiced daily, like meditation or yoga:

> I think that one of our most accessible disciplines now is paying attention to more than one thing at a time. If we can do that with equanimity, then I propose paying attention to three things at the same time. You can practice it as a discipline; I think it is more effective than sitting cross-legged (Kostelanetz 1988, 20).

Above all, the relations we establish between diverse stimuli in a Cunningham/Cage collaboration are flexible. We can choose to radically alter our mode of perception many times in the course of a single performance; the key word here is "choose." The vernacular glance promotes perceptual choice. And it's this freedom of choice that constitutes the moral and political dimension of the Cunningham/Cage aesthetic. In the final analysis, there's a profound correspondence between what we choose to look at and the way we live our lives. As Richard Harris says to Monica Vitti in Antonioni's great film *Red Desert*: "You wonder what to look at. I wonder how to live. Same thing."

I first encountered Cunningham's work in 1968, a year in which the world seemed engulfed in chaos. Now, post-9/11, the world feels that way again. And in both historical contexts, Cunningham's work proves both relevant and useful. No one has ever said it better than the great theater director Peter Brook, who once described Merce Cunningham's work as "a continual preparation for the shock of freedom" (Brook, 1964, n.p.).

Bibliography

Acocella, Joan. *The Reception of Diaghilev's Ballets Russes by Artists and Intellectuals in Paris and London, 1909–1914*. Rutgers University Doctoral Dissertation, University Microfilms International, 1984.

Arnheim, Rudolf. *Toward a Psychology of Art*. Berkeley: University of California Press, 1966.

Artaud, Antonin. *The Theater and Its Double*, trans. Mary Caroline Richards. New York: Grove Press, 1958.

———. "To Have Done with the Judgement of God (1947)" in *Selected Writings*, ed. Susan Sontag, trans. Helen Weaver. New York: Farrar, Strauss and Giroux, 1976, 553–571.

Baer, Van N. *Bronislava Nijinska: A Dancer's Legacy*. San Francisco: The Fine Art Museum of San Francisco, 1978.

Balanchine, George. *By George Balanchine*. New York: San Marco Press, 1984.

Banes, Sally. *Democracy's Body: Judson Dance Theater 1962–1964*. Ann Arbor: UMI Research Press, 1983.

Barber, Benjamin R. *Jihad vs. McWorld*. New York: Random House Times Books, 1995.

Barnes, Clive. Review of "*Canfield.*" *New York Times*, January 1970. Library of the Performing Arts, Lincoln Center, NY, Cunningham Company clipping file, n.p.

Barthelme, Donald. *Not-Knowing: The Essays and Interviews of Donald Barthelme*, ed. Kim Harzinger. New York: Random House, 1997.

Barthes, Roland. *Mythologies*, trans. Jonathan Cope. New York: Hill and Wang, 1970.

———. "Objective Literature," in *Critical Essays*, trans. Richard Howard. Evanston IL: Northwestern University Press, 1972, 13–24.

———. *S/Z*. New York: Hill and Wang: 1974.

———. *The Grain of the Voice: Interviews 1962–1980*, trans. Linda Coverdale. New York: Hill and Wang, 1985.

Baudelaire, Charles. "The Dandy" in *The Painter of Modern Life and Other Essays*, trans. & ed. Jonathan Mayne. New York: Phaidon, 1965, 26–29.

Bayles, Martha. *Hole in Our Sole*. Chicago: University of Chicago Press, 1994.

Bentley, Eric. *In Search of Theater*. New York: Alfred A. Knopf, 1953.

———. "Martha Graham's Journey," in *In Search of Theater*. New York: Alfred A. Knopf, 1953, 174–183.

Berg, Shelley C. *Le Sacre du Printemps: Seven Productions from Nijinsky to Martha Graham*. Ann Arbor: UMI Research Press, 1988.

Bernstein, Roberta. *Jasper Johns' Paintings and Sculptures: 1954–1974*. Ann Arbor, MI: UMI Research Press, 1985.

Blofeld, John, ed. and trans. *I Ching: The Book of Change*. New York: Penguin, 1965.

Brecht, Bertolt. *Brecht on Theatre*, trans. and ed. John Willett. New York: Hill and Wang, 1964.

Brook, Peter. Program note for Cunningham Company performance, Sadler's Wells Theater, London, July 1964, Laban Centre Library, London, England.

———. *The Empty Space*. New York: Avon, 1972.

———. *US Playscript 9*. London: Calder and Boyers, 1968.

Brooks, Peter. "Death of/As Metaphor," *Partisan Review*, 1979, vol. XLVI No. 3, 438–439.

Brown, Carolyn, et al. "Cunningham and His Dancers," *Merce Cunningham,* ed. R. Kostelanetz. Pennington, NJ: A Cappella Books, 1992, 101–123.

Brown, Earle, Remy Charlip, et al. "The Forming of an Esthetic: Merce Cunningham and John Cage" in *Merce Cunningham*, ed. by Richard Kostelanetz. Pennington, NJ: A Cappella Books, 1992, 48–65.

Brown, Norman O. *Love's Body*. New York: Vintage Books, 1966.

Burroughs, William S. *Naked Lunch*. New York: Grove Press, 1959.

———. *The Ticket That Exploded*. New York: Grove Press, 1967.

Cage, John. *A Year From Monday.* Middletown, CT: Wesleyan University Press, 1967.
———. "On the Work of Nam June Paik" in Nam June Paik : *video time, video space*, ed. Toni Stooss and Thomas Kellein New York: Abrams, 1993, 21–26.
———. *Silence.* Middletown: Wesleyan University Press, 1961.
———. "26 Statements RE Ducahmp" in *Marcel Duchamp in Perspective*, ed. by Joseph Masheck. Englewood Cliffs, NJ: Prentice Hall: 1975, 67–69.
Carroll, Noel, and S. Banes. "Cunningham and Duchamp," *Ballet Review* 11:2 (Summer '83) 73–79
Cateforis, David. "All The Great Modern Things" in *Decade of Transformation: American Art of the 1960s* ed. David Cateforis. Lawrence: University of Kansas, Spencer Museum of Art, 1999, 1–15.
Cavell, Stanley. *The World Viewed: Reflections on the Ontology of Film.* New York: Viking, 1971.
Charbonnier, Georges. "Natural Art and Cultural Art" in *Marcel Duchamp in Perspective*, ed. Joseph Macheck. Englewood Cliffs: Prentice Hall, 1975, 77–83.
Clark, T. J. "Clement Greenberg's Theory of Art" in *Pollock and After*, ed. Francis Frascina. New York: Harper and Row, 1985, 47–63.
Clearwater, Bonnie. *Mark Rothko: Works on Paper.* New York: Hudson Hills Press, 1984.
Clifford, James. *The Predicament of Culture.* Cambridge MA: Harvard University Press, 1988.
Coe, Robert. *Dance in America.* New York: Dutton, 1985.
Cohen, Selma Jeanne, ed. *Doris Humphrey: An Artist First.* Middletown CT: Wesleyan University Press, 1972.
———. *Next Week, Swan Lake.* Middletown CT: Wesleyan University Press, 1982.
Copeland, Roger. "Precise and Free: A Conversation with Merce Cunningham." CORD Newsletter, XXI(2), Fall 2001, 4–7.
Corrigan, Robert W. "The Future of the Avant-Garde and the Paradigms of Post-Modernism," in *The Making of Theater*, ed. Robert W. Corrigan. Glenview IL: Scott, Foresman, and Company, 1981, 329–340.
Coton, A.V. *The New Ballet: Kurt Jooss and His Work.* London: Dennis Dobson, 1946.
Croce, Arlene. *Afterimages.* New York: Knopf, 1977.
———. "Discussing the Undiscussable," *The New Yorker*, Dec. 26, 1994-January 2, 1995, 54–60.
———. *Going to the Dance.* New York: Knopf, 1982.
———. "Essays, Stories, and Remarks about Merce Cunningham," *Dance Perspectives*, no. 34 (Summer 1968), 24–25.
Culler, Jonathan. *On Deconstruction.* Ithaca: Cornell University Press, 1982.
Cunningham, Merce. *Changes: Notes on Choreography*, ed. Frances Starr. New York: Something Else Press, 1968.
———. "Close-Up of Modern Dance Today: The Non-Objective Choreographers," *Dance Magazine* XXXI, no. 11 (Nov. 1957).
———. *The Dancer and The Dance: Merce Cunningham in conversation with Jacqueline Lesschaeve.* New York: Marion Boyers, 1985.
———. "The Impermanent Art," in *7Arts 3*, ed. Fernando Puma. Indian Hills CO: The Falcon Wing's Press, 1955, 69–77.
———. "Time, Space, and Dance" in *Merce Cunningham*, ed. Richard Kostelanetz. Pennington NJ: A Cappella Books, 1992, 37–9.
d'Harnoncourt, Anne. *Marcel Duchamp.* Philadelphia: Philadelphia Museum of Art, 1973.
Dalva, Nancy. "The Way of Merce," *Merce Cunningham*, ed. R. Kostelanetz. Pennington, NJ: A Cappella Books, 1992, 179–186.
Daly, Ann. *Done Into Dance: Isadora Duncan in America.* Bloomington: University of Indiana Press, 1995.
Dancers on a Plane: Cage, Cunningham, Johns. London: Anthony d'offay Gallery, 1989.
Daniels, Don. "Cunningham, In Time," in *Merce Cunningham*, ed. Richard Kostelanetz. Pennington, NJ: A Cappella Books, 1992, 160–72.
Danto, Arthur C. *After the End of Art*, Princeton: Princeton University Press, 1997.
De Mille, Agnes. *Martha: The Life and Work of Martha Graham.* New York: Random House, 1991.
Deleuze, Gilles, and Felix Guattari. *Anti-Oedipus: Capitalism and Schizophrenia.* NY: Viking, 1977.
Denby, Edwin. *Dance Writings.* New York: Knopf, 1986.
———. *Looking at the Dance.* New York: Curtis, 1949.

Derrida, Jacques. *Of Grammatology*, trans. Gayatri Chakravorty Spivak. Baltimore: Johns Hopkins University Press, 1976.

Doctorow, E. L. *Ragtime*. New York: Bantam Books, 1976.

Duberman, Martin. *Black Mountain*. London: Wildwood House, 1972.

Duncan, Isadora. *My Life*. Garden City NJ: Garden City Publishers, 1927.

———. *The Art of the Dance* (1928), ed. Sheldon Cheney. New York: Theatre Arts Books, 1977.

Eliot, T. S. "Tradition and the Individual Talent" in *Modern Criticism*, ed. by Walter Sutton and Richard Foster. New York: Odyssey Press, 1963, 140–145.

Ellis, Havelock. "The Dance of Life" in R. Copeland and M. Cohen, *What is Dance?* New York: Oxford University Press, 1983, 478–496.

Ewen, Frederic. *Bertolt Brecht: His Life, His Art, and His Times*. New York: Citadel Press, 1969.

Fenton, James. "The Voracious Eye," *New York Review of Books*, November 6, 1997, 13–15.

Fisher, John Andrew. "What the Hills are Alive With: In Defense of the Sounds of Nature." *Journal of Aesthetics and Art Criticism* 56.2 (Spring 1998): 167–79.

Forti, Simone. *Handbook in Motion*. Halifax: Press of the Nova Scotia College of Art and Design, 1974.

Foster, Susan Leigh. "Confluences of Race, Gender, and Sexuality in American Modern Dance, Part II," paper delivered at the "Confluences" Conference, University of Capetown, S. Africa, July 19, 1997, 20–21.

———. *Reading Dancing: Bodies and Subjects in Contemporary American Dance*. Berkeley: University of California Press, 1986.

Francis, Richard. *Jasper Johns*. New York: Abbeville, 1984.

Frank, Joseph. "Spatial Form in Modern Literature," in *Criticism*, eds. Mark Schorer, Josephine Miles, Gordon McKenzie. New York: Harcourt, Brace, and World, 1958, 379–392.

Franzen, Jonathan. "Talk of the Town: Comment: Tuesday, and After" *The New Yorker*, September 24, 2001, 29.

Freud, Sigmund. *Civilisation and Its Discontents*. London: Hogarth, 1930.

———. "Jokes and the Comic," in *Comedy, Meaning and Form*, ed. Robert Corrigan. San Francisco: Chandler, 1965, 253–263.

Friedman, B. H. *Energy Made Visible: Jackson Pollock*. New York: McGraw-Hill, 1972.

Gale, Joseph. Review of Cunningham Company, in *Newark Evening News*, April '69, exact date and page not readable, Cunningham Company Clipping File, Dance Collection Library of the Performing Arts, New York City.

Glaser, Bruce. "Questions to Stella and Judd," in *Minimal Art*, ed. G. Battcock. New York: Dutton, 1968, pp. 148–164.

Gann, Kyle. *American Music in the Twentieth Century*. New York: Schirmer Books, 1997.

Gold, Mick. "Europe After The Rain" London: Arts Council of Great Britain, 1998.

Goldman, Michael. *The Actor's Freedom*. New York: Viking, 1975.

Graham, Martha. "Graham: A Modern Dancer's Primer for Action" in *Dance as a Theater Art*, ed. Selma Jeanne Cohen. New York: Dodd, Mead, 1974.

———. *Notebooks*. NY: Harcourt Brace Jovanovich, 1973.

———. "Seeking an American Art of the Dance" in *Revolt of the Arts*, ed. Oliver Saylor. New York: Brentano's [1930] 87.

Greensberg, Clement. "Modernist Painting" (1965), in *The New Art*, ed. Gregory Battcock. New York: Dutton, 1973, 66–77.

———. "Towards a Newer Laocoon" (1940) in *Pollock and After, the Critical Debate*, ed. Francis Frascina. New York: Harper and Row, 1985, 35–46.

Grotowski, Jerzy. *Towards A Poor Theatre*. New York: Simon and Schuster, 1969.

Grubbs, Henry A. *Paul Valery*. New York: Twayne Publishers, 1968.

Hamilton, Anita "Merce Cunningham Leaps into the Digital Age," *Time Magazine*, August 2, 1999, 89–90.

Hanhardt, John G. *Nam June Paik*. New York: Whitney Museum of American Art, 1982.

Hansen, Robert C. *Scenic and Costume Design for the Ballets Russes*. Ann Arbor: UMI Research Press, 1985.

Harrison, Jane. "Ancient Art and Ritual," in *What Is Dance?* eds. Roger Copeland and Marshall Cohen. New York: Oxford University Press, 1983. 502–506.

Hayman, Ronald. *Artaud and After*. Oxford: Oxford University Press, 1977.

Hering, Doris. "Suite By Chance," review in *Dance Magazine* XXVIII, no.2 (Feb. 1954), 70.

Hoberman, J. "Love and Death in the American Supermarketplace." *The Voice Literary Supplement* November 1982, 1–2.

Hoffman, Abbie. *Revolution for the Hell of It.* New York: Dial, 1968.

Holden, Stephen. "Review of *Pollock*" *New York Times* National edition, December 15, 2000, B23.

Hollander, Anne. *Seeing Through Clothes.* New York: Avon Books, 1980.

Howard, Richard. "Preface," in Barthes, Roland, *S/Z.* New York: Hill and Wang: 1974.

Hughes, Alan. Dance review in *New York Times*, August 1963. Library of the Performing Arts, Lincoln Center, NY, Cunningham clipping file.

Hughes, Robert. "The Medium Inquisitor," *New York Review of Books*, October 21, 1993, p. 43.

Humphrey, Doris. *The Art of Making Dances.* New York, Chicago: Holt, Rinehart and Winston, 1959.

———. "What the Dancer Thinks About" (1937) in *The Vision of Modern Dance*, ed. Jean Morrison Brown. 2nd ed. Princeton, NJ: Princeton Book Co., Publishers, 1998, p. 55–64.

Hutera, Donald. "Glimpses into the Rehearsal Studio of a Master," *The New York Times* 1 March 1987, sec. 2, p. 8.

Huyssen, Andreas. *After the Great Divide: Modernism, Mass Culture, Postmodernism.* Bloomington, IN: Indiana University Press, 1986.

Hyde, Lewis. *Trickster Makes This World: Mischief, Myth and Art.* New York: Farrar, Strauss, 1998.

Jameson, Frederic. *Formations of Pleasure.* London: Routledge, 1983.

———. "Postmodernism, or, The Cultural Logic of Late Capitalism," in *Storming the Reality Studio*, ed. Larry McCaffery. Durham NC: Duke University Press, 1991, 219–228.

Johnson, Ellen. *Modern Art and the Object: A Century of Changing Attitudes.* London: Thames and Hudson, 1976.

Johnston, Jill. *Jasper Johns: Privileged Information.* New York: Thames and Hudson, 1996.

———. "The New American Modern Dance," *Salmagundi*, no. 33–34 (Spring – Summer 1976), 156.

———.'My Memory about certain things', *Dance Perspectives* (34), 21, 1968.

Jones, Amelia. *Body Art: Performing the Subject.* Minneapolis: University of Minnesota Press, 1998.

Jowitt, Deborah. *Time and the Dancing Image.* New York: William Morrow, 1988.

Joyce, Cynthia. "Merce Cunningham: The *Salon* Inteview." *www.salon.com/weekly/interview960722. html*, 1999 [accessed 2002].

Junkerman, Charles. "'nEw/foRms of living together': The Model of the Musicircus" in *John Cage Composed in America*, eds. Junkerman and Marjorie Perloff. Chicago: University of Chicago Press, 1994, 39–64.

Kaiser, Paul. "Biped," on-line essay, *www.riverbed.com/duoframe/duobipedessay.htm*, accessed June 18, 2000.

———. Website: *http://www.kaiserworks.com/artworks/loops/loopsmain.htm*, accessed April 12, 2003.

Karmel, Pepe. *Jackson Pollock.* New York: Museum of Modern Art, 1998.

———. "Pollock at Work: The Films and Photographs of Hans Namuth" in *Jackson Pollock*, ed. Kirk Varnedoe with Pepe Karmel. New York: Harry N. Abrams, 1998, 87–137.

Katz, Jonathan. "The Art of Code: Jasper Johns and Robert Rauschenberg," *Significant Others*, eds. Whitney Chadwick and Isabelle de Courtivron. London: Thames and Hudson, 1993, 189–207.

Kermode, Frank. "Poet and Dancer Before Diaghilev" in *What Is Dance?* eds. Roger Copeland and Marshall Cohen. New York: Oxford University Press, 1983, 145–160.

King, Kenneth. "Space Dance and the Galactic Matrix," in *Merce Cunningham*, ed. R. Kostelanetz. Pennington, NJ: A Cappella Books 1992, 187–213.

Kirstein, Lincoln. "Classic Ballet: Aria of the Aerial," in *What Is Dance?* ed. by R. Copeland and M. Cohen. New York: Oxford University Press, l983., 238–243.

———. *Movement and Metaphor.* New York: Praeger Publishers, 1970.

———. *Thirty Years: The New York City Ballet.* New York: Alfred A. Knopf, 1978.

———. *Three Pamphlets Collected.* New York: Dance Horizons, 1967.

———. Untitled contribution to *Merce Cunningham* ed. by James Klosty. New York: Dutton, 1975 89–90.

Kiselgoff, Anna. "Cunningham Spirit at Heart of Premiere", *New York Times*, March 11, 1988, C3.

Klosty, James ed. *Merce Cunningham*. New York: Dutton, 1975.

Kosinski, Jerzy. *Being There*. New York: Harcourt Brace Jovanovich, 1970.

Kostelanetz, Richard. "Anarchist Art: The Example of John Cage." in Howard Ehrlich, ed., *Reinventing Anarchy, Again*. San Francisco: AK Press, 1996, pp. 293–96.

———, ed. *Conversing With Cage*. New York: Limelight Editions, 1988.

———, ed. *John Cage*. New York: Preager, 1970.

———, ed. *Merce Cunningham: Dancing in Space and Time*. Pennington, NJ: A Cappella Books, 1992.

Kramer, Hilton. "Jackson Pollock and The New York School, II," *New Criterion*, February 1999, 14–19.

Krauss, Rosalind. *The Optical Unconscious*. Cambridge MA: MIT Press, 1993.

Kren, Alfred. *Robert Rauschenberg: Haywire: Major Technological Works of the 1960s*. Ostfildern-Ruit, Hatje, 1997.

Kuper, Adam. *The Invention of Primitive Society*. London: Routledge, 1988.

Kuspit, Donald. "Collage: The Organizing Principle of Art in the Age of the Relativity of Art," in *Collage: Critical Views*, ed. Katherine Hoffman. Ann Arbor: UMI Research Press, 1989, 39–57.

Laban, Rudolf van. *A Life For Dance*, trans: (Lisa Ullmann) London: Macdonald and Evan, 1975.

Landau, Ely. Souvenir Program for American Film Theater Production of Pinter's The Homecoming, 1973.

Langer, Susanne K. From *Feeling and Form*, in *What Is Dance?* eds. Roger Copeland and Marshall Cohen (New York: Oxford University Press, 1983), 28–47.

Lasch, Christopher. *The Culture of Narcissism*. New York: Norton, 1978.

Leach, Sir Edmund R. "A Tobriand Medusa?" in *Art and Aesthetics in Primitive Societies*, ed. Carol F. Jopling. New York: Dutton, 1971, 45–54.

Levinson, André. "The Spirit of the Classic Dance," in *Dance as a Theater Art*, ed. Selma Jeanne Cohen. New York: Dodd, Mead, 1974, 113–117.

Levi-Strauss, Claude. *Structural Anthropology*, trans. Clair Jacobson and Brooke Grundfest Schoepf. New York: Basic Books, 1963.

Lippard, Lucy. *Surrealists on Art*. Englewood Cliffs NJ: Prentice Hall, 1970.

Litvinoff, Valentina. *The Use of Stanislavsky Within Modern Dance*. New York: American Dance Guild, 1972.

Lorenz, Edward. "The Butterfly Effect," in *The Chaos Avant-Garde: Memories of the Early Days of Chaos Theory*, eds. Ralph Abraham and Yoshisuke Ueda. London: World Scientific, 2000, pp. 91–94.

Ludlow, Lynn. "Dance, Music Parting Way: Independent Existence Cited By Cunningham," Champagne-Urbana Courier, March 4, 1959, 10.

Mailer, Norman. *The White Negro*. San Francisco: City Lights Books, 1968.

Manchester, P. W. "Merce Cunningham and Dance Co.," *Dance News* XXXVI no. 3 (March 1960), 11.

Manning, Susan. *Ecstasy and the Demon*. Berkeley: University of California Press, 1993.

Marcus, Greil. *Lipstick Traces: A Secret History of the 20th Century*. Cambridge MA: Harvard University Press, 1989.

Marcuse, Herbert. *Conservation Foundation Letter*, University of California, June 1980, *http://www.netwalk.com/~vireo/Marcuse Herbert.html* (accessed October 13, 2002).

Martin, John. "The Dance" (1946) in *What Is Dance?* eds. Roger Copeland and Marshall Cohen (New York: Oxford University Press, 1983), 22–23.

The Modern Dance. New York: Dance Horizons, 1972.

Macaulay, Alastair. "The Merce Experience," *Merce Cunningham*, ed. Richard Kostelanetz. Pennington, NJ: A Cappella Books, 1992, 173–178.

McEvilly, Thomas. "Art in the Dark," *Artforum*, Summer 1983, 63–71.

———. "Doctor, Lawyer, Indian Chief: Primitivism in 20th Century Art at the Museum of Modern Art in 1984," Artforum, November, 1984, 54–60.

McLuhan, Marshall. *The Gutenberg Galaxy*. Toronto: University of Toronto Press, 1962.

"Merce Cunningham Receives Guggenheim Award," *Dance Observer*, 21 no. 7 (August–September 1954), 107. (no author listed).

Meyer, Ursula. *Conceptual Art*. New York: EP Dutton, 1972.

Mitchell, W. J. T. "The Politics of Genre: Space and Time in Lessing's *Laocoon*." *Repesentations*, Spring 1984, 98–115.

Mumma, Gordon. "Four Sound Environments for Modern Dance" *Impulse: The Annual of Contemporary Dance*. San Francisco: Chapman Press, 1967.

Munk, Erika. "Cross Left," column, *Village Voice*, March 28, 1988, 119.

Nadeau, Maurice. *The History of Surrealism*, trans. Roger Shattuck. New York: Macmillan, 1965.

Nagler, Alois. *Shakespeare's Stage*. New Haven, CT: Yale University Press, 1981.

Nietzsche, Frederick. "The Birth of Tragedy" in *Philosophies of Art and Beauty: Selected Readings in Aesthetics from Plato to Heidegger,* ed. Albert Hofstadter and Richard Kuhns. NY: The Modern Library, 1964, 498–554.

O'Doherty, Brian. *American Masters: The Voice and The Myth*. New York: Ridge Press, Random House, 1973.

Odom, Selma Landen. "Wigman at Hellerau" *Ballet Review* 14:2 (Summer 1986) 41–53.

O'Mahony, John "The Dancing Master" *The Guardian On-Line,* October 7, 2000 *www.guardian.co.uk/Archive/Article/0,4273,4073205,00.html* (accessed December 18, 2000).

Paik, Nam June. *Video n' Videology, 1959–1973,* ed. Judson Rosebush. Syracuse NY: Everson Museum of Art, 1974.

Peraldi, François. "A Schizo and the Institution (a non-story)." *Semiotext*, III(2) (1978), 20–28.

Pridden, Deirdre. *The Art of the Dance in French Literature*. London: Adam and Charles Black, 1952.

Pynchon, Thomas. *Gravity's Rainbow*. New York: Viking, 1973.

Rainer, Yvonne. *Work 1961–73*. Halifax: The Press of the Nova Scotia College of Art and Dance, 1974.

Ramsay, Burt. *Alien Bodies*. London: Routledge, 1998.

Raynor, Vivien. "Jasper Johns," *Art News* 72, no. 3 (March 1973): 20–21.

Reinhardt, Ad. "Writings" in *The New Art*, ed. Gregory Battcock. New York: EP Dutton, 1973, 167–177.

Retallack, Joan. "Poethics of a Complex Realism," *John Cage: Composed in America*, eds. Majorie Perloff and Charles Junkerman. Chicago: University of Chicago Press, 1994, 242–273

Reynolds, Nancy. *Repertory in Review*. New York: Dial Press, 1977.

Rhode, Eric. *A History of the Cinema*. New York: Hill and Wang, 1976.

Rilke, Rainer Maria. *Duino Elegies*, trans. Gary Miranda. Portland OR: Breitenbush Books, 1981.

Rivers, Larry. Program Notes for "American Film Theater" souvenir program, screening of Peter Hall's film version of Harold Pinter's *The Homecoming*, 1974, n.p.

Robbe-Grillet, Alain. "A Future for the Novel," trans. Richard Howard, in *Modern Culture and the Arts*, eds. James B. Hall and Barry Ulanov. New York: McGraw-Hill, 1967, 272–280.

Rogers, Clark. "Appia's Theory of Acting: Eurythmics for the Stage," in *Total Theatre*, ed. E.T. Kirby. New York: Dutton, 1969, 20–28.

Rogers-Lafferty, Sarah. *Body Mécanique*. Columbus, OH, Wexner Center for the Arts, 1998.

Rose, Barbara "ABC Art," in *Minimal Art: A Critical Anthology*, ed. Gregory Battcock. New York: EP Dutton, 1968, 274–297.

Rosenberg, Harold. "The American Action Painters," *Art News*, 51 No. 8 December 1952, 22–23, 48–50.

"The Mythic Act," cited in Amelia Jones, *Body art/performing the subject/Amelia Jones*. Minneapolis: University of Minnesota Press, 1998.

Roth, Moira. "The Aesthetic of Indifference" *ArtForum*, November 1977, 46–53.

Difference/Indifference: musings on postmodernism, Marcel Duchamp and John Cage / Moira Roth, introduction and text; commentary Jonathon D. Katz Amsterdam : G + B Arts International, 1998.

Rubin, Jerry. *Do It: Scenarios of the Revolution*. New York: Simon and Schuster, 1970.

Rubin, William. *Dada, Surrealism, and their Heritage*. New York: Museum of Modern Art, 1968.

———. "Picasso" in *"Primitivism" in 20th Century Art: Affinity of the Tribal and the Modern*, ed. William Rubin. New York: Museum of Modern Art, 1984, Vol. 1, 241–342.

Sawin, Martica. *Surrealism in Exile and the Beginning of the New York School*. Cambridge MA: MIT Press, 1995.

Schjeldahl, Peter. *Art of Our Time*. London: Lund Humphries, 1984.

———. Column *The Village Voice*, October 7, 1997, n.p.

Schlossman, David A. *Actors and Activists: Politics, Performance, and Exchange Among Social Worlds*, New York: Routledge, 2002.

Schwartz, Tony. *The Responsive Chord*. Garden City NY: Anchor Press, 1972.

Seitz, William Chapin. *The Art of Assemblage*. New York: Museum of Modern Art, 1961.

Shattuck, Roger. *The Banquet Years*. New York: Random House, 1968.

Shelton, Suzanne. "Jungian Roots of Martha Graham's Dance Imagery," *Dance History Scholars Proceedings*, Sixth Annual Conference at The Ohio State University, February 11–13, 1983, 119–132.

Shiff, Richard. "Performing an Appearance: On the Surface of Abstract Expressionism" in *Abstract Expressionism: The Critical Developments*, ed. Michael Auping. New York: Harry N. Abrams, 1987, 94–123.

Shklovsky, Victor. "Arts as Technique," *Russian Formalist Criticism*, eds. Lee Lemon and Marion Reis. Lincoln NE: University of Nebraska Press, 1965.

Siegel, Marcia. "Come In, Earth. Are You There?" in *Merce Cunningham*, ed. Richard Kostelanetz. Pennington, NJ: A Cappella Books, 1992, 71–76.

———. *Watching the Dance Go By*. Boston: Houghton Mifflin, 1977.

Skinner, B. F. *Beyond Freedom and Dignity*. New York: Knopf, 1972.

Smith, Patrick S. *Andy Warhol's Art and Films*. Ann Arbor: UMI Research Press, 1981.

Smoliar, Stephen. "Merce Cunningham in Brooklyn" (1970) in *Merce Cunningham*, ed. Richard Kostelanetz. Pennington, NJ: A Cappella Books, 1992, 77–91.

Sobieszek, Robert A. *Ports of Entry: William S. Burroughs and the Arts*, Los Angeles County Museum of Art, Thames and Hudson 1996.

Solomon, Deborah. "How to Succeed in Art," *The New York Times Magazine*, June 27, 1999, 38–41.

Sontag, Susan. *Against Interpretation*. New York: Dell, 1966.

———. "Francis Bacon: About Being in Pain" *Vogue* magazine (March 1975), 136–7.

"In Memory of Their Feelings" *Dancers on a Plane* London : Anthony d'Offay Gallery, 1989, 13–23.

Spector, Nancy. Rauschenberg and Performance, 1963–67: A "Poetry of Infinite Possibilities," in *Robert Rauscheberg: A Retrospective*. NY: Guggenheim Museum, 1997, 226–46.

St. Denis, Ruth. Uncatalogued journals (1919). UCLA Dance Collection.

Stein, Gertrude. *Lectures in America* (1935). New York: Vintage Books, 1975.

Steinberg, Leo. *Other Criteria*. New York: Oxford University Press, 1972.

Steinberg, Micheline. *Flashback: One Hundred Years of Stratford-Upon-Avon and the Royal Shakespeare Company*. London: RSC Publications, 1985.

Stelarc, "Obsolete Body" *www.stelarc.va.com.au/obsolete/obsolete.html*, accessed August 21, 2001.

Stern, Robert A.M. *New Directions in American Architecture*. New York: Braziller, 1977.

Stockhausen, Karlheinz. "The Golden Bruce Awards" Quoted on the website *http://kalvos.org/gbruce.html#dear*, accessed 2001.

Stone, Allucquere Rosanne. "Will the Real Body Please Stand Up?" in *Cyberspace*, ed. Michael Benedikt. Cambridge MA: MIT Press, 1991, 81–118.

Straus, Erwin. "Born to See, Bound to Behold…" in *The Philosophy of the Body*, ed. S. Spicker. New York: Quadrangle, 1963.

———. "The Upright Posture" (1948) in *Essays in Phenomenology*, ed. Maurice Natanson. The Hague. Martinus N. Jheff, 1966.

Sundell, Nina Castelli. *Rauschenberg/performance, 1954–1984*. Cleveland, Ohio: Cleveland Center for Contemporary Art, 1984.

———. *The Turning Point: Art and Politics in 1968*. Cleveland: Cleveland Center for Contemporary Art, 1988.

Sypher, Wylie. *Literature and Technology*. New York: Random House, 1968.

Taylor, Paul. *Private Domain*. New York: Knopf, 1987.

Terry, Walter. *I Was There: Selected Dance Reviews and Articles, 1936–1976*, comp. & ed. Andrew Mark Wentink. New York: Dekker, 1978.

Tharp, Twyla. *Push Comes To Shove*. New York: Bantam, 1992.

Tobias, Tobi. "The New York Interview: Mark Morris," *New York Magazine*, December 11, 1995, 58.

Todd, Mabel E. *The Thinking Body*. Brooklyn: Dance Horizons, 1968.

Toepfer, Karl Eric. *Empire of Ecstasy: Nudity and Movement in German Body Culture, 1910–1935*. Berkeley: University of California Press, 1997.

Tomkins, Calvin. "On Collaboration" in *Merce Cunningham*, ed. R. Kostelanetz. Pennington, NJ: A Cappella Books, 1992, 44–47.

———. *The Bride and the Bachelors.* New York: Penguin, 1965.

———. *Off The Wall: Robert Rauschenberg and the Art World of Our Time.* New York: Doubleday, 1980.

———. "Merce At Seventy-Five," *The New Yorker,* March 7, 1994.

Torgovnick, Mariana. *Gone Primitive.* Chicago: University of Chicago Press, 1990.

Treichler, Paula A. "AIDS, Homophobia, and Biomedical Discourse: An Epidemic of Signification," in *October 43: AIDS Cultural Analysis, Cultural Activism,* ed. Douglas Crimp. Cambridge MA: MIT Press, Winter 1987, 31–70.

Trilling, Lionel. "Freud: Within and Beyond Culture" (1955) in *Beyond Culture.* New York:Viking Press, 1968, 89–118.

Umland, Anne, ed. *Pop Art: Selections from the Museum of Modern Art.* New York: Museum of Modern Art, 1998.

Updike, John. "Jackson Whole" in *The New York Review of Books,* December 3, 1998, 11–12.

Valery, Paul. "Philosophy of the Dance," in *What Is Dance?* eds. Roger Copeland and Marshall Cohen. New York: Oxford University Press, 1983, 55–65.

Varnedoe, Kirk. "Abstract Expressionism" in *"Primitivism" in 20th Century Art: Affinity of the Tribal and the Modern,* ed. William Rubin. New York: Museum of Modern Art, 1984, Vol. II, 615–659.

Vaughan, David. "Dance of the Avant-Garde: Cunningham and the Post-Cunningham Generation," in *Dance of the Twentieth Century: Slide Text and Catalogue.* New York: Pictura Dance, 1978, 43–55.

———. *Merce Cunningham: Fifty Years, Chronicle and Commentary,* ed. Melissa Harris. New York: Aperture, 1997.

Venturi, Robert. *Complexity and Contradiction in Architecture.* NY: Museum of Modern Art, 1966.

Venza, Jack, prod. *Trailblazers of Modern Dance* (videotape). NY: WNET/13, 1979.

Volinsky, A. K. *The Book of Exultation,* excerpted in *What Is Dance?* eds. Roger Copeland and Marshall Cohen. New York: Oxford University Press, 1983, 255–257.

Ward, Geoffrey. "Letter to the Editor," in *New York Review of Books,* March 29, 2001, 51.

Warhol, Andy. *The Andy Warhol Diaries,* ed. Pat Hackett. New York: Warner, 1989.

Warren, Larry. *Anna Sokolow, The Rebellious Spirit.* Princeton, NJ: Princeton Book Company, 1991.

Wasserman, Jacob. *The World's Illusion,* trans. Ludwig Lewisohn. New York: Harcourt, Brace, 1920.

Willet, John. *The Theatre of the Weimar Republic.* New York: 1988.

———. *The Weimar Years: A Culture Cut Short.* New York: Abbeville Press, 1984.

Winterson, Jeanette. *Art Objects: Essays on Ecstasy and Effrontery.* New York: Alfred A. Knopf, 1996.

Wolheim, "Minimal Art" in *Minimal Art: A Critical Anthology,* ed. Gregory Battcock. New York: E. P. Dutton, 1968, 387–399.

Wynne, Shirley. "Complaisance, An Eighteenth Century Cool" in *Dance Scope* V(1), Fall 1970, 22–23.

Index